Comparative Constitutional Law in Asia

Comparative Constitutional Law in Asia

Edited by

Rosalind Dixon

Professor of Law, University of New South Wales, Australia

Tom Ginsburg

Leo Spitz Professor of International Law, Ludwig and Hilde Wolf Research Scholar and Professor of Political Science, University of Chicago, USA and Research Professor, American Bar Foundation

Edward Elgar

Cheltenham, UK • Northampton, MA, USA

Published by
Edward Elgar Publishing Limited
The Lypiatts
15 Lansdown Road
Cheltenham
Glos GL50 2JA
UK

Edward Elgar Publishing, Inc.
William Pratt House
9 Dewey Court
Northampton
Massachusetts 01060
USA

A catalogue record for this book
is available from the British Library

Library of Congress Control Number: 2013949801

This book is available electronically in the ElgarOnline.com Law Subject Collection, E-ISBN 978 1 78100 270 4

ISBN 978 1 78100 269 8 (cased)

Typeset by Columns Design XML Ltd, Reading
Printed and bound in Great Britain by T.J. International Ltd, Padstow

Contents

Contributors

Tom Allen is Professor of Law, Durham Law School (UK).

Justin Blount is Ph.D. candidate in the Department of Political Science, University of Illinois.

José Antonio Cheibub is Professor in the Department of Political Science, University of Illinois at Urbana-Champaign.

Sujit Choudhry is Cecilia Goetz Professor of Law and Faculty Director of the Center for Constitutional Transitions at the New York School of Law.

Rishad Chowdhury is a JSD Candidate at the University of Chicago Law School.

Martin Clark is a Research Fellow at Melbourne Law School at the University of Melbourne.

Rosalind Dixon is Professor of Law, University of New South Wales (Australia).

Tom Ginsburg is Professor, University of Chicago Law School.

Ran Hirschl is Professor of Political Science and Law, and Canada Research Chair in Constitutionalism, Democracy, and Development, University of Toronto (Canada).

Madhav Khosla is a Ph.D. Candidate in Government at Harvard University.

Fernando Limongi is Professor, Universidade de São Paulo (Brazil).

Kate O'Regan is former Justice, Constitutional Court of South Africa.

Victor V. Ramraj is Associate Professor, Faculty of Law, National University of Singapore.

Cheryl Saunders is Laureate Professor, University of Melbourne Law School (Australia).

Adrienne Stone is Professor, University of Melbourne Law School (Australia).

Mark Tushnet is William Nelson Cromwell Professor of Law, Harvard Law School.

Acknowledgements

This project is a collective effort in which many contributed to the final product. The chapters were originally presented at a conference hosted by the University of Hong Kong in December 2011. Generous financial and in-kind support was provided by the Beijing Center of the University of Chicago, the University of Hong Kong, the University of Chicago Law School, and its Russell Baker Scholars Fund. Our thanks to Deans Johannes Chan and Michael Schill, and to Professor Dali Yang. Special thanks to Dr. Christopher and Mrs. Chermy Lai, who hosted our group with exceptional generosity and grace. Flora Leung and Claudia Lai provided essential support, and Kayla Ginsburg, Natalia Ginsburg, Emily Heasley, and Jeyshree Ramachandran provided superb research assistance in preparing the manuscript. We would also like to thank our respondents at the conference who contributed their country expertise to round out the chapters: Wen-chen Chang, Diane Desierto, Bjoern Dressel, John Gillespie, Teilee Kuong, HP Lee, Tokujin Matsudaira, Fritz Siregar, Kai Tu, and Po-Jen Yap. Others from the University of Hong Kong community were also generous with their expertise.

Chapter 2 draws on material from Justin Blount, Tom Ginsburg and Zachary Elkins, "Citizen as Founder: Public Participation in Constitutional Approval", 81 *Temple U.L. Rev.* 361–82 (2008). Chapter 3 draws from Tom Ginsburg, "Constitutional Courts in East Asia: Understanding Variation", *Journal of Comparative Law* 3(2): 80–100 (2008). Thanks to the respective journals for permission to use the material.

1. Introduction

Rosalind Dixon and Tom Ginsburg

I. CONSTITUTIONALISM IN ASIA

The newly revitalized field of comparative constitutional law has tended to let North America and Europe dictate the agenda. From one point of view, this is understandable, of course: modern written constitutions were first developed in the Atlantic world and spread to the new nation states of Latin America, well before Japan adopted the first national constitution in Asia in 1889. But Asia has also been home to vibrant constitutional discourses for 150 years, as indigenous elites sought to fuse Western institutional forms with the grand East Asian legal and political traditions. This discourse is now returning to the fore with speculation about China's ongoing experiment in developmental authoritarianism. In South Asia and Southeast Asia, too, old traditions of government informed constitutional discussions, although the experience of colonialism was a more immediate factor.

In the early 21st century, Asian countries have developed increasingly vibrant practices of constitutional law. Written constitutions are now the norm, and routinely influence the politics even of authoritarian states including Myanmar or China. Constitutional courts have spread throughout the region, and are deciding many of the major social and political questions of the day. And social and political movements invoke the constitution at key junctures in many countries.

The timing is good for an examination of constitutional law in Asia. One of the great themes of constitutions in Asia is their basic stability (Yeh and Chang 2011). Vibrant constitutional democracies are now well established in Japan, South Korea, Mongolia and Taiwan. Indonesia's transition to a constitutional democracy in the early years of this century was remarkable on many dimensions (Horowitz 2013), and as of this writing, Southeast Asia is as democratic as it has ever been, with stable democracies in the Philippines and Indonesia, a more fragile stability in Thailand, relatively liberal periods in Singapore and Malaysia, and a remarkable evolution under an authoritarian-drafted constitution in

1

Myanmar. In fact, taking the estimate that the average constitution can be expected to live 19 years (Elkins et al. 2009) as a baseline, we see that most countries in the region have surpassed that. Only Thailand has written a new constitution in the past decade, and so Asia stands in sharp contrast with other regions of the world. This statistic does not mean that constitutions have been stagnant, however. Instead, countries have adopted a kind of gradualist evolution, emphasizing constitutional amendment, and relatively cautious judicial adjustment (Yeh and Chang 2011).

Some scholars also emphasize the political character of Asian constitutionalism, in contrast with the heavy emphasis on the judiciary in the Western tradition. For example, Yeh and Chang (2011) argue that judicial review in Northeast Asia has been underdeveloped. Michael Dowdle has criticized as ahistorical the notion that constitutionalism necessarily involves judicial control (Dowdle 2009). Both as an understanding of Western development and what we are calling the East Asian analogues, judicial enforcement of constitutional norms is the exception rather than a *sine qua non*. We agree with Dowdle that the contemporary emphasis on judicialized constitutionalism is incomplete as an account of how effective constitutions have developed and actually operate. On the other hand, as detailed in Chapter 3, Asian constitutional courts have become quite active, and are deciding central questions in many countries.

Another angle to examine Asian countries' experience is to look at the formal text of constitutions. As noted by Yeh and Chang in the context of Northeast Asia, all the countries in the region share, more or less, the idea that constitutional state building was a part of the modernization project. Constitutions in the region have very rarely been a bottom-up project or the result of hard-fought struggles for rights on the part of a people. Instead, constitutions in the region are generally speaking elite projects that only later, if ever, became part of the lived experience of the public. Constitutional politics as a terrain of social struggle is a relatively recent development.

This volume surveys Asian experience on several important constitutional topics. Two linked questions inform the exercise: to what extent is Asian experience distinctive, and to what extent can it inform debates in the rest of the world? In some areas, the jurisprudence and practices of constitutional law may be quite derivative from those of other countries, either within or outside the region. In other cases, the Asian experience may be innovative, in ways that are either obvious or subtle.

With this framework in mind, our introduction examines some of the distinctive patterns revealed in the various chapters, and connects those patterns to broader debates about "Asian values," traditions of political thought, and political and economic conditions.

II. THREE DISTINCTIVE PATTERNS: A BIRDS-EYE VIEW FROM ASIA

A. Convergence/Similarity

One important pattern identified by many of the authors in this volume is a pattern of *convergence*, or similarity or overlap between global constitutional norms and constitutional structures, concepts and principles in Asia.

Tom Ginsburg, for example, in writing about constitutional courts in East Asia, notes the same shift in many Asian countries as has occurred globally "away from traditional notions of parliamentary sovereignty toward the idea of constitutional constraint by expert courts". Cheryl Saunders, in writing about judicial engagement with comparative law in Asia, notes that the 13 Asian countries she surveys with regard to engagement with comparative sources follow the same pattern she found in a prior, more general global survey of constitutional court decision making (Saunders 2013). This pattern also applies across both common and civil law systems in Asia. It includes countries, such as Korea, in which members of the constitutional court have explicitly endorsed the idea of learning or borrowing from other countries, and those such as Singapore where a "four walls" interpretive principle means that comparative engagement tends to be more deliberative or aversive in nature (Saunders, compare Choudhry 1999). This pattern, she suggests, also fits with the three broad explanations for comparative engagement by courts developed by comparative constitutional scholars on a more global scale: it reflects the capacity of foreign jurisprudence to legitimize domestic decisions, which are otherwise lacking in constitutional legitimacy; it reflects the degree to which citing leading courts can bolster the prestige of domestic courts; and it reflects "genealogical" influences within families of legal systems (Saunders, compare Choudhry 1999).

In the context of the constitutional division of power, José Antonio Cheibub and Fernando Limongi note the presence in Asia of all the major archetypal models of executive–legislative relations: presidential systems (e.g. Indonesia, the Philippines and South Korea), semi-presidential systems (e.g. Taiwan and Mongolia), and parliamentary systems (e.g.

India and Japan). Likewise, Sujit Choudhry notes the same broad diffusion in Asia of "post-conflict" federalism as a constitutional design tool that he and Nathan Hume identified in a prior chapter on the global pattern (Ginsburg and Dixon 2011). India, Malaysia and Pakistan, Choudhry notes, have all had federal systems for large parts of the 20th century, against a backdrop of serious religious and ethnic tensions. Federalism has also been proposed, in recent decades, as a design solution to ethnic conflicts in Nepal (which has been trying to adopt such a system over several years of failed negotiation), Sri Lanka, Indonesia and the Philippines. With regard to emergency regimes, Victor Ramraj notes the same broad provision for emergencies in Asian constitutions as is found in most modern constitutions elsewhere. He also notes the presence of the same variety of emergency regimes in Asia as elsewhere – including those that vest the power to declare an emergency in the executive (Singapore and Malaysia), parliament (the Philippines) or in some combination thereof (India); those that generally retain, versus oust, judicial review (e.g., East Timor, versus Singapore and Malaysia); or that potentially allow indefinite emergency rule (Taiwan), as opposed to imposing some express time limit (East Timor).

In the context of constitutional rights provisions, Adrienne Stone, Rishad Chowdhury and Martin Clark note the same broad recognition of rights to free speech, and the same structure of constitutional speech guarantees as Stone previously noted on a global scale: constitutional democracies in Asia generally recognize some form of right to freedom of "speech" "communication" or "expression". Further the interpretation and enforcement of such rights generally follows a three-part structure, examining first, the question of scope of coverage; second, the question of permissible limitations; and third, the question of positive and negative protection. In the context of constitutional rights to property, Tom Allen notes the same presence in Asia, as elsewhere, of competing "liberal" and "social democratic" ideas about property, or property rights. He notes that social democratic ideas, for instance, were influential in the drafting of the Indian constitution, and have underpinned land reform programs in Japan, South Korea and Taiwan, as well as India. Liberal ideas have played a dominant role in court decisions interpreting and enforcing constitutional rights to property in countries such as India and the Philippines. He also suggests that constitutional property rights in Asian constitutions generally take a similar form, and involve a similar logic, to equivalent rights elsewhere: they provide that the government may only acquire property by a process laid down by law, for a public use or purpose, and on terms that provide the owner with compensation.

As for equality clauses and rights to non-discrimination, Kate O'Regan and Madhav Khosla note the degree to which all three of the Asian jurisdictions they study (i.e. India, Japan and Malaysia) have adopted a form of "rational basis" or reasonableness view, in the interpretation and enforcement of constitutional equality clauses. With regard to constitutional regulation of religion, including norms of (anti-)establishment and religious freedom, Ran Hirschl notes the presence, in Asia, of the same three archetypical "religion and state" models he identified on a more global scale in our 2011 handbook (Ginsburg and Dixon 2011): a form of "securalist" model in India and Turkey; a "preferential treatment" model in the Philippines; similar forms of "weak establishment" model in Japan, Nepal (prior to 2006), Thailand, Sri Lanka, Myanmar, Cambodia, Tajikistan, Uzbekistan, Indonesia and Malaysia; and forms of "constitutional theocracy" in other countries in Asia, including, Iran, Pakistan, Iraq, Afghanistan and Saudi Arabia.

One reason for this pattern in Asia undoubtedly has to do with constitutional "borrowing" in Asia, or the *direct* influence of North American, and European (i.e. primarily British and German) constitutional ideas on the design and interpretation of Asian constitutions. In Japan, for example, successive periods of German and American influence have led to competing "schools" of constitutional and legal thought, sometimes leading to conflicts over the shape of reforms. Indeed, there have been dueling associations of constitutional law scholars in Northeast Asia. Scholars in Korea and Taiwan also have similar ties with both German and American networks. French influence in Vietnam has led more to a kind of anti-model for the socialist constitutional model, but still informs some legal thinking. Constitutional design is thus informed by developments in other regions. At the level of constitutional interpretation, as Cheryl Saunders notes in her chapter on comparative engagement by courts in Asia, "[t]he Constitutional Court of Germany and the apex courts of the United States and the United Kingdom are influential in Asia as elsewhere, reflecting historical practice, legal systemic links, continuing reputation and the accessibility of judgements".

B. Complexity and Nuance in Existing Constitutional Categories

A second pattern our authors highlight is the degree of distinctiveness, or *variation*, in Asian constitutional systems, compared to North American, European or Commonwealth archetypes.

For example, Cheryl Saunders notes the distinctive pattern of inter-regional comparison among constitutional courts, especially among courts within East Asia, and by references by Asian courts to the constitutional jurisprudence of the Korean constitutional court and Indian Supreme Court. Likewise in the context of judicial review, and its "strength" or finality, Rosalind Dixon and Mark Tushnet note that in Asia, weak-form review has generally existed (if at all) only via sub-constitutional review and constitutional amendment, rather than the kind of formally weakened judicial review that has become increasingly common in many Commonwealth countries.

In the context of constitutional rights to freedom of expression, Adrienne Stone, Rishad Chowdhury and Martin Clark note the degree to which, as a general proposition, Asian legal systems are often more willing than Western constitutional democracies to restrict speech, via laws criminalizing blasphemy (Malaysia, Indonesia and Pakistan) or defamation (Thailand), laws allowing defamation suits against public figures (Japan and Singapore), or laws restricting speech on the grounds of public morality (India and Singapore), public welfare (Japan), and peace, order and security (Japan, Malaysia, India). Similarly, in the context of constitutional equality rights, Kate O'Regan and Madhav Khosla note the degree to which, at least in the three jurisdictions they study (Japan, India and Malaysia), there has been a noticeable absence of the kind of "disparate impact" equality, or anti-discrimination, jurisprudence found in many other leading constitutional systems, such as Canada, South Africa and Germany. And in the context of religion, Ran Hirschl notes the degree to which "there is far lesser adherence" in Asia than in any other continent to the "classic separation of church and state model".

One potential explanation for this pattern of Asian constitutional distinctiveness, or difference, is the role of culture, or so-called "Asian values". In the early 1990s, scholars and political leaders in the region began to articulate the notion that Asians should not simply adopt Western political forms uncritically, but instead should be governed by regimes consistent with traditional values. These claims were subjected to criticism, but retain rhetorical power in some quarters. In the free speech context, for example, Adrienne Stone, Rishad Chowdhury and Martin Clark note – albeit with some real skepticism – the potential explanatory value of "pragmatic and neo-Confucianist or 'communitarian' norms" in East Asian countries, such as Singapore and Malaysia, in explaining the relatively broad set of limitations on speech upheld by courts, under constitutional free speech guarantees. They also note the potential role of cultural norms of "consensus" in explaining the formally deferential approach of the Supreme Court of Japan to restrictions on speech.

This cultural story, however, seems to overlook the importance of *politics,* or political and economic factors in explaining various patterns of Asian constitutional difference. A striking feature of constitutional dialogue in Japan and India, Rosalind Dixon and Mark Tushnet suggest, is the degree to which it has played out "against ... near complete dominance by a single political party" (Chapter 5). Single party dominance of this kind, they suggest, seems to make some form of weak-form (or at least weakly exercised) review far more likely than in systems with stable forms of two-party competition. Similarly, in the context of constitutional free speech guarantees, Adrienne Stone, Rishad Chowdhury and Martin Clark note the degree to which "democratic norms are undoubtedly weak in many Asian nations" than in leading constitutional systems in North America or Europe, and there are also often weaker legal and political commitments to norms of judicial independence. This also explains why a broader range of limitations on such rights is permitted in Asian countries as diverse as Thailand, Pakistan and Japan – and not just in East or Southeast Asian countries that share a strong Confucian heritage.

One could also argue that in countries such as India, Japan and Malaysia, the dominance of a single political party helps explain the relatively weak, or deferential, enforcement by constitutional courts of universal equality guarantees (see O'Regan and Khosla): as Tom Ginsburg notes in his chapter on constitutional courts in East Asia, in such settings, there is often less space for robust (and successful) judicial review in highly contentious areas than there might be in countries that have a longer history of two-party competition. In a like vein, while noting the degree to which Asia is a distinctly "religion-steeped continent", Ran Hirschl explains the prevalence of some form of religious establishment model in Asia in part by reference to the distinctive political legacies and traditions of relevant Asian countries.

A purely cultural theory also seems poorly equipped to explain the pattern of *intra*-Asian diversity identified by many authors. In the context of courts and constitutional interpretation, for example, Tom Ginsburg notes the emergence of *more* powerful constitutional courts in countries such as South Korea, Taiwan and Indonesia, than in countries such as Thailand, Mongolia or Myanmar, and Leninist states such as China and Vietnam. Culture does not seem to do the work in understanding the differences.

In the context of constitutional divisions of power, Chiebub and Limongi note the degree to which, unlike in Europe, Latin America and Eastern Europe, in Asia "there is no one form of government that predominates". Rather there is enormous variety in which of the three broad global models (i.e. presidential, semi-presidential or parliamentary) various countries adopt, and in the relationship between the executive and the monarchy, and military, in different Asian countries. Sujit Choudhury likewise notes the degree to which models of federalism and decentralization have taken a distinctly more symmetric form in South Asian countries such as India and Sri Lanka, than in Southeast Asian countries such as Indonesia and the Philippines.

A similar diversity is apparent in the context of constitutional rights. In discussing the right to freedom of expression, for example, Adrienne Stone, Martin Clark and Rishad Chowdhury note both the common thread of deference to government limitations running through the jurisprudence in Japan, Singapore, Malaysia and India. But they also identify great diversity in doctrinal approaches (from hypothetical strict scrutiny to the most demanding form of rational basis review) and case selection – from those involving incivility and unrest (Japan, India), to cases of political dissent (Japan and Singapore), to the treatment of religion or religious minorities (India and Malaysia). Similarly, in the context of the right to property, Tom Allen notes the presence of social democratic ideas about property rights in some countries, but their near total absence in other countries, such as China, which are grappling with issues of land reform and economic transition more generally. He also notes patterns of successful land reform in certain Asian countries, such as Japan, South Korea and Taiwan, and largely unsuccessful or abandoned reform in others, such as India and the Philippines. In discussing models of the relationship between religion and the state, Ran Hirschl notes similar variation in how global archetypes have been applied, or played out, in Asia: "secular" constitutional ideals he suggests, have tended to look far more absolutist in Turkey than in India, and weak forms of establishment have been far more compatible with religious freedom in Thailand, Sri Lanka or Myanmar than in Tajikistan, Uzbekistan or Vietnam (Hirschl). Similarly, social democratic ideas about the right to property have appeared to support successful land reform programs in several Asian countries, including Japan, South Korea and Taiwan, but have largely been trumped by liberal ideas, or have been unsuccessful in supporting similar efforts, in countries such as India and the Philippines.

Again, these patterns of intra-Asian difference also seem more to do with differences in history, politics and social and economic conditions, than any form of pan-Asian cultural values or approach. Tom Ginsburg, for example, in explaining the apparent success of constitutional courts in South Korea, Taiwan and Indonesia, compared to those in Thailand, Mongolia and Myanmar, notes the degree to which these countries have systems of divided government (i.e. presidential or semi-presidential system), or some real degree of diffusion in political power, in a way that opens up space for successful judicial review. Tom Allen, in explaining the relative success of land reform programs in countries such as Japan, South Korea and Taiwan, compared to India and the Philippines, notes the importance of external and internal political influences in these countries: in each of these countries, he notes, American influences were important, and the American view at the relevant time was that redistribution was an important means of checking the advance of communism; internal political circumstances in these countries also favored redistribution, in that in Japan and Taiwan, agricultural landlords had lost large amounts of their political influence, and in South Korea, understood "that the threat of a peasant revolution meant that they were better off accepting reforms than challenging them".

In work that complements this volume, Ginsburg (2013) examines the formal features of Asian constitutions, and following Chen (forthcoming), identifies three distinct "Asian" patterns: an evolutionary Leninist variant, a stable liberal constitutionalist variant, and a hybrid, semi-authoritarian variant. He also considers the extent to which these can be seen as distinctly Asian patterns by comparing them with constitutional orders in Latin America, Eastern Europe, South Asia and Africa. The conclusion, in this context, is that what makes Asia as a region distinctive in constitutional terms is a distinctly political set of ideas, or institutions – i.e. the presence of a vital tradition of socialist constitutions, which have distinctive institutional features. China and Vietnam, from this perspective, ought not to be at the periphery of the analysis, but at the center, and their current battles over constitutionalism (Zhang 2010) may well determine whether Asia as a whole can be said to have converged with other regions of the world or remained distinctive.

Culture, however, may still have an important role to play in explaining the distinctive constitutional patterns observed by various authors in Asia – if it is understood as connected to specific historical traditions, or traditions in political thought, that exhibit great internal diversity. The Asian legal tradition goes back for thousands of years, and there are certainly elements that could be characterized as quasi constitutional. This was obscured by early orientalism in the study of Asian political institutions, but recent scholarship has begun to explore this rich history for data (Ruskola 2013; Ginsburg 2012). A brief elaboration of pre-modern antecedents of constitutionalism helps to demonstrate the breadth of thinking and nuance.

Because China is the wellspring of East Asian thinking about law, it is important to think about Chinese contributions to proto-constitutionalism. Accounts of the imperial Chinese legal system have long emphasized the combination of a theoretically unconstrained "son of heaven" at the center of the system with an elaborate system of institutionalized structures that provided actual constraint. Not long ago, scholars drew on this tradition to argue that contemporary Asian political systems retained a degree of comfort with one-party or "one-and-a-half" party rule (Pye 1988).

At an ideal level, the Confucian tradition had natural law elements, instantiated in the concept of ritual propriety, or *li* in Chinese, and scholars have analogized these constraints to constitutionalism. The rules of decorum known as *li* provided normative constraints on the behavior of ruler and ruled alike (Ginsburg 2002). Others have focused on other "constitutionalist" elements of the Confucian tradition, including the rectification of names (*zheng ming*) and the notion of rule by the sage (Bui 2012).

The "constitutional" texts of the Chinese dynasty focused decidedly on agency control. The Ch'in procedural manual, discovered in 1975, shows that from the very outset, the Chinese empire was concerned with the problem of arbitrary decision-making by local officials, and provided detailed, written guidelines aimed to keep Ch'in functionaries account-able in their administrative functions (Turner 1992: 9–10). The T'ang codes elaborated a complex structure of government and lawmaking, providing detailed limitations on what could be done (Liang 1989; Johnson 1979). The Q'ing codes likewise had elaborate rules for punish-ing administrative officials.

Yet the formal ideas of legalized constitutionalism constraining the sovereign himself were not developed in China. One sees constraint through legality – the prior specification of rules and punishments – and an elaborate system of legal orders directed at state agents, but virtually no positive announcements of legal constraint on the will of the Son of Heaven himself. The emperor surely has duties, and is exhorted to behave in accordance with an elaborate set of rules, many of which are written down and have the people's welfare in mind.

For this reason, few scholars have argued that anything approaching constitutionalism can be found in the Chinese tradition. Indeed, this was part of the critique of 19th-century reformers such as Liang Qichao and Sun Yat-sen, and is implicitly carried on by latter-day proponents of building constitutionalism in China (Balme and Dowdle 2009). Perhaps the critics overstate the case; but the overall sense is of an authoritarian legality, with limited areas of pre-commitment used mainly to motivate agents by ensuring their trustworthiness and fidelity.

Elsewhere in Asia, the constitutional legacy is rich with documents that serve to exhort public officials without providing institutional constraints on the ruler himself. In South Asia and Southeast Asia, Hindu and Buddhist ideas also drew on natural law thinking. The Hindu Dharmaśāstra, for example, was treated as a source of "law" by the British, but in fact integrated religion and law into a single normative order. Buddhist thought distinguished the wheel of dharma from the wheel of power, implying that the former constrained the latter. An ideal society would be led by a righteous ruler, whose state was to embody good policy that upheld the dharma. These traditions provide rich resources that inform the modern relationship between religion and state, as well as ideas about legitimate rule (Harding 2007).

Japan's earliest "constitutional" document is the Seventeen-Article Constitution (*Jūshichijō kenpō*) of Shōtoku Taishi, the state-building patron of Buddhism of the Asuka era. Written in 604 CE and adopted as part of a broad set of Sinicizing reforms, the document reads as a Buddhist and Confucian exhortation to maintain harmony, chastise evil, and to obey authority (Steenstrup 1991). It certainly plays the important function, often ascribed to modern constitutions, of helping to bind the nation and define its ideals. But its aspirational character has led to scholarly dispute as to whether or not the document can properly be considered a constitution. Carl Steenstrup (1991: 17), in particular, contends that Shotoku Taishi's "constitution" was not a constitution at all because it did not restrict any extant legislature.

Several centuries later, the laws of the Kamakura period (1185–1333, the period of the first shogunate) have been argued to have a constitutional character (Ginsburg 2012; Mass 1976, 1999). This was a period marked by a split of authority between the emperor and shogunate (bakufu), located in Kyoto and Kamakura respectively. There was competition and conflict over power during the period. A central concern of the bakufu government was the resolution of disputes over land, particularly among its vassals. By specializing in dispute resolution among its vassals, the bakufu enhanced its legitimacy (Mass 1990, 1999). The shogunate promulgated a set of documents to guide the vassals and to govern land ownership (Adolphson 2000: 188–9; Grossverg 1981; Mass 1990, 1999). Some have analogized these documents to constitutions (Mass 1976, 1999).

Perhaps the greatest body of work on the constitutional character of pre-modern law has been done in Korea, of which the recent work of Chaihark Hahm (2009) stands out. Korea's Chosŏn Dynasty (1392–1910) was the most enduring regime in any East Asian country. Korean scholars have not been hesitant to find constitutionalist analogies in the neo-Confucian institutions of the Chosŏn dynasty (Kihl 2005, Hahm 2003a; 2003b). These institutions were embodied in written codes, closely modeled on the Ming codes, which Korean scholars argue limited the authority of rulers. Scholars have focused special attention on the *Kyongguk Taejon* of 1471, seen as embodying a proto-constitutionalism by stating that it "provided a legal framework within which society could function, as far as that function was directly relevant to the state" (Duechler 2002: 122).

The thrust of Hahm's (2009) argument is that paying attention to the category of ritual is important in understanding the Confucian analogue to constitutional law, meaning the norm that regulates and restrains the activities of the ruler. The fact that there was no formal institutionalized constraint on the emperor in the form of a judge or other actor who could challenge his failure to act according to ritual does not mean that there is no constraint at all. The crucial mechanism of remonstrance facilitated correction of the sovereign by loyal officials.

It is worth noting further that these constraints of remonstrance, deliberation and institutionalized *ex ante* review are arguably as extensive as any institutional constraint found in modern constitutional democracies. Many conventional analysts see judicial review as the *sine qua non* of constitutionalism. But empirical studies of constitutional courts, in Asia and elsewhere, emphasize the relative weakness of courts as constraining actors (Ginsburg 2003). A powerful political force usually gets its way when it wants to; courts are rightly seen as the least dangerous branch. Mostly, what courts do in the exercise of constitutional review is facilitate a second look at policies, and require deliberation. And this is perhaps best understood as a form of remonstrance in which the courts are encouraging deliberation in policymaking (Ginsburg 2002).

C. Missing Categories

A third pattern in Asian constitutionalism revealed by our authors is one of "blind spots" (compare Dixon 2008, 2009) or missing categories in existing constitutional scholarship. In Chapter 2, for example, Justin Blount and Tom Ginsburg explore the distinctive pattern of popular *non-participation* in the drafting of some of Asia's most successful, or enduring constitutions – i.e. the constitutions of Japan, Korea, Taiwan and Indonesia. This success, they suggest, also helps cast doubt on the conventional wisdom in comparative constitutional scholarship that "maximum public participation is necessary for constitutional legitimacy," and thus also, constitutional endurance. This fits with the broader pattern we noted at the outset of this introduction that, with few exceptions, constitutions in the region have generally speaking been elite projects that only later, if ever, became part of the lived experience of the public. In this sense, a focus on Asian constitutional experience also helps highlight a broader missing category in existing comparative constitutional scholarship, driven by Europe, North America or the Commonwealth, namely: the prevalence of "elite constitutionalism" as the driving force behind initial constitutionalization projects.

In her analysis of Asian courts, Cheryl Saunders notes the hybrid or overlapping nature of references to foreign and international legal sources. Focusing on this pattern, she suggests, helps us to see more clearly the degree to which it is becoming increasingly difficult – as a matter of general constitutional practice – to distinguish between foreign and international law sources, as distinct sources of law, in ways that challenge our understanding of the monist–dualist distinction, and the basis or nature of transnational engagement itself. Likewise, in their analysis of different modes of judicial review, Rosalind Dixon and Mark Tushnet suggest that Asia helps us see more clearly the degree to which debates over the strength of judicial review are inextricably linked to questions of political structure and competition. In Europe, North America and the Commonwealth, for example, there is widespread agreement over the desirability of weakening the finality of judicial review in some way, but significant debate over the feasibility of doing so. In Asia, in contrast, at least for dominant party democracies, weak judicial review seems a more or less inevitable feature of constitutional self-government – because of a single party's control of the judicial appointments, transfer and removal process, and control over constitutional amendment – but far greater questions remain as to the desirability of weak review, because of less robust political contestation and competition. The focus on Asia, therefore, helps highlight the need for ongoing scholarship by comparative constitutional scholars on a previously overlooked category – i.e. what might be called "authoritarian" forms of weak-form review (see Tushnet 2013), or weak-form review by courts in dominant party democracies more generally.

Similarly, in the context of various constitutional structural provisions, José Antonio Cheibub and Fernando Limongi note the degree to which Asian experience provides important, but to date under-explored, support for "later" generation approaches to questions of legislative–executive relations. These later generation approaches place reduced emphasis on formal separation-of-powers models, and focus instead on the complexity of the relationship between institutional structures, incentives and political party formation and behavior; they also challenge the consensus of "earlier" scholarship on the dangers of presidential government, emphasizing that executive rule may sometimes represent "delegation" rather than unilateral action; that de facto cooperation or coalition formation does in fact occur quite frequently in presidential and parliamentary systems; and that minority governments also occur with some frequency under all three models of legislative–executive relations. A close study of Asian systems, Cheibub and Limongi suggest, also has the potential to shed new light on the explanation for these patterns: In India, for example, there is a long history of minority government, and coalition formation, on a national level, and a tendency for political parties to have a strong regional identification – this may also explain one of the conditions under which coalition formation, or minority government, is most likely to succeed. In Taiwan, the control of the executive over many years by the DPP, against the backdrop of KMT legislative majority support, also helps shed light on the *social* conditions that promote stable minority government – or the kind of cross-cutting social and political conditions that can help sustain stable minority government of various forms.

Likewise, in the federalism context, Sujit Choudhry finds that a close study of Asian constitutional systems helps to highlight important questions about the relationship between federalism and linguistic diversity, and federalism and amendment: in India, Choudhry notes, linguistic diversity has created pressure, at a minimum, for "linguistic federalism" in the internal workings of government, but at the same time, had feedback effects on opportunities for government employment, and access to political resources, in ways that have complicated ethnolinguistic tensions. Similarly, a focus on federalism debates in Sri Lanka and the Philippines helps highlight the tension between (existing) unitary procedures for constitutional amendment and the idea of federalism as a conflict-management device: in Sri Lanka, the Sinhalese majority have contended that a federal model could be introduced by ordinary constitutional amendment, whereas the Tamil minority has argued that such changes could only be passed by the Sinhalese and Tamils as two distinct peoples, or polities; and in the Philippines, the Supreme Court has invalidated attempts to amend the constitution to create a form of asymmetric federalism to resolve the long-standing conflict with the Moro majority in Mindanao, as inconsistent with existing constitutional provisions establishing a unitary state. While such tensions have been evident elsewhere, the Asian experience also undoubtedly brings this tension into much sharper relief. In addition, Choudhry suggests, a detailed study of federalism in Asia helps reveal the degree to which post-conflict justifications for federalism often overlaps with more conventional or "classical" justifications for federalism – such as those based on the value of checks and balances, or government closer to the people. Indeed, Choudhry suggests, "the lessons from the Asian cases may be that the classical and post-conflict justifications for federalism not only overlap in particular cases but often interrelate at a conceptual level." Connecting a range of quite different Asian cases – including India, Sri Lanka, the Philippines, and even China – makes it easier for Choudhry to elucidate these insights.

Similarly, in his chapter on emergencies, Victor Ramraj finds that a close study of Asian constitutional cases helps reveal the importance of social norms – or the "socio-legal" – gap in the regulation of emergency power. One of the most striking features of constitutional practice in this area in Asia, Ramraj notes, is the sheer frequency with which emergency powers have been invoked in different Asian countries. This is just as true in countries "with a diverse array of institutional checks" as in those that have "none at all"; and thus, one of the lessons from Asia, Ramraj concludes, is that as comparative constitutional scholars, we must go beyond formal legal analysis, and our focus on courts and judicial practices, and engage far more closely with social norms and practices on the ground, if we are truly to understand constitutional practices and regimes from either an empirical or normative perspective.

Tom Allen finds that the Chinese experience (especially between 2004 and 2008) helps to reveal a potentially important tension in liberal ideas about the right to property, namely: the possibility that, by incorporating still nascent private-law ideas about property, liberal understandings of constitutional property rights may for some period be a mere "empty vessel, awaiting content from the development of private law" (Allen). Lessons such as this seem crucial for constitutional designers working in the context of major political, economic and legal transitions.

With regard to equality rights, Kate O'Regan and Madhav Khosla find that a focus on Asian countries such as India and Malaysia helps highlight the relationship between the litigation of equality issues and the development of an equality jurisprudence based on notions of disparate impact. In India, for example, they note that after dozens of cases addressing the constitutionality of affirmative action measures or "reservations" for scheduled castes, tribes and "other backward classes," the Supreme Court of India has taken steps toward developing a disparate impact jurisprudence; whereas in Malaysia, there is almost no trace of such an approach. In part, they further note, this is because there is a criminal prohibition in Malaysia on all acts questioning "any matter, right, status, position, privilege, sovereignty, or prerogative established" by those parts of the constitution that protect affirmative action measures for ethnic Malays (or the Bumiputra). A detailed study of Asian countries thus helps highlight the same lesson identified by Victor Ramraj in the context of constitutional emergency regimes: constitutional practices are ultimately deeply shaped by the actions of civil society, and thus, without empowering civil society to enforce and contest the meaning of particular provisions, constitutions will rarely create meaningful social change.

Ran Hirschl's examination of models of religion and the state identifies three different forms of secularism in the Indian case: the "universalist," or neutralist form, often associated with Western-like modernization and progress; the "populist" version often associated with Hindu right-wing parties, such as the Bharatiya Janata Party (BJP); and the "multicultural" or pluralist version associated with the legal status quo, under which various religious minorities have some degree of jurisdictional autonomy. This second, more populist version of secularism also helps draw attention to a largely entirely missing dimension to Western constitutional understandings of secularism – i.e. the extent to which it may be a Trojan horse for distinctly religious, non-neutral political ideas and interests. Seeing secularism in this way may also help us see appeals to secularism elsewhere in a new and distinctly more critical light.

III. WHY ASIA? ASIA AND BEYOND

Regionally focused forms of comparison of this kind also pose distinctive challenges for comparative constitutional scholars. For most comparative scholars, there are a range of jurisdictions they know best, or are most familiar with, and thus, which provide the most natural starting point for developing general comparative insights on particular topics. Asking scholars to focus on a particular region therefore disrupts this general comparative constitutional methodology – by asking scholars to start with constitutional systems they may know little about, and which may also have little in common, other than geography.

One response to this problem by prior authors and editors in the field has been to invite regional, or country, experts to take the lead in developing this kind of regionally focused comparative study. This approach has also generated a number of fine volumes on comparative constitutional topics, including volumes on Asia. The danger we see in this approach, however, is that in adding richness to our understanding of national constitutional systems, it may lose sight of the complexity of global constitutional archetypes – and the importance, and difficulty, of locating regional constitutional patterns within their full global context.

The approach we take in this volume, therefore, is somewhat different to that in existing work on constitutional law in Asia – i.e. to invite leading voices on *global* constitutional law, many of whom contributed to our prior volume on *Comparative Constitutional Law*, to engage more closely with Asian constitutional systems and experiences. Those who wrote on new topics, not directly covered in our 2011 volume, also sought directly to engage with those chapters and the archetypes they set out: thus in his chapter on constitutional courts in Asia, Tom Ginsburg, for example, benefited greatly from prior chapters in our 2011 handbook by Victor Fererres Comella, Frank Michelman and David Fontana on the jurisdiction and agenda/docket control of constitutional courts; and in his chapter on constitutions and emergency regimes in Asia, Victor Ramraj was greatly assisted by the prior work of Oren Gross in our 2011 volume.

For the most part, of course, "global" authors in this project cannot hope to bring the same depth of knowledge to Asia, and Asian constitutional developments, as scholars whose work focuses largely or exclusively on Asia, or who are true experts on particular countries within the region. As the various chapters in this volume attest, however, they have capacity to enrich and deepen scholarship on Asian constitutional law in a different way – by connecting it more closely to global theoretical and empirical debates about constitutional design, change, interpretation and enforcement.

The editors and authors were also extremely fortunate, in this context, to have the benefit of the expertise and generous assistance of many leading experts on constitutional law in Asia. In adapting their prior work to engage more closely with Asian constitutional experiences, most of the contributors to this volume met at a conference co-hosted by the University of Chicago and the University of Hong Kong, in Hong Kong in December 2011. We also invited some of Asia's most distinguished constitutional law experts to attend that conference, and act as commentators there on prior chapters from our volume on *Comparative Constitutional Law* (2011). Scholars who accepted this invitation, and were unfailingly generous in giving of their time and expertise in this context included: Wen-Cheng Chan (Taiwan) (National Taiwan University); Albert Chen (China, Hong Kong) (University of Hong Kong); Rishad Chowdhury (India) (University of Chicago/Delhi Bar); Diane Desierto (the Philippines) (University of Hawaii); Björn Dressel (Thailand) (Australian National University); John Gillespie (Vietnam) (Monash University); Chaihark Hahm (South Korea) (Yonsei University); Madhav Khosla (India) (Harvard University); H.P. Lee (Malaysia) (Monash University); Tokujin Matsudaira (Japan) (University of Tokyo); Fritz Siregar (Indonesia) (UNSW); and Po-Jen Yap (Singapore) (Cambridge University). We would like to take this opportunity to thank them for their contribution to the volume: all of the chapters, and the volume as a whole, are so much richer for their involvement.

The dialogue they helped create also stands as a model, we believe, of how we may all be able to produce the best kind of globally *and* regionally focused constitutional scholarship: dialogue of this kind allows us both to add breadth and nuance to existing global constitutional scholarship, and to bring greater theoretical richness and broader context to existing country-focused constitutional scholarship.

Such an approach could, of course, be applied to almost any region – and indeed, it is our hope that the project we have begun in this volume may be extended, and repeated with appropriate modification and refinement, to other regions in the future. Asia, however, was where it made sense for us to begin – because of both our own expertise and geography. Asia itself is also a region of immense internal diversity: as Ran Hirschl notes in his contribution to this volume, "the term 'Asia' (as in say, 'Asian food' or 'Asian values') is often invoked to refer to what is actually a sub-region that includes East and Southeast Asia," but the region is actually far larger – stretching from the Middle East to the edge of the Pacific Rim, or including 48 countries, or roughly 60 percent of the world's population. As a region, it is thus also in many ways the perfect place in which to start our own attempts to meld truly global and regional comparative constitutional scholarship: in its enormous diversity, Asia is in some sense simply a microcosm of the world, but one that is distinct in noticeable – and often previously unnoticed – ways.

We are therefore delighted to offer you this new volume on Comparative Constitutional Law … *In Asia*, which can be read either independently from, or in conjunction with, our prior volume on *Comparative Constitutional Law*.

REFERENCES

Adolphson, Mikael S. 2000. *The Gates of Power: Monks, Courtiers and Warriors in Premodern Japan*. Honolulu: University of Hawaii Press.

Balme, Stéphanie and Michael W. Dowdle, eds. 2009. *Building Constitutionalism in China*. New York: Palgrave Macmillan.

Bui, Ngoc Son. 2012. "Confucian Constitutionalism: Classical Foundations." *Australian Journal of Legal Philosophy* 37: 61–98.

Choudhry, Sujit. 1999. "Globalization in Search of Justification: Toward a Theory of Comparative Constitutional Interpretation," 74 *Indiana Law Journal* 74: 819–892.

Dixon, Rosalind. 2008. "A Democratic Theory of Constitution Comparison." 56 *American Journal of Comparative Law* 947.

Dixon, Rosalind. 2009. "A New Theory of Charter Dialogue: The Supreme Court of Canada, Charter Dialogue and Deference". 47 *Osgoode Hall Law Journal* 235.

Dowdle, Michael. 2009. "Beyond 'Judicial Power': Courts and Constitutionalism in Modern China". In *Building Constitutionalism in China*, edited by Stéphanie Balme and Michael Dowdle. New York: Palgrave Macmillan.

Duechler, Martina. 2002. *The Confucian Transformation of Korea.* Cambridge, MA: Council on East Asian Studies, Harvard University Press.

Elkins, Zachary, Tom Ginsburg and James Melton. 2009. *The Endurance of National Constitutions*. Cambridge: Cambridge University Press.

Ginsburg, Tom. 2002. "Confucian Constitutionalism? Globalization and Judicial Review in Korea and Taiwan". *Law and Social Inquiry* 27(4): 763–800.

Ginsburg, Tom. 2003. *Judicial Review in new Democracies: Constitutional Courts in Asian Cases.* New York: Cambridge University Press.

Ginsburg, Tom and Rosalind Dixon, eds. 2011. *Comparative Constitutional Law*. Cheltenham, UK: Edward Elgar.

Grossverg, Kenneth A., ed., Kanamoto Nobuhisa, tr. 1981. *The Laws of the Muromachi Bakufu: Kemmu Shikimoku (1336) and Muromachi Bakufu* Tsuikahō. Tokyo: Sophia University.

Hahm, Chaihark. 2003a. "Constitutionalism, Confucian Civic Virtue, and Ritual Propriety." Pp. 31–53 in *Confucianism for the Modern World*, edited by Daniel A. Bell and Hahm Chaibong. Cambridge: Cambridge University Press.

Hahm, Chaihark. 2003b. "Law, Culture, and the Politics of Confucianism." *Columbia Journal of Asian Law* 16(2): 253–291.

Hahm, Chaihark. 2009. "Ritual and Constitutionalism: Disputing the Ruler's Legitimacy in a Confucian Polity." *American Journal of Comparative Law* 57(1): 135–204.

Harding, Andrew. 2007. "Buddhism, Human Rights and Constitutional Reform in Thailand." *Asian Journal of Comparative Law* 1: 1–25.

Horowitz, Donald L. 2013. *Constitutional Change and Democracy in Indonesia*. Cambridge: Cambridge University Press.

Kihl, Young Whan. 2005. *Transforming Korean Politics: Democracy, Reform, and Culture*. New York: M.E. Sharpe.

Liang, Zhiping. 1989. "Explicating 'Law': A Comparative Perspective of Chinese and Western Legal Culture." *Journal of Chinese Law* 3: 55–91.

Mass, Jeffrey P. 1976. *The Kamakura Bakufu: A Study in Documents*. Stanford: Stanford University Press.

Mass, Jeffrey P. 1990. "The Kamakura Bakufu," in *The Cambridge History of Japan*, vol 3, edited by Kozo Yamamura. Cambridge: Cambridge University Press.

Mass, Jeffrey P. 1999. *Yoritomo and the Founding of the First Bakufu: The Origins of Dual Government in Japan*. Stanford: Stanford University Press.

Pye, Lucien. 1988. *Asian Power and Politics: The Cultural Dimensions of Authority.* Cambridge: Belknap Press.

Ruskola, Teemu. 2013. *Legal Orientalism*. Cambridge, MA: Harvard University Press.

Saunders, Cheryl. 2013. "New Challenges for Constitutional Theory." Pp. 149–157 in *Constitutionalism and Constitutional Pluralism: One Supreme Law Many Communities: Contemporary Issues in India, South-East Asia, China, and Europe*, edited by P. Bhat. New York: LexisNexis

Steenstrup, Carl. 1991. *A History of Law in Japan Until 1868*. Leiden: E.J. Brill.

Turner, Karen. 1992. "Rule of Law Ideals in Early China?" *Journal of Chinese Law* 6(1): 1–44.

Tushnet, Mark. 2013. "Authoritarian Constitutionalism: Some Conceptual Issues." Pp. 36–49 in *Constitutions in Authoritarian Regimes*, edited by Tom Ginsburg and Alberto Simpser. New York: Cambridge University Press.

Yeh, Jiunn-Rong and Wen-Chen Chang. 2011. "The Emergence of East Asian Constitutionalism: Features in Comparison." *Journal of Comparative Law* 59(3): 805–839.

Yi, Tang Lu Shu and Ming Li. Wallace Johnson trans. 1979. *The T'ang Code: Volume I: General Principles*. Princeton: Princeton University Press.

Zhang, Qianfan. 2010, "A Constitution Without Constitutionalism? The Paths of Constitutional Development in China." *International Journal of Constitutional Law* 8: 950–976.

PART I

CONSTITUTIONAL DESIGN,
AMENDMENT AND INTERPRETATION

2. Participation in constitutional design: Asian exceptionalism

Justin Blount and Tom Ginsburg

Ours is an era of constitution-making. Approximately one-quarter of the world's written constitutions have been promulgated since the third wave of democracy began around 1974 (Comparative Constitutions Project 2009). The trend over this period has been toward increasing public participation in the constitutional design process – either in the design, drafting or approval of the constitutional text. To cite but one example, more than 40 percent of constitutions currently in force that describe their own promulgation procedure required public ratification via referendum. The comparable figure for 1950 was approximately 5 percent (Ginsburg, Elkins and Blount 2009).[1]

The new constitutionalism that has emerged over this period places as much emphasis on process as it does on outcomes (Hart 2001). In light of this, the formal provision of democratic institutions is no longer sufficient to establish the democratic bona fides of a constitution. Because a constitution is the highest level of lawmaking and provides the ultimate rule of recognition for lawmaking processes (Kelsen 1945; Hart 1961), it requires the greatest possible level of legitimation in democratic theory. This need for legitimation dictates that a democratic constitution must be fashioned by democratic means in acknowledgment of the moral claim of a people to the right to participate in the creation of the rules under which they will be governed (Hart 2001, 2003; Samuels 2005). The 2012 struggle over the constitution of Egypt provides a tragic illustration of the consequences of constraining participation: the Muslim Brotherhood rammed through a document without involvement of other groups in the constituent assembly, generating a backlash of bloody protests.

While a consensus has emerged on the international plane that maximum public participation is necessary for constitutional legitimacy, the

---

[1] This was true even though the proportion of texts specifying any promulgation procedure whatsoever is roughly equivalent in the two periods.

23

claims about the merits of participation have not been subject to much rigorous analysis. This chapter examines participation in constitution-making in East and Southeast Asia, and argues that the Asian experience provides a striking contrast to the conventional wisdom. Many of the most successful constitutions in East Asia – those of Japan, Korea, Taiwan, Indonesia, for example – were produced with a minimum of popular involvement. Others, such as the Philippines People-Power Constitution, produced in the aftermath of the popular revolution that unseated strongman Ferdinand Marcos, involved a referendum, but little popular input into the drafting. In short, there does not appear to be a pattern of popular participation in Asian constitution-making. Instead, Asian constitution-making tends to be an elite affair. This calls into question the conventional wisdom as a positive matter, although it does not imply that participation is bad as a normative matter.

I. PARTICIPATION IN CONSTITUTIONAL DESIGN

The constitutional design literature is rapidly expanding with a plethora of contributions touting the justifications for mass participation in constitution-making and speculating on its prerequisites, effects and consequences.[2] Like constitution-making in general, popular constitution-making takes many forms with frequent variation.[3] No single template exists but the most participatory processes combine elements of representation, consultation, popular ratification and oversight in varying degrees.[4] A quick summary of the various claims, and counter-claims, about public constitutional design will serve as a useful reference point for the discussion to follow as well as illustrating the contradictory nature of a number of hypotheses.

A. Justifying Participation

The most frequently cited, and most intuitively plausible, claim for participation is that it enhances constitutional legitimacy (Hart 2001,

---

[2] For a handful of recent examples, see Bannon 2007; Benomar 2004; Elkins, Ginsburg and Blount 2008; Ginsburg, Elkins and Blount 2009; Moehler 2008; Samuels 2006; Voigt 2004; and Widner 2008.

[3] See Ginsburg, Elkins and Blount 2009, p 205.

[4] Mendez and Triga (2009) conceptualize participation in an analogous manner, comparing constitutional design processes in terms of modes of representation, communicative interaction and legitimation.

2003; Samuels 2006; Voigt 2004; Karli 2009). Legitimacy reduces the likelihood of opposition and future renegotiation, imparting stability to a constitutional order (Voigt 2004). Voigt further suggests that even the perception or possibility of participation is sufficient to capture the legitimacy-conferring benefits of inclusive constitution-making.

In addition, participation is theorized to make 'better citizens' through the inculcation of democratic skills, habits and values (Mansbridge 1995: 1; Barber 1984). These newly acquired or burnished citizen attributes then provide a foundation for the efficacious functioning of formal democratic institutions enumerated in a new constitution (Barber 1984; Pateman 1970). Participation is also educative; it instructs citizens on matters of public import, accelerates the acquisition of political information and equips citizens for more critical evaluations of their government (Mansbridge 1995; Moehler 2008). In the constitutional setting, these arguments suggest that participation in, for example, ratification, promotes democratic values in citizens and educates them in the operations of democratic processes as well as the contents of the constitution (Barber 1984; Finkel 1987). This may increase the likelihood of the success of democracy at the regime level. Thus participation in the constitutional approval process will carry over to governance under the constitution once adopted.

The preceding arguments dovetail with another in support of mass participation in constitutional design: participation increases a constitution's ability to constrain government. If citizens are to effectively police the actions of government, it must be sufficiently clear what constitutes a violation of the limits of governmental power so that citizens can mobilize to prevent it (Carey 2000). Constitutions help resolve this coordination problem by generating common knowledge about the scope of acceptable government behavior and by providing a focal point for citizens to coordinate enforcement efforts (Weingast 1997). To the extent that popular ratification of a constitutional design process serves to construct focal points, it will facilitate the coordination needed to deter potential constitutional violations by government. In the most optimistic scenario, the presence of a focal point in the written text, when coupled with the more robust civil society that emerged as part of a participatory design process, will ensure that the constitution will be enforced and not serve as a mere parchment barrier (Carey 2000).

Finally, scholars think participatory processes will include more rights provisions and better enforcement mechanisms to protect them, including super-majoritarian institutions, and more public involvement in selecting government agents (Hart 2001; Samuels 2006; Ginsburg 2003; Voigt 2004).

B.   Uncertain Benefits

Much of the uncertainty and doubt surrounding the presumed virtues of participatory constitution-making are practical in nature rather than philosophical. Common themes include the quality of the text, the difficulty of reaching agreement and concerns about the post-adoption operation and duration of a constitution.

Rather than maximizing the common good by providing a more representative sample of interests, it has been suggested that participation will produce documents dominated by self-interest (Scaff 1975), particularly if it is the case that citizens are motivated more by self-interest than are elites (Cusack 2003). In this view, participation is largely instrumental, providing citizens an additional avenue to capture state benefits, protect interests or gain power. Rather than promoting civil society and building democratic citizens, such self-interested participation may have the opposite effect (Ghai and Galli 2006; Scaff 1975; Salisbury 1975).

Voigt (2004) voices a practical concern related to the consequences of participatory constitutional design processes for textual coherence. As Horowitz (2002) notes, even under the best of circumstances, constitutional "design" – a term he reserves for a cohesive process – is quite rare, with some process of incremental construction more the norm. Constitution-making frequently consists of a combination of institutional borrowing, wholesale grafting, log-rolling and improvisation (Horowitz 2002). As new, and more, actors become involved in the process, bargaining and negotiation become both more extensive and intensive (Horowitz 2002). The constitution that emerges from this process will almost certainly be an ad hoc creation, rife with internal inconsistencies and institutional mismatches. While the loss of design consistency may be compensated for by the resultant gains in legitimacy, it may also render the constitutional scheme unworkable (Horowitz 2002).

A different line of critique emphasizes the difficulty of reaching agreement itself. More actors will, *ceteris paribus*, increase the transaction costs of negotiation (Karli 2009), particularly when participants have veto powers over the adoption of new rules (Tsebelis 2002). If the cardinal measure of the success of a design process is the adoption of a new constitution, then participation-induced procedural inefficiencies that prevent agreement on and the promulgation of a new text are serious matters (Karli 2009).

Finally, an older line of theory hypothesizes that mass participation in the design process has the capacity to destabilize fragile societies either by exacerbating conflicts over resources, activating latent identities such as ethnicity, or both (Huntington 1968).[5] Given the large number of constitutional design episodes occurring in post-conflict or conflict-prone societies, this criticism is of more than academic interest (Widner 2005b; Reynolds 2002) although it has also not been subjected to empirical verification.[6]

C. Deliberation

Democracy theorists agree on the value of participation in constitution-making though disagreement about methods exists. There is a natural tension between direct or mass democracy and deliberative democracy. This tension is most evident in terms of public oversight (see "Transparency, Self-interest and Arguing" below) but manifests itself in other ways as well. Generally speaking, the emphasis on popular legitimacy in the mass democracy literature lends itself to particular modes of participation in constitution-making. Representation, inclusiveness and ratification via referendum are key to establishing procedural and constitutional legitimacy. The best practices guidelines of the Commonwealth Human Rights Initiative (1999) urging the adoption of a design process that "engages the largest majority of the population" (p 4) are consistent with this view.

Deliberative theorists such as Fishkin (2009) distinguish between institutions of "refined" and "raw" opinion. Refined opinion is that "tested by the consideration of competing arguments and information conscientiously offered by those who hold contrasting views" (p 14). Raw opinion is untested, generally unsystematic and pervasive in modern democracies. Focus groups, opinion polls and direct democracy instruments like the referendum inhabit the universe of raw opinion. In terms of constitution-making, legitimate popular consultation is an instrument of refined opinion while popular ratification, with its simple yes or no format, is an expression of raw opinion. The Burkean emphasis on representation as a filter rather than a mirror is another difference of import for constitution-making. The purpose of representative institutions is not to ascertain what citizens think but what citizens would think if they were better informed (Fishkin 2009). Inclusiveness in deliberation then is not justified on equitable grounds but as a means of reaching the "true" counter-factual of refined opinion.

---

[5] But see Lipset (1959) noting that although intergroup conflict can lead to societal disintegration, social cleavages strengthen democratic institutions.

[6] Widner notes more than 150 episodes in the 1975–2003 period, for instance.

The tension between deliberative and mass democracy has historical roots. As Fishkin (2009) argues, the arc of democratic development in the United States is one of a transition from more deliberative, filtering political structures to more mass-based, popular ones. Early institutions such as the indirect election of senators, the Electoral College and even the Philadelphia convention itself were consciously designed to promote measured deliberation. Changes in the conduct of elections, including the candidate-nominating process, and the functional dismissal of the Electoral College have worked to make institutions more reflective of raw public opinion.

II. REPRESENTATION

Popular election of representatives to the body responsible for debating and adopting a constitution is the most straightforward method of engaging the public in the design process. Other selection methods such as appointment by the head of state, the legislature or other corporate bodies like peak associations are used but the trend is toward popular election.[7] Indeed, Widner (2008) reports that since 1987, 65 percent of all processes included elected delegates. From another perspective, one-quarter of new constitutions during this period "were drafted by bodies that would not be considered representative either in terms of the method of authorization or composition" (p 1524).

The concept of representative constitution-making involves more than just the identity of those debating and adopting a draft text. It is also a matter of choice about institutional venue. Excluding executive-centered processes as a priori undemocratic and non-participatory, constitutional reformers typically choose between either a legislature-centered reform process or a constituent assembly-centered one. As will be discussed below, it is generally assumed that an elected constituent assembly is more representative and "other-regarding" than an elected legislature tasked with crafting a new constitution (Ghai 2004: 9; Elster 2006, 2009).

---

[7] Widner's (2005b) survey of 194 constitution-writing processes held between 1975 and 2003 in conflict-prone societies indicates that only 15 percent of cases are the exclusive domain of the executive branch. Our survey of more than 400 episodes of constitutional design since 1789 found a predominant role for the executive in approximately 20 percent of cases.

A. Elections

As noted above, direct election of delegates to the deliberating and/or adopting body is a common means of securing mass participation in the constitution-making process. It is important to note though that elections are simply a means to an end, and not an end in and of themselves. Popular election is simply a mechanism through which to seek full, inclusive representation of citizen interests, preferences and beliefs. It is not a magic bullet and the popular election of delegates is no guarantee of a representative, inclusive body. Election rules, electoral formulas, polling access, citizen information and physical (in-)security of voters can all distort the expression of a people's preferences. To counter this, some countries have allowed social and/or economic groups to select delegates to the deliberating/adopting body in addition to the delegates chosen by the citizenry at large. In contexts in which elections are seen as easily manipulatable by political elites, such arrangements may produce a more popularly credible assembly (Widner 2008). Ideally, this combination of both generalized and specialized constituencies is a way to combine the credibility of elections with the legitimacy conferred by the inclusion of as wide a swath of society as is practicable.

The Ugandan constitutional experience in this regard is illuminating. To begin with, it is likely that public pressure was largely responsible for the ruling National Resistance Council's (NRC) decision to allow a popularly elected constituent assembly to debate and adopt the draft constitution prepared by the Ugandan Constitutional Commission (UCC). There was public skepticism about the initial plan for the NRC to simply transform itself into a constituent assembly to debate and adopt the final draft as well as a concern that the UCC itself lacked any kind of popular mandate or sanction (Furley and Katalikawe 1997; Moehler 2008). Elections were agreed upon in no small part in order to secure legitimacy.

In Uganda, approximately 75 percent of the 284 delegates to the constituent assembly were chosen by direct election.[8] Seats were specifically set aside for women with one woman being elected from each of 39 districts by women leaders within her district. In addition, various groups within Uganda elected delegates to represent their interests. Ten delegates were chosen by the military, two by the National Organization of Trade Unions, one by the National Organization of

---

[8] The elections were legally non-partisan, hampering coordination of would-be opposition groups to the National Resistance Movement. Rallies and demonstrations "in support of or against any candidate" were prohibited (National Resistance Council. Constituent Assembly Statute No. 6 of 1993).

Disabled People, four youths elected by youth leaders of each region, four elected political leaders and ten presidential appointees (Waliggo 2001). Despite concerns about the true motivations of the government (see Furley and Katalikawe 1997) and caveats about individual-level effects of participation, the 1995 Constitution enjoys some of the highest levels of public support in Sub-Saharan Africa, surpassing even that of the highly participatory South African process (Moehler 2006, 2008).

B.   Risks of Elections

A critical assumption of some is that representation secured through popular election is an unqualified good. Some cautionary words are perhaps in order. First, elections can remove the veil of ignorance from rival groups or parties. Removing the uncertainty surrounding the "true" level of support for a group has the capacity to reduce the incentive to compromise. In extreme cases, such as Egypt in 2012, constitution-making becomes an exercise in majoritarianism, or more cynically, census-taking, rather than consensus. Notable cases in Asia include East Timor in 2002 and the ongoing Nepalese process, uncompleted at the time of this writing.

The East Timor constitutional assembly was dominated by Fretilin, which won 55 of 88 seats in elections in 2001. The electoral results so skewed power in the assembly that Fretilin had no need to compromise on its proposals while other groups lacked negotiating leverage (Ghai and Galli 2006). Although the assembly (which later transformed into a working legislature) accepted drafts from each of the interested political parties, the Fretilin draft was used as the working draft by the drafting committee and the draft ultimately produced by the committee very closely resembled the draft originally submitted by the Fretilin party. The other parties' drafts were not considered. In addition, the assembly was criticized by Muslim residents as "unrepresentative since the electoral law prevented many of them from voting" (Widner 2005b), further attenuating the legitimacy of the process. Fretilin's dominant position within the assembly enabled it to ignore the results of an initial round of public consultation in creating the draft constitution. Ultimately, Fretilin was able to push through a final version of the text following only a seven-day period for public review and comment (Benomar 2004; Kritz 2003; Widner 2005b).

It must be noted, however, that despite these procedural concerns, the East Timor constitution has been in operation for over a decade and Fretilin's once dominant position has eroded. In 2007 elections, it won less than a third of the seats. The East Timor experience provides a clue that participation need not always produce a more legitimate outcome, but also that a flawed negotiation need not doom the country forever.

In the case of Nepal, where the legislature is also doubling as a constituent assembly, the 2008 elections that gave the Unified Communist Party of Nepal (Maoist) a sizable plurality may have undermined the consensual elements of the 2006 Comprehensive Peace Agreement (International Crisis Group 2009). The mix of legislative and constituent functions appears to have made an already precarious situation even more fragile. Unable to govern, the Maoists (and others) have pushed constitution-making to the back burner amidst other political crises, making it unlikely that the assembly will meet the May 2010 deadline for a new text. It seems improbable that in cases marred by breakdowns in elite-level cooperation and deliberation such as these, meaningful mass participation will continue (Benomar 2004).

Elections, and popular participation more generally, also have the capacity to foment polarization and civil strife.[9] In the Iraqi case, elections contributed to communal polarization and led to the Sunni boycott (Ghai and Galli 2006); likewise, Chad's participatory process resulted in a heightening of Francophone–Arab tensions (Bannon 2007; Widner 2005b). Bannon urges careful consideration of local contexts in designing participatory processes, noting that a single "participatory model" does not exist. Would-be reformers would likely do well to heed her advice and resist the temptation to understate the potential non-pecuniary costs of participatory constitution-making and be flexible in designing the methods for and rules governing popular input, particularly given the noticeable regional variation in Widner's (2005) analysis of the relationship between representation and post-ratification violence reduction.

C. Elite Selection

In some cases, a drafting commission can be selected by elites but designed to include people from a wide swath of society. This was the model chosen by President Aquino after the People Power Revolution in the Philippines. She appointed a 50-member commission to draft a new constitution, which was written in six months. Members included Supreme Court Justices, representatives of civil society, a Catholic bishop, academics and a film director. The draft constitution was ratified

---

[9] See Lipset (1959) and Huntington (1968) about the potentially destabilizing effects of mass participation. Bannon (2007: 1842–1849) reiterates some of these arguments in her review of Kenya's constitutional design experience.

by an electorate in a referendum with a three-fourths' majority in February 1987. The 1987 Constitution replaced the interim constitution, which "lacked democratic credentials" because of its broad executive and legislative powers. This constitution "served chiefly as a presidential device to dismantle the remnants of the Marcos regime" (Ruland 2003: 463).

The 1987 Constitution revived the presidential system of the 1935 Constitution, which was patterned on the American system due to colonialism. This includes a directly elected president, an executive–legislative relationship characterized by checks and balances, a bicameral Congress, and, unlike the American system, a unitary state. Because the constitution was drafted hastily, it left major articles to be specified by congressional legislation, thus leaving constitutional debate open long after its ratification.

The current constitution restored the separation of powers that corroded under the Marcos regime, which in turn empowered a judiciary that had been severely weakened under the Marcos regime. Aquino "almost immediately reestablished a Supreme Court, staffed with several new Justices, and this Court quickly ascended to a position of respect that nearly matched that of its pre-martial law predecessor" (Gatmaytan-Magno 2007: n 31). Under the Marcos regime, the Supreme Court had gained a reputation for corruption as an extension of the president's office. The Court's response to charter change reflects its enlarged and redefined role in Philippine society.

III. THE ROLE OF INTERNATIONAL ACTORS

Constitution-making is, increasingly, a transnational enterprise, and the history of constitution-making in Asia is ridden with circumstances in which outside actors were shaping processes to various extents. This section reviews the experience.

A. Japan

Asian countries' experience with constitution-making illustrates the sometimes critical role of international actors in the process. The most extreme case, of course, is that of Japan. In the aftermath of the defeat in World War II, Japan was occupied by allied forces under the direction of the Supreme Commander of the Allied Powers (SCAP), General Douglas MacArthur. MacArthur had originally intended to leave constitution-making to the Japanese themselves, but a conservative commission produced a draft that was seen as insufficiently democratic (Moore and Robinson 2002). In February of 1946, MacArthur ordered a small group of his staff to draft a constitution within a period of ten days, to be presented to the Japanese government. He issued his famous note, outlining a few features of the future Japanese constitution, including an instruction to preserve the Imperial institution and to prohibit the maintenance of an army.

One remarkable participant was a young woman named Beate Sirota Gordon, and she was (as her autobiography put it) "The Only Woman in the Room" (Gordon 2001). Gordon single-handedly drafted the provisions on women's rights, informed by her experiences growing up in Japan and her familiarity with the trials of Japanese women. There is little doubt that the provisions would have been less progressive, and maybe even absent, had the drafting been left up to the Japanese themselves. This illustrates the point that outside involvement need not always be an imposition, but can facilitate the rights of subaltern voices in domestic contexts.

The Japanese government made some minor changes to the draft, which was then sent to a newly elected Diet for deliberation. The government maintained the fiction that the draft had been produced internally. The summer 1946 sessions of the Diet can be considered a form of indirect popular participation, and in the end the constitution was passed without the need for a popular referendum. However, it would be too much to say that there was no input whatsoever (Law 2013; Elkins, Ginsburg and Melton 2008). In a couple of instances, the Japanese participants in the process fought back attempts to change fundamental norms. For example, the SCAP drafters, who had been influenced by the New Deal, sought to declare that all land belonged to the state. The Japanese, who had a long feudal and agrarian tradition, found this to be anathema and insisted on a right to private property. The Japanese also insisted on retaining a bicameral parliament from the Meiji Constitution, though the American draft had included only one house of the legislature.

Ultimately, it seems that elite buy-in was accomplished primarily through allowing the Diet to translate the American-written, English-language text into Japanese, thereby creating an indigenous, "Japanese" constitution (Moore and Robinson 2004). Interestingly, several attempts at revising the constitution since 1946 have failed, although another attempt is being pushed by Prime Minister Shinzo Abe at the time of this writing.

B. East Timor

East Timor and Cambodia both marked constitutional transitions that
were shepherded by United Nations missions. Unlike the comparable
effort in Cambodia after 1989, there was no peace agreement specifying
that a constitution would be a component of East Timor's state-building
effort (Aucoin and Brandt 2009). When the pro-independence group
Conselho Nacional da Resistencia Timorense (CNRT) held a meeting in
Tibar, it asked for a constitutional working committee to be formed to
draft the constitution in a fully participatory process. But the United
Nations Transitional Authority in East Timor (UNTAET) decided on an
alternative model that was based on an elected constituent assembly that
would then be transformed into the country's working legislature (Aucoin
and Brandt 2009). This model was quite different in that it placed much
less emphasis on public consultation. Many questioned why the CNRT
ideas had been ignored, but the UN went ahead with the plan for an
elected body that would have to draft, debate and adopt the constitution
within 90 days.

The pro-independence resistance movement Fretilin dominated the
subsequent elections, winning 55 of the 88 seats in the assembly.
Because of their links with some minor parties, this gave Fretilin the
effective ability to adopt the constitution without building broader
consensus or compromising with a unified opposition. The subsequent
process was heavily supported by outside organizations, but ended up
drawing heavily on a draft that had been produced by Fretilin in 1998.
Although the elected assembly organized its work into various committees, these drew heavily on the Fretilin draft and paid little attention to
proposals from outside the assembly. The Constitution was ultimately
adopted on March 22, 2002, by a vote of 72 to 14.

UNTAET appeared to be focused on elections as the main mode of
legitimating constitutional drafting, and did not pay sufficient attention to
other modes of participation. Furthermore, in the context of East Timor,
it was clear that Fretilin would dominate any electoral process. This
meant that the possibility of a broader, more diverse body, or one that
relied more heavily on independent technical expertise, was foreclosed.
Aucoin and Brandt (2009: 257) suggest that a two-phased approach
would have been more appropriate. This would have involved "the
formation of an appointed, broadly representative constitutional commission to develop a draft constitutional text and adoption of a final
constitution by an elected body or a body that is both selected and
elected to ensure the diversity of the nation is represented." (Id.)

The story of East Timor's independence constitution reveals the benefits and risks of outside involvement. As much as UNTAET did to shepherd the birth of the state, it also imposed its own agenda on the process of constitution-making, which had the effect of reinforcing Fretilin's political dominance. As in other situations in which outsiders heavily influenced constitution-making, such as the Japanese case noted above or the more recent experience of the Americans in Iraq, speed was privileged over inclusion. The lessons are that participation must be treated in a contextual manner, and that elections alone may be insufficient to provide for broad-based access to constitution-making.

C. Cambodia

Cambodia's 20-year civil conflict came to an end under the Paris Peace Accords, which called on the country to elect a constituent assembly to produce a liberal democratic constitution. This body would present the draft to Prince Sihanouk for promulgation. As in East Timor, this constituent assembly would then become a working legislature after the constitution was adopted.

The election was administered in May 1993 by the United Nations, and was won by the royalist political party, FUNCINPEC, which won around 45 per cent of the votes. The ruling Cambodian People's Party (CPP) finished second with 38 per cent of the votes. A 12-member Drafting Committee was formed, and this group produced a draft over the summer of 1993, releasing it in only September. Meanwhile, the FUNCINPEC party produced its own draft. While the Committee's draft was republican in character, the FUNCINPEC version restored the monarchy. The two drafts were then presented to Sihanouok, who made some edits to the FUNCINPEC draft, and sent it to the Assembly. The Assembly then adopted the text, and it was ratified by Sihanouk on September 24. Cambodia's monarchy was restored.

The constitution-making process in Cambodia accomplished its short term goal of re-establishing legitimate government, and can be said to have reflected the results of the election in that the monarchist party had the dominant role. Nevertheless, in terms of the broader theme of this chapter, the entire process was nearly free of public participation. Neither civil society, which was then in a nascent state, nor the broader public had much input into the draft. The process of drafting was conducted in secret. Although the UN played a role in ensuring a formal veneer of liberal democracy, the CPP eventually deposed FUNCINPEC and continues to dominate the country's politics today. It is hardly an illustration of the advantages of outsider involvement.

D. Fiji

Another model of outside involvement occurred in Fiji in 1997, when a three-person commission headed by an outsider, Sir Paul Reeves of New Zealand, was selected to review the 1990 Constitution. That document had explicitly involved racial allocation of seats to ensure indigenous Fijian dominance. The review process was well designed in terms of balance, with one Indo-Fijian and one indigenous member, but far too small to ensure that a wide range of interests was directly represented within the commission. The commission ultimately produced a document that essentially contained drafting instructions for an entirely new constitution (Ghai and Cottrell 2007).

The Fiji process was based on a two-stage model, involving both technical expertise and political deliberation. First, the commission would prepare a draft in the course of its review. Second, the Parliament would debate and enact the constitution. There would not be a special constituent assembly, nor a referendum involving public approval. The Reeves Commission took its work very seriously, giving very high priority to public participation. It engaged in an extensive set of meetings with the public, and commissioned a variety of background papers on specific questions. After more than a year of work, it compiled its findings into an 800 page report that was then presented to the president and published in September 1996.

The action then moved to the Parliament where a Joint Parliamentary Select Committee with representation from all the political parties had primary responsibility for reviewing the draft and preparing a formal bill for constitutional amendment. The Committee took about six months to complete its task, and produced a compromise on many of the key points. This reflected the competing positions of the Fijian members, who were by and large happy with the 1990 constitution, and the Indo-Fijians, who wished for greater representation. The closed-door compromise led to an amendment bill, introduced in June 1997 and adopted nearly as drafted.

In short, outsiders can have a crucial role to play in structuring the process, and even leading drafting processes, and especially in providing expertise. But notwithstanding positive rhetoric from international actors, their involvement is not always a panacea for local participation, at least in the Asian experience.

E. Deliberations, Where Art Thou?

An additional aspect of representation in popular constitution-making is the choice of reform model (Widner 2008). The most common approaches are to house such power either in the existing legislature, which will assume such a task in addition to its regular legislative functions, or in a specially convened assembly with no other purpose than to deliberate upon and/or adopt a proposed constitution. This choice has implications for the extent to which the benefits of a particular method of delegate selection will be realized.

There is a long tradition of debate relating to the legitimacy of the exercise of constituent power. In *The Rights of Man*, Thomas Paine emphasized the need for a distinction between ordinary law and the supreme law of a constitution. Legislative drafting of the constitution blurs this distinction as legislators may seek to inject policy or partisan concerns into the deliberations or constitutional text itself.[10] This certainly appeared to be the case in the Polish parliament where "in the course of parliamentary debates, constitutional compromise was increasingly overwhelmed and obscured by political compromise" (Spiewak 1997). The distinction may likewise be blurry for voters as their constitutional preferences get traded off against other concerns when choosing a representative.

In the same vein, it was frequently noted during the Massachusetts Constitutional Convention of 1779 that the "body charged with creating the fundamental law could not be the same body that enacts ordinary law" (Breslin 2009). Gouverneur Morris made this point as well when the Provincial Congress of New York was debating whether it possessed the authority to draft a constitution (Elster 2009). Similar themes are echoed in the constitutional histories of France and Italy of the late 19th century in which parliaments sought to exercise constituent power with only a vague mandate (Arangio-Ruiz 1895; Currier, 1893; Saleilles 1895). Elster's (2006) concern with parliamentary drafting has a long pedigree.

In contrast to the legislature-based reform model, the constituent assembly-based model of constitutional reform is an unequivocal representation of a people's constituent power (Ghai 2004). Its prima facie legitimacy is unquestioned and largely avoids the conflicts of interest and credibility issues facing legislative drafting. Constituent assemblies are

---

[10] There is skepticism that legislators will not seek to advantage their own institution at the expense of other branches (Elster 2006; but see Ginsburg, Elkins and Blount 2009).

also perceived as more broadly representative (Ghai 2004). One reason for this is that unlike a legislature where selection rules are typically designed with an eye to governability, and hence majority formation, constituent assemblies seek to include as broad a range of interests as possible (Elster 2006). Of course, an expansive membership may also complicate the process of agreement and risk deadlock. Secondly, in countries in need of systematic political reform, and thus a new constitution, citizen access to power is likely limited so even if the drafting and deliberation of a new constitution occurs under the auspices of an elected legislature, it is clearly less participatory than an elected constituent assembly. For these reasons, constituent assemblies are hypothesized to enable a more wide-open, reform-minded agenda capable of transformational change than legislatures (Ghai, 2004). Other things being equal, constituent assembly-based models are generally more participatory and representative.

Tushnet (2008) argues that while popular support is important, it is secondary to elite buy-in. Including relevant elite stakeholders minimizes the opportunity for entrepreneurial elites to seek political gain by "appealing to members of the public who would not have bought in" (pp 1490, 1491). In this perspective, popular participation functions as an additional layer of insurance against attacks on the constitutional order. Ultimately, this is a difference more of degree than of kind as the need to include relevant stakeholders is a frequent constitutional prescription (Benomar 2004; Hart 2003) but it does suggest that the potential costs of expanded participation should be more carefully weighed against its supposed benefits.[11]

IV. RATIFICATION

Since the early 20th century, there has been an increasing trend of popular ratification of constitutions (Elkins, Ginsburg and Blount 2008; 2009). Despite its growing popularity as a mode of public involvement, the referendum is clearly a limited one in that it involves only an up or down vote over a package of provisions.[12] Even under ideal conditions, ratification via referendum probably does not represent a Pareto-efficient

---

[11]   Exclusion of key stakeholders introduces a downstream constraint on the successful operation of a constitution as the Ethiopian case, in which opposition groups were excluded from the process, illustrates (Benomar 2004).

[12]   Interestingly, the 1978 Ecuadorian referendum held by the military government provided for a choice of constitutions. A 'yes' vote indicated support for

outcome though it is certainly to be hoped that it signifies a Pareto improvement over the status quo. Majority support of a sub-optimal text is easily envisaged, if one considers that as voters, citizens may bundle non-constitutional concerns with constitutional ones in deciding how to vote, just as legislative drafters undoubtedly do. A notable example of this is the Democratic Republic of the Congo (DRC), whose voters in 2005 overwhelmingly approved at referendum a constitution they had almost no part in writing. Voters' views on the proposed institutional arrangements were less important than their belief that accepting the constitution would end the war and bring peace (Gathii 2008).

A. Logistical Constraints on Referendum Efficacy

While it is common to think of referenda as primarily a downstream constraint on drafters, it is worth remembering that referenda are not immune to elite manipulation. State control of the logistics of elections can be a substantial upstream constraint as existing governments or political elites may function as gatekeepers. Even when referenda are allowed to proceed, elites may yet retain significant influence over events. A notable achievement of the Cherokee Nation process was the constitution commission's insistence that its enabling legislation gave it the sole authority to call and conduct a ratification referendum (Lemont 2006a). With the tribal government held in such low regard, this independence enhanced the credibility of the commission and the process.

The timing of referenda can also be manipulated to influence the result. Sufficient time should be devoted to a referendum campaign that allows for public education and debate. Too short a time prevents debate as civil society may not have time to collectively organize while waiting too long may subsume the constitutional issue into other matters of political import or allow public interest in the process to wane altogether (International IDEA 2008). The former problem is likely more of a concern in non-democratic contexts as the recent Thailand experience demonstrates. Among the many procedural complaints against the 2007 constitutional design process was the scant 19 days allowed for review of the 300-article draft produced by the military government (International IDEA 2008). Other complaints highlight the concerns discussed above. It was suggested that approval of the draft would result in an early return of

---

the newly drafted text while a 'no' vote indicated support for the previously abrogated 1945 constitution.

democratic elections while its rejection would "create continuing problems and a chaotic situation" (International IDEA 2008). Given this, it is difficult to say what proportion of the 57 percent of Thais voting "yes" did so out of support for the constitution rather than out of a desire for a return to democratic government or simple fear of the unknown.

B. Approval Thresholds

An additional consideration in the structure of referenda is the question of a minimum turnout threshold. A number of states impose such thresholds for the adoption of new constitutions or amendments. While a requirement that at least 50 percent of eligible voters must participate for a vote to be valid is normatively appealing on democratic grounds, it can have perverse consequences that can reinforce the status quo and frustrate legitimately popular aims. With a 50 percent threshold, a proposal enjoying unanimous support will be disqualified with 49 percent turnout while a proposal with 26 percent support but 25 percent opposition is a valid result. The incentive for referendum opponents to boycott the process rather than engage in it is obvious and woe to the referendum that fails to be enacted because it did not generate enough opposition (Gallagher 2001)!

Compulsory voting laws can mitigate this problem but currently only 16 countries both have and enforce such provisions (International IDEA 2008). Voting in referenda is mandatory in Australia but like Switzerland, it also imposes a double majority requirement; referenda must be approved by a majority of the national electorate as well as majorities in four of six states (International IDEA 2008). Since 1924, three referenda items approved by a majority of Australians have failed to reach the territorial threshold including one in May of 1977 that received 62 percent of the national vote (Australian Electoral Commission 2010).

C. Autocratic Referenda

One feature of the use of referenda in the constitution-making process is its frequent employment by autocrats. Approximately half of all referenda from a sample of 460 constitutional design episodes were used in executive-centered processes (Ginsburg, Elkins and Blount 2009). In these cases, referenda were motivated more by a desire to legitimize the autocrat's control of a polity than to allow the citizens to render a considered verdict on the constitution (Brunner 2001). The contrast between the early use of ratification referenda in post-Communist

Eastern Europe and the later use of ratification as instruments of acclamation in Central Asia makes the point nicely (Brunner 2001).

Given the advantages of executives in referendum campaigns such as more control of the process and greater access to state resources including media, one would expect them to be nearly universally successful in their efforts. Indeed, the record looks quite grim. Referenda in Belarus (1996) and Kazakhstan (1995) succeeded in preparing the way for super-presidentialism while executives in Turkmenistan, Uzbekistan and Kyrgyzstan similarly employed referenda to expand power or extend their term of office (Brunner 2001).

More encouragingly, however, the recent past also provides examples of referenda as binding constraints and not simply rubber stamps. Examples of this include the well-known case of Kenya in 2005 but also Albania in 1994 and Seychelles in 1992. All three cases share a similarity of attempted executive/elite manipulation of established processes. Mid-process changes to drafting and adoption procedures in Kenya undermined the credibility of political elites as good-faith agents of constitutional reform (Cottrell and Ghai 2007; Bannon 2007; Whitaker and Giersch 2009). Likewise, in Albania in 1994, President Berisha attempted an end-run around established constitutional procedures but was thwarted by voters (Brunner 2001; Widner 2005b). In Seychelles, efforts by President Rene to ensure himself a legislative majority following the return of multi-party elections were rebuffed in a November 1992 referendum (Hatchard 1993; Tartter 1995).

Even the admittedly sporadic success of peoples in blocking executive attempts to manipulate the referendum instrument for their own advancement is an encouraging sign for it signals that with elite commitment to a democratic process of constitution-making, referenda can function as binding constraints on drafters. Evidence of such a function is the preliminary general support for Samuels' (2006) findings that in non-authoritarian settings, referenda encourage the inclusion of a broader menu of rights provisions and direct democracy devices (Elkins, Ginsburg and Blount 2008; 2009).

V. PUBLIC OVERSIGHT

The complement to public participation is public oversight of the design process. If it is believed that delegates will behave differently when facing the nation than they will when facing their colleagues, then such oversight can be consequential. However, the case for transparency is not clear cut. A tension exists between transparency and secrecy; finding the right mix between sunlight and shadow can go a long way toward determining the overall success of a design process.

A.   Transparency, Self-interest and Arguing

While transparency is a general good with regard to the normal operations of a legislature, it is not necessarily the case that this is so with regard to constituent bodies. Constitution-building is a political process as well as a legal one, and a more enduring compact is likely to be established if participants are able to freely deliberate (Arato 1995; Elster 1995; Horowitz 2002; Sunstein 2001). Certain types of transparency such as monitoring and/or publishing the speeches and votes of individual delegates can have a stifling effect on the deliberative process as the human emotions of vanity and fear conspire to reduce the quality of debate (Elster 2009). Vanity, which prevents people from changing their mind as a result of argument, undermines the fundamental rationale of deliberation (Voigt 2004). Elster reports James Madison as averring that the secrecy of the Philadelphia Convention allowed each delegate to maintain his position only so long as he was convinced of its truth; in a deliberative setting, consistency is not a virtue. Elster notes that French delegates in September 1789 "feared for their lives" if they voted for bicameralism or the executive veto (p 26).

There is reason to think that transparency will have decisive effects on the manifestations of self-interest. In an ideal world, delegates would be dispassionate judges, calmly deliberating in the interests of the common weal, paying little heed to their own concerns. This will never be the case but transparency may be able to induce at least its pretense. At best, the "civilizing force" of this hypocrisy will serve to move the "most self-serving proposals off the agenda" (Elster 2009: 27).

In Elster's formulation, secrecy is amenable to hard bargaining, whereas publicity facilitates arguing. Though arguing is preferable to bargaining in his view, thus tending to favor a more transparent process, secret arguing, if it occurs, will be superior to public arguing (Elster 2009). As a solution to this tension between transparency and secrecy, Elster (2006) employs an hourglass metaphor to describe the optimal role of the public in the process with participation via public hearings at the upstream stage and some form of ratification possible at the downstream stage. The actual writing and deliberation (the neck of the hourglass) should be shielded from the public eye to avoid the pitfalls described above. The Spanish constitutional design process of 1977–78 mostly achieved this ideal though not entirely by design (Banting and Simeon 1985; Gunther 1985).

VI. CONCLUSION

As this brief discussion and cursory glance at a handful of cases revealed, there is a fair amount of constrained variation in the constitutional design procedures used by countries. While some forms of public participation are doubtless linked inextricably to their context, others offer up examples and innovations suitable for export. All of them, however, function in varying degrees as a constraint on the adoption of new institutions and rules. Though causal relationships are methodologically difficult to demonstrate, especially given the presence of selection bias in choice of process, participation should be expected to make a difference. Process should matter and there is accumulating evidence that it does – that the counter-factual constitution and subsequent constitutional order with no popular participation would be noticeably different.

REFERENCES

Arangio-Ruiz, G. 1895. "The Amendments to the Italian Constitution." *Annals of the American Academy of Political and Social Science* 6: 31–57.

Arato, Andrew. 1995. "Forms of Constitution Making and Theories of Democracy." *Cardozo Law Review* 17: 191–231.

Aucoin, Louis and Michelle Brandt. 2009. "East Timor's Constitutional Passage to Independence." Pp. 245–74 in *Framing the State in Times of Transition*, edited by Laurel Miller. US Institute for Peace Press.

Australian Election Commission, *Constitutional Referendums*, available at http://www.aec.gov.au/Education/files/constitutional-referendums-brochure-nov-2010-fa.pdf.

Bannon, Alicia L. 2007. "Designing a Constitution-Drafting Process: Lessons from Kenya." *Yale Law Journal* 116: 1824–1872.

Banting, Keith G. and Richard Simeon, eds. 1985. *Redesigning the State: The Politics of Constitutional Change*. Toronto: University of Toronto Press.

Barber, Benjamin. 1984. *Strong Democracy: Participatory Politics for a New Age*. Berkeley: University of California Press.

Benomar, Jamal. 2004. "Constitution-Making After Conflict: Lessons for Iraq." *Journal of Democracy* 15: 81–109.

Breslin, Beau. 2009. *From Words to Worlds: Exploring Constitutional Functionality*. Baltimore: The Johns Hopkins University Press.

Brunner, Georg. 2001. "Direct vs. Representative Democracy" in *Direct Democracy: The Eastern and Central European Experience*, edited by A. Auer and M. Butzer. Aldershot: Ashgate.

Carey, John M. 2000. "Parchment, Equilibria, and Institutions." *Comparative Political Studies* 33: 735–761.

Commonwealth Human Rights Initiative. 1999. Promoting a Culture of Constitutionalism and Democracy in Africa. Recommendations to the Commonwealth Heads of

Government. Available at http://www.humanrightsinitiative.org/publications/const/constitutionalism_booklet_1999.pdf.

Cottrell, Jill and Yash Ghai. 2007. "Constitution Making and Democratization in Kenya (2000–2005)." *Democratization* 14: 1–25.

Cottrell, Jill and Yash Ghai. 2009. "Between Coups: Constitution Making in Fiji." pp. 275–310 in *Framing the State in Times of Transition: Case Studies in Constitution Making*, edited by Laurel Miller. Washington DC: United States Institute of Peace.

Currier, Charles F.A. 1893. "Supplement: Constitutional and Organic Laws of France." *Annals of the American Academy of Political and Social Science* 3: 1–77.

Cusack, Thomas. 2003. *A National Challenge at the Local Level: Citizens, Elites and Institutions in Reunified Germany*. Burlington: Ashgate Publishing.

Elkins, Zachary, Tom Ginsburg and Justin Blount. 2008. " Citizen as Founder: Public Participation in Constitutional Approval." *Temple Law Review* 81: 361–382.

Elkins, Zachary, Tom Ginsburg and James Melton. 2008. "Baghdad, Tokyo, Kabul: Constitution-making in Occupied States." *William and Mary Law Review* 49: 1139–78.

Elster, Jon. 1995. "Forces and Mechanisms in the Constitution-Making Process." *Duke Law Journal* 45: 364–396.

Elster, Jon. 2006. "Legislatures as Constituent Assemblies." In *The Least Examined Branch: The Role of Legislatures in the Constitutional State*, edited by R.W. Bauman and T. Kahana. Cambridge: Cambridge University Press.

Elster, Jon. "The Optimal Design of a Constituent Assembly." Paper read at Conference on Comparative Constitutional Design, 16 October 2009 at University of Chicago.

Finkel, Steven E. 1987. "The Effects of Participation on Political Efficacy and Political Support: Evidence from a West German Panel." *The Journal of Politics* 49: 441–464.

Fishkin, James. 2009. *When the People Speak: Deliberative Democracy and Public Consultation.* New York: Oxford University Press.

Furley, Oliver and James Katalikawe. 1997. "Constitutional Reform in Uganda: The New Approach." *African Affairs* 96: 243–260.

Gallagher, Michael. 2001. "Popular Sovereignty and Referendums." In *Direct Democracy: The Eastern and Central European Experience*, edited by A. Auer and M. Butzer. Aldershot: Ashgate.

Gathii, James Thuo. 2008. "Popular Authorship and Constitution Making: Comparing and Contrasting the DRC and Kenya." *William and Mary Law Review* 49: 1109–1138.

Gatmaytan-Magno, D. 2007. "Changing Constitutions: Judicial Review and Redemption in the Philippines." *UCLA Pacific Basin Law Journal* 25(1): 1.

Ghai, Yash. "The Constitution Reform Process: Comparative Perspectives." Paper read at Toward Inclusive and Participatory Constitution Making, at Kathmandu, 2004.

Ghai, Y and J Cottrell. 2007. "A Tale of Three Constitutions: Ethnicity and Politics in Fiji." *Icon-International Journal of Constitutional Law* 5(4):639–669.

Ghai, Yash and Guido Galli. 2006. "Constitution Building Processes and Democratization." In *Democracy, Conflict, and Human Security*. Further Readings. IDEA.

Ginsburg, Tom. 2003. *Judicial Review in New Democracies: Constitutional Courts in Asian Cases*. Cambridge: Cambridge University Press.

Ginsburg, Tom, Zachary Elkins and Justin Blount. 2009. "Does the Process of Constitution-Making Matter?" *Annual Review of Law and Social Science* 5: 201–223.

Gordon, Beate Sirota (2001), *The Only Woman in the Room: A Memoir*, New York: Kodansha International.

Gunther, Richard. 1985. "Constitutional Change in Contemporary Spain." In *Redesigning the State: The Politics of Constitutional Change*, edited by K. G. Banting and R. Simeon. Toronto: University of Toronto Press.

Hart, H.L.A. 1961. *The Concept of Law*. Oxford: Oxford University Press.

Hart, Vivien. 2001. "Constitution-Making and the Transformation of Conflict." *Peace & Change* 26: 153–176.

Hart, Vivien. 2003. "Democratic Constitution Making." Special Report. United States Institute of Peace.

Hatchard, John. 1993. "Reestablishing a Multi-Party State: Some Constitutional Lessons from the Seychelles." *Journal of Modern African Studies* 31: 601–612.

Horowitz, Donald L. 2002. "Constitutional Design: Proposals Versus Processes." In *The Architecture of Democracy,* edited by A. Reynolds. New York: Oxford University Press.

Huntington, Samuel. 1968. *Political Order in Changing Societies*. New Haven: Yale University Press.

International Crisis Group. "Nepal's Future: In Whose Hands?" 2009. Retrieved October 20, 2009. (http://www.crisisgroup.org/home/index.cfm?id=6269&l=1).

International IDEA. 2008. "Direct Democracy: The International IDEA Handbook." Stockholm: International IDEA.

Karli, Mehmet. 2009. "A Constitutional Convention for Cyprus: Costs, Benefits and Shortcomings." *Journal of Balkan and Near Eastern Studies* 11: 397–411.

Kelsen, Hans. 1945 (1961). *General Theory of Law and State*. Translated by A. Wedberg. New York: Russell & Russell.

Kritz, Neil. 2003. "Constitution Making Processes: Lessons for Iraq." In *Briefings and Congressional Testimony*. Washington, DC: United States Institute of Peace.

Law, DS. 2013. "The Myth of Imposed Constitutionalism" in *The Social and Political Foundations of Constitutionalism*, edited by Denis Galigan and Mila Versteeg. New York: Cambridge University Press.

Lemont, Eric. 2006a. "Overcoming the Politics of Reform: The Story of the Cherokee Nation of Oklahoma Constitution Convention." In *American Indian Constitutional Reform and the Rebuilding of Native Nations*, edited by E. Lemont. Austin: University of Texas Press.

Lipset, Seymour Martin. 1963. *Political Man: The Social Bases of Politics*. Garden City, NY: Doubleday.

Mansbridge, Jane. "Does Participation Make Better Citizens?" 11–12 February 1995. Retrieved 7 November 2007. (http://www.cpn.org/crm/contemporary/participation. html).

Mendez, Fernando and Vasiliki Triga. 2009. "Constitution-making, Constitutional Conventions and Conflict Resolution: Lesson Drawing for Cyprus." *Journal of Balkan and Near Eastern Studies* 11: 363–380.

Moehler, Devra. 2006. "Public Participation and Support for the Constitution in Uganda." *Journal of Modern African Studies* 44: 275–308.

Moehler, Devra. 2008. *Distrusting Democrats: Outcomes of Participatory Constitution-Making*. Ann Arbor: University of Michigan Press.

Moore, Ray A. and Donald L. Robinson. 2002. *Partners for Democracy: Crafting the New Japanese State under MacArthur*. New York: Oxford University Press.

Pateman, Carole. 1970. *Participation and Democratic Theory*. Cambridge: Cambridge University Press.

Reynolds, Andrew, ed. 2002. *The Architecture of Democracy: Constitutional Design, Conflict Management, and Democracy*. Oxford: Oxford University Press.

Ruland, J. 2003. "Constitutional Debates in the Philippines: From Presidentialism to Parliamentarism." *Asian Survey* 43(3): 461–484.

Saleilles, R. 1895. "The Development of the Present Constitution of France." *Annals of the American Academy of Political and Social Science* 6: 1–78.

Salisbury, Robert H. 1975. "Research on Political Participation." *American Journal of Political Science* 19: 323–341.

Samuels, Kristi. 2005. "Post-Conflict Peace-Building and Constitution-Making." *Chicago Journal of International Law* 6: 663–682.

Samuels, Kristi. 2006. *Constitution Building Processes and Democratization: A Discussion of Twelve Case Studies*. International IDEA.

Scaff, Lawrence A. 1975. "Two Concepts of Political Participation." *The Western Political Quarterly* 28: 447–462.

Spiewak, Pawel. 1997. "The Battle for a Constitution." *East European Constitutional Review* 6: 2–3.

Sunstein, Cass. 2001. "Deliberative Trouble." In *Designing Democracy*. Oxford University Press.

Tartter, Jean R. 1995. "Seychelles: A Country Study." In *Indian Ocean: Five Island Countries*, edited by H. C. Metz. Washington: GPO for the Library of Congress.

Tsebelis, George. 2002. *Veto Players: How Political Institutions Work*. Princeton University Press.

Tushnet, Mark. 2008. "Some Skepticism About Normative Constitutional Advice." *William and Mary Law Review* 49: 1473–1495.

Voigt, Stefan. 2004. "The Consequences of Popular Participation in Constitutional Choice – Towards a Comparative Analysis." In *Deliberation and Decision: Economics, Constitutional Theory and Deliberative Democracy*, edited by A. van Aaken, C. List and C. Luetge. Aldershot: Ashgate.

Waliggo, John. 2001. "The Main Actors in the Constitution Making Process in Uganda." In *Constitution-Making and Democratization in Africa*, edited by G. Hyden and D. Venter. Pretoria: Africa Institute of South Africa.

Weingast, Barry R. 1997. "The Political Foundations of Democracy and the Rule of Law." *American Political Science Review* 91: 245–263.

Whitaker, Beth Elise and Jason Giersch. 2009. "Voting on a Constitution: Implications for Democracy in Kenya." *Journal of Contemporary African Studies* 27: 1–20.

Widner, Jennifer. 2005. "Constitution Writing and Conflict Resolution." *The Round Table* 503–518.

Widner, Jennifer. 2008. "Constitution Writing in Post-Conflict Settings: An Overview." *William and Mary Law Review* 49: 1513–1541.

3. Constitutional courts in East Asia

Tom Ginsburg[1]

After decades of authoritarian rule, East Asia has experienced a wave of democratization since the mid-1980s. Transitions toward more open political structures have been effectuated in South Korea, Taiwan, Thailand, Mongolia, Myanmar and Indonesia, and even the Leninist states of China and Vietnam have experienced tentative moves toward more participatory politics (Balme and Sidel 2007). These political transitions have been accompanied by an important but understudied phenomenon: the emergence of powerful constitutional courts in the region. In at least three countries, Indonesia, South Korea and Mongolia, constitutional courts created during the democratic transition have emerged as real constraints on political authority. In Taiwan, the Council of Grand Justices reawakened after years of relative quiet to play an important role in Taiwan's long political transition to democracy. In other countries, such as Thailand and Myanmar, courts found themselves in the middle of significant political conflicts, and had less success.

Given the cultural and political history of the region, this is a phenomenon that might be seen as surprising. After all, most political systems in the region were until the 1980s dominated by powerful executives without effective judicial constraint. The political systems of non-Communist Asia involved varying degrees of "authoritarian pluralism," wherein a certain degree of political openness was allowed to the extent it did not challenge authoritarian rule (Scalapino 1997: 150). Thus there was little precedent for active courts protecting rights or interfering with state action.

Furthermore, traditional perspectives on Asian governance, resuscitated by proponents of "Asian values," have tended to view political culture in East Asia as emphasizing responsibilities over rights and social order over individual autonomy (Jacobsen 2000; Mahbubani 2002; Davis 1998; Bell 2000; Bauer and Bell 1998). Both Buddhist and Confucian religious

---

[1]   Thanks to Robert Meyer and Sonali Maulik for research assistance.

traditions emphasize the ideal of concentrating power in a single right-eous ruler (the Buddhist *dhammaraja* or the Emperor enjoying the Mandate of Heaven) rather than establishing multiple seats of competing power and authority as a means of effective governance.[2] These trad-itional images of a single righteous leader have been exploited by rulers in the region, from Ho Chi Minh to Chiang Ching-kuo, usually to justify and perpetuate authoritarian rule.

Although the extent of the new constitutional constraint varies across countries and issue areas, it seems apparent that the phenomenon is real and lasting. It seems appropriate, even at this early juncture, to take stock of the phenomenon from a comparative perspective to determine what factors might explain the emergence and success of constitutional review in East Asia. There is a brief description of the emergence of each court, followed by an analysis of institutional design and court performance in comparative perspective. Finally several possible factors that might help explain the emergence of effective constitutional constraint by courts are considered. The chapter concludes with thoughts on the global lessons of the Asian cases.

I. THE EMERGENCE OF CONSTITUTIONALISM IN ASIA

Traditional Asian political thought provides few resources for developing an indigenous theory of judicial review of legislation (Ginsburg 2002: 763; Ginsburg 2003). Most East Asian societies had some influence from the imperial Chinese tradition, in which judicial and executive functions were not separated and all power emanated from a single figure at the center of the political system. Even in systems where power and authority were separated, as in Japan, the notion of an *independent* constraint on power was absent in traditional politics.

The strong history of centralized political authority throughout the region has continued in the twentieth century, and many have connected

---

²   The situation is of course a bit more complicated than this characterization would suggest. In classical Confucianism, particularly as manifested in Korea rather than post-Ming China, advisors to the emperor exercised significant authority and can be seen as a competing power center. See Palais, J (1975) *Politics and Policy in Traditional Korea* Harvard University Press. In classical Buddhist thought, the wheel of power was also to be constrained by the wheel of *dharma*, so the *sangha* might serve as an alternative power center to state authority.

Asian authoritarianism with more general notions of political culture, arguing that there was a strong resonance between classical political traditions and the modern systems of one-party, or one-and-a-half party, a form of governance that was remarkably consistent from Japan to Indonesia (Pye 1995). In South Korea, a series of military authoritarian regimes governed, with one brief interlude in 1961, from the end of Japanese colonialism through 1987. In Taiwan, the Kuomintang (KMT) relied on traditional Chinese notions of government as modified by Sun Yat-sen's political thought to legitimize a quasi-Leninist authoritarian party regime. Thailand experienced a cycle of alternating periods of corrupt civilian and military governments. Mongolia had a governmental structure parallel to that of the Soviet Union, headed by a classically Leninist party. In all four of these countries, a meritocratically selected state apparatus provided continuity and exercised much influence, though of course the precise extent of that influence in the capitalist economies is an issue subject to intense controversy (Gownder and Pekkanen 1996: 363; Johnson 1982; Rosenbluth 1989; Kernell 1991). The situation in Myanmar and Indonesia is less clear, in that the state bureaucracy was never as fully developed.

Historically, the exercise of judicial review in East Asia was constrained, even though it formally existed in many systems. Only the Philippine Supreme Court can be seen as exercising review with regularity. The Japanese Supreme Court has been constrained by the long rule of the Liberal Democratic Party and has issued only seven decisions on unconstitutionality of legislation (Ramseyer and Rasmusen 2003; Beer and Itoh 1978). In other countries, including Malaysia, Korea and Taiwan, judicial efforts to constrain the state were met with harsh attacks on the courts.

Beginning in the 1980s and accelerating in the 1990s, a global wave of democratization and political liberalization led to significant changes in East Asia and beyond. In many countries, this was accompanied by a shift away from traditional notions of parliamentary sovereignty toward the idea of constitutional constraint by expert courts. The causes were complex, and the pressures were global in character. The next section describes the constitutional courts under consideration in more detail.

A. Taiwan

Taiwan continues to be governed under an amended version of the 1947 Constitution of the Republic of China (ROC) adopted in Nanjing. This Constitution, which nominally governed all of China, was emasculated for many years through the use of so-called "Temporary Provisions" that legitimated one-party government by the KMT. Democratic transition in Taiwan began in earnest only in the mid-1980s, when President Chiang Ching-kuo announced reforms and tolerated the creation of the opposition Democratic Progressive Party (DPP). After Chiang's death, Taiwan-born President Lee Teng-hui presided over a long and complex democratic transition, culminating in the election of DPP leader Chen Shui-bian as President in 2001.

The power of judicial review formally existed throughout this period, to be exercised by the Council of Grand Justices of the Judicial Yuan. Under the 1947 Constitution, the Council was composed of 17 members who were appointed by the President with approval of the Control Yuan (a separate branch of government) for renewable nine-year terms.[3] Constitutional amendments have lowered the number of Grand Justices to 15, shortened the terms to eight years, transferred approval power to the legislature, and provided for staggered appointments that coincide with the four-year presidential election cycle.[4] These amendments also assigned the power to declare political parties unconstitutional to the Council of Grand Justices, removing regulation of parties from the executive branch. The Council's primary functions are to issue uniform interpretations of law and to interpret the Constitution upon request from litigants or government agencies.[5]

After some early efforts to constrain the exercise of political power by government, the Grand Justices were punished by the legislature in the late 1950s. The legislature raised the voting threshold to issue constitutional interpretations and restricted interpretations to the constitutional text. From then until the recent liberalization, the Justices were cautious. Indeed, in the early era, the Council can be seen as an instrument of the KMT regime. It never accepted a case on the (dubious) constitutionality of the Temporary Provisions, which were the basis of authoritarian rule. The Temporary Provisions suspended the two-term limitation for the Presidency and allowed the President to govern through decree powers

---

[3]   Although Article 81 of the Constitution grants "judges" life tenure, the Grand Justices are not considered to fall into that category.

[4]   Additional Articles of the Constitution of the Republic of China, Article 5. The Article also provides that the Judicial Yuan's draft budget may not be eliminated or reduced by the Executive Yuan in their submission of the budget to the Legislative Yuan.

[5]   Under the 1947 Constitution there are five branches of government (yuan), three corresponding to the Montesquieuan framework and two drawn from the Chinese imperial tradition, the Control Yuan for audit and the Examination Yuan for entry into the civil service.

without legislative approval.[6] The Council declined to hear challenges to these Provisions and issued a number of decisions that facilitated KMT rule within the confines of at least nominal constitutionalism. Most prominently, it issued a decision suspending elections to the National Assembly during the "national emergency", so that representatives elected on the mainland in 1948 to represent all of China continued to serve in power for several decades.

After the election of Lee Teng-hui in 1987, however, the Council gradually became more active (Ginsburg 2003: ch 4 n 4). It began to strike administrative actions that were vague or delegated too much power to the executive branch. In 1990, the Council was called on to rule on the constitutionality of the continued sitting in the National Assembly of members elected on the mainland in 1948. These members had become a major obstacle to reform since the Assembly was the body solely responsible for constitutional amendment. The Assembly thus had an effective veto over efforts to abolish it, as well as to undertake other institutional reforms desired by the reformers.

Council Interpretation No. 261, announced on June 21, 1990, called for new elections and forced the retirement of the decrepit old guard of the KMT. This was undoubtedly the most important case in the history of the Council of Grand Justices and removed the last legal barrier to rapid institutional reform in Taiwan. Without this decision of the Grand Justices, the democratization process would have remained at a standstill, with the possible consequence that then-President Lee Teng-hui would never have cultivated his strong position within the KMT, and reform would have been delayed indefinitely. Following the decision, several stages of constitutional amendments transformed the governmental structure of Taiwan to be more effective, only nominally retaining the fiction of governing all China.

After appointment of a new set of Grand Justices in 1994, the Council became more active in striking legislation and constraining executive authority. Many of the new Justices were Taiwan-born and thus more likely to share Lee Teng-hui's vision of an independent Taiwan. They systematically dismantled the quasi-Leninist system of KMT control, for

---

6   "Temporary Provisions Effective During the Period of Communist Rebellion." These were adopted in 1948 at the first meeting of the First National Assembly in Nanjing, and came into effect on May 10 of that year. For a discussion of the constitutionality of the Temporary Provisions, see Mendel, F.F. (1993) 'Judicial Power and Illusion: The Republic of China's Council of Grand Justices and Constitutional Interpretation' *Pacific Rim Law and Policy Journal* 2: 157–89.

example by ending the ban on rallies advocating secessionism or communism as a violation of free speech; allowing universities to refuse to allow military "counselors," whose presence in dorms had formerly been mandatory; and allowing teachers to form a union outside the "official" union structure.

The Council has also played a major role in introducing international norms of criminal procedure into Taiwan, forcing a complete revision of the Criminal Procedure Code. It struck provisions of an anti-hooligan law that had reduced procedural protections for those designated by police as hooligans, and when the legislature modified the statute in question, the court demanded further revisions. It has also constrained both police and prosecutors in significant ways.

The Council has been involved in political controversies as well. After the election of the DPP's Chen Shui-bian as President in 2001, the Council embarrassed his government by preventing it from halting construction of a major nuclear power plant. It was also thrust into the center of political controversy when President Lee Teng-hui sought to retain Vice President Lien Chan as "acting prime minister" after the 1997 presidential election. The legislature had protested against this as a violation of the Constitution. Although the Constitution does not clearly state that the Vice President cannot serve as Prime Minister, the Council found that this was not consistent with the spirit of the Constitution. It thus allowed Lien to retain office, though a few months later his government was removed for political reasons.

Constitutional amendments in 1992 provided for the Council of Grand Justices to hear (sitting as a Constitutional Court) challenges against "unconstitutional" political parties, defined as those whose "goals or activities jeopardize the existence of the ROC or a free democratic constitutional order." These clauses were thinly targeted at the DPP, particularly its pro-independence factions, which would eliminate the ROC and declare a new state of Taiwan which would no longer claim to be the titular government of all of China. The transfer of the power of regulating political parties to the Grand Justices reflects continuing German influence in Taiwan's constitutional law,[7] and was seen as progressive in that it took the determination of party unconstitutionality away from an Executive Yuan "Political Party Screening Committee,"

---

[7]   Under the German Basic Law, the Constitutional Court also has the power to disband political parties that "seek to impair or abolish the free democratic basis order." Basic Law, Article 21. Kommers, D (1997) *The Constitutional Jurisprudence of the Federal Republic of Germany* (2nd ed.) Duke University Press at 223–29.

which had the previous January agreed to punish the DPP for its pro-independence plank. Giving this power to the Council is an important step in the Taiwan context.

The Council has thus been active in using the power of judicial review to strike legislation and administrative action. It has served as an *instrument* of democratization, both by giving life to the constitutional text and elaborating on the text in accordance with the constitutional spirit and international norms. It has also become involved in major controversies of a political character, though it has thus far avoided any major attacks on its powers. It is an exemplar of the role a constitutional court can play in facilitating democratization.

B. South Korea

South Korea's last military regime, headed by Chun Doo-hwan, took power in a coup in 1979. In part because of a massacre of hundreds of non-violent protestors at Kwangju in May 1980,[8] the government enjoyed little legitimacy, and opposition politicians demanded that the regime allow direct elections and liberalization. The Korean democratization process began in earnest in 1986, when widespread demonstrations involving the middle class led military dictator Chun Doo-hwan to resign the Presidency. His successor, former general Roh Tae-woo, gave in to opposition demands for a directly elected Presidency and oversaw a process of political negotiation that produced the 1987 Constitution.

One of the central features of this Constitution was the design of a new Constitutional Court, roughly along the lines of the German model. The Court is composed of nine members who serve renewable six-year terms, with three members each nominated by the President, National Assembly and Supreme Court. I characterize this appointment method as "representative" because each institution has the ability to pick its nominees unimpeded (Ginsburg 2003). The Court has the power to consider the constitutionality of legislation or administrative action at the request of political bodies or a court, can resolve competence disputes among governmental institutions, and can respond to constitutional complaints from citizens if fundamental rights have been abused by government action or omission, or if an ordinary court fails to refer a constitutional question to the Constitutional Court.

---

[8] The precise facts of the incident are hotly disputed, including the number of dead, estimates of which range between the official figures of 191 up to 2000.

Although earlier Korean Republics had formal provisions for judicial review, oscillating between centralized and decentralized models, judicial review in Korea had never effectively served to constrain the state. In the early 1960s, a Supreme Court decision striking a legislative act upset President Park Chung-hee, who shortly afterwards moved to concentrate his authority in the so-called Yushin Constitution of 1972. After these reforms, Park fired all the judges who had voted against his position in the earlier case. Constitutional review power under the Yushin Constitution was centralized in a Constitutional Council that remained dormant. It is thus not surprising that most observers of the 1987 constitutional reforms did not expect the Korean Constitutional Court to play a major role in the society (Ginsburg 2003: ch 7).

However, the Court has surprised these observers by regularly overturning legislation and administrative action (West and Yoon 1992: 73; Yang 1993: 1; Ahn 1997: 71). Indeed, in its very first case, it struck as a violation of the equality principle of the Constitution a law providing that the state could not be subject to preliminary attachment orders in civil cases. The Court insisted that equality under the law requires treating the state no differently than a private citizen or corporation. In doing so it challenged the philosophical underpinnings of the postwar Korean political economy, wherein the state played a major role in directing private economic activity.

One sign of the Court's boldness has been its willingness to create new rights by reading the text of the constitutional document quite broadly. For example, in 1989 the Court found an implied "right to know" based on several clauses of the Constitution, echoing Japanese constitutional case law. It subsequently strengthened that provision by referring to the Universal Declaration of Human Rights. In 1991, the Constitutional Court read Article 10 of the Korean Constitution, which grants citizens a right to pursue happiness, to encompass a right to freedom of contract (Ahn 1997: 71). Again, this is fairly radical in the formerly *dirigiste* Korean context.

The Court has also been involved in sensitive political issues. For example, it was drawn into efforts to achieve retroactive justice for the bloody Kwangju incident of the Chun regime. Many believe that President Kim Young-sam, who in 1992 became the first civilian to assume the Presidency, had agreed not to pursue claims against his predecessors, the Generals Roh Tae-woo and Chun Doo-hwan, as part of the deal that allowed Kim to take power and democratization to proceed. Early in Kim's term, prosecutors had investigated the two generals and dropped all charges related to treason during the 1979 coup or the deaths in the 1980 incident at Kwangju. Later, however, responding to public pressure and seeking to deflect allegations of corruption, Kim changed his mind. The Constitutional Court was asked to rule on the constitutionality of special legislation, passed at Kim's instigation, to facilitate prosecution even after the normal period of statutory limitations had expired. In a carefully worded decision, the Court found that the legislation had been passed after the expiry of the period of statutory limitations for the 1979 coup, but that prosecutions for the Kwangju incident could proceed. The Court's analysis highlighted Kim Young-sam's failure to take action against Chun and Roh early in his Presidency when the statute of limitations would not have been an issue. Ultimately, both men were found guilty, and subsequently pardoned at the instigation of President-elect Kim Dae-jung in December 1997.

The Court has been especially important in dealing with the legacies of the authoritarian regime, particularly the National Security Act (NSA) and the Anti-Communist Act. These laws were used to suppress independent political organizations by providing draconian sanctions against dissenters and loosely defined illegal associations. The laws were therefore a target of human rights activists and regime opponents. The statutes operated by carving out exceptions to normal requirements of criminal procedure. For example, Article 19 of the NSA allowed longer pre-trial detention for those accused of particular crimes, and this was struck by the Constitutional Court in 1992 as a violation of the right to a speedy trial. The Court also found a clause criminalizing anyone who "praises, encourages, or sympathizes with the activities of an anti-state organization or its members, or … by any means whatever benefits an anti-state organization" to be vague and overbroad, and to threaten constitutional guarantees of freedom of the press and speech, freedom of academic study, and freedom of conscience. The Court did not strike the NSA, but rather sought to limit and channel its application to constitutional purposes.

Perhaps the greatest political controversy the Court has had to deal with was the impeachment of President Roh Moo-hyun, an activist labor lawyer who took office in 2003 with a reformist agenda (Lee 2005: 403). Roh faced a hostile National Assembly, and was soon beset by a split in his party and a corruption scandal related to campaign contributions erupted that October. Roh staked his future on a mid-term legislative election, but – in violation of South Korean law – appeared to campaign for his own party by urging voters to support it. The majority in the National Assembly responded with a motion for impeachment which passed by the necessary 2/3 vote.

Under Korean law, Roh was suspended from office and the Prime Minister assumed the duties of the President. The case was then sent to the Constitutional Court for confirmation, as required under the Constitution. During the deliberations of the case, however, the mid-term election was held and Roh's party received overwhelming support, winning an absolute majority in the Assembly.

Perhaps responding to the public's preferences, the Constitutional Court rejected the impeachment motion one month later. In addressing the issue, the Court bifurcated the issue into the question of whether there was a "violation of the Constitution or other Acts," the predicate for impeachment, and whether those violations were severe enough to warrant removal. Although the Court found that Roh had violated the election law provisions that public officials remain neutral, along with other provisions of law, they decided that it would not be proportional to remove the President for the violation. Instead, they asserted that removal is only appropriate when the "free and democratic basic order" is threatened. Roh's violations were not a premeditated attempt to undermine constitutional democracy. The Court further rejected some of the charges, namely those concerned with campaign contributions, that took place before he took office.

In short, the Korean Constitutional Court has been playing a significant role in Korean politics and society. It has become an important site of political contestation, as interest groups have begun seeking to use the Court to achieve social change. The Court frequently strikes legislative action and also regularly overturns prosecutorial decisions, particularly important given the central role of prosecutors in the authoritarian period. At the same time, the Court has trodden on careful ground in those cases likely to lead to political backlash, as in the impeachment case and in its handling of the NSA. At the time of this writing, the Constitutional Court is the most popular government institution in Korean society.[9]

C. Indonesia

The Indonesian Constitutional Court was created in 2003 as part of a series of constitutional reforms and amendments that ran from the late 1990s to the early 2000s, beginning just after the resignation of President Soeharto in May of 1998. Beginning in 1999, the People's Consultative Assembly (MPR), the Indonesian Legislature, made four rounds of

---

[9]   JoongAng Daily, July 3, 2007, available at http://joongangdaily.joins.com/article/view.asp?aid=2877553.

amendments to the 1945 Indonesian Constitution. The third of these amendments, passed in 2001, created the Indonesian Constitutional Court.

That third amendment was passed in the upheaval regarding the impeachment and eventual removal of President Abdurrahman Wahid. After sustained political conflict between President Wahid and the MPR, the MPR voted to impeach Wahid in the absence of clear constitutional guidance over how the process should move forward. The impeachment process was in part a consequence of differing interpretations of the 1945 Constitution, and the absence of a judicial mechanism for constitutional interpretation exacerbated the conflict (Indrayana 2005: 178). The Indonesian Supreme Court functioned only as the highest court of appeals, and was not charged with hearing questions of constitutional interpretation (Tabulajan 2002). The MPR was reluctant to give these responsibilities to the Supreme Court due in part to "concern about [its] integrity," and after representatives from the Supreme Court told the MPR that "the court did not consider it possible to take on additional functions – not with a backlog of more than 20,000 cases," the MPR found it easier to create a new court (Indrayana 2005: 15; Stockmann 2007: 15). At the end of those negotiations, the Third Constitutional Amendment to the 1945 Indonesian Constitution created the Indonesian Constitutional Court.

The new court was modeled largely on the South Korean Constitutional Court, with three Justices each nominated by the President, Supreme Court and MPR, and was intended to fill the space left by the Supreme Court's limited jurisdiction. The Amendment gave the Constitutional Court power to "[review] laws against the Constitution, [determine] disputes over the authorities of state institutions whose powers are given by this Constitution, [decide] over the dissolution of a political party, and [decide] disputes over the results of general elections," as well as "the authority to issue a decision over an opinion of the DPR concerning alleged violations by the President and/or Vice-President of this Constitution."[10] Soon thereafter, the MPR passed Law 24 of 2003, specifying among other things the qualifications for Justices and the method of selection. There were to be nine judges, each required to have a law degree, banned from holding a position in the legislature or a post as another state official, and required to go on leave from any academic post they may have had.[11]

---

[10]   1945 Indonesian Constitution, Article 24C Paragraphs 1 and 2.
[11]   Law number 24 of year 2003 on the Constitutional Court. Government of Indonesia. August 2003.

One of the first questions in front of the Court pertained to its own jurisdiction. Article 50 of Law 24 from 2003, the statute specifically establishing the Constitutional Court and outlining everything from judicial selection procedures to finances, limited the judicial review powers of the Court to "those which have been enacted after the introduction of the amendment to the 1945 Constitution."[12] The First Amendment to the Constitution was passed in 1999, effectively limiting judicial review to post-1999 laws, ostensibly to prevent an influx of cases regarding decades-old legislation. Unsurprisingly, a petition for judicial review was lodged against a pre-1999 law soon after the Court opened, putting that limitation on review in the spotlight. In its decision for that case, the Court could "not act *suo moto*, on its own initiative," to invalidate the prohibition on reviewing pre-1999 laws, as "Article 50 was not itself under review," but it decided by a six to three majority to review the statute in question anyway, a 1985 law, in spite of Article 50.

Soon after, a second set of plaintiffs brought another petition for review of a pre-1999 law, in combination with a petition directly asking for review of Article 50 from Law 24/2003. Directly reviewing Law 24/2003 gave the Court the legal authority to officially strike down Article 50, and it did so, again by a six to three margin. The majority cited the amended Indonesian Constitution, arguing that there was no temporal limitation on review in the constitutional language. (Article 24C said simply that "The Constitutional Court shall have the authority to hear cases at the first and final level and shall have the final power of decision in reviewing laws against the Constitution.") The majority noted that Article 50 of Law 24/2003 was in the "Procedural Law" section of the statute, but argued that limiting judicial review to post-1999 laws was not a procedural matter, but a limit on the Court's judicial review authority, and that laws outside the Constitution cannot reduce or increase the Court's authority to that extent. The majority also suggested that leaving such a limit intact would create a double standard between the laws applied before the First Amendment and the laws applied after the Amendment.[13]

This decision created some controversy, both inside and outside the Court, and many drew attention to the fact that the Court had essentially just given a ruling on its own power. Some, such as a representative from the Indonesia Law Reform Consortium, saw the verdict "as a step

---

12   Law 24/2003, Article 50.
13   Constitutional Court of Indonesia. Decision on case No. 066/PUU-II/2004. Pages 10–11.

forward and in line with the hopes and the wishes of the people," but others viewed it as an exercise in self-dealing (Stockmann 2007: 32). Two other controversial decisions of the Court that are helping to define its young image are a ruling on a law restricting citizens' rights to stand for election and a decision on a retrospectively imposed terrorism law. The first of those decisions, from early 2004, invalidated a section of a 2003 law that barred former members of "the banned Indonesian Communist Party ..." and anybody "directly or indirectly involved in the G30S/PKI", an alleged coup attempt in 1965.[14] The Court found by an eight to one majority that the law violated constitutional protections against discriminatory treatment and equal standing under the law (Stockmann 2007: 36).

The response was overwhelmingly positive from the human rights community in Indonesia, but several government officials disagreed with the Court's decision. However, in a positive sign for the rule of law in Indonesia, those officials who were disapproving of the verdict made sure to express respect for the Court's power and ability to make a legal determination on legislation: the Armed Forces Chief stated: "I feel disappointed about the Constitutional Court Verdict ... but it's already done," and the Vice President commented: "... this matter is already decided by the Constitutional Court, well, what more do we want ... ?" despite his qualms about the content of the ruling (Stockmann 2007: 36).

The second case involved Law 16 of 2002, an anti-terrorism law passed in response to the Bali terrorist bombings of October 2002. The statute was worded to allow the retrospective prosecution of those guilty for the bombing. The Court ruled in a narrow five to four majority that the Law contradicted Article 28I (1) of the amended Indonesian Constitution, which sets aside several rights, the protection from retroactive prosecution among them, as non-derogable. The minority opinion argued that these rights could in fact be limited by the subsequent Article, 28J, which allows "restrictions established by law for the sole purposes of guaranteeing the recognition and respect of the rights and freedoms of others and of satisfying just demands based upon considerations of morality, religious values, security and public order in a democratic society."[15] The Court struck down the anti-terrorism law "in the face of

---

[14]   Draft of Law Number 12 of the Year 2003 Concerning General Elections for the Members of the People's Representative Council, the Regional Representative Council, and the Regional People's Representative Council. Unofficial translation. International Foundation for Electoral Systems. www.ifes.org.

[15]   1945 Indonesian Constitution, Article 28I Paragraph 1 and Article 28J Paragraph 2.

enormous political and popular pressure" to uphold the legislation (Harijanti and Lindsey 2006: 138–50).

The Indonesian Constitutional Court is still very young, but is an innovative new addition to the Indonesian government that fills several gaping holes in the Indonesian judiciary. Thus far, it has proven independent of the executive and legislative branches of the Indonesian government, and made several unpopular but legally sound rulings. There is then great hope that the Constitutional Court will continue to contribute to the protection of democracy and human rights in Indonesia.

D. Thailand

The Thai Constitutional Court was established with the 1997 Constitution. This emerged as part of a dramatic transition to democracy designed to break the cycle of coups and political corruption that had plagued Thailand's history since the end of the absolute monarchy in 1932. Depending on how one counts, Thailand had experienced between 17 and 19 coups, and had 16 different constitutions during this period (Harding and Leyland 2008). However, a coup in 1992 had provoked the ire of the middle class when protests were violently suppressed. Pressure grew for the renewal of democracy, accelerating after the King intervened to castigate the coup leaders. Ultimately the citizens' movement prevailed. The result was the so-called "people's constitution," adopted after widespread public input and debate. It was the first ever of Thailand's constitutions to include such input from the public.

Faced with the history of instability, and with an endemic form of electoral corruption that had made civilian rule as ineffective as the military was illegitimate, the drafters of the Thai Constitution focused on limiting governmental power. Academics played an important role in the drafting process, as the drafting commission was led by Chulalongkorn University Law Professor Bovornsak Uwanno. The Constitution emerged as a kind of mega-constitution, with 336 articles covering over 100 pages of text. In part this reflected the desire to specify rights in detail so as to avoid the possibility of misinterpretation.

The Constitution had a number of radical features designed to increase participation and accountability. First, it tried to decentralize power to the hitherto moribund local governments. Second, it established extensive administrative rights to information, to sue the government and receive reasons for adverse decisions by government. It introduced elections for the upper body of Parliament, the Senate, and made it into a non-partisan body. It also created several new institutions to enhance participation and human rights protection. Two powerful new independent bodies were set up to improve the political process, an Election Commission and a National Counter-Corruption Commission (NCCC). The former was designed to minimize the chronic problem of vote-buying; it had the power to monitor elections, ban candidates and political parties, and order a re-run of any election it deemed to have been fraudulent.[16] The NCCC collected reports on assets from politicians and senior bureaucrats to ensure that there were no mysterious increases during the time they were in public service. Those who failed to report assets could be barred from office, subject to approval from the new Constitutional Court.

The new Constitutional Court was one of the key institutions designed to enhance legality and check a Parliament traditionally seen as a hotbed of corruption and special interest. It was to be a permanent body with 15 members appointed by the King upon advice of the Senate for nine-year non-renewable terms. Members had to be 40 years of age. In keeping with the need to secure various kinds of expertise in constitutional interpretation, the body included a variety of qualifications and appointment mechanisms. Cases could be referred to the Constitutional Court by ordinary courts in the course of litigation, the presidents of each house of Parliament, the Prime Minister and other designated political bodies. As in Fifth Republic France, there was a provision for minority groups of legislators to submit legislation before promulgation by the King, but no power of direct petition from the public.

In addition, the Court exercised a wide array of ancillary powers. Besides the power to confirm findings of, and evaluate disclosures submitted to, the Election Commission and NCCC described above, the Court could, *inter alia*: review whether any appropriations bill would lead to involvement of an elected official in the expenditure of funds (section 180); determine whether an Emergency Decree is made in a real emergency (section 219); determine whether Election Commissioners should be disqualified (section 142); and decide whether political party regulations violate the Constitution or fundamental principles of Thai governance (section 47). Because of the overarching concern with corruption that animated the 1997 Constitution, the Court had the power to demand documents or evidence to carry out its duties. In this sense it was a kind of inquisitorial Constitutional Court. The Court's early history was mostly uneventful but it quickly became embroiled in the politics surrounding billionaire populist Thaksin Shinawatra, who became Prime Minister in 2001.

---

[16] In the first Senate election in 2000, the Election Commission threw out 78 out of 200 election results because of fraud.

Just before the election won by his Thai Rak Thai Party, Thaksin was found by the NCCC to have filed a false assets report. The Constitutional Court was called on to confirm the finding, and was put in a difficult position. In a divided decision that has been described as confused, the Court found that the false report had not been filed deliberately and allowed Thaksin to take the post of Prime Minister. Thus began a long chapter in which Thaksin used his money and influence to dominate Thai politics, undermining many of the guardian institutions that were supposed to protect the constitutional scheme (Leyland 2007: 151). The Court was tainted in some eyes for allowing Thaksin to take power, but on some occasions did constrain him. For example, it ruled that a couple of appointments, including those of an Election Commission and the Auditor General, had not followed proper procedure (Leyland 2007: 159). Still, the general perception was that these did not function as they should have. Following widespread allegations of electoral corruption in 2006, the Constitutional Court found that a legal case against him was non-justiciable (Leyland 2007: 168).

Frustrated with political institutions, opposition forces took to the streets. Thaksin called a snap election for April 2006, but this was boycotted by the opposition, leading to a constitutional crisis when too few members of Parliament could be seated. At this point, on April 26, 2006, the King met with the leaders of the Constitutional, Supreme and Administrative Courts and publicly called for them to resolve the constitutional crisis, suggesting they should void the April election. The Constitutional Court responded by annulling the election, and three Election Commissioners were jailed on the grounds that the time allowed for the election campaign had been too brief and that some polling booths had been positioned to allow others to view the ballots as they were cast. Five new Election Commissioners, who had just been chosen after months of deadlock, would be replaced. Nevertheless, with political institutions at a standstill, the appointment process could hardly operate. The Constitutional Court seemed to have failed to resolve the problem completely. This is a paradigm example of the politicization of the judiciary, which is a risk of constitutions placing so much power in the hands of guardians.

Thaksin's domination of politics eventually provoked a reaction from the military and in September 2006 he was replaced in a coup. Pointedly, the Interim Constitution promulgated by the military disbanded the Constitutional Court, even though most of the other guardian institutions were allowed to continue operating. In August 2007 a new constitution was approved by referendum, and a new Constitutional Court established.

The new Court is a nine-member body, serving a single nine-year term selected in simpler fashion by a selection committee.[17]

The Thai story is of a court that disappointed many of those who had high hopes in it, yet it is not fully clear exactly what the court could have done to resist the billionaire populist whose reach extended into virtually every institution in Thailand. If anything, the story cautions against expecting courts to be able to do too much, and to single-handedly save a democratic system from itself.

E. Mongolia

The world's second communist country, Mongolia, was governed for many years as a de facto satellite of the Soviet Union. This changed only in 1989 when demonstrations led by intellectuals led the ruling Mongolian People's Revolutionary Party (MPRP) to revise the political system and allow for multi-party elections. After a brief period of transition, these reforms were crystallized in the 1992 Constitution.

The Constitutional Court (called the *Tsets* from the traditional word for a judge in Mongolian wrestling) was designed to supervise the Constitution. Although the drafters of the Constitution briefly considered the institution of American-style decentralized judicial review, the adoption of the Kelsenian centralized model was considered more compatible with Mongolia's civil law tradition. The Court had nine members, three selected by each of the President, the Parliament and the Supreme Court. Cases can be brought by ordinary citizens through constitutional petition, as well as referral by various political institutions.

In its early years, the Court's primary role was in resolving competence disputes between the powerful legislature and the directly elected President. The Court also responded to citizen complaints and issued a number of decisions overturning government actions that violated the constitutional text. However, the Court's own decision that the Constitution did not give it jurisdiction over ordinary court decisions meant that certain areas important for human rights protection, most notably criminal procedure, were outside its purview (Ginsburg 2003: ch 6).

The Court has been somewhat hampered by a peculiar institutional design that allowed the Parliament to reject initial findings of the Court. In the event the Parliament rejected the decision, the Court could hear the case again *en banc* and issue a final, binding decision by a two-thirds vote. This institutional design probably reflected residual socialist notions

---

[17] Constitution of Thailand 2007, sections 200, 202.

of parliamentary sovereignty, as well as a similar scheme that existed in the Polish Constitution before amendments in 1997. Although the Mongolian Court's initial decisions were accepted by the Parliament, the election of an overwhelming majority of MPRP to the Parliament in 1998 meant that the party had the ability easily to reject Court decisions as a matter of course.

This situation was exacerbated by a particular series of poorly considered decisions by the Court on the shape of the political system (Ginsburg and Ganzorig 2001; Ginsburg 2003: ch 6). Following the first election victory of the opposition coalition in 1996, the Court decided that a constitutional clause that said "members of parliament shall have no other employment" prevented the government from forming the cabinet out of sitting parliament members. This question went to the core of the nature of the political system: was it a parliamentary system or a presidential one? The case produced a series of institutional conflicts between the Parliament and the Court. After the Court rejected legislation passed to allow the government to be formed out of Parliament as unconstitutional, the Parliament passed a series of constitutional amendments designed to remedy the defect. These amendments were themselves rejected by the Court as unconstitutional. The crisis was only resolved some five years later in 2001, when the Court finally backed down and allowed a second round of constitutional amendments to go forward. The story of the Mongolian Court is thus one of poor decision-making that squandered institutional capital that had been built up in the very first years of the institution.

F. Myanmar

At this writing, Myanmar is in the midst of an extraordinary political transition whose ultimate outcome is quite unclear. After spending 17 years drafting a new constitution, the military junta in Myanmar initiated a process of political reform under President Thein Sein. Elections followed, and were won by a military-backed political party, but forces associated with long-time oppositionist Aung San Suu Kyi also won seats. A Constitutional Tribunal was formed with nine members, three nominated by each house of the Parliament and three by the President. The Court had the responsibility for deciding disputes related to the allocation of powers as well as interpretation of the Constitution.

As we have seen in other cases, the Tribunal was thrust into the midst of complicated disputes about the separation of powers. In March 2012 the Court was called on to interpret the powers of the Parliament vis-à-vis the government, and it decided that parliamentary committees and commissions were not "national" bodies. This meant that they had limited power to summon government ministers for questioning. The Parliament, which perhaps had been expected to be a mere rubber stamp, became quite upset and initiated impeachment proceedings against all nine members of the Tribunal. In September 2012 the judges were all removed. At this writing, the Tribunal has not been reformed, and so it joins the Thai Constitutional Court of 1997 as an example of a tribunal that overreached, triggering severe punishment.

G. Summary

These six cases illustrate a range of environments in which constitutional courts operate. They include former Communist regimes and former military regimes. They range geographically and culturally. But all five courts have become involved in major political conflict, and with the exceptions of those in Myanmar and Mongolia, have by and large helped to resolve these conflicts effectively. All the courts have played a role in underpinning and facilitating democratization. The next sections consider some comparative questions in light of these brief case studies.

II. UNDERSTANDING INSTITUTIONAL DESIGN

The several courts under consideration exhibit a range of features. Yet all reflect the Kelsenian model of a centralized institution, paradigmatically embodied in the German Constitutional Court, rather than the American decentralized model in which any court can make a declaration of unconstitutionality. This choice of the continental model was made despite substantial American influence on the law and politics of Korea and Taiwan, and American input into the Mongolian constitutional drafting process. In this sense, courts in Asia are reflecting the dominant role of the continental model in most legal systems except those subject directly or indirectly to British colonialism. In a global sense, only a very few courts without British or American colonial experience have adopted a decentralized model of judicial review.

The following table summarizes several features of institutional design of the courts.

Table 3.1 Features of institutional design

	Thailand	Korea	Taiwan	Indonesia	Myanmar	Mongolia
Date of establishment	1997–2006	1989	1947; as modified by constitutional amendments	2003	2008	1992
Members	15	9	15	9	9	9
How appointed	7 elected by top courts; 8 selected by a mixed commission as qualified in law and political science; confirmed by Senate	3 each from President, Parliament and Supreme Court	By President with approval by the National Assembly	3 each from President, Parliament and Supreme Court	3 each from President, and two houses of Parliament	3 each from President, Parliament and Supreme Court
Term length in years	9	6	8	5	5	6
Terms renewable?	No	Yes	No	Yes	Not clear	Yes
Constitutional petitions from public?	No	Yes	No	Yes	No	Yes

Table 3.1 continued

	Thailand	Korea	Taiwan	Indonesia	Myanmar	Mongolia
Abstract/ concrete review	Both	Concrete	Abstract but includes referrals from ordinary courts	Both	Both	Both
Review of legislation *ex post/ex ante*	Both	*Ex post*	*Ex post*	*Ex Post*	*Ex post* (though text not fully clear)	*Ex post*
Decisions final?	Yes	Yes	Yes	Yes	Yes	Initial decisions can be rejected by the legislature, but subsequently confirmed by *en banc* sitting of court
Important ancillary powers	Overseeing corruption and electoral commissions	Impeachment, dissolution of political party	Declare political parties unconstitutional	Impeachment	Intra-regional disputes	Impeachment, overseeing electoral commission

While the prestige of the German model may explain the decision to centralize review in a single designated body, the details of institutional design are likely to reflect in large part the political configuration during the time of constitutional drafting. Thus the appointment mechanisms are most complex in Thailand, wherein drafters sought to insulate the Justices from politics by setting up an intricate array of appointment mechanisms and committees. Although many American states and several countries use mixed committees to appoint ordinary judges, the Thai scheme is particularly byzantine and reflects the importance of various professional factions in the drafting process. In Taiwan, in contrast, the drafting of the constitutional text in 1947 reflected the dominance of Chiang Kai-shek in the KMT. The President plays the major role in appointing the Grand Justices, a desirable feature for a powerful figure certain to win the Presidency.

Mongolia, Indonesia and Korea utilize the Italian model of representative appointments by each of three political branches, while Myanmar also uses multiple appointing authorities. This representative model may be desirable when parties are uncertain of their position in government after the constitution is adopted. Whereas Chiang Kai-shek knew he would be able to appoint the Grand Justices and was happy to keep the power centralized in the Presidency, situations of greater political uncertainty are likely to lead drafters to ensure wide representation on the court (Ginsburg 2003: ch 6). When each institution appoints a third of the members, no institution can dominate the court.

This dynamic is best illustrated in Korea, where the Constitution was drafted behind closed doors by three factions with roughly equal political support.[18] Situations of such uncertainty mean that each faction believes it is likely to be *out* of power. This may also give the drafters the incentive to include the power of constitutional petition by citizens. Constitutional petition guarantees that political losers will have access to the Constitutional Court in the event the winners trample their rights.

Another issue in constitutional court design is that of term length. It is usually suggested that longer terms are likely to lead to more independent adjudication. There seems to be a tradeoff in our cases between short renewable terms (Indonesia, Korea and Mongolia) and longer non-renewable terms (Thailand and Taiwan). While this does not reflect any

---

[18] Other institutions of the 1987 Constitution, including the single term Presidency, reflect the uncertainty that any one of these three factions would win the first election. The single term has allowed the presidency to be rotated by the three major political figures involved in the drafting – Roh Tae-woo, Kim Young-sam, and Kim Dae-jung.

apparent political pattern, it is interesting that the shift to non-renewable terms in Taiwan only took place after democratization began in earnest; in the one-party period it may have been politically useful for the KMT to wield the threat of non-reappointment over the Grand Justices.

This illustrates that dominant party regimes may be in a better position to hinder strong review power in constitutional design. Strong parties that believe they are likely to control the legislature are likely to want weaker courts. In both Mongolia and Taiwan, strong party regimes built in controls over the court in the design process: in Mongolia through the anomalous institution of parliamentary approval of initial decisions by the court on constitutionality, and in Taiwan, through the centralized appointment mechanism. The more diffuse political environments of Thailand and Korea, wherein multiple political parties were competing for power, may have contributed to more powerful court design.

Other features of institutional design reflected political concerns associated with particular circumstances. Examples include the emphasis on anti-corruption and the mechanism of abstract pre-promulgation review of legislation in the Thai Constitutional Court design. These features both reflect the overarching distrust of partisan politics in Thailand. As the French experience has shown, abstract pre-promulgation review tends to lead to the insertion of the constitutional court into the legislative process (Stone 1992).

In short, institutional design of constitutional courts should be understood as reflecting a process of adapting foreign models to local institutional needs. This account suggests that political considerations play an important role in understanding court design in Asia and elsewhere.

III. UNDERSTANDING COURT PERFORMANCE

What about the performance of these constitutional courts? What roles are they playing? While of course each court presents its own story in a distinct political, social and cultural context, several broad themes emerge from the regional snapshots provided above.

First, constitutional courts have been useful in striking, one at a time, elements of the old system. They served as consolidators of democracy, rather than the bodies triggering the process. This function was particularly important in the relatively gradual transitions from authoritarian rule in Taiwan and Korea. In Thailand, the military regime was not systematically entrenched in the society, having been in power only a short time and reflecting the less pervasive character of the Thai state in controlling the ordinary lives of its citizens. The primary threat to democracy was seen to be the corrupt political process itself, and the constitutional text reflected that concern. In Mongolia, the Court played less of a rights-protecting role than in Korea and Taiwan; this may have been appropriate since the complete break with the past marked by the transition from socialism meant that by definition the old regime was less intact.

Second, ancillary powers of constitutional courts are important, though they have received relatively little scholarly attention in Asia and elsewhere. In Thailand, for example, cases involving constitutional review of legislation were not nearly as important as the Court's role in supervising the electoral process (Harding and Leyland 2008). The most prominent case in Korea's constitutional history was an impeachment case – far from the exercise of judicial review as classically defined. Giving the Council of Grand Justices on Taiwan the ability to declare political parties unconstitutional marked a major step in ensuring that such declarations would be conceived of in legal rather than political terms, and reflected a shift toward the rule of law.

Third, many of the constitutional courts have been involved in issues related to the composition of government. In Thailand, the high-profile case approving Thaksin's appointment as Prime Minister is the best example; in Taiwan and Korea the courts adjudicated interim appointments of the Prime Minister by a President in a split executive system, and the Korean impeachment also involved government composition in one sense. The Mongolian Constitutional Court was called on to determine the fundamental character of the political regime as parliamentary or presidential. In all these cases, the transfer of political struggle from the streets to the courtroom is a significant step. Regardless of the outcome, the fact that political forces have an alternative place to resolve core questions may facilitate democratic consolidation.

These types of disputes, however, place constitutional courts in difficult positions in that they are called on to wield expertise that they may not have, and may have to substitute for more democratic processes. One need only consider the reaction to the United States Supreme Court's system in *Bush v. Gore* (531 U.S. 98 (2000)) to understand the perils associated with these kinds of decisions. Arguably the Korean and Taiwanese Courts took the best approach by ducking the issue and letting the political process decide the outcome. In Thailand, the Court could not avoid the issue, but in the end it took a similar approach by deferring to the democratic majority that had elected Thaksin despite reports of his failure to file a complete declaration of assets with the NCCC. In contrast, the Mongolian Court derailed the entire constitutional system by refusing to allow the newly elected majority to form a government of its choosing. This led to a severe conflict with the political branches and the depletion of the Court's authority. Indeed, the Myanmar Constitutional Tribunal provides an extreme example of this dynamic. The lesson then, is one of caution on core issues of the political process for courts in new democracies (Croissant 2010).

This leaves attention to fundamental rights and constraint of state authority as the areas in which the courts can have a real role to play. Here the Courts of Korea and Taiwan have been active in introducing international norms into new contexts, with both Courts forcing significant reforms in criminal procedure. The Mongolian Court also played such a role, at least early in the post-socialist period. The Indonesian Court's decision on the anti-terrorism law was also a blow for fundamental rights. Given the less severe character of Thai criminal justice even under the military government, it is perhaps understandable that the Court has not yet emerged as a major voice in this area.

This discussion has implicitly assumed that courts are strategic actors. Courts make choices as to what cases to hear and how to handle them. Because judicial behavior and motivation in general is so poorly understood, it is difficult to develop predictive conclusions about how courts will act in particular cases (Baum 1997). What we *can* conclude, however, is that variations in performance may also be affected by broader cultural, political and social factors. The next section considers some of these.

IV. EXPLAINING THE EMERGENCE OF CONSTITUTIONAL REVIEW

What are the implications of this story for broader comparative understanding of the emergence of constitutional review? Because the adoption of constitutional review is intimately bound up in the broader phenomena of global political liberalization and expansion of judicial power, it implicates issues much larger than can be resolved here. However, we will use our case studies to draw some conclusions on factors that might be relevant to the conditions for the successful emergence of constitutional review.

Cultural traditions are sometimes seen to provide important supporting conditions for the exercise of legal authority. From this perspective, judicial review is the ultimate expression of a tradition of autonomous law associated with the modern West. The four environments considered here have no cultural tradition of autonomous law. The robust exercise of judicial power in all settings helps to confirm that cultural factors are not insurmountable obstacles to judicial review. We need not rehash the entire debate over "Asian values" except to note that, too often, those arguing for Asian exceptionalism reason backward from the existence of illiberal regimes to the values that allegedly support those regimes. At a minimum, we can conclude that the existence of non-Western values at one point in history is not an insurmountable barrier to the later emergence of constitutional constraints on politicians.

One factor that might be called cultural concerns the *receptivity* of the society to foreign ideas, a factor particularly important in an era of "globalization." All four countries considered here are drawn from small countries. Three of them have historically been subject to Western influence while a fourth, Mongolia, has recently turned to the West as a counterweight to Chinese and Russian influence. Such small countries may be particularly open to influence from the modern West because of their fear of cultural and political domination by more proximate large states. Judicial review from this point of view is one element of a package of modernizing reforms that are adopted because of their very Western-ness, as part of a complex security strategy.

One might also expect that *prior history of judicial review* would provide an important source of support for constitutional judges in new democracies. After all, it is generally hypothesized that democratization has been easier in those countries where authoritarian regimes had displaced prior democracies. History, the argument runs, provides a source of inspiration as well as models of institutional design for new democracies (Elster et al. 1998: 60–1). In the Eastern European context, for example, the inter-war history of democracy in Czechoslovakia and Hungary is thought to support the more rapid democratization of those countries than the ambivalent cases of Romania and Bulgaria (Sadurski 2002).

Yet prior experience can constrain as well as inspire. In particular, when an institution exists under authoritarianism, it may develop an institutional culture that favors restraint. Further, it is unlikely to be seen as legitimate in the very early years of democratization. In the case of Taiwan, the Grand Justices existed under the authoritarian regime, and this may have hindered rather than supported the emergence of a more activist conception of judicial review. The Council of Grand Justices in Taiwan was quite cautious in building up its power, treading very carefully, in part because its legacy complicated the task of identifying core constituencies. Even its most famous decision, forcing the retirement in 1990 of the legislators who had been elected on the mainland decades earlier, is perhaps best understood as siding with one ascendant faction of the KMT over another, and not truly about the constraint of power. The Korean and Mongolian Constitutional Courts, as new institutions, had a bit more freedom to operate. In Thailand, formal provision for the exercise of judicial review in earlier constitutions lay dormant. This suggests that prior history is neither a necessary nor sufficient condition for the successful functioning of a particular constitutional court.

Some scholars have attempted to tie the exercise of judicial power to the *type of previous regime*, with a peculiar threat posed by military authoritarians (Ackerman 1997). Our cases provide counter-evidence to the assertion that military authoritarian regimes hinder the development of judicial review. The Korean Constitutional Court has developed active judicial review in the shadow of a departing military authoritarian regime. Thailand's 1997 Constitution, embodied in the Constitutional Court itself, was designed in part to secure the permanent removal of the military from politics. Taiwan's Council of Grand Justices has also systematically dismantled the military-Leninist system of control of civil society. It may be helpful that the only tool the military has to influence the court is to overturn the entire constitutional order, the political equivalent of a nuclear warhead; civilian political parties and institutions have more subtle ways of engaging with the court to communicate their preferences and to encourage judicial modesty. Paradoxically, this means military regimes may actually be associated with judicial autonomy – after all, both officers and judges see themselves as professionals insulated from the dirty politics of legislatures and parties.

The *pace of transition*, in particular the timing of constitutional reform, may affect the exercise of judicial review. In Korea, as well as Mongolia and Thailand, constitutional reform was accomplished quickly at the outset of the transition process (though other democratic reforms were gradual in Korea). This provided the courts with an identifiable constitutional moment to invoke. Where constitutional reform is a gradual process, as in Taiwan, the court must fear the real possibility of constitutional override of any unpopular decisions and therefore will likely be more cautious. Further research on other countries is necessary to evaluate this hypothesis, but our cases suggest that quick transition can support judicial review.

Ackerman (1997) has suggested that *strong presidencies* are helpful for the exercise of judicial review. In this regard, one might add that the adoption of a French-style split executive creates a need for independent courts to arbitrate institutional disputes. Three of our countries have such split executive systems, while Thailand relies on a traditional parliamentary structure of government. Korea and Taiwan were both more strongly weighted toward presidential power than the weak semi-presidential system in Mongolia.

Probably more important is the type of party system. The party system is the crucial factor that determines how the institutions interact, not the mere fact of presidentialism. If a single dominant party exists and controls the legislature and executive, inter-institutional conflict is likely to be minimal. Where divided government holds, however, institutional conflicts will provide the court with a role to play and more policy space in which to render decisions. Split executive systems often produce divided government, and Korea and Taiwan, the two cases with arguably the most robust exercise of judicial review, both had periods of divided government in the 1990s. In Mongolia, the Court's challenge of an overwhelming parliamentary majority after 1998 put it into a battle it could not win; ultimately it had to capitulate.

Certain other variables may affect demand for judicial review by creating incentives for plaintiffs to bring cases to courts. In particular, a *vigorous civil society* provides interest groups that may seek to challenge government action in courts (Voigt 1998: 191). Furthermore, an *un-restricted legal profession* may create incentives for individual lawyers to act as entrepreneurs by pursuing constitutional litigation. These two demand-side variables would support plaintiffs' propensity to bring constitutional cases. Charles Epp has argued that these are necessary underpinnings for a "rights revolution" (Epp 1998).

On both of these scores, Korea provides counter-evidence to the hypothesis. In contrast with Taiwan and Mongolia, associational life has been limited in Korea (Koo 1993). While certain types of private associations exist, for the most part these are not focused on public-interest issues of the type that would lead to greater demand for judicial review. If anything, the presence of an increasingly active system of judicial review has encouraged the formation of new interest groups, suggesting that the causal relationship runs in the opposite direction. Similarly, Korea and to a lesser extent Taiwan have historically placed significant restrictions on the practice of law, limiting entry into the profession to a greater extent than Thailand. This should dampen demand for judicial review. But Korea's activist system of judicial review existed and thrived prior to recent efforts to liberalize the profession.

More broadly, however, the emergence of a *middle class*, seen to be so important in the broader process of democratization, may be a necessary condition for constitutional review to thrive. Most of the countries under consideration here can be said to have vigorous middle classes that played an important role in demanding democratic reforms (Compton 2000). The presence of this broader middle class allows the court to have an alternative means of legitimation – the court can protect itself from attack by political institutions through building up a wellspring of popular support. Of course, such a move requires the court to take a particular strategy in choosing cases of most interest to the middle class and their rights-claims. The Mongolian Court notably declined to do this, and found itself without much public support when it became embroiled in conflicts with the Parliament and government. In contrast, Korean and Taiwanese societies have seen the development of some interest groups that seek to advance their causes through litigation. Such groups by definition have a stake in the courts' continued independence and vitality.

Table 3.2 summarizes some of the possible explanatory variables discussed here. The obvious conclusion is that constitutional courts can emerge and thrive in a variety of environments. Even the rather odd Mongolian case should not be generalized to other post-socialist contexts, for some such courts have been very effective at building up effective support and constraining their politicians. The Hungarian case is perhaps best known in this regard.

V. CONCLUSION

In recent decades, judicial review has expanded around the globe from the United States, Western Europe and Japan to become a regular feature of constitutional design in Africa and Asia. Constitutional courts have exercised review to challenge political authorities when conflicts arise among government institutions or governments impinge on individual rights. Although the formal power to exercise judicial review is now nearly universal in democratic states, courts have varied in the extent to which they are willing to exercise this power in practice.

The courts described above all emerged as major political actors as part of the democratization process. We draw four main conclusions from this account of the Asian cases. First, these cases highlight the important role of constitutional courts in mediating the political process, sometimes by using powers ancillary to the primary, high-profile function of reviewing legislation for constitutionality. Here the existence of the constitutional court can facilitate institutional dialogues among political actors, encouraging peaceful resolution of political disputes and facilitating consolidation.

Second, the emergence of constitutional review in Asia suggests that supposed cultural barriers to the emergence of constitutional constraint are no longer operative, if they ever were so.

Table 3.2 *Explanatory variables*

	Thailand	Korea	Taiwan	Indonesia	Myanmar	Mongolia
Confucian cultural tradition	No	Yes	Somewhat	No	No	No
Colonialism	None	Japanese	Japanese	Dutch	British	Russian
Previous judicial review?	Minimal	Yes	Yes	No	Yes	No
Previous democracy?	Yes	Yes	No	No	No	No
Type of previous regime	Military	Military	Dominant Leninist party	Military/personalist	Military	Dominant Leninist party
Type of transition	Quick	Quick	Gradual	Quick	Gradual	Quick
Governmental structure	Parliamentary	Semi-presidential	Semi-presidential	Presidential	Presidential	Semi-presidential
Divided government?	No	Yes	Yes	Yes	No	No
Middle class?	Yes	Yes	Yes	Yes	No	Yes
Capitalist economy?	Yes	Yes	Yes	Yes	No	No
History of authoritarian pluralism	Yes	Yes	Yes	Yes	No	No

Third, although a wide variety of social contexts can support constitutional review, the existence of a middle class appears to be an important factor in creating a bulwark of support for constitutional courts.

Fourth, it seems that political diffusion matters. Dominant parties are less likely to design open and powerful systems of judicial review, and are less likely to tolerate powerful courts exercising independent power once the constitution enters into force. In contrast, constitutional design in a situation of political deadlock is more likely to produce a strong, accessible system of judicial review as politicians seek political insurance. Political diffusion creates more disputes for courts to resolve, and hinders authorities from overruling or counter-attacking courts. In this sense, the emergence of powerful constitutional courts in Asia *reflects* democratization, and is not counter-democratic as has been argued in the US context.

REFERENCES

Ackerman, Bruce. 1997. "The Rise of World Constitutionalism." *Virginia Law Review* 83: 771–797.

Ahn, Kyong Whan. 1997. "The Influence of American Constitutionalism on South Korea." *Southern Illinois Law Journal* 22: 71–118.

Balme, Stephanie and Mark Sidel, eds. 2007. *Vietnam's New Order: International Perspectives on the State and Reform in Vietnam*. New York: Palgrave Macmillan.

Bauer, Joanne R. and Daniel A. Bell, eds. 1998. *The East Asian Challenge for Human Rights*. New York: Cambridge University Press.

Baum, Lawrence. 1997. *The Puzzle of Judicial Behavior*. Ann Arbor: University of Michigan Press.

Beer, Lawrence Ward and Hiroshi Itoh. 1978. *The Constitutional Case Law of Japan: Selected Supreme Court Decisions, 1961–70*. Seattle: University of Washington Press.

Bell, Daniel A. 2000. *East Meets West: Human Rights and Democracy in Asia*. Princeton: Princeton University Press.

Compton, Robert W. 2000. *East Asian Democratization: The Impact of Globalization, Culture and Economy*. Westport: Praeger.

Croissant, Aurel. 2010. "Provisions, Practices and Performances of Constitutional Review in Democratizing East Asia." *The Pacific Review* 23(5): 549–578.

Davis, Michael C. 1998. "The Price of Rights: Constitutionalism and East Asian Economic Development." *Human Rights Quarterly* 20: 303–337.

Elster, Jon, Claus Offe and Ulrich K. Preuss. 1998. *Institutional Design in Post-communist Societies*. New York: Cambridge University Press.

Epp, Charles R. 1998. *The Rights Revolution: Lawyers, Activists and Supreme Courts in Comparitive Perspective*. Chicago: University of Chicago Press.

Ginsburg, Tom. 2002. "Confucian Constitutionalism? The Emergence of Judicial Review in Korea and Taiwan." *Law and Social Inquiry* 27(4): 763–799.

Ginsburg, Tom. 2003. *Judicial Review in New Democracies: Constitutional Courts in Asian Cases*. New York: Cambridge University Press.

Ginsburg, Tom and Gombosuren Ganzorig. 2001. "When Courts and Politics Collide: Mongolia's Constitutional Crisis." *Columbia Journal of Asian Law* 14(2): 309–26.

Gownder, Joseph P. and Robert Pekkanen. 1996. "The End of Political Science? Rational Choice Analyses in Studies of Japanese Politics." *Journal of Japanese Studies* 22(2): 363–384.

Harding, Andrew and Peter Leyland. 2008. "The Constitutional Courts of Thailand and Indonesia: Two Case Studies from South East Asia." *Journal of Comparative Law* 3(2): 118–137.

Harijanti, Sisi Dwi and Tim Lindsey. 2006. "Indonesia: General Elections Test the Amended Constitution and the New Constitutional Court." *International Journal of Constitutional Law* 4(1): 138–150.

Indrayana, Denny. 2005. *Indonesian Constitutional Reform 1999–2002: An Evaluation of Constitution-making in Transition.* Thesis. University of Melbourne. Retrieved from University of Melbourne Library Digital Repository.

Jacobsen, Michael and Ole Bruun, eds. 2000. *Human Rights and Asian Values: Contesting National Identities and Cultural Representations in Asia.* Oxford: RoutledgeCurzon.

Johnson, Chalmers. 1982. *MITI and the Japanese Miracle: The Growth of Industrial Policy, 1925–1975.* Stanford: Stanford University Press.

Kernell, Samuel, ed. 1991. *Parallel Politics: Economic Policymaking in Japan and the United States.* Washington DC: Brookings Institution.

Kommers, Donald P. 1997. *The Constitutional Jurisprudence of the Federal Republic of Germany.* 2nd ed. Durham: Duke University Press.

Koo, Hagen, ed. 1993. *State and Society in Contemporary Korea.* Ithaca: Cornell University Press.

Lee, Youngjae. 2005. "Law, Politics, and Impeachment of Roh Moo-Hyun from a Comparative Constitutional Perspective." *American Journal of Comparative Law* 53(2): 403–432.

Leyland, Peter. 2007. "Thailand's Constitutional Watchdogs: Dobermans, Bloodhounds or Lapdogs?" *Journal of Comparative Law* 2(2): 151–177.

Mahbubani, Kishore. 2002. *Can Asians Think? Understanding the Divide Between East and West.* South Royalton VT: Steerforth Press.

Palais, James B. 1975. *Politics and Policy in Traditional Korea.* Cambridge MA: Harvard University Press.

Pye, Lucian W. 1995. *Asian Power and Politics: The Cultural Dimensions of Authority.* Cambridge MA: Harvard University Press.

Ramseyer, J. Mark and Eric B. Rasmusen. 2003. *Measuring Judicial Independence: The Political Economy of Judging in Japan.* Chicago: University of Chicago Press.

Rosenbluth, Frances. 1989. *Financial Politics in Contemporary Japan.* Ithaca: Cornell University Press.

Sadurski, Wojciech. 2002. *Constitutional Justice, East and West: Democratic Legitimacy and Constitutional Courts in Post-Communist Europe, in a Comparative Perspective.* The Hague: Kluwer Law International.

Scalapino, Robert. 1997. "A Tale of Three Systems." *Journal of Democracy* 8(3): 150–155.

Stockmann, Petra. 2007. *The New Indonesian Constitutional Court: A Study Into Its Beginnings and First Years of Work.* Hanns Seidel Foundation.

Stone, Alec. 1992. *The Birth of Judicial Politics in France: The Constitutional Council in Comparative Perspective.* New York: Oxford University Press.

Tabulajan, Benny S. "Features – The Indonesian Legal System: An Overview." *Indonesian Legal System: An Overview*. Retrieved 2 December 2002 (www.LLRX. com).

Voigt, Stefan. 1998. "Making Constitutions Work: Conditions for Maintaining the Rule of Law." *Cato Journal* 18(2): 191–208.

West, James and Dae-Kyu Yoon. 1992. "The Constitutional Court of the Republic of Korea: Transforming the Jurisprudence of the Vortex." *American Journal of Comparative Law* 40(1): 73–119.

Yang, Kun. 1993. "Judicial Review and Social Change in the Korean Democratizing Process." *American Journal of Comparative Law* 41(1): 1–8.

4. Judicial engagement

Cheryl Saunders

I. INTRODUCTION

This chapter examines whether and how judges of courts in Asian jurisdictions engage with foreign and international sources of law in resolving constitutional cases. 'Engagement' is used in a neutral sense, to encompass any reference to transnational legal sources, whether positive, negative or bland (cf. Jackson 2010). It extends to consultation of transnational sources by courts, even where this is not reflected in their published reasons. Like the other chapters in this book, this one builds on earlier work, which examined the topic from a more global perspective (Saunders 2011). By adopting an exclusive focus on courts in the Asian region, the chapter seeks both to throw light on constitutional review in Asia and to deepen understanding of judicial engagement as a practice. In doing so, it has the potential also to identify any distinctive characteristics of judicial engagement in the Asian region and thus to provide insight into the utility of regions as a tool of analysis in comparative constitutional law.

The earlier chapter took into account experience with judicial engagement in a small number of selected Asian jurisdictions: Japan, Taiwan and Singapore. The approach in this chapter is to determine the extent to which conclusions based on a global sample of jurisdictions are verified, qualified, elaborated or altered by an exclusively Asian focus. In one important respect, which itself is instructive, I depart from the parameters of the earlier study, by including judicial engagement with international, as well as foreign law. While I have previously excluded the former, on the grounds that its status raises different considerations, I have also foreshadowed the possibility that, in time, this may no longer be practicable (Saunders 2011: 572). The extent to which references to international and foreign law are intermingled in at least some Asian jurisdictions suggests that this point has been reached, at least in the context of the present study.

The earlier chapter concluded that, globally, judicial engagement with foreign law in constitutional cases is common and increasing. It is driven by the forces of internationalisation, including the operation of regional human rights regimes and supra-national arrangements, the ready availability of constitutional information and the general degree of interdependence of myriad aspects of public and private life across national jurisdictional boundaries. Explicit references to foreign law are notably more common in some jurisdictions than others, along lines that correlate broadly with adherence to common law and civil law legal systems. Here as elsewhere the distinction between legal systems is breaking down, making it decreasingly useful as a predictor of attitudes towards engagement with foreign law. Nevertheless, for the moment at least, it retains explanatory value, in relation to both the frequency and the manner of references to foreign law. Inhibitions arising from the assumptions of the legal system aside, there is relatively little concern about the legitimacy of judicial engagement as a practice per se, outside the United States, where for a period it became a cause célèbre (Tushnet 2006). Concern about legitimacy can be prompted by the manner of use, however, in relation to which there are considerable variations between states. Given burgeoning interest in comparative constitutional method, as the practice of judicial engagement increases, closer scrutiny of how and why foreign law is used can be expected.

This chapter broadly follows the outline of the earlier argument. It begins with a section on Asia, in which it identifies the range of jurisdictions on which the study draws and examines collective characteristics of the region that are relevant to understanding the patterns of judicial engagement with foreign and international law. The next sections deal, respectively, with the extent and manner of judicial engagement, with considerations of legitimacy, and with methodology. To anticipate the conclusions: while judicial engagement with foreign and international law in Asian jurisdictions broadly mirrors global experience, there are variations in practice and new perspectives on theory that enrich earlier understandings of this application of comparative constitutional law and endorse the relevance of regionalism as a technique for comparative study.

II. ASIA

Asia may be an artificial region from the standpoint of geography, but on any view of its boundaries it is hugely diverse in terms of history, government, culture, language and economic development. This chapter focuses primarily on eastern, southern and south-eastern Asia, excluding the western and central Asian sub-regions (for details, see United Nations Statistics Division) and excluding states without a recognised system of judicial review on grounds of constitutionality. Even this smaller catchment area, however, comprises 20 distinct and varied polities, within three quite different sub-regions, superimposed on ancient civilisations and cultures.[1] The following observations about the region, thus defined, provide context for the analyses of judicial engagement that follow.

First, the Asian region supports a rich mixture of legal systems, creating a 'comparative law paradise' (Black and Bell 2011: 22). The legal systems of most polities have features that are characteristic of either the civil law or the common law, adapted to the local context. Each legal system bears witness to the historical influence of one or more of a range of western powers, whether as coloniser or in some other guise: the United Kingdom, the United States, France, Germany, the Netherlands, Spain or Portugal. It may be noted in passing that these influences also left a mark on constitutional arrangements in Asian polities, including the form of government, although this has tended to erode over time as changes are made in response to local conditions. To a greater or lesser degree, most Asian legal systems also are pluralist, formally or in practice, combining Western-style law with forms of customary, religious or personal law (Khilnani et al. 2013).

One consequence of the variety of legal systems across the region is that arrangements for constitutional adjudication are similarly diverse. In states with a predominantly common law legal system, constitutional questions typically are resolved by generalist courts, albeit sometimes only at the upper levels of the judicial hierarchy, together with other types of legal dispute.[2] The other accoutrements of common law adjudication generally follow: a formal doctrine of precedent; individual access to courts; an adversarial process; discursive reasons for decision. States with a civilian legal system, by contrast, tend to vest constitutional jurisdiction in a specialist constitutional court, following the Kelsenian model of judicial review. In these jurisdictions, there may be no formal

---

[1]   Hong Kong, Japan, Mongolia, Republic of Korea, Taiwan, Macao (eastern Asia); Bangladesh, Bhutan, India, Maldives, Nepal, Pakistan, Sri Lanka (southern Asia); Cambodia, Indonesia, Malaysia, Philippines, Singapore, Thailand, Timor-Leste (south-eastern Asia).

[2]   Modification of both a diffused and concentrated system in a way that confines constitutional jurisdiction to higher courts while still enabling an avenue of appeal is expressly recognised and discussed by the Royal Court of Justice of Bhutan in *Royal Government v Opposition Party* (SC Hung 11.-1) 5.5, 6.4.

doctrine of precedent, reasons for decision may be less elaborate, procedures may be inquisitorial and individual complaints may not be admissible. The dichotomy is by no means neat, as the example of Japan shows; an essentially civilian legal system in which a generalist Supreme Court has jurisdiction in constitutional matters (Anderson and Ryan 2011: 126–129). The dominance of civil law assumptions nevertheless is consistent with the relative reticence of the Japanese court to engage explicitly with foreign law.

Secondly, modern constitutionalism has had a distinctive trajectory in Asia, in contrast to the rest of the world. All Asian constitutions post-date World War II and many matured as frameworks for democracy towards the end of the 20th century. Constitutional democracy invariably followed a period of authoritarian rule, in one form or another. In some cases, authoritarianism has returned intermittently, often in the guise of emergency rule, widespread provision for which can be ascribed, at least in part, to a continuation of mechanisms originally developed for control in colonial times (Kalhan et al. 2006: 114; Welikala 2013). In relation to a range of states the impetus for constitutional government, when it came, has been described as instrumentalist, linking constitutionalisation to the project of modernisation or to legitimation of a new regime, rather than for the more obviously direct purposes of constraining public power or securing rights (Yeh and Chang 2011; Tan 2011a). Of course, this is not universally true across the region, as the otherwise different examples of India, Hong Kong and Indonesia show. It is sufficiently widespread, however, to have some explanatory power. For Yeh and Chang it constitutes an element of the distinctive form of transitional constitutionalism in eastern Asia, pursuant to which a constitution originally introduced to assist with the project of state-building gradually evolves into an instrument of democracy, with relatively little fundamental change, alongside a 'reactive and cautious' approach to constitutional review that nevertheless protects social and economic as well as civil and political rights (Yeh and Chang 2011: 816).

Thirdly, as a generalisation, Asian constitutionalism occupies a distinctive space on the spectrum between universalism and particularism in the world of the 21st century. Arguably, many Asian constitutional forms, including the very concepts of the modern state and a formal written constitution have been inherited from Western sources, voluntarily or involuntarily and directly or indirectly (Chen 2010). Even on this assumption, however, the leading Asian constitutional systems have now been in existence for some time and integration and organic growth are well advanced. Some states, of which India and Korea are examples, are role models for others in the region (eg Omara 2008). If the incidence of new constitutions is a guide, constitutional stability is greater in Asia than across the world as a whole (Ginsburg 2013), possibly because of its grounding in economic prosperity (Yeh and Chang 2011: 811–812). There now is a considerable body of scholarship on Asian constitutionalism (eg I.CON symposium 2010), identifying and theorising its modes and patterns, some of which also explores its roots in Asian historical experience and tradition (eg Hahm 2001; Sen 2009: 330–332).

International law, with all its implications of universalism, is a significant source of influence in Asian constitutional adjudication. This might be explained in several ways: by the relative neutrality of international law (Hoque 2011: 221); by its familiarity to constitutional systems that came into existence in the latter part of the 20th century (Desierto 2010); as a bulwark against the 'Asian values' debate of the 1980s (Yeh and Chang 2011: 809). Whatever the cause, however, a willingness to invoke international norms co-exists with an appreciation of the significance of local context and preservation of a substantial measure of effective national sovereignty. In stark contrast with Europe, moreover, there is no pan-Asian regional arrangement that seeks to deepen economic integration or to enhance human rights protection and any such arrangements in place at the sub-regional level are still relatively respectful of national autonomy (Tan et al. 2010: 214). This mixture of attitudes towards the international and the local provides a potentially productive platform from which to examine the methodology of judicial engagement with foreign law, with results that are examined in part V of this chapter.

III. USE

Judicial engagement with foreign and international law in the course of constitutional litigation is a familiar phenomenon in the Asian region. The barrier of language makes it difficult to be categorical about both the extent and manner of engagement in all jurisdictions with arrangements for constitutional review. Nevertheless, the reasoning of courts with constitutional jurisdiction is available in English in at least 13 of the jurisdictions covered in this study: Bangladesh, Bhutan, Cambodia, Hong Kong, India, Japan, Korea, Malaysia, Pakistan, Philippines, Singapore, Sri Lanka and Taiwan. Between them, these jurisdictions are drawn from all three sub-regions and represent civil law, common law and mixed legal systems. There is also a body of scholarship on judicial engagement in particular jurisdictions or groups of jurisdictions, to which reference is made below. This material is sufficient to enable at least tentative conclusions to be drawn about the extent to which engagement in Asia reflects patterns of use elsewhere in the world and about whether and, if so, how, Asian experience adds new insights.

All the Asian courts with constitutional jurisdiction for which data is readily available use foreign legal experience as an aid although not, of course, as a binding source of law, in resolving constitutional questions brought before them. This consistency of use, across common law and civil law legal systems, appears to distinguish Asia, at least for the moment, from patterns across the world as a whole. Even so, however, in Asia as elsewhere, identification of the general legal system with either the common law or the civil law tradition respectively offers a rough guide to the manner in which foreign legal experience is used and how usage is manifested. Judges of common law courts including, in this study, Bangladesh, Bhutan, Hong Kong, India, Malaysia, Pakistan, Singapore and Sri Lanka, explicitly refer to foreign legal experience in their published reasons for decision.[3] Typically, such references are an unexceptional aspect of legal reasoning, although frequency varies between jurisdictions, over time and with the political or cultural context of a particular case (see in relation to India, Smith 2006: 238–266). The experience on which they draw often, although by no means always, takes the form of a judicial decision. By contrast, as a generalisation, judges in civil law systems are less likely to refer explicitly to external sources. Studies of both Japan (Ejima 2013) and Taiwan (Law and Chang 2011), for example, show that such references are few and more likely to be found in minority opinions.[4] They are also as likely to draw

---

[3] Cases that illustrate the point include *Kazi Mukhlesur Rahman v Bangladesh* (1974) 26 DLR (AD) 44 (Bangladesh); *Royal Government v Opposition Party* (SC Hung 11.-1) (Bhutan); *W v Registrar of Marriages* [2011] HKEC 1546 (Hong Kong); *Naz Foundation v Government of NCT of India* 160 DLT 277 (2009); *Sugumar Balakrishnan v Pengarah Imigresen Negeri Sabah* [1998] 3 MLJ 289 (CA) (Malaysia); *Munir Hussain Bhatti v Federation of Pakistan* Const.P. 10 of 2011 (Pakistan); *Castro v Judicial and Bar Council (JBC)* GR No 191002, March 17, 2010 (Philippines); *Ramalingam Ravinthram v Attorney-General* [2012] SGCA 2 (Singapore); *Re the Thirteenth Amendment to the Constitution and the Provincial Councils Bill* (1987) 2 Sri LR 312 (Sri Lanka).

[4] In her study of constitutional decisions in Japan between 1 January 1990 and 31 July 2008, Ejima reports only two very general references in majority opinions ('foreign countries') and 13 references in concurring or dissenting opinions (Ejima, 2013). Similarly in relation to Taiwan, Law and Chang identify only eight cases in which a majority opinion expressly referred to foreign legal experience, over the period from 1949 to 2008 although in a much larger number

conclusions from foreign legislation or practice as from judicial decisions. On the other hand, the evidence is equally strong that foreign experience in fact is taken into account in many and perhaps most constitutional cases during judicial deliberation, with consequential impact on judicial reasoning. Despite the paucity of explicit references to foreign experience, the Japanese and Taiwanese studies suggest its influence in developing principles of proportionality, due process, justiciability and strict scrutiny, amongst others (Ejima 2013; Law and Chang 2011: 560). In at least some courts, information about foreign experience is systematically made available to judges. The Constitutional Research Institute of the Constitutional Court of Korea is a distinctive example (Constitutional Research Institute 2011), but the appointment of clerks may provide a similar service elsewhere (Law and Chang 2011: 561).

The explanation for these differences in approach lies in the characteristic features of each of these legal systems (Saunders 2011). Judges of common law courts are used to reasoning by analogy from a wide variety of authorities and to justifying their conclusions in discursive legal reasons. Common law adversarial procedures provide the primary vehicle through which foreign experience is fed into constitutional adjudication, preclude extensive further judicial research behind the scenes and encourage an explicit response to the parties' arguments in published reasons. Judges of courts in the civil law tradition are less comfortable with judge-made law, through both education and professional experience, and employ a 'legislative model' of reasoning from previous decisions (Komárek 2013: 157). They are somewhat less inclined than their common law counterparts to write lengthy discursive reasons although styles in fact vary considerably, from the relatively detailed analytical reasoning of the Constitutional Court of Korea to the syllogistic format of reasons published by the Constitutional Council of Cambodia (eg [2009] KHCCl 2 March 16, 2009). Courts in civil law jurisdictions also typically follow inquisitorial procedures, which may involve an oral hearing but will not always do so and which enable foreign experience to be taken into account in the course of deliberation in ways that will not necessarily be reflected in written reasons (in relation to Taiwan, see Law and Chang 2011: 558–567). The character of the legal system by reference to this binary ordering is by no means either a consistent or stable guide to the use of foreign law, however, as legal systems converge on some points and diversify in relation to others, in response to the complex

---

(21.8% of the total) concurring or dissenting opinions drew on foreign legal experience (Law and Chang 2011: 557).

interaction of globalisation and local context. Thus the Indonesian Constitutional Court, established relatively recently in 2003, will consider both international law and 'other relevant laws in other countries' in accordance with the 'customary practices' of other constitutional courts (Omara 2008: 38–39).

The pattern of references to external sources is distinctive in Asia in some respects. The Constitutional Court of Germany and the apex courts of the United States and the United Kingdom are influential in Asia as elsewhere, reflecting historical practice, legal systemic links, continuing reputation and the accessibility of judgments. Preference for one over another may also be influenced by the education or training of a judge or a researcher for the court (Law and Chang 2011: 558). Less usually, however, reference can be found to the case law of a wide range of other jurisdictions, including those within Asia itself. The Supreme Court of India and the Constitutional Court of Korea are particularly influential in their respective sub-regional and systemic spheres, but cross-jurisdictional references to other Asian courts are familiar as well. Thus, to take only one specific and not particularly unusual example, in *W v Registrar of Marriages*[5] the Hong Kong Court of Appeal cited authorities from Singapore, Malaysia and the Philippines, as well as from Australia, New Zealand, the United Kingdom and the European Court of Human Rights (ECHR). Intra-regional cross-referencing is likely to be encouraged by increased collegial contact between Asian courts through, for example, the recently formed Association of Asian Constitutional Courts and Equivalent Institutions.[6]

As noted earlier, the external sources on which Asian courts draw typically include international as well as foreign law, without necessarily distinguishing between them. At a general level, this development reflects both the increasingly pervasive character of international law and the growing familiarity of jurists with it. In any event, there are signs that more recently established courts, of which the Constitutional Court of Indonesia is an example (Butt and Lindsey 2012: 189ff), rely heavily on international law, and that older courts, such as the Supreme Court of

---

[5] *W v Registrar of Marriages* [2011] HKEC 1546. On appeal, the Hong Kong Court of Final Appeal cited authorities from the United Kingdom, the ECHR, New Zealand, Australia and the United States: *W v Registrar of Marriages* [2013] HKCFA 39.

[6] In March 2013, the Association had 11 members: the apex courts with constitutional jurisdiction from Indonesia, Korea, Malaysia, Mongolia, Pakistan, the Philippines, the Russian Federation, Tajikistan, Thailand, Turkey and Uzbekistan, http://www.aaccei.org.

India, now rely on it to a greater extent (Smith 2006: 257). These developments present a challenge in traditionally dualist states, the significance of which is declining, as the understanding of domestic rights is harmonised with international norms (Hoque 2011: 223).

IV. LEGITIMACY

The initial focus of the debate on judicial engagement that attracted so much attention in the United States in the first decade of the 21st century was the legitimacy of the practice, as a matter of principle (Tushnet 2006). In its most extreme form, the critique denied recourse to any legal sources external to the state that post-dated the Constitution in order to throw light on contemporary constitutional meaning and application. While it was articulated in various ways, the critique rested on a compound conception of a constitution as a distinctive national compact, to be interpreted and understood on the terms originally laid down, by national courts accountable to a sovereign people (Saunders 2011). As this part demonstrates, with one arguable exception that does not withstand scrutiny, the legitimacy of judicial engagement with foreign law is not questioned from the standpoint of principle in adjudication in Asia. In this respect, practice in Asia is no different from that in most of the rest of the world, where reference to external sources in the course of determining constitutional questions before a court is common and appears to be increasing (Saunders 2011). Some features of Asian constitutionalism nevertheless cast further light on the issue of legitimacy, in ways that are examined below. Relevantly also, while the legitimacy of the practice is accepted in Asia in principle, there is a parallel discourse about method, which has indirect implications for legitimacy and is the subject of the next part.

The proposition that the legitimacy of judicial engagement per se is not an issue in Asia is inferred from the extent of engagement with foreign and international law without significant apparent criticism in the reasoning of other judges or the secondary literature. An earlier fracas in Taiwan over the placement of a foreign citation in the text of a majority opinion rather than in a footnote may be attributable to legal systemic considerations and in any event is said to have been 'ignored' (Law and Chang 2011: 559).[7] States in which external sources are cited explicitly appear to accept it as the norm. Studies in states where this does not

---

[7] Law and Chang also note, however, that the views expressed by this Justice were also held by others, even though they caused no change in practice.

occur nevertheless claim that external sources are influential and urge more open acknowledgement of their use (Ejima 2013). In his inaugural remarks on being sworn in as a Justice of the Constitutional Court of Korea, Justice Lee Jin-Sung said, in explicit acknowledgement of the practice: 'I will hold fast to the ideas and spirit of the Constitution and do my best to figure out, referring to the judicial systems of other countries as well as our own Constitution and legal system, a constitutional solution to the conflicts and disputes of our time ...' (Constitutional Court of Korea 2012).

One arguable challenge to the legitimacy of the practice is, or was, the 'four walls' doctrine that was invoked by courts in both Singapore and Malaysia in the latter part of the 20th century (Thio 2006). The doctrine gained prominence when, in 1994, the High Court of Singapore held that an observation in the Malaysian *Kelantan*[8] decision, that the Constitution was 'primarily to be interpreted within its own four walls', applied also in Singapore (*Colin Chan v Public Prosecutor*[9]). The High Court's decision seemed to chime with an earlier government critique of the use of 'foreign case law and precedents' as creating an 'untenable position' in which Singaporean law was 'governed by cases decided abroad' (Ramraj 2002: 319).

There is a fine line between denial of the legitimacy of any use of foreign law and repeated denial of its relevance on the grounds of local difference, pursuant to a comparative methodology that favours particularism. Nevertheless, the four walls doctrine, even in its heyday, clearly was an example of the latter rather than the former. In *Colin Chan* itself the court referred to judicial decisions from the United Kingdom and Australia as well as Malaysia[10] and the formulation of the four walls doctrine in *Kelantan* drew on observations of the Privy Council in *Adegbenro v Akintola*[11] with reference to the new Constitution of Western Nigeria. In context, the court in *Colin Chan* invoked the four walls doctrine in order to repudiate the relevance of 'analogies' with the

---

[8] *Government of the State of Kelantan v Government of the Federation of Malaya* (1963) 1 MLJ 355.

[9] *Colin Chan v Public Prosecutor* (1994) 3 *Singapore Law Reports* 662 at 681.

[10] For example, *O'Reilly v Mackman* [1983] 2 AC 237; *Adelaide Co of Jehovah's Witnesses Inc v Commonwealth* (1943) 67 CLR 116. The UK cases were cited for points of common law, statutory interpretation and procedure, in an illustration of the difficulty of separating constitutional from non-constitutional points in common law adjudication.

[11] *Adegbenro v Akintola* (1963) 3 All ER 544.

Constitution of the United States in resolving a question about religious freedom in Singapore where 'social conditions ... are markedly different' (681). With hindsight, the early cases in this series can be understood as part of a process whereby former colonies of the United Kingdom, with its uncodified constitutional tradition, adapted to the logic of interpreting and applying new written constitutions. The later cases coincided with the debate on 'Asian values' and are also consistent with what Kevin Tan has described as the emergence of a 'much more autochthonous' legal system (2011a: 356). In any event, while the comparative methodology of the courts of Singapore and Malaysia remains a subject of considerable interest, the courts of both countries continue to cite foreign law in the course of constitutional adjudication.[12]

The relative willingness of Asian courts to use external legal sources to inform decisions in constitutional cases makes the region useful to explore various hypotheses about why some courts engage with foreign law without concern about legitimacy while others do not. One hypothesis is that a common genealogy explains and helps to legitimise references by the courts of one state to the constitutional experience of another with which it has a 'family relationship' (Choudhry 1999: 868). Another is that new courts, interpreting new constitutions, necessarily draw on foreign authority because they lack sufficient jurisprudence of their own (Goldsworthy 2012: 709). A third is that the constitutional decisions of courts that are well established and highly regarded may be cited in the constitutional reasons of other courts to bolster their own authority and prestige (Slaughter 1994: 133–134).

All of these possibilities potentially are in play in constitutional adjudication in Asia, as the following examples demonstrate. References by the courts of Singapore and Malaysia to decisions of each other or of the Supreme Court of India or of United Kingdom courts could be understood in terms of genealogy. The willingness of the Constitutional Court of Indonesia or the Supreme Court of Bhutan to draw on external legal sources could be explained on the basis that both are relatively new courts that lack an established jurisprudence. Across Asia, courts have variously adapted decisions of the Constitutional Court of Germany, the Supreme Court of the United States and the House of Lords to their own purposes. But actual experience shows that these explanations are incomplete. Asian courts also draw on constitutional experiences of states with

---

[12] Eg *Meor Atiqulrahman bin Ishak & 2 Lagi v Fatimah Binti Sihi* [2006] MYFC 18, citing, without following, a series of Indian decisions; *Ramalingam Ravinthran v Attorney-General* [2012] SGCA 2, citing authority from India, the United States and the United Kingdom.

which they have no genealogical relationship; Asian courts with a considerable jurisprudence of their own continue to consider the decisions of others, although the rate at which they do so may vary; influential sources of foreign law in Asia are by no means confined to the small handful of Western constitutional courts with high international prestige. Rather, the explanation for the willingness of Asian courts to consider foreign legal experience almost certainly is more complex. At least in part it reflects the reality that the current constitutions of all Asian states came into effect at a time when there already was considerable world experience with written constitutions, on which they drew, in varying degrees. It is unsurprising in these circumstances that the courts that interpret and apply these constitutions assume the capacity to draw on wider experience as well, albeit selectively and employing a wide range of different methodological approaches, with which the next part deals.

V. METHODOLOGY

The attitude of courts towards any substantive consideration of foreign law in the course of constitutional adjudication can be envisaged as ranged along a spectrum. At one end, recourse to foreign law effectively is precluded. At the other, foreign law is treated as authoritative. Over the vast middle ground, courts draw on foreign constitutional experiences of various kinds, in different ways, at different stages in the deliberative and reasoning process, for different purposes and with different outcomes. Vicki Jackson describes this approach as 'engagement' (Jackson 2010: 9). Her terminology has been adapted for the purposes of this chapter, where it is used more broadly, but still in roughly the same sense. In another helpful contribution to the methodology of the role played by foreign law in constitutional reasoning, Sujit Choudhry has characterised this approach to adjudication as 'dialogical' (Choudhry 2013; cf Law and Chang 2011: 527). While these two accounts may differ in matters of detail and emphasis, each explains the process as one in which a court uses foreign law to inform its own deliberation, both as an aid to deeper self-understanding and as a guide to the course of action that it ultimately takes. In the course of this exercise, the foreign law itself may be relied upon or rejected, in whole or in part. Typically, rejection is taken to suggest particularism or localism while reliance is associated with convergence, but both equations depend on context and neither is universally true.

As this chapter has shown, courts in Asia do not regard themselves as precluded from reference to foreign legal experience in constitutional adjudication as a matter of principle. Equally, however, nor do they regard it as authoritative, in a formal sense. In Asia as elsewhere, however, there is some discussion in the literature about whether there are circumstances in which foreign law might effectively be authoritative, even if it is not binding in law. Thus, in his analysis of the decision in *Naz Foundation*,[13] in which the Delhi High Court held unconstitutional a provision of the Indian Penal Code criminalising homosexuality, Madhav Khosla raised the possibility that an 'overwhelming set' of foreign authorities might have exerted a 'kind of force' on the decision of the Court that was independent of their persuasive content (Khosla 2011: 926). Commenting also on *Naz Foundation,* Sujit Choudhry has drawn attention to passages in the reasoning where the Court tended to treat 'Indian and American jurisprudence ... as if they were one integrated body of case law' responding to a 'transcendent constitutional norm' (Choudhry 2013). Both point to pressures for convergence that are products of the dynamics of globalisation, but neither remove from the Court the capacity to make a choice and the responsibility to explain it. And elsewhere in *Naz Foundation,* as will be seen, the Court goes to some lengths to ground its conclusions in the values of the Indian Constitution (*Naz Foundation* at [129], [130]).

In Asia, as in much of the rest of the world, the approach of courts to the use of foreign law in the course of constitutional adjudication can be described broadly in terms of engagement. As elsewhere also, however, there is considerable variation in the manner of engagement, which extends to the receptiveness of the courts of different states to the influence of foreign law and to the types of law and particular jurisdictions with which they engage. Nor is the picture static: methodological approaches to the use of foreign law, as with interpretive method more generally, may vary between judges or panels within a court, with the issues before a court, and over time (in relation to India, for example, see Mate 2010: 231). Even allowing for these differences, however, there are features of engagement in the Asian region that arguably give it a distinctive, regional cast. By and large, Asian jurisdictions are conscious of their own traditions, are engaged in an ongoing process of nation-building in local contexts with particular characteristics and challenges and have gained increasing measures of constitutional self-confidence over the past 20 years. The willingness of Asian courts to engage with the

---

[13]   *Naz Foundation v Government of NCT of Delhi* (2009) 160 DLT 277.

constitutional law of other jurisdictions, some of which formerly exercised hegemonic authority in Asia, sets up an interesting dynamic.

Not surprisingly in these circumstances, there is a burgeoning literature in and in relation to Asia on the methodology of judicial engagement with foreign constitutional sources. At least two distinct, if related, issues can be identified. The first deals with the question of when to apply and when to distinguish foreign law. The second concerns the selection of foreign jurisdictions to which consideration is given. The discussion below necessarily draws largely on courts that engage explicitly with foreign law and publish their decisions in full in English. All courts that engage with foreign law confront the same issues, although the answers may differ in courts that consider foreign law during the deliberative process at the instance of the judges themselves.

A variety of factors potentially bears on the relevance of foreign constitutional experience to an issue before the court. Most obviously, these include the text and structure of the home and foreign constitution(s), together with the accepted interpretive tools; values associated with the respective constitutions including priorities as between values; and the practical context in which each constitution falls to be applied. As far as the first of these is concerned, there is almost always textual difference, broadly understood, between constitutions, despite the considerable if 'qualified' convergence of rights provisions that has taken place in recent times (Elkins and Ginsburg 2012: 1). A critical question for a court considering foreign law in determining a question on which the local constitutional text is inconclusive and local authority is regarded as not determinative is the extent to which the particular textual difference matters. The answer is likely to depend partly, although not entirely, on the relative formalism of the court's general interpretive approach.[14] Values sometimes are articulated in a constitution but often are not, at least in precise and comprehensive form. Engagement with foreign law can assist a court to identify the values that underlie both constitutions so as to determine whether they are sufficiently comparable to make foreign experience applicable (Choudhry 2013). Difference does not inevitably imply rejection; local values thus uncovered may be outdated, disputed, or otherwise vulnerable. Finally, even where foreign experience otherwise appears relevant, there may be local conditions that render it inappropriate, generally or in the context of the particular case.

---

[14] Comparative constitutional reasoning is an emerging area of interest in comparative constitutional law, which is inextricably linked with engagement with foreign law: see, for example, Dyevre and Jacob 2013.

As with constitutional interpretation generally, these factors leave
considerable discretion to a court, which nevertheless is bounded by the
constraints of locally accepted interpretive method and institutional
design. In jurisdictions where engagement with foreign law is explicit,
judicial reasons for distinguishing or drawing on foreign law can be
examined and criticised as long, at least, as they are adequately explanatory. In fact, there has been surprisingly little analysis of this aspect of
judicial reasoning in relation to courts around the world that cite foreign
law freely. It has attracted somewhat more attention in Asia, where
decisions either to distinguish or to apply foreign authority sometimes
have been controversial.

Colin Chan is an example at one end of the scale, where the High
Court of Singapore tersely distinguished United States first amendment
doctrine on the grounds of differences in both constitutional text and
social conditions, in determining whether a government order deregister-
ing the Singapore Congregation of Jehovah's Witnesses, in the face of its
attitude to military service, infringed the right to 'profess and practice
religion' under the Constitution of Singapore.[15] Towards the other end is
Naz Foundation, in which the Delhi High Court accepted that a Union
law criminalising homosexuality was contrary (inter alia) to the right to
privacy inherent in the right to life under the Constitution of India, on the
basis of an analysis that drew on an extraordinarily wide range of foreign
and international authorities, in addition to decisions of the Supreme
Court of India, in a manner that at times treated the question as
susceptible of a universal answer. At the same time, however, the court
grounded its reasoning at critical points deeply in Indian constitutional
tradition, invoking Ambedkar in support of its recognition of constitutional, but not public, morality as a compelling state interest (at [79]) and
Nehru on inclusiveness as an underpinning value of the Indian Constitution (at [129],[130]).

---

[15]   Article 15(4) of the Constitution excepted 'any act contrary to any general
law relating to public order, public health or morality'. In context, however,
surprisingly, the textual basis on which the Court relied was the US prohibition
of 'establishment of religion', although it subsequently pointed to the limitation
clause (in approving Malaysian authority) (at 19, 21). Difference in social
conditions was asserted but not elaborated, apart from an observation that
conscientious objection would cause 'the whole system of universal National
Service' to 'come unstuck' (at 19, 22). *Colin Chan* was the case credited with
reviving the 'four walls' doctrine and its peremptory dismissal of selected foreign
experience should be understood in that context.

The method of engagement of the courts in both cases has been criticised: in *Colin Chan* for distinguishing foreign doctrine too readily and with insufficient warrant (eg Ramraj 2002) and in *Naz Foundation* for treating it as a 'conclusive answer' (Singh 2009: 363). They nevertheless have served the useful purpose of opening up debate on the respective relevance of textual difference, shared values and local context in judicial engagement and the importance of explanation and justification on the part of the courts themselves (Ramraj 2002: 239–331). Despite the vast differences between them, moreover, it is possible to understand the courts in both these cases as seeking to strike a balance between cosmopolitanism, in the sense of a willingness to draw on global constitutional resources, and local ownership. This is an enterprise that is shared with other jurisdictions. With particular reference to Bangladesh, for example, Ridwanal Hoque has called for a 'national context-focused but globality-conscious comparative method' that avoids 'judicial or legal imperialism' on the part of jurisdictions either outside or within the Asian region (Hoque 2011: 245).

A second issue on which Asian experience casts light is the choice of jurisdictions and laws with which to engage. It underlies the familiar concern that a court can 'cherry-pick' a wide array of foreign authorities to select those that favour its own views. It is connected also with the earlier issue of the relevance of foreign law, buttressed by concerns about imperialism and identity (Khilnani et al. 2013: ch 6).

In a still influential and sceptical article written in 1957, Pradyumna Tripathi identified five reasons that influenced the choice of foreign law in constitutional adjudication: 'cultural jealousy of, or admiration for' the jurisdiction concerned; 'political apprehension' of the consequences of preferring eg the United States over Commonwealth authority; the 'cultural and educational background' of the judges; any 'strong personal views' of the judges that strengthened the lure of particular jurisdictions; and the accessibility of particular sources, not least in terms of language (Tripathi 1957: 345). More recent research confirms the continuing influence of the educational background of judges, under both common law and civil law procedures. Accessibility now is much enhanced, however, through technology, ready availability of translations, judicial networks and, occasionally, deliberate provision for research capacity on foreign law. This supports the distinctively wide range of jurisdictions on which Asian courts collectively draw, including considerable cross-fertilisation between courts within Asia itself. Thus, between them, the courts of Singapore and India, in *Colin Chan* and *Naz Foundation*, referred to decisions from Australia, Canada, Fiji, Hong Kong, India, Malaysia, Nepal, South Africa, the United Kingdom and the United

States in addition to some international legal sources that are mentioned below. The common law bias is evident and continuing; the range is unusual by international standards, nevertheless.

The preparedness of Asian courts to draw on a wide range of jurisdictions feeds into the methodology of engagement in other ways. First and most obviously, it may present a court with alternative lines of foreign authority on the issue in question, each of which merits consideration. This situation is exemplified by *W v Registrar of Marriages*, in which the Court of Appeal of Hong Kong held that the right to marry in the Basic Law and the Hong Kong Bill of Rights did not apply to a post-operative transsexual woman who sought to marry her male partner. While the case subsequently was overturned on appeal, the manner of the use of foreign law makes the point for present purposes. The Court of Appeal preferred the reasoning of courts in the United Kingdom, the Philippines and some US states over that of courts in Australia, New Zealand, other US states and the ECHR, partly on the ground of the compatibility of the former with local legal context (at [101]–[104]), (for critique, see Yee 2010). The conclusion of the Court in this case could have been reached without reference to foreign sources; one consequence of these references is to highlight the breadth of the discretion exercised by the Court, requiring it to justify the choices that it made. On the other hand, where a broad range of jurisdictions supports a particular course of action, a court can draw some conclusions from its 'geographical neutrality', as in *Naz Foundation* (Khosla 2011: 11). In either case, the dangers of cherry-picking are diminished, although not eradicated altogether (Khosla 2011: 23–24).

International legal sources frequently are commingled with references to foreign law. In *Naz Foundation*, for example, the Court referred to United Nations human rights treaties, the Yogyakarta Principles, the decision of the Human Rights Committee in *Toonen v Australia*,[16] a declaration of the United Nations General Assembly and a general comment of the Committee on Economic, Social and Cultural Rights, in addition to the range of foreign authorities identified earlier. International sources raise somewhat different methodological issues, however, for present purposes. In states with a dualist tradition there may be threshold questions about whether they can be considered at all; in states with a monist tradition some may require application as operative law. With reference to the impediments that stem from dualism in Bangladesh,

---

[16]   *Toonen v Australia* (1994) No.488/1992 CCPR/C/ 50/D/488/1992.

Ridwanal Hoque has endorsed an 'infusionist' approach, already emergent in India and Sri Lanka, under which courts read into domestic rights provisions treaties that are 'harmonious' with the 'spirit' of the constitution, to which the state is a party, 'so as to strengthen constitutional guarantees' (Hoque 2011: 223, 226).

These problems aside, in principle international law offers a neutral source on which domestic courts can draw, representing universal norms, emanating from the international community of which each state is part and thus deserving respect (Khosla 2011: 8, 9; Mate 2010: 251; for the unusual position of Taiwan in this regard, see Law and Chang 2011: 540–544). On the other hand, suspicion of its provenance remains (Hoque 2011: 221). And more significantly still, international law often is indeterminate in relation to the types of issues that come before domestic courts, sometimes requiring a different form of recourse to foreign practice before it can be used. The decision of the Hong Kong Court of Appeal in *W v Registrar of Marriages* (2011) once again offers an example. International law was directly relevant to the issue before the Court because the International Covenant on Civil and Political Rights (ICCPR) was incorporated into domestic law by the Hong Kong Bill of Rights. The text of the ICCPR does not deal explicitly with the position of post-operative transsexual women, however, and there was no decision of the Human Rights Committee directly on point, to which the Court was referred. The appellant and the International Commission of Jurists, intervening, attempted to overcome the difficulty by directing the Court to the practice of State parties to the ICCPR. The attempt failed at this point because, in the view of the Court, there was insufficient evidence of 'relevant consensus' ([150]–[152]).

VI. CONCLUSION

This study of judicial engagement in Asia in the course of constitutional adjudication offers at least three general insights for comparative constitutional law.

First, it shows that judicial engagement is a significant vehicle for the global dissemination of constitutional ideas. Through judicial engagement, constitutional doctrines that originated outside Asia were introduced into the jurisprudence of particular Asian states. Examples given in this chapter include proportionality, due process, justiciability and strict scrutiny. Equally, through judicial engagement constitutional doctrines have circulated within Asia. An obvious example is the adoption of the basic structure doctrine by most southern Asian states. Asian jurisprudence presently is cited less frequently outside Asia, although citations can be found, particularly within the network of Commonwealth countries.[17] The increasing accessibility of Asian case law provides a means by which this can increase.

Second the study confirms, if confirmation is needed, that the internationalisation of constitutional law is a catalyst for considerable convergence in constitutional doctrine, as well as other aspects of constitutional law. Equally importantly, however, it also warns against overstating its effects. The evidence of this chapter is that both local constitutional difference and national constitutional identity are significant phenomena with which judicial engagement, as well as other applications of comparative constitutional law, must deal. In consequence, constitutional doctrines received through judicial engagement typically are mixed with others, modified to suit local needs and explained in terms that facilitate local ownership. Thus in *Naz Foundation* the Delhi High Court notes that Indian jurisprudence has adopted both proportionality and strict scrutiny and understands the latter as having no application to cases of affirmative action (at [107]–[111]). In an example of a different kind, in discussing the application of a basic structure doctrine in Bangladesh, Radwanal Hoque notes that it was 'definitely fed by the mandates of the country's Constitution', although 'greatly assisted by similar developments in … neighbouring … India' (Hoque 2011: 247).

Finally, the chapter demonstrates the potential benefits for the global understanding of comparative constitutional law of analyses that take a particular region as a focus. As in all regions, Asian states are diverse and generalisation is fraught. In many respects, also, the pattern of judicial engagement in Asia is similar to that elsewhere in the world. There are some features of judicial engagement in Asia that are distinctive, however. Not the least of these is the willingness of Asian jurisdictions to draw on a diverse range of foreign legal experience, further intermixed with international law. Recourse to this variety of sources, in the context of Asian constitutionalism, has been a catalyst for advances in the methodology of judicial engagement, which should be of interest elsewhere.

---

[17] In *Fose v Minister for Safety and Security* (1997) (3) SA 786, for example, the Constitutional Court of South Africa cited both Indian and Sri Lankan authority in considering the public law nature of the remedy for infringing a constitutional right.

REFERENCES

Anderson, Kent and Trevor Ryan. 2011. "The Importance and Evolution of Legal Institutions at the Turn of the Century." In *Law and Legal Institutions of Asia*, edited by E. Ann Black and Gary F. Bell. Cambridge: Cambridge University Press.

Black, E. Ann and Gary F. Bell, eds. 2011. *Law and Legal Institutions of Asia.* Cambridge: Cambridge University Press.

Butt, Simon and Tim Lindsey. 2012. *The Constitution of Indonesia.* Oxford: Hart Publishing.

Chen, Albert H.Y. 2010. "Western Constitutionalism in Southeast Asia: Some Historical and Comparative Observations." (http://ssrn.com/abstract=1723658).

Choudhry, Sujit. 1999. "Globalization in Search of Justification: Towards a Theory of Comparative Constitutional Interpretation." *Indiana Law Journal* 74(3): 819–892.

Choudhry, Sujit. 2013. "How to do Comparative Constitutional Law in India: *Naz Foundation*, Same Sex Rights, and Dialogical Interpretation." In *Constitutionalism in South Asia*, edited by S. Khilnani et al. New York: Oxford University Press.

Constitutional Council of Cambodia. 2009. "Request of the 15 Members of Parliament, requesting the Constitutional Council to interpret Article 29 of the Law on the Elections of the Capital Council, Provincial Councils, Municipality Councils, District Councils and Khan Councils, and to examine its constitutionality as well as to interpret Article 16 of the Law on the Commune/Sangkat Administrative Management." KHCCl 2.

Constitutional Court of Korea (2012), *Newsletter 144*.

Constitutional Research Institute. 2011. *About CRI* (http://ri.ccourt.go.kr/eng/ccourt/about/greetings.html).

Desierto, Diane A. 2010. "A Universalist History of the 1987 Philippine Constitution (II)." 11 *Historia Constitucional* 427.

Dyevre, A. and A. Jacab. 2013. "Foreword: Understanding Constitutional Reasoning." *German Law Journal*, forthcoming.

Ejima, Akiko. 2013. "Enigmatic Attitude of the Supreme Court of Japan towards Foreign Precedents – Refusal at the Front Door and Admission at the Back Door." Forthcoming in *The Use of Foreign Precedents by Constitutional Judges*, edited by Tania Groppi and Marie-Claire Ponthoreau. Oxford: Hart Publishing.

Elkins, Zachary and Tom Ginsburg. 2012. "Getting to Rights: Treaty Ratification, Constitutional Convergence, and Human Rights Practice." (http://works.bepress.com/tom_ginsburg/32).

Ginsburg, Tom. 2013. "East Asian Constitutionalism in Comparative Perspective." Forthcoming in *Constitutionalism in Asia in the Early Twenty First Century*, edited by Albert Chen. Cambridge: Cambridge University Press.

Goldsworthy, Jeffrey. 2012. "Constitutional Interpretation." In *Oxford Handbook of Comparative Constitutional Law*, edited by Michel Rosenfeld and Andras Sajo. Oxford: Oxford University Press.

Hahm, Chaihark. 2001. "Conceptualizing Korean Constitutionalism: Foreign Transplant or Indigenous Tradition." *Journal of Korean Law* 1(2): 151–196.

Hoque, Ridwanal. 2011. *Judicial Activism in Bangladesh: A Golden Mean Approach.* Newcastle upon Tyne: Cambridge Scholars Publishing.

I.CON symposium. 2010. "The Changing Landscape of Asian Constitutionalism." 8 *International Journal of Constitutional Law* 766–987.

Jackson, Vicki C. 2010. *Constitutional Engagement in a Transnational Era.* Oxford: Oxford University Press.

Kalhan, Anil et al. 2006. "Colonial Continuities: Human Rights, Terrorism, and Security Laws in India." *Columbia Journal of Asian Law.* 20: 93–234.

Khilnani, Sunil, Vikram Raghavan and Arun K. Thiruvengadam. 2013. *Comparative Constitutionalism in South Asia.* Oxford: Oxford University Press.

Khosla, Madhav. 2011. "Inclusive Constitutional Comparison: Reflections on India's Sodomy Decision." *American Journal of Comparative Law* 59(4): 909–934.

Komárek, Jan. 2013. "Reasoning with Previous Decisions: Beyond the Doctrine of Precedent." *American Journal of Comparative Law* 61(1): 149–171.

Law, David and Wen-Chen Chang. 2011. "The Limits of Global Judicial Dialogue." *Washington Law Review* 86: 523–577.

Mate, Manoj. 2010. "The Origins of Due Process in India: The Role of Borrowing in Personal Liberty and Preventive Detention Cases." *Berkeley Journal of International Law* 28(1): 216–260.

Omara, Andy. 2008. "Lessons from the Korean Constitutional Court: What can Indonesia Learn from the Korean Constitutional Court Experience?" A comparative study prepared for the Korean Legal Research Institute.

Ramraj, Victor V. 2002. "Comparative Constitutional Law in Singapore." *Singapore Journal of International and Comparative Law* 6: 302–334.

Saunders, Cheryl. 2011. "Judicial Engagement with Comparative Law." In *Comparative Constitutional Law*, edited by Tom Ginsburg and Rosalind Dixon. Northampton, Mass: Edward Elgar.

Sen, Amartya. 2009. *The Idea of Justice.* Cambridge: Harvard University Press.

Singh, Mahendra. 2009. "Decriminalisation of Homosexuality and the Constitution." *NUJS Law Review* 2: 361–380.

Slaughter, Anne-Marie. 1994. "A Typology of Transjudicial Communication." *University of Richmond Law Review* 29: 99–136.

Smith, Adam M. 2006. "Making Itself at Home Understanding Foreign Law in Domestic Jurisprudence: the Indian Case." *Berkeley Journal of International Law* 24(1): 218–272.

Tan, Kevin Y.L. et al. 2010. "History and Culture: Complexities in Studying Southeast Asian Constitutionalism Roundtable." *National Taiwan University Law Review* 5(2): 187–224.

Tan, Kevin Y.L. 2011a. "Singapore: A Statist Legal Laboratory." In *Law and Legal Institutions of Asia*, edited by E. Ann Black and Gary F. Bell. Cambridge: Cambridge University Press.

Tan, Kevin. 2011b. "Constitutionalism in Burma, Cambodia and Thailand: Developments in the First Decade of the 21st Century." Forthcoming in *Constitutionalism in Asia in the Early Twenty First Century*, edited by Albert Chen. Cambridge: Cambridge University Press.

Thio, Li-Ann. 2006. "Beyond the 'Four Walls' in an Age of Transnational Judicial Conversations: Civil Liberties, Rights Theories, and Constitutional Adjudication in Malaysia and Singapore." *Columbia Journal of Asian Law* 19: 428–518.

Tripathi, P. 1957. "Foreign Precedents and Constitutional Law." *Columbia Law Review* 57(3): 319–347.

Tushnet, Mark. 2006. "When is Knowing Less Better than Knowing More? Unpacking the Controversy over Supreme Court Reference to Non-US Law." *Minnesota Law Review* 90: 1275–1302.

United Nations Statistics Division, *Composition of macro geographical (continental) regions, geographical sub-regions and selected economic and other groupings* (http://unstats.un.org/unsd/methods/m49/m49regin.htm).

Welikala, Asanga. 2013 "The Sri Lankan Conception of the Unitary State: Theory, Practice and History." In Amaranth Amarasingham and Daniel Bass (eds.) (forthcoming 2014) *Post-War Sri Lanka: Problems and Prospects*. Lexington, KY: University Press of Kentucky.

Yee, Karen Lee Man. 2010. "*W v Registrar of Marriages*; from Transsexual Marriage to Same-sex Marriage." *Hong Kong Law Journal* 40(3): 549–562.

Yeh, Jiunn-Rong and Wen-Chen Chang. 2011. "The Emergence of East Asian Constitutionalism: Features in Comparison." *American Journal of Comparative Law* 59: 805–839.

5. Weak-form review and its constitutional relatives: An Asian perspective

Mark Tushnet and Rosalind Dixon

I. INTRODUCTION

Weak-form constitutional review was one of the late twentieth century's major innovations in constitutional design. Specific forms vary, but all share the characteristic that a court decision ultimately resolving a constitutional matter can be followed by a legislative or popular response short of constitutional amendment that differs in whole or in part with the court's decision (and the interpretation of the *existing* constitution on which the court's decision rests).

What Lorraine Weinrib calls the "post-war paradigm" of constitutional law includes institutions to perform constitutional review in a systematic way (Weinrib 2006). Weak-form review was developed in response to concerns that conforming to the paradigm by establishing a system of full-fledged or strong-form constitutional review in nations with deep traditions of parliamentary supremacy would disrupt the established scheme of things too substantially, and with unknowable follow-on effects. Proponents of weak-form review contended that it was a better institutional embodiment of the post-war paradigm's accommodation of constitutional review and democratic self-governance. As experience accumulated with weak-form review, another feature emerged: weak-form review could promote valuable constitutional dialogues about the constitution's meaning (Hogg and Bushell 1997; Symposium 2007), especially where legislatures might have overlooked constitutional problems lurking in the details of otherwise defensible legislation, where political considerations led legislatures deliberately to finesse constitutional questions, or where long-standing legislation had become problematic in light of changes in constitutional understandings (Dixon 2008).

Yet, weak-form review has largely been absent in Asia at the level of formal constitutional design. Rather, with the exception of Mongolia, constitutional courts in East Asia typically have broad powers to invalidate legislation for inconsistency with the constitution, similar to those exercised by the German Constitutional Court. Most non-specialized courts in the region (other than in China, and possibly Hong Kong) also enjoy US-style powers of judicial review, even in countries with a long history of British-style parliamentary government.

But, substance as well as form matters when it comes to judging the strength of judicial review. To say that review is strong in form does not mean that constitutional review is strong in practice, taken to mean that a constitutional court regularly sets its constitutional interpretations against those implicit in the legislation it reviews. Some Asian constitutional courts, such as those in Taiwan and South Korea, have exercised powers of constitutional review that are strong both in form and in practice. Others, such as the Japanese Supreme Court, have tended to be more restrained in the exercise of their powers of constitutional review, thereby creating a weaker model of judicial review in practice. Yet even in these systems, practices of statutory interpretation – whether in the form of expansive interpretations to advance what the courts perceive to be constitutional values or in the form of "reading statutes down" through narrow interpretation to avoid interference with those values – are similar enough to weak-form review to be worth considering as a part of a broader family of practices.

The actual strength of judicial review is linked in Asia, as elsewhere, to various countries' rules for constitutional amendment. The more easily a constitution may be amended, the more readily the amendment process can serve functions similar to that of weak-form review in supporting legislative and public involvement in constitutional interpretation and the like.[1] In several Asian countries, constitutional amendment processes have in fact played exactly this kind of role in allowing parliament to override or "trump" particular court decisions (Dixon 2011; cf. Denning and Vile 2002). This, for example, has been true in India in the context of battles between the Indian Supreme Court (SCI) and Parliament over the scope of affirmative action and the constitutional right to property,

---

[1]   Weak-form review and easy amendment processes differ formally, of course, in that weak-form review promotes dialogue with respect to the existing constitution while amendments change the constitution.

though the SCI has also responded by purporting to review the substantive validity of these amendments, thereby at least partially reasserting the strength of judicial review in certain "core" constitutional areas.

A striking feature of the constitutional dialogue in many Asian countries, such as Japan and India, has also been the degree to which the relevant constitutional dialogue has played out against the backdrop of near complete dominance by a single political party (the Liberal Democratic Party (LDP) in Japan, and the Congress Party in India). Asian constitutional systems provocatively raise questions about the relationship between weak-form review and dominant-party democracy.

This chapter examines these potential functional substitutes for weak-form review – sub-constitutional review and constitutional amendment – and their limits (both positive and normative), using Japan and India as case studies.

It considers how each mechanism can serve the goals that weak-form review does, in promoting legislative participation in constitutional decision-making, but also how each may be unstable in promoting true balance, or dialogue, between courts and legislatures. It also considers the degree to which such questions are affected by the background conditions of political competition, and thus how models of weak-form review relate to broader questions of democratic consolidation.

It suggests, for example, there may in fact be a certain paradox to the idea of weak-form review, or its constitutional equivalents or "relatives", in a dominant-party democracy: the argument for weak-form review seems less compelling in such countries than in those with stronger norms of electoral competition, but at the same time, some weakening in the strength of review also seems more likely (Choudhry 2009). This, we suggest, is potentially the most interesting and important lesson provided by attention to Asian constitutional developments in this context.

II. WEAK-FORM REVIEW IN ASIAN CONSTITUTIONAL DESIGN

As noted, weak-form review was an innovation in constitutional design. Before the innovation became available, constitutional designers had several models to follow – the Kelsenian specialized constitutional court, the US generalist one, the diffuse versus the concentrated system of constitutional review, and others – but all of these models were for strong-form review in which constitutional courts had the last word on constitutional interpretation subject only to the possibility of constitutional amendment. The possibility of an alternative not even being on the horizon, then, the Japanese Constitution of 1947, developed by the US occupying forces and therefore modeled on the US Constitution, established a system of strong-form review. Many scholars and judges in Japan and elsewhere in the region received an initial legal training strongly influenced by German concepts and scholars, and had post-graduate training in Germany. The post-war German paradigm was one of strong-form review as well.

One can find glimmerings of weak-form review in East Asia. The version closest to real weak-form review exists in Mongolia. There the 1992 Constitution created a constitutional court (Ginsburg and Ganzorig 2001: 310–11). After an initial screening stage, a three-person panel of the nine-member Court considers constitutional challenges to legislation. If the panel finds the legislation unconstitutional, its decision is sent to the nation's Parliament. The Parliament then considers whether to accept or reject the Court's interpretation. If it rejects the interpretation, the case is sent back to the Constitutional Court, and all nine judges deliberate. But, if the full Court agrees with the panel, the decision is final and binding, subject of course to constitutional amendment. The amendment rule has two components: a referendum called when two-thirds of the Parliament so recommend, with a quorum rule requiring participation by a majority of the nation's eligible citizens and a rule that a majority of those voting prevail; and a legislative process in which amendments can occur with the agreement of three-fourths of the Parliament. The amendment rules are thus rather stringent, and the weak-form component of the Mongolian system is only a modest incursion on strong-form review.

Hong Kong provides an example of a similarly outlying version of weak-form review. After 1999 Hong Kong has a constitution in the form of a Basic Law that establishes the "one nation, two [legal] systems" regime for the Hong Kong Special Administrative Region within the People's Republic of China (PRC). A High Court within Hong Kong has responsibility for interpreting the Basic Law. The relation between that Court's interpretations and PRC law is contested. The High Court has asserted the power to hold Hong Kong legislation unconstitutional because it is inconsistent with the Basic Law (*Ng Ka Ling v. Director of Immigration*, 1 HKC 291 (1999)). In a case with high political salience, the Court held that a regulation aimed at restricting the right of people from China to relocate to Hong Kong was invalid because it was inconsistent with the definition of the "right to abode" in Hong Kong's Basic Law.

The modest position and, unsurprisingly, the stronger one have been contested by PRC representatives. In their view Hong Kong legislation finds its ultimate foundation not in the Basic Law but in PRC law. So, they contend, a decision to find a Hong Kong statute inconsistent with the Basic Law amounts to a decision that some aspect of PRC law is unconstitutional. And, as a creation of PRC law the Hong Kong High Court has no power to hold PRC legislation unconstitutional or even unenforceable because of its inconsistency with a subordinate body of law, the Basic Law. For example, the Hong Kong executive obtained a decision from the Standing Committee of the National People's Congress stating that the "right to abode" ordinance was valid law. The Hong Kong High Court indicated even before that decision that it "did not question the authority" of the Standing Committee to give binding interpretations of the Basic Law (*Ng Ka Ling v. Director of Immigration* [2], 1 HKC 425 (1999)).

The state of affairs in Hong Kong continues to develop. At present, the PRC asserts a position that transforms the Hong Kong High Court into a weak-form court. According to the PRC, it can choose to override a High Court decision by having the Standing Committee interpret the Basic Law. Of course, locating this practice in the same conceptual field as weak-form review is itself problematic, not least because the accommodation of democratic self-government with constitutionalism works in the wrong direction, so to speak: High Court decisions with some, perhaps modest, claim to democratic pedigree are displaced by a decision of a political body that, in authoritarian China, has none.

III. QUASI-WEAK-FORM WITHIN FORMALLY STRONG-FORM SYSTEMS: JAPAN AND SUB-CONSTITUTIONAL REVIEW

The relation between the strength of and formal powers of legislative override is a structural one, part of the constitution's design. Other ways of reducing the difference between strong- and weak-form systems, however, are functional, arising from actual practice rather than built into the design.

Consider the final stage of a dialogue in a weak-form system. The constitutional court has held a statute unconstitutional based on its interpretation of the constitution. The legislature has responded by re-enacting (or, in some weak-form systems, deliberating and choosing not to alter) the statute. The constitutional challenge is renewed. The weak-form court is then required, in theory at least, to defer to the legislature's interpretation, treating that interpretation as displacing its own.

Turn now to a strong-form system. A court in such a system clearly has the *option* of deferring to the legislature's interpretation of the constitution at either the initial, or the second, stage. At an initial stage, it may choose wholly to defer (in which case, judicial review may in fact be so weak as to be non-existent), or simply signal a willingness to defer in the future, if needed, by relying on explicitly sub-constitutional grounds (Coenen 2001). At the second stage, it again has the option of deciding to show deference: it can persist in its own interpretation but acknowledge the legislature's power to disagree and support the statute with a different interpretation, or it can defer to the legislature's interpretation, treating that interpretation as displacing its own. Deference occurs in both systems, and to that extent we might treat deference by strong-form courts as similar to one path that weak-form courts might take.

This, we suggest, is also more or less the equivalent to weak-form review that has developed in Japan. Japan's Supreme Court is usually described as "conservative" in two senses (Matsui 2011; Law 2011). Its substantive rulings on constitutional issues that have some substantial political overtones are said to be resolved systematically in a conservative direction, and it rarely exercises its formally strong powers of constitutional review to invalidate government-supported legislation. These two senses are perhaps not readily distinguishable, for reasons explored in the literature on the Court's role in the Japanese political system. The LDP, a conservative party, has dominated Japanese politics since the end of World War II. In broad outline, Japanese governments do not enact "liberal" statutes. So, refusals to exercise the power of constitutional review to invalidate legislation – a "conservative" use of the power – leave in place substantively conservative statutes, and the doctrine that emerges from such decisions will also be substantively conservative, though perhaps laced with some references to deference to legislative authority.

There is, however, one important difficulty with this account: it takes as its predicate the Court's failure to exercise strong-form constitutional review against legislation. Yet a fair amount of sub-constitutional adjudication results in substantively liberal decisions. Frank Upham describes numerous cases in which the Court gave sometimes aggressively liberal interpretations of enacted statutes (Upham 2011). In one, the Court found it disproportionate for an employer to fire a worker for missing two early-morning and time-sensitive job assignments because he overslept, accommodating statutes that appear to make employment "at will" to the "common sense of society" as expressed in the Civil Code's general clauses. In addition, administrative law decisions finding executive action unauthorized by statute sometimes appear to be similarly inflected by constitutional concerns. Shigenori Matsui describes a case in which the Court overturned a student's expulsion for refusing on religious grounds to participate in martial arts training, on grounds resonant with proportionality concerns (Matsui 2011: 1398–99).

These decisions, we suggest, can be understood as a subtype of weak-form review, which, though always a part of the account of such review, has sometimes been obscured by the stark contrasts drawn between the two forms of constitutional review.

Consider the cases involving review and invalidation of executive action. Such review is familiar within systems of parliamentary supremacy, that is, familiar entirely independent of the post-war paradigm. Courts in such systems regularly engage in what used to be called judicial or administrative review, that is, review of executive action to determine whether the action is consistent with the authority the legislature has given the executive. Administrative review of this sort has many of the features of weak-form review. After a judicial decision that the legislature had not authorized the challenged executive action, the legislature can respond by granting express authority. Like some variants of weak-form review, administrative review shifts the burden of inertia from those challenging legislation to those supporting it. Further, courts can adjust their scrutiny of the statutes on which the executive purports to rely in light of the constitutional sensitivity of the subject matter, requiring greater clarity in authorizing legislation the more constitutionally sensitive the subject is.

The cases involving statutory construction are similar (Coenen 2001). Statutes that in the court's view promote constitutional values can be construed generously, as in the employment cases. The legislature can respond by enacting a narrower statute. Similarly with statutes the court views as constitutionally problematic: a narrow construction promotes the court's view of the constitution's meaning, while giving parliament the opportunity to respond by insisting that it did indeed want to intrude on what the court saw as constitutional values.

IV. QUASI-WEAK-FORM REVIEW WITHIN FORMALLY STRONG-FORM SYSTEMS: INDIA AND CONSTITUTIONAL AMENDMENT

Another way in which strong-form review can be weakened, in practice, is via processes of constitutional amendment. Constitutional amendment processes play a number of different functions under an entrenched constitution. For one, they allow major constitutional change, or revision, to occur within an existing constitutional framework (see Denning and Vile 2002; Ginsburg and Dixon 2011; Griffin 1998; Lutz 1995); and for another, legislatures can correct or "update" specific constitutional rules via formal legal means, rather than less orthodox forms of constitutional "workaround" (see Dixon 2009b; Ginsburg and Dixon 2011; Murphy 1995: 165; cf Tushnet 2009a). They thus help promote values of transparency, and rule-of-law adherence, in the process of constitutional change (see e.g. Ginsburg and Dixon 2011; Griffin 1998: 42, 52).

Another important function of constitutional amendment rules, however, is to provide a vehicle by which legislatures, or popular actors, can engage in dialogue with courts – both by jump-starting or generating new interpretations of the constitution by courts (see Forbath 2003), and creating pressure for courts to defer to attempts by the legislature to modify, or trump, prior judicial interpretations (see Dixon 2010; Dixon 2011; Denning and Vile 2002; Vermeule 2006).[2] The way in which amendment procedures do this is also in much the same way as formal powers of legislative override: by both changing the *textual basis* for subsequent processes of constitutional interpretation and creating a clearer *evidentiary record* of legislative or popular constitutional understandings (see Ginsburg and Dixon 2011; Levinson 2001: 273). The only difference is that, compared to such powers, amendment procedures tend to produce broader, more enduring forms of text-based change.[3] The level, or kind, of political disagreement required for legislatures to use such procedures may therefore be somewhat greater than under a system of true weak-form review (see e.g. Waldron 2004; Dixon 2009a).

The best example of amendment procedures performing this kind of "trumping" function, in Asia, is in India, where there have been over 80 amendments to the Constitution since it was first adopted in 1950, and a large number of amendments designed explicitly to override, or trump, decisions of the SCI (see e.g. Neuborne 2003). The Indian Constitution's

---

[2] Of course, where a legislature's objection to a court's approach is that it is unduly restrained, the two functions may merge into one, but the distinction nonetheless remains useful in other cases.

[3] In weak-form systems, changes to the text are generally limited to a particular statute (because of the exercise, for example, of a power of express or implied repeal) or more temporary in nature: see e.g. the five-year sunset that applies under s 33 of the Canadian *Charter.*

amendment rule, stated in Article 368, is simple: amendments can be adopted by a majority vote in each House of Parliament.[4]

The first amendment to the Indian Constitution,[5] for example, added language to the Constitution designed to override at least three prior decisions of the SCI: language in Article 15 of the Constitution expressly permitting the state to make "special provision for the advancement of any socially and educationally backward classes of citizens or for the Scheduled Castes and the Scheduled Tribes"; language in Article 19 permitting the state to impose "reasonable restrictions" on the right to free speech and expression "in the interests of the security of the State, friendly relations with foreign States, public order, decency or morality, or in relation to contempt of court, defamation, or incitement to an offence;" and language immunizing laws "for the acquisition by the State of any estate or of any rights therein or for the extinguishment or modification of any such rights" from challenge based on the right to property in Article 31 of the Constitution and adding various land reform statutes to the schedule of laws deemed non-justiciable under the 9th schedule to the Constitution. The first change was made in response to the SCI's holding, in *State of Madras v. Champakam Dorairajan*, A.I.R. 1951 S.C. 227, that the reservation by a state medical school of places based on caste violated the prohibition on non-discrimination under (the unamended) Article 15(1); the second in response to a decision of the SCI, in *Romesh Thapar v. State of Madras*, A.I.R. 1950 S.C. 124, striking down an attempt by the government of Madras to ban a communist-leaning magazine under the state's anti-sedition laws; and the third, to the decision of various high courts striking down land reform statutes, including statutes designed to abolish the "zamandari" system of feudal landholding.

The SCI responded by showing *partial* deference to all three attempts at legislative override (see e.g. Mehta 2002: 183). The year after the amendment was passed, it adopted a quite different notion of equality, and non-discrimination, under Articles 14, 15 and 16 of the Constitution, thereby permitting far broader scope for measures designed to promote substantive equality (see e.g. *State of Kerala v. Thomas*, A.I.R. 1976 S.C. 490; *Vasanth Kumar v. State of Karnataka*, A.I.R. 1985 S.C. 1495). In the context of free speech, it adopted a more intermediate standard of

---

[4] Amendments to certain fundamental aspects of the Constitution, such as its provisions governing the representation of the states and the scheduled castes, are subject to the additional hurdle of ratification by a majority of state legislatures.

[5] Constitution (First Amendment) Act, 1951.

scrutiny review for public order-based restrictions on speech (see e.g. *Superintendent, Central Prison v. Ram Manohar Lohiya*, A.I.R. 1960 S.C. 633) (requiring a "proximate connection" between an incitement and a breach of public order for the purposes of Article 19(2)). And in the context of land reforms, initially at least, it held that the ninth schedule to the Constitution was sufficient to preclude any challenge to such laws based on the right to property (see *Shankari Prasad Singh v. Union of India*, A.I.R. 1951 S.C. 458).

As the Indian experience also makes clear, however, constitutional amendment procedures do not guarantee deference by a court. Soon after the decision in *Shankari Prasad*, for example, the SCI began once again to assert a power to review the constitutionality of land reform legislation, under the unamended Constitution (see Neuborne 2003: 487–95). In 1952, in *State of Bihar v. Kameshwar Singh*, A.I.R. 1952 S.C. 252,[6] it held that the first amendment was insufficient to oust review of whether an acquisition of property was for a "public purpose", and thus within the scope of Parliament's power of eminent domain under Article 246 of the Constitution. And a decade later, in *Karimbil Kunhikoman v. State of Kerala*, A.I.R. 1962 S.C. 723, it held that the word "estate", in the first amendment, did not in fact include zamandari holdings.

When the Parliament responded by passing yet another amendment to the Constitution designed to oust judicial review (i.e. the 17th amendment, expanding the definition of those laws included in the ninth schedule to the Constitution), the SCI again refused to defer to both this text-based and evidentiary change, and instead responded by developing a doctrine of "unconstitutional constitutional amendments" (see e.g. Jackson 2010).

In *Golak Nath v. State of Punjab*, A.I.R. 1967 S.C. 1643, the Court held that amendments to the Constitution were "laws" within the meaning of, and thus subject to judicial review under, the fundamental rights provisions in Article 13(2) of the Constitution. Similarly, in *Kesavananda Bharati v. State of Kerala*, A.I.R. 1973 S.C. 1461, while narrowing its previous holding in *Golak Nath*, the Court held that the amendment power could not be used to alter the "basic structure" of the Constitution as a whole. Based on this reasoning, in *Minerva Mills v. Union of India*, A.I.R. 1980 S.C. 1789, the SCI also held that it was unconstitutional for Parliament to attempt to insulate laws implementing the directive principles from review via the 42nd Amendment.

---

[6] Striking down certain provisions of the Bihar Land Reform Act that sought to eliminate zamandari estates.

A similar position, of course, also applies in weak-form systems of review, given the ability of courts to rely on so-called powers of "reading down" to deprive legislation of almost all practical effect (see Dixon 2009a). However, in a system of strong-form review, structural factors make courts more reluctant to show complete deference to attempts at legislative override.

Judicial review – or judicial supremacy – in a system of strong-form review is generally understood to be part of the basic constitutional framework. Where the legislature attempts to remove review in a particular area, courts may therefore see such efforts as threatening that entire constitutional architecture, not simply the force of a particular decision. In a system of weak-form review, by contrast, legislative override – or parliamentary sovereignty – is the norm. Specific attempts at override are thus capable of being interpreted as actually affirming, rather than undermining, the "integrity" of that system.

The SCI in *Golak Nath*, for example, suggested that one important reason for holding the 17th amendment unconstitutional was that the amendment departed from – or "destroyed" – a norm of judicial supremacy, and accordingly was not an "amendment" (rather than revision, or indeed revolution) properly so called (see e.g. Baxi 1985: 65–66; Baxi 1997; Dhavan 1977: 407–8; and more generally, Ginsburg and Dixon 2011; Simeon 2009; Zohar 1995: 318).[7] Similar reasoning was endorsed by various justices in *Kesavananda* in upholding (narrower) limits on the power of amendment under Article 368.[8]

In a weak-form system such as Canada, by contrast, the Supreme Court of Canada in *Ford v. Quebec (Attorney-General)* [1988] 2 S.C.R. 265 para 33, held that the power of override under section 33 of the Charter of Rights and Freedoms "lays down requirements of form only, and there is no warrant for importing into it grounds for substantive

---

[7]   Bachawat and Ramaswami JJ (concurring): "The word 'amendment' implies such an addition or change within the lines of the original instrument as will effect an improvement or better carry out the purpose for which it was framed and it cannot be so construed as to enable the Parliament to destroy the permanent character of the Constitution."

[8]   See e.g. Sikri CJ (reading the amendment power as impliedly limited to changes consistent with, or designed to carry out the basic objectives of the Constitution as set out in the preamble); Hegde and Mukherjea, JJ (noting limits on power of Parliament to alter basic features set out in the preamble); Khanna J (noting limits inherent in the word 'amendment' in terms of alterations to the basic structure). On the relationship between *Golak Nath* and *Kesavananda* in this context, and the argument that it was narrowed rather than overruled, see also Dhavan 1977 at 412–13.

review of the legislative policy in exercising the override authority in a particular case." In doing so, it also stressed the fundamental nature of the legislature's authority to decide certain questions of policy, under the *Charter*, without interference from the courts (para 35).

V. WEAK-FORM REVIEW, ITS RELATIVES, AND DOMINANT-PARTY DEMOCRACIES

What explains the development of these sub-constitutional and amendment-based substitutes for weak-reform review in Japan and India, when other Asian countries have had relatively robust histories of strong-form judicial review? Though many factors are in play, we suggest that in each country the dominance of a single political party is important to explaining the development of this effectively weak form of judicial review.[9]

Persistent single-party legislative domination provides no reason for the dominant party to seek insurance for its policies, through constitutional review, in the event of its loss of a legislative majority.[10] Japanese Supreme Court justices are appointed by the Cabinet, with the Chief Justice's recommendations playing a large role. The LDP can assure itself of a compliant Court by investing relatively limited resources in picking a Chief Justice. The Court must contain a significant number of members who have served as judges in relatively high positions, and the judicial bureaucracy is said to ensure political reliability through its control of judicial promotions, thereby seeding the pool from which Supreme Court justices are chosen. And, the justices are typically appointed late in life. Not only will the appointing authorities have a good sense of the nominees' substantive views, but even a maverick justice would have a relatively short time to develop innovative constitutional doctrines. Judges are chosen in ways that ensure in practice that they will understand their role to be enforcing a national consensus

---

[9] On the narrowest definition, neither India nor Japan is in fact a dominant-party democracy, because there has been at least one change in the party in power at a national level since the inception of electoral democracy: see e.g. Huntington 1991: 267, cited in Choudhry 2009: 20–21. However, both parties have also had extremely long periods of uninterrupted and extremely dominant rule, at a national level, by a single party, thus making them 'dominant-party democracies' in this looser sense.

[10] On insurance-based accounts of judicial review, see Ginsburg 2003; Stephenson 2003; Hirschl 2004.

represented concretely by legislation. They see themselves as faithful agents of the nation and its dominant political party. As agents, they have some discretion in interpreting statutes and in finding executive action unauthorized, but their actions as agents can always be overridden by the principle itself. Sub-constitutional review is consistent with this notion of agency; strong-form constitutional review is not.

As noted above most constitutional amendments in India require the support of only a simple majority of the Parliament present and voting (provided this is also no less than two-thirds of the total number of representatives). The overwhelming political dominance of the Congress Party, for most of India's history, has also meant that, the 1990s aside (see Mehta 2002: 187), it has almost always enjoyed a majority in both houses of Parliament sufficient to adopt any amendment proposed by the dominant party (see e.g. Sripati 1998: 471–81).

Dominant-party democracy of this kind also raises distinctive questions about the desirability and stability of attempts to establish weak-form review in many countries. The dialogic characteristics of weak-form review flow primarily from a "linguistic" feature of constitutions, and a political one. The linguistic feature is that many constitutional provisions are stated in general terms, so that reasonable disagreements arise over their meaning and application in specific circumstances. The political feature is the existence of robust party competition.

The linguistic feature enables vigorous discourse about the constitution's meaning, both in the courts and in the political culture more generally. Such a discourse might exist in the absence of robust party competition, but it is far more likely to arise when more than one political party has a realistic chance of taking office. Party platforms and leaders may offer competing constitutional interpretations purely opportunistically, for example as criticisms of each other's policy positions. Yet, even opportunistic uses of constitutional disagreement can contribute to sustaining a culture of constitutionalism, because politicians who use constitutional rhetoric must believe that voters care about the constitution. In dominant-party systems, in contrast, the dominant party can be completely opportunistic about the constitution, forcing through whatever policies they prefer and changing the constitution if necessary. Weak-form review is thus generally unsuitable for dominant-party political systems.

Yet, at the same time, the status of a country as a dominant-party democracy also undermines the chances of a constitutional designer effectively being able to establish strong-form review in substance, not just form.

Consider the power of judicial appointment, and how the executive may make strategic use of such a power to override constitutional decisions with which it disagrees.[11] In most democracies, competition between political parties will mean that there is either some real formal or de facto constraint on the ability of a government to use the power of judicial appointment, promotion or assignment in order to weaken the strength of judicial review – because attempts to "pack" or "stack" a court will generally meet with strong partisan opposition. In a dominant-party democracy, by contrast, the degree of control over parliament by the government will often mean that there is extremely broad power to use such powers in this way.

The degree to which this is the case will of course ultimately depend even in a dominant-party democracy on norms governing judicial appointment. Even in India, however, strict norms of seniority governing the appointment of the Chief Justice have not always been sufficient to prevent the government from passing over judges (such as three judges in the majority in *Kesavananda*) who have authored opinions with which it disagrees (see Neuborne 2003: 484–5, 492).

The experience in India also demonstrates the importance in this context of the degree of turnover on a country's constitutional court: the more norms of mandatory retirement, or fixed judicial terms, for the constitutional judiciary create natural turnover on a court, the greater the opportunity for the executive to use its power of judicial appointment, transfer, or promotion strategically. In many cases, the government of Indira Gandhi also did just that (see Baxi 1985: 79; Neuborne 2003). Similar claims have been made about assignment and promotion of judges in Japan, though there the scholarship has focused on strategic assignment and promotion policies with respect to lower-court judges (see Ramseyer and Rasmussen 1997).

VI. CONCLUSION

Deliberate acts of constitutional design are one important way in which constitutional archetypes are created. Design processes of this kind also

---

[11] Departmentalist theories in the US, for example, explicitly endorse the use of the judicial appointment processes, and the control of a court's size, as a means of popular control of constitutional meaning: see e.g. Paulsen 1994; Tushnet 2003; Whittington 2002. While developed in the context of Presidential systems such as the US, departmentalist theories also have a clear overlap with more legislative-focused theories of weak-form review.

often produce a certain degree of commonality, or convergence, among constitutional systems.[12] Constitutional ideas are often "borrowed" across national lines, so that design innovations in one country influence the design, or redesign, of constitutions in other parts of the world (on borrowing, see e.g. Tushnet 1999).

Borrowing of this kind, however, also tends to occur most among countries with strong religious, linguistic, geographic or legal-historical ties (see e.g. Simmons and Elkins 2004; Linos 2006). This may be one reason that several Commonwealth countries have recently adopted weak-form review (see e.g. Gardbaum 2001): Commonwealth countries, for legal-historical and cultural reasons, tend be influenced by one another in matters of constitutional design; and many such countries have gone through processes of constitutional redesign in the last 30 years.

Asia is a region that, as a whole, lacks these kinds of ties (see e.g. Lewis and Wigen 1997). It is home to 11 different mainstream religions (i.e. Buddhism, Confucianism, Judaism, Hinduism, Christianity, Lingayatism, Jainism, Sikhism, Taoism, Islam and Zoroastranism) and more than 2,000 languages, is the world's largest continent, and has a history of having been colonized by numerous different foreign powers (including France, Portugal, Russia and the United Kingdom), as well as internally (see e.g. CIA World Factbook, Linguistic Society of America). It is no surprise, then, that there is no clear archetype of either weak- or strong-form review in Asia.

Attention to Asian constitutionalism, however, offers insights not necessarily apparent from focusing on constitutionalism from a global perspective. The most basic is that there are a range of potential functional equivalents – or close relatives – to weak-form review. One such relative, highlighted by Japanese constitutional experience, is a model of sub-constitutional review that relies on statutory interpretation or "reading down" as a means of enforcing constitutional values. Another relative, which exists in India, is a system of relatively flexible formal constitutional amendment, which allows legislatures to create text-based and evidentiary pressures for courts to defer to their preferred constitutional understandings. Both these models have also developed less by deliberate design than by constitutional accident.[13]

A second important insight is that background political conditions, or political party competition, are likely to matter to both the desirability

---

[12] For debates over constitutional convergence, see Law 2008; Tushnet 2009b; Dixon and Posner 2011.

[13] On the drafting history to Art. 368, for example, and the suggestion that it was potentially too onerous, see e.g. Prateek 2008.

and stability of any attempt actually to design a system of weak-form review. To date, the fact that, for the most part, weak-form review has been adopted in mature, two-party democracies has tended to obscure this insight.[14] Attention to Asia, however, helps remind us of the unspoken assumptions that sometimes lie in scholarship on comparative constitutional law, and thus of the value of more fine-grained, regionally focused forms of constitutional comparison.

REFERENCES

Baxi, Upendra. 1985. *Courage, Craft, and Contention: The Indian Supreme Court in the Eighties.* Bombay: N. M. Tripathi.

Baxi, Upendra. 1997. "A Pilgrim's Progress: The Basic Structure Revisited." *Indian Bar Review* 24: 53–72.

Choudhry, Sujit. 2009. "'He Had a Mandate': The South African Constitutional Court and the African National Congress in a Dominant Party Democracy." *Constitutional Court Review* 2: 1–86.

Coenen, Dan T. 2001. "A Constitution of Collaboration: Protecting Fundamental Values with Second-Look Rules of Interbranch Dialogue." *William and Mary Law Review* 42: 1575–870.

Denning, Brannon P. and John R. Vile. 2002. "The Relevance of Constitutional Amendments: A Response to David Strauss." *Tulane Law Review* 77: 247–82.

Dhavan, Rajeev. 1977. *The Supreme Court of India: A Socio-legal Critique of Its Juristic Techniques,* Bombay: N. M. Tripathi.

Dixon, Rosalind. 2008. "A Democratic Theory of Constitutional Comparison." *American Journal of Comparative Law* 56: 947–98.

Dixon, Rosalind. 2009a. "A Minimalist Charter of Rights for Australia: The UK or Canada as a Model?" *Federal Law Review* 37: 335–62.

Dixon, Rosalind. 2009b. "Updating Constitutional Rules." *Supreme Court Review* 2009: 319–46.

Dixon, Rosalind. 2010. "Partial Constitutional Amendments." *University of Pennsylvania Journal of Constitutional Law* 13: 643–85.

Dixon, Rosalind. 2011. "Constitutional Amendment Rules: A Comparative Perspective." Pp. 96–111 in *Comparative Constitutional Law,* edited by Tom Ginsburg and Rosalind Dixon. Cheltenham: Edward Elgar.

Dixon, Rosalind and Eric A. Posner. 2011. "The Limits of Constitutional Convergence." *Chicago Journal of International Law* 11: 399–423.

Forbath, William E. 2003. "The Politics of Constitutional Design: Obduracy and Amendability? A Comment on Ferejohn and Sager." *University of Texas Law Review* 81: 1965–84.

Gardbaum, Stephen. 2001. "The New Commonwealth Model of Constitutionalism." *American Journal of Comparative Law* 49: 707–60.

---

[14] Mongolia, of course, is potentially an exception to this within Asia, as is Hong Kong, if one regards it as a true weak-form system, with a more fragile democratic system post-1997.

Ginsburg, Tom. 2003. *Judicial Review in New Democracies: Constitutional Courts in Asian Cases*. New York: Cambridge University Press.

Ginsburg, Tom and Rosalind Dixon, eds. 2011. *Comparative Constitutional Law*. Cheltenham: Edward Elgar.

Ginsburg, Tom and Gombosuren Ganzorig. 2001. "When Courts and Politics Collide: Mongolia's Constitutional Crisis." *Columbia Journal of Asian Law* 14: 309–26.

Griffin, Stephen M. 1998. "The Nominee is ... Article V." Pp. 51–3 in *Constitutional Stupidities, Constitutional Tragedies,* edited by William N. Eskridge and Sanford Levinson. New York: New York University Press.

Hirschl, Ran. 2004. *Towards Juristocracy: The Origins and Consequences of the New Constitutionalism*. Cambridge, MA: Harvard University Press.

Hogg, Peter W. and Alison A. Bushell. 1997. "The Charter Dialogue Between Courts and Legislatures (Or Perhaps the Charter of Rights Isn't Such a Bad Thing After All)." *Osgoode Hall Law Journal* 35: 75–124.

Huntington, Samuel P. 1991. *The Third Wave: Democratization in the Late Twentieth Century*. Norman, OK: University of Oklahoma Press.

Jackson, Vicki C. 2010. "Unconstitutional Constitutional Amendments: A Window into Constitutional Theory and Transnational Constitutionalism." (unpublished, copy on file with authors).

Law, David S. 2008. "Globalization and the Future of Constitutional Rights." *Northwestern University Law Review* 102: 1277–350.

Law, David S. 2011. "Why Has Judicial Review Failed in Japan?" *Washington University Law Review* 88: 1425–66.

Levinson, Sanford. 2001. "Designing an Amendment Process." Pp. 271–87 in *Constitutional Culture and Democratic Rule*, edited by John Ferejohn, Jack M. Rakove and Jonathan Riley. Cambridge: Cambridge University Press.

Lewis, Martin W. and Kären E. Wigen. 1997. *The Myth of Continents: A Critique of Metageography*. Berkeley: University of California Press.

Linos, Katerina. 2006. "When Do Policy Innovations Spread? Lessons for Advocates of Lesson-Drawing." *Harvard Law Review* 119: 1467–87.

Lutz, Donald S. 1995. "Toward a Theory of Constitutional Amendment." Pp. 237–74 in *Responding to Imperfection: The Theory and Practice of Constitutional Amendment*, edited by Sanford Levinson. Princeton: Princeton University Press.

Matsui, Shigenori. 2011. "Why Is the Japanese Supreme Court So Conservative?" *Washington University Law Review* 88: 1375–423.

Mehta, Pratap Bhanu. 2002. "The Inner Conflict of Constitutionalism: Judicial Review and the 'Basic Structure.'" Pp. 179–206 in *India's Living Constitution: Ideas, Practices, Controversies*, edited by Zoya Hasan, E. Sridharan and R. Sudarshan. London: Anthem Press.

Murphy, Walter F. 1995. "Merlin's Memory: The Past and Future Imperfect of the Once and Future Polity." Pp. 163–90 in *Responding to Imperfection: The Theory and Practice of Constitutional Amendment*, edited by Sanford Levinson. Princeton: Princeton University Press.

Neuborne, Bert. 2003. "The Supreme Court of India." *International Journal of Constitutional Law* 1: 476–510.

Paulsen, Michael Stokes. 1994. "The Most Dangerous Branch: Executive Power to Say What the Law Is." *Georgetown Law Journal* 83: 217–345.

Prateek, Satya. 2008. "Today's Promise, Tomorrow's Constitution: 'Basic Structure', Constitutional Transformations and the Future of Political Progress in India." *NUJS Law Review* 1: 417–98.

Ramseyer, J. Mark and Eric B. Rasmussen. 1997. "Judicial Independence in a Civil Law Regime: The Evidence from Japan." *Journal of Law, Economics & Organization* 13: 259–86.

Simeon, Richard. 2009. "Constitutional Design and Change in Federal Systems: Issues and Questions." *Publius: The Journal of Federalism* 39: 241–61.

Simmons, Beth A. and Zachary Elkins. 2004. "The Globalization of Liberalization: Policy Diffusion in the International Political Economy." *American Political Science Review* 98: 171–89.

Sripati, Vijayashri. 1998. "Toward Fifty Years of Constitutionalism and Fundamental Rights in India: Looking Back to See Ahead (1950–2000)." *American University International Law Review* 14: 413–95.

Stephenson, Matthew C. 2003 "'When the Devil Turns …': The Political Foundations of Independent Judicial Review." *Journal of Legal Studies* 32: 59–89.

Symposium. 2007. "*Charter* Dialogue: Ten Years Later." *Osgoode Hall Law Journal* 45.

Tushnet, Mark V. 1999. "The Possibilities of Comparative Constitutional Law." *Yale Law Journal* 108: 1225–309.

Tushnet, Mark V. 2003. "Alternative Forms of Judicial Review." *Michigan Law Review* 101: 2781–802.

Tushnet, Mark. 2009a. "Constitutional Workarounds." *Texas Law Review* 87: 1499–516.

Tushnet, Mark. 2009b. "The Inevitable Globalization of Constitutional Law." *Virginia Journal of International Law* 49: 985–1006.

Tushnet, Mark. 2009c. *Weak Courts, Strong Rights: Judicial Review and Social Welfare Rights in Comparative Constitutional Law*. Princeton: Princeton University Press.

Upham, Frank K. 2011. "Stealth Activism: Norm Formation by Japanese Courts." *Washington University Law Review* 88: 1493–505.

Vermeule, Adrian. 2006. "Constitutional Amendments and Common Law." Pp. 229–73 in *The Least Examined Branch: The Role of Legislatures in the Constitutional State*, edited by Richard W. Bauman and Tsvi Kahana. Cambridge: Cambridge University Press.

Waldron, Jeremy. 2004. "Some Models of Dialogue between Judges and Legislators." In *Constitutionalism in the Charter Era*, edited by Grant Huscroft and Ian Brodie. Markham, ON: LexisNexis Canada.

Weinrib, Lorraine E. 2006. "The Post-War Paradigm and American Exceptionalism." Pp. 84–112 in *The Migration of Constitutional Ideas*, edited by Sujit Choudhry. Cambridge: Cambridge University Press.

Whittington, Keith E. 2002. "Extrajudicial Constitutional Interpretation: Three Objections and Responses." *North Carolina Law Review* 80: 773–851.

Zohar, Noam. 1995. "Midrash: Amendment through the Molding of Meaning." Pp. 307–18 in *Responding to Imperfection: The Theory and Practice of Constitutional Amendment*, edited by Sanford Levinson. Princeton: Princeton University Press.

PART II

CONSTITUTIONAL STRUCTURE

6. The structure of legislative–executive relations: Asia in comparative perspective

José Antonio Cheibub and Fernando Limongi[1]

I. INTRODUCTION

Legislative–executive relations refers to the institutions that govern and the processes that characterize the interactions between two of the three conventional branches of a democratic political system (the third being, of course, the judiciary). This entails a consideration of the legal (constitutional and statutory) provisions that regulate the formation of the government, the rules for electing the legislative assembly, the way the formation of each of these branches affects the performance of the other, the rules for producing legislation, and the behavior (strategic or otherwise) of the actors that make up the "executive" (the head of government and the ministers) and the "legislative" (individual legislators and political parties). This is a large area of research, which could reasonably encompass everything that would traditionally go under the heading of "comparative government." A thorough treatment of all these topics here is impossible for reasons of space, and so we offer a selective treatment of the issues based on our particular perspective of how studies of legislative–executive relations have evolved. We provide a general overview of the issues, before turning to the Asian context in the last part of the chapter.

In order to simplify the analysis we divide the vast and heterogeneous literature that concerns us here into two parts, which we call the "earlier" and the "later" generations of studies of legislative–executive relations.

[1] We thank Tom Ginsburg and Rosalind Dixon for comments on an earlier draft of this chapter.

The distinctive feature of the earlier studies is that they analyze inter-branch relations as being essentially shaped by the way the chief executive and the legislators obtain their mandates, with "presidential-ism" and "parliamentarism" being the organizing concepts. The in-dependence or the dependence of the executive's mandate with respect to the legislature is the key factor determining whether the relationship between the two powers will likely be characterized by conflict or cooperation, and whether it will remain within the bounds prescribed by the constitution. In these studies executives and legislatures tend to be conceived as unified actors who compete for influence over policy outcomes. The institutional framework shapes the nature of the inter-action between the two branches, determining which one, if any, will dominate the policy process. The institutional embodiment of this distinc-tion is, of course, represented by the contrast between parliamentary and presidential systems. Whereas the former represents a system of mutual dependence between the government and the legislature, the latter represents a system of independence of the two (Stepan and Skach 1993). The best example of this approach can be found in the comparative studies of parliamentary and presidential systems, which we review below.

It is only more recently that inter-branch conflict has begun to give way to more complex models, in which executive–legislative relations are conceived not necessarily as the interaction between two branches of the government, but as the relationship between the government, political parties and groups of legislators, all of whom must cooperate with one another in order to govern, and yet must also compete to gain votes in periodic elections. From this perspective, the question is not so much what triggers conflict or cooperation between the executive and the legislature, but about the institutions and the strategies that allow governments to obtain the support of a majority in the legislature to implement policy change. These more recent studies are quite hetero-geneous; what allows us to group them together is the recognition, first, that relevant actors seek multiple goals that may be in conflict with one another, and, second, that factors internal to the legislative process itself are crucial for understanding how a majority organizes itself in the two branches and is effective in the pursuit of its policy objectives.

In what follows we seek to characterize both the earlier and the later studies of legislative–executive relations. Section II deals with the former, focusing on parliamentary (section IIA) and presidential (section IIB) systems. We also discuss studies of semi-presidential systems (section IIC), which are of more recent origin but increasingly popular after the end of the Cold War. Yet, as we will show, the research questions guiding studies of semi-presidentialism have been informed primarily by the questions raised by the earlier paradigm contrasting parliamentary and presidential systems. In section III we turn to the later studies of legislative–executive relations, highlighting three substantive areas that helped redefine the field. Section IV surveys the scholarship on executive–legislative relations in Asia, highlighting the ways in which the perspective adopted in later studies helps understand some of the cases in the region. Section V concludes the chapter.

II. EARLIER STUDIES

Early studies of legislative–executive relations were primarily concerned with understanding how governments are formed, based on the assumption that politicians are primarily office-seekers. In this perspective, the analysis of inter-branch relations reduced to the identification of the incentives office-seeking politicians might have to cooperate in governing a country. In spite of the common preoccupation with government formation and the common assumption about politicians' goals, the early literature was bifurcated; it evolved into two separate and independent bodies of work, with very little exchange between the two. One literature focused on parliamentary systems and the other on presidential systems.

A. Parliamentary Democracies

The literature on parliamentarism focused on the process of government formation. Government formation is crucial because, it was believed, it is the moment in which the government's ability to act throughout its existence is determined. Empirically, the focus of this literature is Western Europe, with only a few studies including two of the long-lasting democracies in Asia: India and Japan.

In the most basic view, the very nature of parliamentarism is such that parties operate under a majoritarian imperative; that is, the requirement that governments must be composed by parties that together command more than 50 percent of legislative seats. In this view, governments are formed as parties exchange cabinet positions for legislative support: a party is considered to be in government if it controls one or more cabinets; when in government, a party's members of parliament are expected to vote in support of government measures.

If a party alone commands more than 50 percent of the seats in the legislature, it forms a single-party government; it keeps to itself all the benefits of being in the government as it does not need the support of other parties to remain in power. If no party controls more than 50 percent of the legislative seats, then parties must form a coalition government by sharing cabinet positions. Given the fact that in the majority of parliamentary democracies no party commands more than 50 percent of the seats, two of the central research questions in the early studies of executive–legislative relations are: (a) Which parties will come together into the government? (b) How will they share the limited number of portfolios?

There is a vast literature that deals with coalition formation and termination, and here is not the place to review it in detail.[2] For our purposes, it is sufficient to say that formation and termination are directly associated in most accounts, implying that the operation of the government between these two moments does not require attention or explanation. The primary function of parliaments is to make or break governments (Laver 2006: 122). Regarding coalition formation specifically, the most popular and influential theory assumes purely office-seeking politicians and predicts the formation of minimum-winning coalitions (Riker 1962). Parties try to form the smallest possible coalition and to keep as much as possible of the spoils of government, subject to the constraint that these coalitions have to be majoritarian. As Laver and Schofield (1998) note, the failure of the minimum-winning coalition theory to predict actual outcomes led scholars to revise some of Riker's assumptions and broaden their search for the criteria that would guide the coalition-formation process (e.g., Axelrod 1970 and De Swaan 1973).

In most theories of coalition formation (always in parliamentary regimes) one constraint that parties always face, regardless of their motivation, is the majoritarian one. In this sense, minority governments – governments formed by one or more parties that together control less than 50 percent of legislative seats – necessarily represent a failure of the government-formation process. They result from crises that are induced by high levels of political fragmentation and polarization. Minority governments, therefore, cannot be explained except as anomalies induced by a dysfunctional political system.

The type of government that emerges from the formation process matters for its duration. Because minority governments are the product of an underlying situation characterized by fragmentation and polarization, they are the most unstable and ungovernable. Single-party majority governments, on the other hand, are at the opposite end, tending to last

---

[2]   See Laver and Schofield 1998 for the best analysis of the different theories of coalition formation.

long and implement important policy programs. Coalition governments, such as the ones we observe in Japan and India, both of which made the transition from one-party governments after 1990, are the truly interesting political phenomena. After all, they rest on a precarious bargain among parties over how to divide the spoils of government and set major policies. They are fragile in the sense that a coalition may break over major and minor issues. Thus, coalition governments are vulnerable to (parties' anticipation of) even small shifts in voters' preferences, as well as to the idiosyncrasies of each coalition member.

The coalition formation and termination literature took on a life of its own.[3] The relevant points to retain from the perspective of executive–legislative relations is that it privileges office-seeking considerations when it comes to politicians' motivations and concentrates on the two extreme moments in the existence of any government: its formation and its termination. The actual operation of the government, the way executive–legislative relations are structured and unfolded during the ordinary life of the government, was not an object of scrutiny.

B. Presidential Democracies

The preoccupation of those who have studied presidentialism has been different. The fact that the head of government's mandate originates in popular elections leads to a totally different world where coalitions and government duration are irrelevant. The president and the legislature have a fixed term in office and government duration therefore becomes a moot question. The fact that the president does not need to generate majority support in the legislature in order to remain in office, in turn, makes coalition governments unnecessary.

Comparative studies of presidential systems started much later than those of parliamentary ones. There is, of course, a large literature on the United States. But this literature is not comparative in any significant way as it is concerned primarily with accounting for the rather unique features of the overall US political system, and not with analyzing it as one among many presidential democracies. Moreover, as presidential and legislative studies have developed as independent subfields, and given the more qualitative and anecdotal approach that dominates the former,[4]

---

[3]   See Grofman and Roozendaal 1997 and Laver 2003 for reviews.

[4]   Reviews of presidential studies usually lament their lack of scientific depth and general backwardness when compared to the rest of the discipline. For an example, see Edwards III, Kessel and Rockman (1993: 3–23). For a more optimistic and recent review see Moe 2009.

executive–legislative relations has not been a central lens through which to view the functioning of the US system.

The dearth of early comparative studies of presidential systems was partly due to the scarcity of available cases for analysis. Most presidential democracies outside of the United States, at least until the re-democratization of Latin America in the 1980s, experienced at least one regime breakdown. South Korea and the Philippines are illustrative examples in Asia of democratic presidential systems that gave way to authoritarianism. Scholarly attention, therefore, was redirected to the study of the dictatorships that replaced them or the conditions that produced their demise.

It is not until the 1980s that presidentialism as an institutional form became the object of systematic analysis. Here the work of Juan Linz is absolutely central. In calling attention to the role of incentives generated by a system of separation of powers in the crises that led to democratic breakdowns in Latin America, Linz set out the agenda and the tone for comparative studies of executive–legislative relations under presidentialism.[5]

Linz's argument is well known. Here we provide only a brief sketch of the Linzian view to highlight the steps that connect the separation of powers that defines presidentialism to the eventual breakdown of democratic regimes. According to this view, presidential constitutions, contrary to parliamentary ones, provide few or no incentives for coalition formation. There are three reasons for this: (1) because the president's survival in office does not depend on any kind of legislative support, a president need not seek the cooperation of political parties other than his own; (2) because presidents are independent from the legislature when it comes to survival, and are elected in nationwide contests that provide widespread popular support, they have an inflated sense of power and overestimate their ability to govern alone; and (3) presidential politics is a zero-sum winner-takes-all affair, which is hardly conducive to cooperation or coalition formation. For these reasons, coalitions are difficult to form and do form "only exceptionally" (Linz 1994: 19) under presidentialism (Mainwaring 1990; Stepan and Skach 1993: 20; Linz and Stepan 1996: 181). As Niño (1996: 169) puts it, presidentialism "operates against the formation of coalitions;" for this reason, according to Huang

---

[5]   The initial argument appeared in Linz (1978) and was developed in a paper that was widely circulated before it was published in (1994). See also Linz (1990a and 1990b).

(1997: 138), "the very notion of majority government is problematic in presidential systems without a majority party."

In the Linzian framework, therefore, while parliamentary regimes are supposed to foster cooperation, presidential regimes encourage independence. Under parliamentarism, political parties have an incentive to cooperate with one another and form coalitions. Presidentialism, in turn, is characterized by the absence of such incentives and hence is likely to generate either minority governments or governments that are only nominally majority governments. The lack of incentives for coalition formation and the resulting high incidence of minority governments under presidentialism, particularly multiparty presidentialism (Mainwaring 1993; Jones 1995), imply conflict between the executive and the legislature as well as governments that are legislatively ineffective. As we will see later, this has been a common diagnosis of presidential South Korea and semi-presidential Taiwan. Presidents who do not have legislative support will try to bypass Congress in order to implement their programs and, in the process will undermine democratic legitimacy (Valenzuela 1994; O'Donnell 1994).

In sum, because there are no incentives for inter-branch cooperation, presidentialism is characterized by frequent minority governments as well as conflict and deadlocks between the government and the legislature. Because these regimes lack a constitutional principle that can be invoked to resolve conflicts between the executive and the legislature, such as the vote of no confidence in parliamentary regimes, minority presidents and deadlock provide incentives for actors to search for extra-constitutional means of resolving their differences. As a consequence, presidential democracies become more prone to instability and eventual death.

The Linzian view, as we said, is widely held.[6] In it, presidential institutions are simply not conducive to governments capable of handling the explosive issues that populate the political agenda in many countries, particularly new democracies in the developing world. These issues make governing difficult under any circumstances. Governing becomes almost impossible when the institutional setup is likely to generate governments with weak legislative support as well as parties and politicians whose dominant strategy is to act independently. Given the lack of constitutional solutions to the crises that are likely to erupt, political actors have no

---

[6] See, for a few examples, Mainwaring and Scully (1995: 33), González and Gillespie (1994: 172), Riggs (1988), Ackerman (2000: 645), Stepan and Skach (1993: 17), Valenzuela (1994: 16).

choice beyond appealing to those with guns to intervene and put an end to their misery.

This broad view has at least three important implications. First, the notion that presidentialism is detrimental to democratic consolidation because of the very nature of the system. The sense that there is something inherently problematic about presidential institutions, something that needs to be neutralized for the system to operate properly and generate positive outcomes, is a legacy of the Linzian framework that is hard to dispel.

Second, in the Linzian view, politicians are strictly office seeking and the pitfalls of presidentialism follow at least partially from this assumption. Yet, once one assumes that politicians also care about policies, it becomes apparent that presidents do have an incentive to seek support in the legislature, even if their survival in office does not depend on a majority in the legislature. Thus, as Cheibub, Przeworski and Saiegh (2004) argue, the undeniable institutional differences between presidential and parliamentary systems are not sufficient to make coalition governments rare under the former.

Finally, the model of executive–legislative relations that underlies the Linzian view is one of potential conflict. The conflict may lead to deadlock or presidential or congressional domination. Under this view, deadlock, as we have seen, is democracy's kiss of death as there is no constitutional solution to it. Presidents will dominate when they have strong constitutional powers. Constitutionally strong presidents will be able to impose their views over the legislature and will, eventually, usurp powers from it. It is only when the president is weak, institutionally incapable of dominating the legislative process, that presidential democracies stand a chance of functioning in a satisfactory way (Shugart and Carey 1992). Consequently, the primary focus of institutional design should be balancing presidential powers so as to prevent them from overwhelming the political process.

There have been many cases of presidential impeachment since the 1990s, both in the Americas and in Asia (Indonesia and the Philippines in 2001, and the failed, but politically important, case of South Korea in 2004). These events raise an important challenge for those who see presidential and parliamentary systems as fundamentally different in the way they operate. The reason is that the same factors that account for the fall of parliamentary governments – failures of coalition formation and management, government overreach, and legislative deadlock – seem to also explain the removal of presidents in the middle of their term (whether by impeachment or popular pressure).[7] Thus, in spite of written constitutional provisions, presidential systems too can display the flexibility of removing the government in a situation of crisis without at the same time abolishing democracy; and this was, according to Linz, the essential advantage of parliamentarism over presidentialism.

C. Semi-presidential Democracies

Systems that combine a government dependent on the confidence of a legislative assembly and a popularly elected president have become very popular in the past two decades or so. These are semi-presidential or mixed systems; they emerged in a few Western European countries (France, Iceland, Portugal), are pervasive in the new democracies of Eastern Europe, and, in Asia, exist in Taiwan and Mongolia.[8] Naturally, the number of scholarly works seeking to evaluate their performance has grown in tandem with the increase in the number of countries that adopted them.[9]

The vast majority of the work on semi-presidential systems has focused on the presidency, seeking to identify the combination of presidential powers that would mitigate what are considered to be the intrinsic difficulties of a semi-presidential form of government. These difficulties are related to the dual nature of the executive, the fact that both the president and the prime minister may claim to be the effective executive leader as both are the product of the democratic process. Problems arise as competencies are not well defined and/or one of the actors seeks to impinge on the domains that the constitution reserves to the other. The potential for conflict increases considerably in situations of "co-habitation," namely the situations in which a president faces a legislative majority – and consequently a prime minister – from a different (or opposition) party. These are the cases in which the system faces the highest threat to its operation, and the ones that have summoned

---

[7] See the chapters in Llanos and Marsteintredet (2010) for analyses that emphasize the increasing "flexibility" of presidential democracies. On impeachment and other forms of interrupted presidencies, see Hochstetler 2006, Pérez-Liñán 2007, Kim and Bahry 2008, Marsteintredet and Berntzen 2008, and Hochstetler and Edwards 2009.

[8] But see Munkh-Erdene (2010) for an argument that Mongolia became a parliamentary democracy with the constitutional amendments passed in 2000.

[9] See Elgie (2011 and 1999), Elgie and Moestrup (2007 and 2008), and Elgie, Moestrup and Wu (2011) for the most comprehensive, both thematically and geographically, analysis of semi-presidentialism.

the greatest level of attention from scholars. Presidents with strong constitutional powers only make matters worse as they will feel more compelled to play an active role in the political process.

Thus, semi-presidential systems are supposed to be inherently problematic, prone to conflicts between presidents and prime ministers and to legislative paralysis, particularly under "co-habitation" and/or when presidents have strong constitutional powers; crises will be frequent, which will be detrimental to the country's democratic standing.

It is fair to say that this perspective represents the mere extension to the study of semi-presidentialism of the usual thinking about pure presidentialism. In a similar vein, extending the concern of those who study parliamentary democracies, considerable effort has been dedicated to understanding the duration of governments in semi-presidential regimes (Roper 2002; Elgie 2004; Nikolenyi 2004; Cheibub and Chernykh 2009). Thus, the same points we raised above concerning studies of parliamentary and presidential systems apply to semi-presidential ones.

This is not to say that semi-presidential systems do not raise interesting issues of their own. Here we want to call attention to two main ones, which have been understudied: the apparent disjuncture between constitutional precepts and practice in semi-presidential systems and the importance of focusing on the powers of the government – as opposed to the powers of the president – when studying semi-presidential democracies.

Regarding the first point, consider the following. Presidential democracies are different in many respects, some of them as crucial and important as the method of election and the existence of constitutional term limits. But in all presidential democracies the president, once chosen, is the head of the government, which, once formed, cannot be dismissed by the assembly. Similarly, not all parliamentary systems are alike, and the differences may be as consequential as the formal process of governmental investiture and dismissal. However, in all parliamentary democracies, the government is subject to the confidence of a legislative majority, which, if lost, implies the dismissal of the government as a whole.

Semi-presidential systems do not share such a common feature. Although all semi-presidential systems have constitutions that combine a directly elected president, who is in varying degrees constitutionally allowed to influence the existence of the government, with a government that needs the confidence of parliament in order to exist, not all of them have presidents who effectively participate in the political process and share governing responsibilities with the prime minister.

On the one hand we have systems like France and Taiwan, where the president is an effective power in the process of government formation and dismissal, actively participates in governing, and is regarded as being at least partially responsible for policies; the presidency is a desirable post, and increasingly so as attested by the competitiveness of presidential elections in those countries. On the other hand, we have systems such as Iceland, where presidential elections are often uncontested and the directly elected president is commonly perceived as "a figurehead and symbol of unity rather than a political leader" (Kristinsson 1999: 87), and Finland, where even before the 2000 constitution, which codified a more ceremonial role for the president, the system had functioned like a parliamentary democracy (Raunio 2004). Thus, identifying a democratic constitution as semi-presidential does not really convey the way the system actually operates. We need more information to know if it is a system in which the president really matters or if the president plays a more ceremonial, symbolic role. The president matters if the government is effectively dependent on the president in order to exist and this cannot be known from the constitutional text alone.

To pursue the point a little further, constitutions that allow for equally strong presidents may have very different patterns of interaction between the head of state and the head of government. Consider the constitutions of Iceland (1944), Germany (1919) and France (1958). Regarding government formation and assembly dissolution, the German and French constitutions read, in many ways, very much like the Icelandic constitution. Yet, Iceland's political system is considered to function like a parliamentary democracy, Weimar is considered to be the epitome of a "presidential-parliamentary" system, characterized not only by the government's assembly responsibility but also by the primacy of the president (Shugart and Carey 1992: 24), and France is considered to be the prototypical mixed, semi-presidential, or "premier-parliamentary" system (Duverger 1980; Shugart and Carey 1992; Sartori 1994). Thus, according to the Weimar constitution, the prime minister is appointed and dismissed by the president (article 53); the same is true, however, of the prime minister in France (article 8) and in Iceland (article 15). In Iceland, article 24 allows the president to dissolve the assembly with no limitations to this power; in France, according to article 12, the president must consult the prime minister and the presidents of the assemblies before dissolving the assembly, and must wait a year in order to be able to do it again; in Weimar, article 25 allowed the president to dissolve the assembly, but only once for the same reason.

So, the powers of the president described in the constitution do not match the powers of the president as practiced in each of the countries.

France has a weaker president than Iceland, and yet the president in France is a more important political actor than the president in Iceland. It is intriguing, thus, why similarly designed constitutions entail practices that are as divergent as the ones we observe in countries such as Iceland, Austria, Cape Verde, Central African Republic, France, Iceland, Madagascar, Russia, Taiwan and Ukraine.

Part of the issue may be merely definitional, that is to say, some semi-presidential regimes are simply parliamentary regimes with an elected president. It is possible to argue that what distinguishes contemporary forms of democratic governments is whether they have assembly confidence or not. Given assembly confidence, whether the president is directly elected may be of little relevance. In all likelihood the adoption of semi-presidential constitutions in most recent democracies was not driven by the explicit goal of carefully dividing authority between a directly elected president and a government responsible to the parliament. It is more likely that the choice was to create an assembly confidence system and, at the same time, to institute a head of state who, by virtue of his independence from the parliamentary majority, would somehow guarantee the continuity of the state. That this head of state was to be elected by popular vote is almost the default option, given the lack of legitimacy of the alternatives.

This brings us to the second point: the exclusive focus on the powers of the president when studying semi-presidential systems may be misleading. It is quite possible that governance in assembly confidence systems is guaranteed not by the way the president is elected, or the amount of powers he has, but by other institutional features that strengthen the government, that is, that component of the political structure that needs to obtain the confidence of the legislature: mechanisms that allow the government to shape the legislative agenda, to organize a legislative majority and to keep it reasonably together in the face of the multiplicity of often contradictory interests legislators must reconcile in the course of their careers.

France, the prototypical case of a semi-presidential regime of the more workable variety, provides a good example of how relatively unimportant the role of the president may be in accounting for the system's overall performance. There is general agreement that France under the semi-presidential Fifth Republic became a more stable and governable system than it was under the parliamentary Fourth Republic. One of the most notable features of the new constitution was the introduction of a strong presidency, shaped, it is often said, to fit the personality of the man who was the force behind it.[10] Yet, to say that France became governable as it moved from the Fourth to the Fifth Republics *because* of the constitutional provisions regarding the presidency is to disregard other, probably more significant, constitutional changes also introduced with the 1958 constitution. Two of these changes were the package vote (article 44.3), which allows the government to close debate on a bill and force an up or down vote on a proposal that only contains the amendments accepted by the government, and the confidence vote procedure (article 49.3), which, when invoked by the government, stops debate on a bill and, if no motion of censure is introduced and adopted, implies approval of the bill shaped by the government. These two reforms strengthened the government vis-à-vis the legislature, and enhanced governability.

We will return to this point in section III. Here it is sufficient to note that provisions such as the ones found in the French 1958 constitution are not rare among existing semi-presidential ones. Cheibub and Chernykh (2009), show that 59 percent of the constitutions in place since 1919 allow the government to request a confidence vote on specific legislation; 48 percent grant the government control over the budget process; 35 percent place restrictions on the assembly's ability to pass a vote of no confidence in the government; 37 percent forbid legislators from serving in the government; and 23 percent contain provisions that allow the government to request urgency in the treatment of legislative proposals. It is remarkable that while a lot of effort has been spent in trying to identify the effects of the constitutional powers of the president in semi-presidential systems, powers which, as we suggested above, are not really descriptive of the way the system actually works, virtually no work has been done on the effect of the powers of the government on the performance of these systems. We attribute this oversight to the fact that much of the literature on semi-presidentialism has been informed by the concerns of the earlier generation of studies of both parliamentarism (as expressed in the preoccupation with the duration of cabinets) and presidentialism (as expressed in the virtual obsession with the powers of the president). Newer studies, however, suggest that we look at legislative–executive relations differently. It is to them that we now turn.

---

[10] Direct presidential election was not introduced until 1962.

III. MORE RECENT STUDIES

What distinguishes the studies we discuss in this section from the
previous ones is that they do not assume that the mode of government
formation completely shapes "governability" or the legislative process.
According to the more traditional view reviewed above, interests generated at the electoral arena ultimately define relations between the two
branches. In this view, governments under parliamentarism have a
built-in mechanism to overcome inter-branch conflict, namely the threat
to dissolve the assembly and provoke early elections. It is the incentive to
avoid new elections that leads the rank-and-file members of parliament to
subject to partisan directives and support the governments of which their
parties are members. Presidents, in turn, cannot count on the dissolution
threat and, for this reason, are deprived of consistent support in the
legislature. Under this view, politicians are primarily office-seekers and
the possibility of losing office is what drives their behavior. The
legislative arena proper, that is, the locus of the interaction between the
executive and the legislature over policy, is completely irrelevant. It is
this arena that is stressed by what we are calling the new generation of
studies of executive–legislative relations. As a matter of fact, it is the
emphasis on the way legislatures organize their business and define who
holds the power to control the agenda that allows us to speak of the
otherwise widely heterogeneous studies we will discuss below as belonging to a common generation.

   There are two other features of the new studies of legislative–executive
relations, which follow from their common emphasis on the legislative
arena. First, the expected pattern of interaction between the two branches
becomes one of coordination rather than conflict. Inter-branch relations
are modeled more as a coordination or bargaining game than as a
zero-sum game where the gains of the executive happen at the expense of
the legislature. Second, there is a marked shift on the assumptions
regarding politicians' motivations. As much as office seeking is associated with the conflict view, the supposition that politicians *also* care
about policy is associated with the coordination view of legislative–
executive relations. And given that policies cannot be enacted unilaterally
by one of the branches, it is only through the continuous existence of a
majority that controls both the executive and the legislature that the
policies preferred by both will become reality. In this sense, the incentive
to coordinate rather than confront is inherent in the democratic political
framework, regardless of the way these bodies are formed.

Finally, these studies recognize the importance of electoral competition among parties, even those who coordinate to support a government. Legislative coordination must be achieved with an eye to the fact that, at elections, parties will fiercely compete for votes. Communication with voters about the party's or the legislator's positions is an essential part of this competition. As will become clear in the discussion below, this fact offers a new perspective on legislative behavior and certain types of governments that, at first sight, appear to be the outcome of irreconcilable conflict among political actors and between the legislative and the executive branches.

We will organize our discussion around three main themes, stressing the empirical regularities associated with them and their implications for the study of executive–legislative relations in democratic regimes. The first is the discovery that minority governments in parliamentary regimes are neither infrequent nor ephemeral; the second is the acknowledgment that coalition governments are neither rare nor uniquely unstable in presidential systems; and the third is the recognition that the executive's use of restrictive legislative tools does not necessarily imply that it is unilaterally imposing its will over the legislature. Each one of these "discoveries" contributed to dilute the divide between presidential and parliamentary forms of government. By employing knowledge generated in the study of one of these systems to understand the other, these studies have demonstrated that the radical distinction that exists between the two systems when it comes to formation and survival does not necessarily extend to their actual operation in practice.

A. Minority Governments in Parliamentary Democracies

Minority governments are vexing under the traditional view of parliamentary democracies. Given office-seeking politicians and the "majoritarian imperative" created by the confidence mechanism, minority governments should never exist. If they do, they must have resulted from some kind of system malfunction and would disappear as soon as these problems were "solved."[11] It was not until Strøm's important book (1990) that this view was radically changed, with consequences for how we think about both parliamentary and presidential systems in general, and legislative–executive relations in particular.

---

[11] Another vexing issue for the traditional view are oversized coalitions, which should also not exist. Yet, they do exist. According to Laver and Schofield (1998: 70), 25% of the cabinets that existed in 12 European democracies between 1945 and 1987 were surplus majority coalitions.

Strøm's contribution is both empirical and theoretical. Empirically he shows that minority governments are not infrequent in European parliamentary democracies and that they do not do worse when compared to majority coalition governments.

Theoretically, Strøm's contribution is to show that minority governments emerge out of party leaders' calculations about the costs and benefits of participating in government. Assuming that politicians care about office and policy (as well as votes), Strøm argues that there are conditions under which rational parties will *prefer* to remain out of the government. The decision to refrain from joining a government is affected by the degree of policy influence parties can exert from the outside, as well as by their expectation regarding electoral returns (positive or negative) of joining the government. Out-of-government policy influence, in turn, depends essentially on the organization of parliament, that is factors such as the existence of standing committees, their degree of specialization, their scope of action, and the way they are allocated. Electoral consequences depend on the decisiveness and competitiveness of the electoral process. When parties can affect policies even if they are not in the government, and the electoral costs of incumbency are perceived to be high, parties will rationally choose to stay out of the government. The emergence of minority governments, therefore, has nothing to do with political systems that are dysfunctional.

Strøm's analysis accounts for variation within parliamentary democracies by highlighting factors related to the internal organization of the legislature. Legislative organization had either been neglected in analyses of parliamentarism or, more commonly, had been assumed to be constant within each form of democratic regime. Thus, discussions of legislative organization were organized around the two paradigmatic cases of Britain and the United States: a centralized and a decentralized legislature, respectively, and, as we know, a parliamentary and a presidential democracy. Arguments about decision making in democracies tended to contrast these two systems and assume, often implicitly, that all legislatures, and, for that matter, the decision-making process, are centralized under parliamentarism and decentralized under presidentialism.

Strøm's analysis suggests that legislative organization varies significantly under parliamentary regimes, at least sufficiently to affect how political parties calculate the value of formally joining a government. In close affinity to models developed to account for the operation of the US Congress, which emphasize the role of standing committees in providing opportunities for all parties to influence policy (Shepsle 1979; Shepsle and Weingast 1987), Strøm shows that minority governments in parliamentary democracies will be more frequent when the parliament is

organized in such a way as to offer "structural opportunities for opposi-
tional influence" (Strøm 1990: 72). It follows from this that the way the
legislature is organized can explain variation in legislative–executive
relations *across* types of democratic regime. An important implication for
studies of Asia is to direct scholarly attention to legislative organization.
With the exception of Japan, where a few studies exist (to be noted in
section IV), there is virtually nothing written about the legislative process
and organization in countries such as India, Taiwan, the Philippines,
South Korea and Indonesia.

The recognition that minority governments may be functional in
parliamentary systems has a direct bearing on the discussions about the
perils of presidentialism stimulated by Linz. As we indicated above,
minority presidents were considered to be ineffective and, consequently,
would have strong incentives to find ways to circumvent or altogether
ignore the legislature. But minority presidents may be as effective as
minority prime ministers if opposition parties care about similar things in
both systems (office, policy and votes) and go through the same
calculation about supporting a government. Since there are no good
reasons to believe that parties have different goals in parliamentary and
presidential systems, it is easy to see that, even though they all aspire to
conquer the presidency in the next election, opposition parties may
cooperate with the incumbent president on policy grounds. Moreover,
since presidents may also form coalition governments, something we
discuss next, minority presidents do not imply minority governments.[12]

B. Coalition Government

At the root of the view that presidentialism causes democratic instability
is the idea that presidential institutions provide no incentive for coalition
formation. This fact, as we have seen, would have disastrous consequences: minority presidents would be unable to obtain the support of a

---

[12] The only exception is, of course, in a two-party presidential system,
where, save for national fronts, which emerge in extraordinary circumstances, a
minority president will imply a divided government. Note, however, that presidential two-party systems are infrequent and exist primarily in Costa Rica and
the United States. The frequency with which, in the latter country, they have
emerged in the post-WWII period has led to the emergence of an enormous
literature, which we will not address here. For our purposes here, suffice it to say
that much of this literature revolves around the seminal book by Mayhew (1991),
which reports no difference in the policy effectiveness of divided and unified
governments and proposes an explanation for this similarity that is compatible
with Strøm's explanation of minority governments.

majority of legislators, deadlock would ensue as legislative activity is brought to a halt and, given the impossibility of constitutionally removing the government from office, actors would have an incentive to invoke extra-constitutional solutions.

Parliamentary and presidential systems are different when it comes to the institutional features relevant for coalition formation. Cheibub, Przeworski and Saiegh (2004) identified two main ones. First, in presidential democracies the president is always the government *formateur*, while in parliamentary democracies any party is a potential *formateur*. Thus, not only is the number of *possible* government coalitions smaller in presidential than in parliamentary systems, the party of the president, regardless of its size, will always be in the government. Second, failure to form a coalition government leads to different outcomes in each system. In parliamentary democracies, with few exceptions, it is the occurrence of new elections: voters are given the chance to return a new distribution of seats, hopefully one that will allow for the formation of a viable government. In presidential systems, failure to form a coalition implies that the party of the president is the only one to hold government portfolios, while policies may or may not remain at the status quo.

But do these differences imply that parties in one system will want to join together to form a coalition government whereas in the other they will want to pursue their goals independently and exclusively strive to achieve the presidency? Cheibub, Przeworski and Saiegh (2004), as well as Cheibub (2007), show that this is not the case. According to them, the conditions under which a coalition government will emerge are identical in presidential and parliamentary systems. These conditions depend on the distance between the party of the president and the next party in the policy space, on the location of the status quo, and on whether the president dominates the legislative process.

There are several implications of this analysis that directly challenge the traditional view of executive–legislative relations. Probably the most important one is that the absence of coalition governments does not automatically imply a lack of cooperation among political parties. The crucial distinction here is that between *government* (or portfolio) and *legislative* coalitions, which do not always coincide: there will be governments composed of one single party that are nonetheless supported by a legislative coalition. Thus, given that no party holds more than 50 percent of legislative seats, some minority governments emerge under presidentialism because no legislative majority wants to replace them since enough parties get policies they like. They are, in this sense, supported minority governments that will be at least as effective legislatively as coalition governments. This is an important insight for the study of executive–legislative relations in Asia, where coalition politics is said to be less important than elsewhere. Given the transition away from one-party governments in both India and Japan, this is certainly no longer true of the parliamentary systems of the region. But it is not true of presidential systems either: although minority presidents have existed in the Philippines, Indonesia and South Korea, in none of these cases, perhaps with the exception of Indonesia as we will see below, is there a sense that governments are immobilized by their minority status. They must be somehow building majority legislative coalitions. Identifying the political and institutional mechanisms that are used in this process is, therefore, crucial for understanding how Asian presidential democracies are governed.

C.   Agenda Power and the Decision-making Process

In the traditional model of legislative–executive relations, a strong government, that is, one endowed with a large array of legislative powers, will use these powers against the legislature. The greater the conflict between the two branches of government, the greater the incentives the executive will have to use these powers in order to see its will prevail over the recalcitrant legislature.

This view has been challenged and the seminal work that does so is Huber's (1996) study of policy making under the 1958 French constitution. Specifically, in his book Huber focuses on the role of the package vote and the confidence vote procedure – two features of the 1958 constitution that strengthens the government's legislative powers[13] – in shaping how the executive and the legislature interact.

Using an adapted version of the classical agenda setter model (Romer and Rosenthal 1978) and drawing heavily from models developed to understand the relations between the floor and committees in the US Congress, Huber redirects the way one should think about the use of restrictive legislative procedures by the executive. He does so in at least three ways. First, he demonstrates theoretically and empirically that the use of restrictive legislative procedures is not a function of the degree of

---

[13]   The package vote (article 44.3) allows the government to close debate on a bill and force an up or down vote on a proposal containing only the amendments proposed or accepted by the government; the confidence vote procedure (article 49.3), when invoked by the government, stops debate on a bill and, if no motion of censure is introduced and adopted, implies approval of the bill shaped by the government.

policy conflict between the government and parliament.[14] Second, Huber shows that not all restrictive legislative procedures are the same. He demonstrates that the package vote is a mechanism used by the government to protect the outcome of bargaining in a multidimensional policy space among parties within the governing coalition, or between the government and the opposition. Finally, Huber shows that the confidence vote allows parties in the majority to compete for votes at the same time that they cooperate to pass legislation. Together, Huber's analysis indicates that while restrictive legislative procedures give some leeway to the government to pick a policy it likes, they cannot be used *against* the legislative majority.

The implications of this perspective are profound when it comes to analyzing executive–legislative relations. To begin with, the analytical focus shifts from outside forces – the way legislators and governments get and retain their mandates – to the specific rules regulating executive–legislative relations. As with Strøm, the relevant variables for understanding policy making are located inside rather than outside the legislature. Second, not all parliaments are rationalized in the sense used by Huber (see also Lauvaux 1988), that is, not all parliaments contain provisions that allow the government to control the flow of legislation. In this sense, government control over the legislative agenda is not intrinsic to the principle that defines parliamentarism. That is to say, the strong cabinet control of the legislative process and the near irrelevance of individual members of parliament in this process, which characterizes Britain, are not inherent to parliamentary governments, as illustrated by the cases of Italy after 1945 and France in the Third and Fourth Republics. Similarly, and by extension, there is nothing in presidentialism that requires that a well-functioning system be one in which a weak president faces a strong Congress. Although this describes the allocation of powers across branches in the US system and the US is the only presidential democracy that has lasted for a long time, it does not follow that the success of the US system can be attributed to the specific way powers are allocated across the presidential and the legislative branches.[15]

If Huber's analysis is correct, and we believe it is, a legislatively strong government, be it under parliamentarism or under presidentialism, does

---

[14]   Huber's argument is analogous to the one developed by Shepsle (1979), Shepsle and Weingast (1987a and 1987b) and Krehbiel (1987a and 1987b) to the effect that congressional committees in the US cannot legislate against the will of the floor.

[15]   But see below for a different account of the institutional power of US presidents.

not imply a powerless legislative majority. Given the near obsession of the comparative literature on presidentialism with the risks resulting from strong presidents, this point needs to be examined in further detail.

1. Strong presidents and decree power

Almost all presidential constitutions give some legislative powers to the presidency. The most important ones are veto, decree, and urgency powers, as well as the government's exclusive prerogative to introduce legislation in specified areas.[16] All these features of presidential agenda powers are rather consequential, and they combine into institutionally weaker or stronger presidencies. Although there are many who believe that strong presidents are problematic in that they will clash with Congress and eventually generate government and even regime crises, there are those who argue that strong presidents are not necessarily bad for the operation of presidential constitutions. For instance, the strong presidential agenda powers established by the post-authoritarian constitutions of countries such as Brazil and Chile are considered to be largely responsible for the high level of legislative success of their governments (Figueiredo and Limongi 2000a and 2000b; Siavelis 2000; Jones and Hwang 2005; Amorin Neto, Cox and McCubbins 2003; and Londregan 2000).

The existence of presidents with strong agenda-setting powers raises a number of interesting questions. Most prominently, it raises the question of whether the president, in his capacity as the head of government, is imposing his preferences over those of the legislative majority. Despite some divergences, the vast majority of the analyses that address this issue adopt a model of conflict between the two branches. The possibility that these instruments – in a way similar to the restrictive procedures analyzed by Huber – can be used as tools for the coordination of a governing majority is not even considered.

There are two broad types of explanations for the variation in the use of decrees by presidents: the political-conditional and the institutional. The first one sees decrees as one among alternative options in a menu of instruments available to presidents seeking to implement their legislative agenda. The choice between these instruments is seen as a function of the political context within which presidents must interact with the legislature, and of circumstantial factors, such as the presidents' popularity, the occurrence of elections, or the existence of pressures for speedy executive action.

---

[16]   See Cheibub 2009 for a brief description of each of these powers.

The political-conditional view of presidential decree usage, in fact, sustains two competing positions, which Pereira, Power, and Rennó (2006) call "unilateral action" and "delegation" theories. In the former, presidents use their decree powers when they do not have the necessary support to get ordinary legislation approved in Congress. In this perspective, the use of decrees constitutes a way for the president to bypass an unfriendly Congress. Thus, the share of decrees in the president's overall legislative strategy will increase when he cannot count on the reliable and steady support of a legislative majority. The share of seats controlled by the parties also holding cabinet positions often indicates this support. Delegation theory, in turn, sees presidential decrees as a convenient means at the disposal of the legislative majority, which may prefer to transfer some of its powers to the executive for a variety of reasons. These may include partisan support for individual governments, collective action problems within the legislature, or electoral incentives of individual legislators (Carey and Shugart 1998).

Both unilateral-action and delegation theories predict that the reliance on decrees by presidents is a function of the political conditions they face; the only difference is that they predict opposite effects. According to unilateral-action theory, the use of decrees will increase when the president faces unfavorable political conditions; according to delegation theory, the use of decrees will increase when the president faces favorable political conditions.

In spite of their differences, both unilateral action and delegation theories see the use of decrees as a decision taken by the executive that does not involve the legislature. Yet, inspired by analyses such as Huber's, we can formulate a more institutional hypothesis that does not postulate any kind of necessary antagonism between the two branches. According to this hypothesis, presidential decree power is a mechanism whereby, through negotiation and bargaining, the executive can lead the process of shaping a legislative majority in support of the policies it wishes to implement. Although he leads, the president does not mandate: the majority in the legislature has the last word and any decree that the president issues that is not preferred by the majority to the *status quo ante* can be rejected. Unilateral action as a way of governing and setting policies contrary to preferences of the majority is simply not feasible. In this sense, the use of decrees by the executive is neither an act of delegation by the legislature nor unilateral power grabbing by the executive.

Attempting to adjudicate between these two perspectives is, we believe, probably futile. Decrees are, by design, instruments that allow the executive to set the legislative agenda; through this action, however, the government is able to bring together a legislative majority, a necessary step if it wants the policies implemented through decrees to become law. Thus, the matter is not whether Congress delegates or the president usurps legislative powers. The question is: how does the president use decrees to shape the legislative agenda and to bring about a legislative majority?

According to the institutional hypothesis, decrees are used both as convenient means to address routine issues and as regular instruments in the negotiations and bargaining that characterize the legislative process. Since they are neither usurpation nor delegation, they do not vary systematically with political factors such as the legislative strength of the president, his ability to manage his coalition, or his popularity. Some circumstantial factors, such as macroeconomic pressures leading to the implementation of emergency stabilization plans, matter; but they do so simply because it is only through decrees that presidents can act with the speed, secrecy and surprise that are sometimes considered to be essential for the policy's success. Even in these cases, however, presidents can be, and often are, successful in transforming their decrees into regular legislation.

Most presidents are endowed with decree power by their respective constitutions. Indeed, recent scholarly work has shown that in some countries where this power is denied to them, presidents have been able to force their way and get some sort of de facto decree power. Argentina from 1983 to 1995 and the United States are two prominent examples. As Rubbio and Goretti (1998) have shown, both Alfonsin and Menén relied on some old precedents to issue "decrees of necessity and urgency" (DNUs). Although primarily aimed at curbing hyperinflation, DNUs were also used to regulate more mundane affairs. The doubtful constitutional basis of this presidential prerogative was resolved with the 1995 constitutional reform, which introduced presidential decree powers that are similar to the ones granted by the 1988 Brazilian constitution.

In the United States, the constitutional provision stipulating that the president "shall take care that the Laws be faithfully executed" led to the unilateral issuing of executive orders, which have been interpreted by the Supreme Court as having the same status as a law passed by Congress. Executive orders have been issued to deal with important matters, including nationalizations, internment of Japanese-Americans during World War II, desegregation of the military, creation of the Peace Corps and the Environmental Protection Agency, federalization of the national guard, multiple health care initiatives, affirmative action policies, and the creation of special military tribunals to try non-US citizens accused of terrorism (Howell 2003: 1–6). Thus, even in the absence of any formal decree power, US presidents can still influence policy in a way similar to the "strong" presidents designed by the Brazilian and Chilean constitutions.

What is important to retain from this discussion, though, is that institutionally strong presidents are not necessarily detrimental to the functioning of presidential democracies. Attempts to weaken them on the ground that they usurp the power that should be located at the assembly must, therefore, be re-evaluated and considered in light of the benefits they bring about in terms of government performance (Croissant 2003; Londregan 2000).

IV. EXECUTIVE–LEGISLATIVE RELATIONS IN ASIA

Unlike Western Europe (parliamentary), Latin America (presidential) and Eastern Europe (semi-presidential), there is no one form of government that predominates in Asia. Adding to this variety is the fact that, outside of Europe and the Middle East, Asia is the only region where we find monarchies, some of which are constitutional and democratic (Japan, Nepal between 1990 and 2002, Bhutan since 2007, Thailand sometimes), others are constitutional but not necessarily democratic (Cambodia, Malaysia), and others are neither constitutional nor democratic (Brunei). It is true that the majority of years spent by Asian countries under a democratic regime between 1946 and 2008, 194 out of 335 (58 percent) to be precise, were parliamentary.[17] This, however, is mostly due to the fact that India and Japan, the two longest-lasting democracies in Asia, are parliamentary.

Parliamentarism has been adopted early in post-colonial Asia, including in Burma (1948–1958, 1960–1962), Laos (1953–1959), Pakistan (1947–1958), Sri Lanka (1948–1976) and, of course, India (1947–present) and Japan (1946–present). Of these, the experiences of Burma and Laos remain understudied and we know of no study (at least in English) that provides significant insights on the pattern of executive–legislative relations during the democratic periods in these countries. Pakistan, in turn, is mired in instability and it is hard to expect that its experience will be of much help in illuminating how executives and

---

[17]   These numbers and the dates below come from Cheibub, Gandhi and Vreeland (2010). They classify political regimes as democracies or dictatorships; they further classify democracies as parliamentary, semi-presidential, and presidential.

legislatures relate under different forms of democratic governance. Thailand, too, has always been parliamentary when democratic, but the spells of democracy have not been sufficiently long to allow for the development of specific patterns of executive–legislative relations.[18] Sri Lanka was characterized by regular alternation in power between the United National Front and the Sri Lanka Freedom Party from independence until a presidential constitution was introduced in 1978. It is thus the experiences of Japan and India, the longest-lived democracies in Asia, that provide the bulk of the raw material for studying democratic executive–legislative relations in the region.[19] As for semi-presidential systems, Asia contains two significant cases: Taiwan, which became democratic in 1996 and Mongolia, which adopted a democratic semi-presidential constitution in 1992.[20] Finally, there are three important cases of presidential democracies in Asia, namely Indonesia (since 1999), the Philippines (before 1973 and after 1987) and South Korea (since 1988).[21]

How, then, do the Asian cases of democracy fit in the map of studies of executive–legislative relations we drew in the previous sections? In what way do they help us understand broad patterns of interaction between these two branches and how do these broad patterns illuminate the experiences of each of the Asian countries?

In spite of the variation in regime form across Asian democracies, the large majority of work focusing on executive–legislative relations in the region has been concerned with the purely presidential (South Korea, the Philippines and Indonesia) and semi-presidential (Taiwan) systems. The issues that are often analyzed have to do with the fact that presidents do not have sufficient legislative support, or if they do, they obtain it at a price that is deleterious to overall political and economic performance. There are warnings about the propensity toward "delegative democracy"

---

[18] But see Ginsburg 2009 for an excellent analysis of constitutional changes in Thailand and an argument for a possible stabilization of politics in that country.

[19] Other parliamentary democracies in Asia include: Bhutan (2007–2008), Mongolia (1990–1991), South Korea (1960), Nepal (1990–2002 and 2008–present) and Bangladesh (1991–2006).

[20] Other cases of semi-presidentialism in democratic Asia include Bangladesh (1986–1990), East Timor (2002–2008) and Pakistan (1973–1976).

[21] Other cases of presidentialism include the Maldives (in 2008) and Sri Lanka (1989–2008). Sri Lanka is often classified as semi-presidential, although this is incorrect. In spite of the fact that reference to the "French model" is often made, the head of the government under this constitution is the president (unlike in France) and he cannot be removed by a legislative majority through a vote of no confidence.

in some of these countries (Croissant 2003), or about the democratic malaise that predominates in them (Cheng 2003); there are concerns with the (lack of) incentives for coalition formation in presidential and semi-presidential systems, the recurrence of minority governments, the problems generated by direct presidential elections, the possibility of co-habitation and divided governments and with the weakness of party systems and its effects on the proper operation of the democratic system.[22] Thus, the themes that one finds running across much of what has been written on the subject reproduce the preoccupations that have characterized "first generation" studies of democratic executive–legislative studies. Yet, some of the Asian cases in each of the three main forms of government – parliamentary, presidential and semi-presidential – raise important questions, which deserve much more attention than they have received in the English-language scholarship. As a matter of fact, the cases in each category illustrate challenges faced by each form of government or contain institutional innovations that may be of great significance for the study of executive–legislative relations in general.

Both India and Japan have experienced a transition from a predominant to a multiparty system, that is a transition from a system in which "one party is consistently supported by a winning majority of the votes" (Sartori 1976: 173) to one in which multiple parties have the capacity to win control of the government. The Indian experience raises important issues for those seeking to understand government formation and survival in parliamentary democracies. It represents a system in which Duverger's law of bipartisan competition in single-member constituencies holds at the district level; however, the two-party contests aggregate into a fragmented multiparty system at the national level.[23] This means that the national party system is, in fact, composed of multiple, non-overlapping regional party systems, and that many of the parties that get national representation, and become relevant as potential coalition partners, are regionally based. Governments, therefore, are composed of an amalgamation of sub-national parties. What is the implication of this fact for the way the government operates? Most coalition theories in parliamentary democracies take the national scope of partisan representation as given and assume that coalition agreements happen over broad-scope policies, both in ideological and territorial terms. Yet, what happens when parties

---

[22]   On the weakness or low level of institutionalization of political parties in Asia, see Chambers (2008), Hicken (2006), and Croissant and Völkel (2012).

[23]   On India, see Nikolenyi (2005) and Heath, Glouharova and Heath (2005); on Japan see Schoppa (2011).

have a strictly regional basis but at the same time provide crucial support for sustaining the national government in power?

We know virtually nothing about the mechanisms that have allowed Indian governments to function; and to function at a level that is probably more than satisfactory. India has undergone important structural transformations in the past few decades and its economy has been performing quite well. This suggests the formation of governments that are capable of changing the status quo and introducing reforms that are, to say the least, contentious. These same governments, however, have faced highly fragmented parliaments and have to accommodate multiple and highly heterogeneous interests in order to survive in power. Since 1996 they have tended to be coalition governments composed of a high number of parties that do not hold a majority of seats in the legislature. In other words, they tended to be minority governments. How this is accomplished is not well known, at least as far as we can determine. There is little research on India that focuses on the institutional instruments – legislative or otherwise – that may be available and which might account for the Indian governments' capacity to navigate the treacherous political environment within which they exist.

Unlike India, the transition from a dominant to a multiparty system in Japan coincided with a deep economic crisis and a general sense that the government's capacity to change the status quo had been considerably eroded. There is a diffuse sense that governments are weak and incapable of governing the country adequately.[24] Recent research, however, shows that governments may count on having some institutional resources which, as we discussed in section IIIC, grant them some power over the definition of the legislative agenda and control over factions in the governing party. For instance, Kim and Shoji (2008) demonstrate that the Japanese prime ministers use rulemaking decrees (*seirei*) to stabilize the government in view of unstable legislative support and the high degree of factionalism within the ruling party. As they state, the "decree is one of the tools at the PM's disposal to ensure timely implementation of necessary reforms so as to win back his base of support" (p 7). Unfortunately their analysis stops in 2005, precisely at the point where the LDP's long domination of Japanese politics ended. It would be interesting to see whether the emergence of new parties and coalition governments changed the way prime ministers use their rulemaking decrees.

---

[24] Kupchan (2012), for instance, believes that Japan, together with Europe and North America, are engulfed in a crisis of governability.

When it comes to semi-presidential systems, the bulk of the focus has been on Taiwan, with only cursory attention paid to Mongolia, in spite of the fact that democracy in the latter is older than in the former.[25] Although there is some disagreement when it comes to labels,[26] the usual narrative about Taiwan is that the system functioned well up to the point when the KMT held both the presidency and a majority of legislative seats, that is, until 2000, when the DPP won the presidency but the KMT held a majority in the Legislative Yuan. What emerged in 2000 was not exactly a situation of "co-habitation" as it is usually understood in the literature on semi-presidentialism. Under co-habitation, a president who faces a hostile legislative majority is forced to appoint a prime minister belonging to that majority given that governments must hold the confidence of parliament. This happened for a short period of time, after President Chen Shui-bian from the DPP "co-habitated" with a prime minister from the KMT (Tang Fei, who served from May through the beginning of October 2000, with at best reluctant support from the KMT). In October 2000 Chen named Chang Chun-hsiung from the DPP as the prime minister in spite of the fact that the DPP did not hold a legislative majority. For the remaining of his term, Chen appointed DPP prime ministers (four in total), in spite of never having held a majority in the Legislative Yuan.

How was this possible? Analysts believe that the 1997 constitutional reforms created the conditions for this situation to come about. One of the reforms approved in that year deprived the Legislative Yuan of its ability to approve the appointment of prime ministers. At the same time, the Legislative Yuan acquired the ability to pass a no confidence vote on the prime minister, a power it did not have before 1997. However, and this is, in our view, the important provision, even though the successful

---

[25]   According to Cheibub et al. (2010), transition to democracy in Mongolia happened in 1990; in Taiwan it happened in 1995.

[26]   Wu (2007: 202) asserts that the 1997 constitutional amendments "turned Taiwan's semi-presidentialism towards what Shugart and Carey (1992, ch 4) call a 'president-parliamentary' system;" and he explains in a footnote (note 3, p 215) that these systems are "considered dangerous for the consolidation of nascent democratic regimes." Cheng (2003: 16), in turn, asserts that "Taiwan's system is largely a premier-presidential system, or a mixed one, with dual legitimacy, the separation of powers, and, since the 1997 constitutional revision, an increasingly strong parliamentary bent." As Shugart (2005: 333) puts it, "under premier-presidentialism, the prime minister and cabinet are *exclusively* accountable to the assembly majority, while under president-parliamentarism, the prime minister and cabinet are *dually* accountable to the president and the assembly majority."

vote of no confidence required the resignation of the government, it also allowed the president to dissolve the Legislative Yuan if he so desired.

Without this provision, the so-called 1997 compromise (Huang 2006: 382–383) would simply make Taiwan look like a large number of assembly confidence systems, whether pure parliamentary or semi-presidential ones. Not all such systems have government investiture votes (for this is what the requirement of a legislative approval of a prime minister is); and whether the existence of such votes is of any conse-quence is a matter of debate among political scientists.[27] What allowed Chen Shui-bian to successfully appoint minority DPP prime ministers was the fact that the KMT majority in parliament found it more palatable to live with such a prime minister than to face the possibility of having to contest new elections... and possibly lose the majority it then held.

We do not know of any study that has systematically examined the legislative success of the Taiwanese government. There are, of course, countless assertions that, under its "unique" semi-presidential formula, Taiwan faced profound problems of governability. Yet, given our discus-sion in section III regarding minority governments and the success of presidents under seemingly intractable adverse conditions, this should not pass as evidence of paralysis or governability crisis. The really interesting question about Taiwan, we submit, is to understand the reasons why the possibility of a no confidence vote by the KMT majority never repre-sented a serious threat to the existence of the DPP government. True, a successful no confidence vote would lead to the fall of the government

---

[27] Strøm (2000: 265), for instance, does not consider that parliamentary participation in the selection of the prime minister is a characteristic of parliamentarism (or, more broadly, of assembly confidence systems). He argues: "what characterizes parliamentary democracies is that the cabinet must be tolerated by the parliamentary majority, not that the latter actually plays any direct role in the selection of the former." The reason is that, given that the parliament can remove the government at will, any government that has not been removed by a vote of no confidence represents a government that would have survived a vote of investiture if one had been required. Bergman (1993), in turn, argues that the vote of investiture deters the emergence of minority government since such governments would not be formed in the first place if they had to obtain the positive support of a legislative majority. Finally, while Martin, Rasch and Cheibub (2012) agree that there is a difference between requiring a majority in favor of the government (the investiture vote) or a majority against (no confidence vote), they hypothesize that what really matters are the specific provisions of the investiture rule, such as whether it precedes the bargaining for government formation, the decision rule, and the number of formation attempts that are allowed.

but also to the dissolution of the legislature by the president. But the possibility of dissolution alone cannot be the reason for the KMT's immobility regarding a no confidence vote. It must be also the case that at least parts of the KMT did not anticipate any significant gains if it were to compete in new elections, and therefore found the status quo not too unattractive. Thus, the issue about Taiwan is to understand the legislative and electoral reasons why a majority of representatives, which cut across the KMT and DPP, preferred the status quo to a chance to increase their power through new elections. In this respect, Cheng (2003: 15–17) suggests a possible answer, even though he belongs to the set of analysts who finds fault with the Taiwanese institutional design. He suggests that the sub-ethnic cleavage between "*mainlanders*" and "*taiwanese*" allowed the DPP to sustain its rule in spite of a formally hostile legislative majority. If this is correct, it is not the institutional design per se, but its combination with the social conditions under which it must operate, that accounts for the persistence of a minority government under a DPP president.

South Korea, the Philippines and Indonesia represent the three cases of presidential democracies in Asia. Work on these countries has been overwhelmingly concerned with the alleged perils of presidentialism – minority presidents facing a hostile majority, low incentives for coalition formation, presidential usurpation of legislative powers and low levels of legislative capacity. In all three countries a president was removed, or almost removed, from office via impeachment (see Fukuyama, Dressel and Chang 2005 for a discussion of these cases). These events for a moment dominated accounts of executive–legislative relations in these countries and reinvigorated complaints about the rigidity of presidential systems, the difficulties in removing an unpopular president from office, and the drastic measures that must be taken when presidents lose their popular appeal.

Yet, the recent literature on executive–legislative relations in these three countries also highlights, even if sometimes inadvertently, some of the mechanisms that account for the reasonably good performance of the systems; or, alternatively, it suggests that some of the difficulties encountered in sustaining smooth and cooperative executive–legislative relations are to be found in institutions other than the form of government.

Concerns with the performance of some of the Asian presidential democracies converge on three issues: the possibility that presidents will bypass Congress and make use of instruments that allow them to act unilaterally, and thus diminish the role of the legislature in the democratic process; the weakness of political parties, which is alleged to feed into the problems inherent to presidentialism; and the low legislative capacity of the systems, which is seen, in part at least, as a result of the first two issues.

Presidential unilateral action is normally discussed in the context of decree powers, which none of the Asian presidents has. South Korea is the only constitution that grants presidents delegated decree powers, stipulating relatively strict conditions for how and when they can be used. But presidents have other instruments that allow them to affect policy unilaterally, even if they are formally deprived of decree powers. These instruments are akin to the "executive orders" issued by US presidents, which we discussed in section IIIC. Thus, for Croissant (2003: 91), "the relationship between the executive and the National Assembly in South Korea [as opposed to that in the Philippines] exhibits clear features of delegative democracy whenever there have been congruent majorities." Delegative democracy emerges, he argues, when presidents use their "proactive decree powers" to alter the balance of power in their favor. As he says, "the more presidents employ them in order to create immediate and permanent law, the more will the executive turn into a supreme legislator and, inversely, the more will the legislature be degraded to a submissive body" (Croissant 2003: 73). Rose-Ackerman, Desierto and Volosin (2010) find that "presidential declarations of emergency" in the Philippines are equivalent to presidential decrees. For them, these declarations "pose important challenges to constitutional checks on presidential powers;" they allow presidents to "manipulate or ignore legal and constitutional constraints to enhance their power and freedom of action" (p 54).

But if we adopt the cooperative perspective suggested in section IIIC, which sees executive decree powers (broadly understood) as instruments to *discipline* or even *generate* a legislative majority, presidential decrees can be seen in a new light, that is, as one among many governing instruments in the presidential toolkit. In this light, the research question becomes understanding the conditions under which presidents choose to use decrees and the effects that their use have. We noted above how Kim and Shoji's (2008) study of rulemaking by Japanese prime ministers fits this perspective. In a different study of decree use in Argentina, South Korea and the United States, Kim (2007) argues that, in general, broadly conceived decree powers do not necessarily constitute usurpation of lawmaking capacity by the executive. He develops a "constrained unilateralist" model of decree use, which places it in the context of the broader constitutional framework; that is, it takes into consideration the actor (the legislative majority or the courts) that has the last word in the legislative process. Thus, he finds, for instance, that in South Korea presidents issue more decrees under unified (when they control a legislative majority) than under divided government (when presidents do not control a legislative majority) (Kim 2007; see also Kim 2010). This, of course, is not what a theory that sees presidential decree use as a way for a president to compensate for the lack of sufficient legislative support would predict.

Regarding the weakness of party systems, nowhere is this seen as an issue that affects the operation of democratic presidential institutions more than in the Philippines. The fluidity of the Philippine party system is notorious and has served as a reference in claims that presidential systems are not conducive to strong political parties. There is a level at which this fluidity may be effective: as Cheng (2003: 23) points out, presidents in the Philippines are always elected with a minority of seats in the lower house, although by the time they take office they can count on majority support. However, the lubricant that fuels this fluidity – patronage politics – is costly, both economically and politically. Yet, one important question to ask is whether the Philippine party system is what it is *because* of presidentialism or other institutions that are not inherent to the system. In other words, are the factors behind legislators' incentives to remain loosely affiliated with political parties and make themselves available as members of ephemeral presidential coalitions a product of presidentialism or of other institutions?

There are, for sure, institutional incentives underlying political parties in the Philippines; but these incentives do not necessarily follow from the fact that the system is presidential. Rather, they follow from secondary institutions, such as the one-term presidency or the possibility of a split ticket in the vote for president and vice-president. This is the argument developed by Kasuya (2005). She shows that Philippine legislators affiliate with parties that have viable presidential candidates, even if this means switching parties. Given this behavior by legislators, the instability of the party system is due to the instability – high volatility – of presidential elections. This instability, in turn, is the product of the no-re-election clause, which prevents the presence of incumbents in the elections. Thus, the removal of incumbents from all presidential contests, Kasuya claims, ultimately affects the way legislators will choose with whom to affiliate when in Congress.

The last point to discuss has to do with the low legislative capacity in the Asian presidential systems. We know of one study that systematically addresses legislative production in an Asian democracy, and this is about Japan (Fukumoto 2008). When it comes to presidential democracies, the generalized sense is that legislative capacity is low, either because presidents bypass Congress or because the fluidity of the party system renders Congress ineffective. Thus, Kawamura (2010: table 2) analyzes legislative production between 1998 and 2009 in Indonesia and finds it to be quite low: in this period, only 392 laws have been proposed in the legislative assembly, of which 270 were initiated by the government; and of these, 99, or 37 percent, became laws (note that the Indonesian president does not have the power to veto legislation that has been approved by the assembly). Croissant (2003: 84) finds that the highest rate of legislative efficacy (proportion of approved bills out of proposed ones) observed in the Philippines between 1987 and 1999 was 4.6 percent in the Senate. In South Korea, legislative efficacy was 51.7 percent and 72.8 percent for the 1988–1992 and 1992–December 1995 periods, respectively; presidential efficacy, in turn, that is, the share of presidential bills that are approved out of all the bills the president introduces, was 87.2 percent and 92.4 percent for the same period (Croissant 2003: 86).

These figures, however, particularly the ones about "legislative efficacy," must be seen as tentative as they lack an appropriate base for comparison. It is not clear, for example, that including the bills initiated by individual legislators in the base for computing legislative efficacy is appropriate. The cost of bill initiation is low and legislators have all sorts of reasons to introduce bills, even when they are sure they will not be approved.[28] If we include bills introduced by individual legislators in the computation of legislative efficacy, the vast majority of parliaments in the world, including those in the established European democracies, would be highly inefficacious, probably as, or even more so, than the one in the Philippines. Systematic comparative data on legislative efficacy are not easy to come by, but see Saiegh (2011: 64) for a comparison of nine countries.

Note that all of these figures are subject to the influence of myriad institutional features of the legislative process. In some cases, such as in Indonesia, they can be misleading. Thus, the fact that the presidential bills in that country have a relatively low passage rate does not imply that presidents fail in implementing their legislative agenda. In Indonesia, for example, the democratic constitutional reforms of 1999–2002 removed the presidential veto (which had existed in the 1945 constitution), but stipulated, in turn, that the president must agree on a piece of legislation *before the legislature can vote on it*. Thus, the president is able to effectively veto *ex ante* any piece of legislation that he does not want to

---

[28] There is a large literature on bill initiation by individual members of Congress in the United States. Crisp et al. 2004 represents one of the few comparative studies on the topic.

see implemented. This certainly helps to account for why the passage rate of individual legislators in Indonesia is quite high relative to that of the president: the president will let legislators initiate policies that he likes, which will then be approved.

Asian democracy is here to stay in many countries. In addition to the venerable democracies in India and Japan, there are now quite a few countries that have already accumulated a considerable stock in terms of democratic years. Unlike other regions of the world that are characterized by the predominance of one form of democratic government, Asia is plural, containing exemplars of all three forms. Scholarship on executive–legislative relations has been somewhat reactive or even derivative, in the sense that it has simply "applied" to the region the perspectives and concerns that emerged in the course of studies of Western and Eastern Europe, as well as Latin America. More recently, however, a new scholarship has been emerging, prompted, on the one hand, by a shift in perspective regarding how the relationship between executives and legislatures is conceptualized, and, on the other hand, by the recognition that some of the Asian countries raise broad theoretical issues. It is this scholarship that holds the most promise in helping us understand executive–legislative relations in general.

V. CONCLUSION

As we said at the beginning, this is a necessarily incomplete review of a large literature. Our goal was to establish a contrast between what we called a "traditional" and a "recent" set of works that, in spite of their heterogeneity, have in common a conception of the way the executive and the legislative interact in a democratic system. "Traditional" works adopt a perspective of conflict between the two powers, which originates from the emphasis they give to the way governments and legislatures are formed, and from a narrow view of politicians' motivations as being purely office oriented. "Recent" works, in contrast, expand their purview to include the legislative process per se, that is the moment of proposing and supporting policies. They also adopt a broader view of motivations of politicians, who, in addition to office, also care about policies and must compete for votes.

One broad consequence of this shift in perspective is a blurring of the distinction between presidential and parliamentary forms of government. Of course this does not mean that presidentialism and parliamentarism are identical; they clearly are not and actors in each system may have available to them strategies that are not feasible in the other. The point is that once we accept that politicians across systems have similar motivations, and that legislative institutions are not dependent on the form of government, it is possible to see that the democratic process of passing laws, which necessarily involves both the executive and the legislature, is in fact quite similar across different types of political systems. This perspective helps bring together the variety of democratic forms that now exist in Asia. It is important to move away from single-country studies, or studies restricted to one regime type. It may very well be the case that one can learn more about Indonesia's presidential system by comparing it to Japan's parliamentary one; that Taiwan's semi-presidential regime can be seen in the light of South Korea's presidential one. It is by crossing the boundaries of broad constitutional frameworks and focusing on the process of governing, which necessarily involves both the executive and the legislature, that we will be able to advance our understanding of Asian democratic regimes.

REFERENCES

Ackerman, Bruce. 2000. "The New Separation of Powers." *Harvard Law Review* 113(3): 642–727.

Amorim Neto, Octávio, Gary Cox and Mathew D. McCubbins. 2003. "Agenda Power in Brazil's Camara dos Deputados, 1989–98." *World Politics* 55(4): 550–578.

Andrews, William. G. 1978. "The Constitutional Prescription of Parliamentary Procedures in Gaullist France." *Legislative Studies Quarterly* 3(3): 465–506.

Axelrod, Robert. 1970. *Conflict of Interest: A Theory of Divergent Goals with Applications to Politics*. Chicago: Markham.

Bergman, Torbjörn 1993. "Formation Rules and Minority Governments," *European Journal of Political Research* 23: 55–66.

Carey, John M. and Mathew Shugart. 1998. "Calling out the Tanks or Just Filling Out the Forms?" Pp. 1–32 in *Executive Decree Authority*, edited by John M. Carey and Mathew Shugart. New York: Cambridge University Press.

Chambers, Paul. 2008. "Factions, Parties and the Durability of Parliaments, Coalitions and Cabinets: The Case of Thailand (1979–2001)." *Party Politics* 14(3): 299–323.

Cheibub, José Antonio. 2007. *Presidentialism, Parliamentarism and Democracy*. New York: Cambridge University Press.

Cheibub, José Antonio. 2009. "Making Presidential and Semi-Presidential Constitutions Work." *Texas Law Review* 88(7): 1375–1408.

Cheibub, José Antonio and Svitlana Chernykh. 2009. "Are Semi-presidential Constitutions Bad for Democracy?" *Constitutional Political Economy* 20(3–4): 202–229.

Cheibub, José A., Jennifer Gandhi and James R. Vreeland. 2010. "Democracy and Dictatorship Revisited." *Public Choice* 143: 67–101.

Cheibub, José Antonio, Adam Przeworski and Sebastian Saiegh. 2004. "Government Coalitions and Legislative Success Under Parliamentarism and Presidentialism." *British Journal of Political Science* 34(4): 565–587.

Cheng, Tun-jen. 2003. "Political Institutions and the Malaise of East Asian New Democracies." *Journal of East Asian Studies* 3: 1–41.

Crisp, Brian, Maria C. Escobar-Lemmon, Bradford S. Jones, Mark P. Jones and Michelle M. Taylor-Robinson. 2004. "Vote-Seeking Incentives and Legislative Representation in Six Presidential Democracies." *Journal of Politics* 66(3): 823–846.

Croissant, Aurel. 2003. "Legislative Powers, Veto Players, and the Emergence of Delegative Democracy: A Comparison of Presidentialism in the Philippines and South Korea." *Democratization* 10(3): 68–98.

Croissant, Aurel and Philip Völkel. 2012. "Party System Types and Party System Institutionalization: Comparing New Democracies in East and Southeast Asia." *Party Politics* 18(2): 235–265.

De Swaan, Abram. 1973. *Coalition Theories and Cabinet Formations*. Amsterdam: Elsevier.

Duverger, Maurice. 1980. "A New Political System Model: Semi-Presidential Government." *European Journal of Political Research* 8(2): 166–187.

Edwards III, George C., John H. Kessel and Bert A. Rockman, eds. 1993. *Researching the Presidency: Vital Questions, New Approaches*. Pittsburgh: University of Pittsburgh Press.

Elgie, Robert, ed. 1999. *Semi-presidentialism in Europe*. Oxford: Oxford University Press.

Elgie, Robert. 2004. "Semi-presidentialism: Concepts, Consequences, and Contested Explanations." *Political Studies Review*, vol. 2, pp. 313–330.

Elgie, Robert. 2011. *Semi-Presidentialism: Sub-Types And Democratic Performance*. Oxford: Oxford University Press.

Elgie, Robert and Sophia Moestrup, eds. 2007. *Semi-presidentialism Outside of Europe: A Comparative Study*. London: Routledge.

Elgie, Robert and Sophia Moestrup, eds. 2008. *Semi-presidentialism in Central and Eastern Europe*. Manchester: Manchester University Press.

Elgie, Robert, Sophia Moestrup and Yu-Shan Wu, eds. 2011. *Semi-Presidentialism and Democracy*. Basingstoke: Palgrave Macmillan.

Figueiredo, Argelina and Fernando Limongi. 2000a. "Constitutional Change, Legislative Performance, and Institutional Consolidation." *Brazilian Review of Social Sciences* 1: 1–22.

Figueiredo, Argelina and Fernando Limongi. 2000b. "Presidential Power, Legislative Organization and Party Behavior in the Legislature." *Comparative Politics* 32(2): 151–70.

Fukumoto, Kentaro. 2008. "Legislative Production in Comparative Perspective: Cross-Sectional Study of 42 Countries and Time-Series Analysis of the Japan Case." *Japanese Journal of Political Science* 9(1): 1–19.

Fukuyama, Francis, Björn Dressel and Boo-Seung Chang. 2005. "Facing the Perils of Presidentialism." *Journal of Democracy* 16(2): 102–116.

Ginsburg, Tom. 2009. "Constitutional Afterlife: The Continuing Impact of Thailand's Post-Political Constitution." *International Journal of Constitutional Law* 7(1): 83–105.

González, Luis Eduardo and Charles Guy Gillespie. 1994. "Presidentialism and Democratic Stability in Uruguay." Pp. 151–178 in *The Failure of Presidential*

Democracy: The Case of Latin America Vol II, edited by J. J. Linz and A. Valenzuela. Baltimore: Johns Hopkins University Press.

Grofman, Bernard and Peter Van Roozendaal. 1997. "Review Article: Modelling Cabinet Durability and Termination." *British Journal of Political Science* 27: 419–451.

Heath, Anthony, Siana Glouharova and Oliver Heath. 2005. "India: Two-Party Contests within a Multiparty System." Pp. 137–156 in *The Politics of Electoral Systems* edited by Michael Gallagher and Paul Mitchell. Oxford: Oxford University Press.

Hochstetler, Kathryn. 2006. "Rethinking Presidentialism: Challenges and Presidential Falls in South America." *Comparative Politics* 38(4): 401–418.

Hochstetler, Kathryn and Margaret E. Edwards. 2009. "Failed Presidencies: Identifying and Explaining a South American Anomaly." *Journal of Politics in Latin America* 1(2): 31–57.

Howell, William G. 2003. *Power Without Persuasion: The Politics of Direct Presidential Action*. Princeton: Princeton University Press.

Huang, The-fu. 1997. "Party Systems in Taiwan and South Korea." Pp. 135–59 in *Consolidating the Third Wave Democracies: Themes and Perspectives*, edited by Larry Diamond, Marc F. Plattner, Yun-han Chu and Hung-mao Tien. Baltimore: Johns Hopkins University Press.

Huang, Thomas Weishing. 2006. "The President Refuses to Cohabit: Semi-presidentialism in Taiwan." *Pacific Rim Law & Policy Journal* 15(2): 375–402.

Huber, John D. 1996. *Rationalizing Parliament*. New York: Cambridge University Press.

Jones, Mark P. 1995. *Electoral Laws and the Survival of Presidential Democracies*. Notre Dame, IN: Notre Dame University Press.

Jones, Mark. P. and Wonjae Hwang. 2005. "Party Government in Presidential Democracies: Extending Cartel Theory Beyond the U.S. Congress." *American Journal of Political Science* 49(2): 267–282.

Kasuya, Yuko. 2005. "The Presidential Connection: Party System Instability and Executive Term Limits in the Philippines." Ph.D. Dissertation. University of California, San Diego.

Kawamura, Koichi. 2010. "Is the Indonesian President Strong or Weak?" Institute of Developing Economies Discussion Paper no. 235. Chiba, Japan.

Kim, James Je Heon. 2007. "Constrained Unilateralism: Comparing Institutional Foundations of Executive Decrees in Presidential Democracies." Ph.D. Dissertation. Columbia University.

Kim, James Je Heon. 2010. "Making Orders to (Re)make Policy: Analysis of Rulemaking Decrees in South Korea, 1988–2005." California State Polytechnic University, Pomona, CA. Unpublished.

Kim, James Je Heon and Kaori Shoji. 2008. "Executive Decrees and Incomplete Information in the Japanese Government." Presented at the Annual Meeting of the Western Political Science Association, San Diego, March 20–22.

Kim, Young Hun and Donna Bahry. 2008. "Interrupted Presidencies in Third Wave Democracies." *Journal of Politics* 70(3): 807–822.

Krehbiel, Keith. 1987a. "Sophisticated Committees and Structure-induced Equilibria in Congress." Pp. 376–402 in *Congress: Structure and Policy*, edited by Mathew McCubbins and Terry Sullivan. Cambridge, Cambridge University Press.

Krehbiel, Keith. 1987b. "Why are Congressional Committees Powerful?" *American Political Science Review* 81: 929–35.

Kristinsson, Gunnar Helgi. 1999. "Iceland." In *Semi-Presidentialism in Europe*, edited by Robert Elgie, 86–103. Oxford: Oxford University Press.

Kupchan, Charles A. 2012. "The Democratic Malaise: Globalization and the Threat to the West." *Foreign Affairs* 91(1): 62–67.

Lauvaux, Philippe. 1988. *Parlementarisme Rationalisé et Stabilité du Pouvoir Exécutif*. Brussels: Bruylant.

Laver, Michael. 2003. "Government Termination." *Annual Review of Political Science* 6: 23–40.

Laver, Michael. 2006. "Legislatures and Parliaments in Comparative Context." Pp. 121–140 in *The Oxford Handbook of Political Economy*, edited by Barry R. Weingast and Donald A. Wittman. Oxford: Oxford University Press.

Laver, Michael and Norman Schofield. 1998. *Multiparty Government: The Politics of Coalition in Europe*. Ann Arbor, MI: University of Michigan Press.

Limongi, Fernando and Argelina Figueiredo. 1998. "As Bases Institucionais do Presidencialismo de Coalizão." *Lua Nova* 44: 81–106.

Limongi, Fernando and Argelina Figueiredo. 2007. "The Budget Process and Legislative Behavior: Individual Amendments, Support for the Executive and Government Programs." *World Political Science Review* 3(3): article 3.

Linz, Juan J. 1978. *The Breakdown of Democratic Regimes: Crisis, Breakdown, and Reequilibration*. Baltimore: Johns Hopkins University Press.

Linz, Juan J. 1990a. "The Perils of Presidentialism." *Journal of Democracy* 1(1): 51–69.

Linz, Juan J. 1990b. "The Virtues of Parliamentarism." *Journal of Democracy* 1(4): 84–91.

Linz, Juan J. 1994. "Presidential or Parliamentary Democracy: Does it Make a Difference?" Pp. 3–87 in *The Failure of Presidential Democracy: The Case of Latin America*, edited by Juan Linz and Arturo Valenzuela. Baltimore: The Johns Hopkins University Press.

Linz, Juan J. and Alfred Stepan. 1996. *Problems of Democratic Transition and Consolidation: Southern Europe, South America, and Post-Communist Europe*. Baltimore: Johns Hopkins University Press.

Londregan, John. 2000. *Legislative Institutions and Ideology in Chile*. New York: Cambridge University Press.

Mainwaring, Scott. 1990. "Presidentialism in Latin America." *Latin American Research Review* 25(1): 157–179.

Mainwaring, Scott. 1993. "Presidentialism, Multipartism, and Democracy: The Difficult Combination." *Comparative Political Studies* 26(2): 198–228.

Mainwaring, Scott and Timothy R. Scully. 1995. "Introduction: Party Systems in Latin America." Pp. 1–34 in *Building Democratic Institutions: Party Systems in Latin America*, edited by Scott Mainwaring and Timothy R. Scully. Stanford: Stanford University Press.

Marsteintredet, Leiv and Einar Berntzen. 2008. "Reducing the Perils of Presidentialism in Latin America through Presidential Interruptions." *Comparative Politics* 41(1): 83–101.

Martin, Shane, Bjørn Erik Rasch and José Antonio Cheibub. 2012. "The Investiture Vote and the Formation and Survival of Minority Parliamentary Governments." Presented at the Annual Meeting of the American Political Science Association, August 30–September 2, 2012, New Orleans, LA, USA.

Mayhew, David R. 1991. *Divided We Govern: Party Control, Lawmaking, and Investigations, 1946–1990*. New Haven, Yale University Press.

Munkh-Erdene, Lhamsuren. 2010. "The Transformation of Mongolia's Political System: From Semi-parliamentary to Parliamentary?" *Asian Survey* 50(2): 311–334.

Nikolenyi, Csaba. 2004. "Cabinet Stability in Post-Communist Central Europe." *Party Politics* 10(2): 123–50.

Nikolenyi, Csaba. 2005. "Party Inflation in India: Why Has a Multiparty Format Prevailed in the National Party System?" Pp. 97–114 in *Duverger's Law of Plurality Voting: The Logic of Party Competition in Canada, India, the United Kingdom and the United States* edited by Bernard Grofman, André Blais and Shaum Bowler. New York: Springer.

Niño, Carlos Santiago. 1996. "Hyperpresidentialism and Constitutional Reform in Argentina." In *In Institutional Design in New Democracies: Eastern Europe and Latin America*, edited by Arend Lijphart and Carlos H. Waisman, 161–74. Boulder, CO: Westview.

O'Donnell, Guillermo. 1994. "Delegative Democracy." *Journal of Democracy* 5: 55–69.

Pereira, Carlos, Timothy J. Power and Lucio Rennó. 2006. "Under What Conditions Do Presidents Resort to Decree Power? Theory and Evidence from the Brazilian Case." *Journal of Politics* 67(1): 178–200.

Pérez-Liñán, Aníbal. 2007. *Presidential Impeachment and the New Political Instability in Latin America.* Cambridge: Cambridge University Press.

Raunio, Tapio. 2004. "The Changing Finnish Democracy: Stronger Parliamentary Accountability, Coalescing Political Parties and Weaker External Constraints." *Scandinavian Political Studies* 27 (2): 133–52.

Riggs, Fred W. 1988. "The Survival of Presidentialism in America: Para-Constitutional Practices." *International Political Science Review* 9(4): 247–78.

Riker, William H. 1962. *The Theory of Political Coalitions.* New Haven: Yale University Press.

Romer, Thomas and Howard Rosenthal. 1978. "Political Resource Allocation, Controlled Agendas, and the Status Quo." *Public Choice* 33: 27–43.

Roper, Steven D. 2002. "Are All Semipresidential Regimes the Same? A Comparison of Premier-Presidential Regimes." *Comparative Politics* 34(3): 253–72.

Rose-Ackerman, Susan, Diane Desierto and Natalia Volosin. 2010. "Leveraging Presidential Power: Separation of Powers without Checks and Balances in Argentina and the Philippines." Faculty Scholarship Series, Paper 31. (http://digitalcommons.law.yale.edu/fss_papers/31).

Rubio, Delia Ferreira and Matteo Goretti. 1998. "When the Presidents Govern Alone: the decreatazo in Argentina, 1989–93." Pp. 33–61 in *Executive Decree Authority*, edited by John M. Carey and Mathew Shugart. New York: Cambridge University Press.

Saiegh, Sebastian M. 2011. *Ruling by Statute: How Uncertainty and Vote Buying Shape Lawmaking.* Cambridge: Cambridge University Press.

Sartori, Giovanni. 1976. *Parties and Party Systems: A Framework for Analysis.* Cambridge: Cambridge University Press.

Sartori, Giovanni. 1994. *Comparative Constitutional Engineering: An Inquiry Into Structures, Incentives and Outcomes.* New York, New York University Press.

Schoppa, Leonard J. ed. 2011. *The Evolution of Japan's Party System: Politics and Policy in an Era of Institutional Change.* Toronto: University of Toronto Press.

Shepsle, Kenneth A. 1979. "Institutional Arrangements and Equilibrium in Multidimensional Voting Models." *American Journal of Political Science* 23: 27–60.

Shepsle, Kenneth A. and Barry Weingast. 1987a. "The Institutional Foundations of Committee Power." *American Political Science Review* 80: 85–104.

Shepsle, Kenneth A. and Barry Weingast. 1987b. "Reflections on Committee Power." *American Political Science Review* 81: 935–945.

Shugart, Mathew. 2005. "Semi-Presidential Systems: Dual Executive and Mixed Authority." *French Politics* 3: 323–351.

Shugart, Mathew and John M. Carey. 1992. *Presidents and Assemblies: Constitutional Design and Electoral Dynamics*. Cambridge: Cambridge University Press.

Siavelis, Peter M. 2000. "Executive–Legislative Relations in Post-Pinochet Chile: A Preliminary Assessment." Pp. 321–365 in *Presidentialism and Democracy in Latin America*, edited by Scott Mainwaring and Mathew Shugart. New York: Cambridge University Press.

Stepan, Alfred and Cindy Skach. 1993. "Constitutional Frameworks and Democratic Consolidation." *World Politics* 46(1): 1–22.

Strøm, Kaare. 1990. *Minority Government and Majority Rule*. Cambridge: Cambridge University Press.

Strøm, Kaare. 2000. "Delegation and Accountability in Parliamentary Democracies." *European Journal of Political Research* 37: 261–289.

Valenzuela, Arturo. 1994. "Party Politics and the Crisis of Presidentialism in Chile: A Proposal for a Parliamentary Form of Government." Pp. 91–150 in *The Failure of Presidential Democracy: The Case of Latin America, Volume 2*, edited by J. J. Linz and A. Valenzuela. Baltimore: Johns Hopkins University Press.

Wu, Yu-Shan. 2007. "Semi-presidentialism – Easy to Choose, Difficult to Operate: the Case of Taiwan." Pp. 201–218 in *Semi-presidentialism Outside Europe*, edited by Robert Elgie and Sophia Moestrup. London: Routledge.

7. Classical and post-conflict federalism: Implications for Asia

Sujit Choudhry[1]

I. INTRODUCTION

Federalism has long been a topic of study for comparative constitutional law. However, the scholarly literature on federalism is in a process of transition. For most of the twentieth century, the study of federalism was oriented around a standard set of cases in the developed world: Australia, Canada, Switzerland and the United States of America. These cases provided the raw material for certain fundamental questions: What is federalism? Why should federations be adopted? What role is there for courts? For the most part, these questions appear to have been answered, often with the aid of comparative analysis. To be sure, important debates persist. For example, scholars disagree over the relative priority to be given to the different goals served by federalism and how those goals should shape the allocation of jurisdiction. In the area of environmental policy, for example, new opportunities for democratic self-government and policy experimentation argue for greater regional authority but also generate inter-jurisdictional externalities, which argue against it. This debate relies on an implicit understanding of its terms and range, and participants in such discussions of federalism often draw on the same standard set of jurisdictions as illustrations of models to be followed and dangers to be avoided.

Recent developments in the practice of constitutional design have challenged this consensus. Many states in the developing world, such as

[1] This chapter draws extensively on Choudhry and Hume 2011. I acknowledge Nathan Hume's contributions to our co-authored work, which I have drawn upon freely here. I thank Tom Ginsburg and Rosalind Dixon for the opportunity to explore these themes within the context of Asia, and for their help in shaping this chapter. I thank Diane Desierto and Kai Tu for their thoughtful commentary. All remaining errors are mine.

Ethiopia, Iraq and Nigeria, have adopted federal solutions to manage ethnic conflict, often as part of a broader package of post-conflict constitutional reforms. In these federations, internal boundaries are drawn to ensure that territorially concentrated national minorities constitute regional majorities. The difference between the standard and emerging cases is not just geographic. Rather, the very mission of federalism is different. Its principal goals are not to combat majority tyranny or to provide incentives for states to adopt policies that match their citizens' preferences, but rather to avoid civil war or secession. Federalism promotes not public accountability or state efficiency but rather peace and territorial integrity. Post-conflict federalism pursues different goals than classical federalism and thus provides an opportunity to revisit the basic assumptions underlying the field.

Advocacy of federalism as a tool for managing ethnic conflict continues to grow, with respect to a diverse set of cases that spans the globe from South and East Asia to Eastern Europe. However, its purported benefits have been challenged by those who argue that federalism exacerbates, instead of mitigates, ethnic conflict. This academic debate about the merits of post-conflict federalism has reached an impasse, largely as a consequence of methodology. Proponents and opponents of drawing boundaries to empower national minorities point to different cases of federal success and failure. But recent scholarship in comparative politics that combines large-sample quantitative analysis with small-sample qualitative case studies promises a way forward. It shows how we might test these competing claims about the ability of federalism to control ethnic conflict across a variety of cases and begin to identify the factors that explain when post-conflict federalism succeeds and when it does not.

These global debates are highly relevant to Asia. This chapter brings those debates to bear on Asia, and draws on an earlier contribution that explored these issues on a global canvas (Choudhry and Hume 2011). It first reviews the literature on classical federalism (Section II), and turns to a discussion of post-conflict federalism (Section III). Finally, it explores the purchase of post-conflict federalism in three Asian cases: India, Sri Lanka, and the Philippines (Section IV).

II. CLASSICAL FEDERALISM

Three questions dominate the classical literature on comparative federalism: What is federalism? Why should we adopt it? What role is there for courts? These questions and the standard answers to them are drawn from the experiences of a few canonical federal states and the dominant academic accounts of those experiences. The model I call "classical federalism" emerges from these analyses.

A. What is Federalism?

What is federalism? In his seminal *Federal Government*, K.C. Wheare provided this influential definition of the "federal principle": for a state to be federal, "the general and regional governments must be coordinate and independent in their respective spheres" (Wheare 1964: 4–5). The constitutional implications of this federal principle included a written constitution expressly conferring powers on the central and regional governments, a system of direct elections for both levels of government, the power of each level of government to act (or not act) independently of the other, and the existence of an independent high court to serve as the "umpire" of federalism. This definition has informed many investigations into the political, social and institutional conditions required for different orders of government to preserve their independence while coordinating their actions (Elazar 1987). It also has inspired scholars to propose other definitions. For example, William Riker criticized Wheare for fostering a legalistic approach to federalism and offered an alternative formula: federalism is "a political organization in which the activities of government are divided between regional governments and a central government in such a way that each kind of government has some activities on which it makes final decisions" (Riker 1975: 101). While Riker's definition does not emphasize the use of constitutions to create and entrench federal arrangements, it is identical in substance (Riker 1964: 11). Ronald Watts, by contrast, elaborated Wheare's constitutional model. He added the formal distribution of legislative and executive authority, the allocation of sufficient revenues to ensure the autonomy of each order of government, the representation of regional views in the central legislature (e.g. through an upper chamber), a constitutional amendment procedure requiring a substantial degree of regional consent, and an enforcement mechanism that included courts, referendums or a special role for the upper chamber (Watts 1966).

Wheare developed his definition from a set of standard cases that embodied the federal principle to varying degrees: Australia, Canada, Switzerland and the United States. To be sure, Watts extended the field to the new federations then emerging from the British Empire (i.e., India, Pakistan, Malaysia, Nigeria, Rhodesia, and the West Indies) and firmly demonstrated that federalism was not confined to Wheare's four original cases. But those classical federal constitutions set the intellectual agenda for the study of federalism, and they continue to serve as the focus, or at least the point of departure, for orthodox engagements in comparative federalism. As the initial and most prominent modern example of federalism, the United States is often considered first among equals. Although Daniel Elazar attributed a biblical pedigree to his preferred definition ("shared rule plus self rule"), he identified American federalism as the prototype for modern federalism and used it to orient his explorations in the field (Elazar 1987: 12, 144–146). Riker also used his model of American federalism to make sense of federal experiments elsewhere (Riker 1964; Stepan 2001). With its rich history and widespread influence, American federalism remains a valuable foil for contemporary developments elsewhere, including the European Union (see, for example, Nicolaidis and Howse 2001). This narrow focus has facilitated comparative investigation, but it also has limited the relevance of the literature. The four central cases are relatively stable, prosperous and democratic. They have rarely faced domestic threats to their very existence. The theories and models that have resulted from elaborating their conditions may illuminate aspects of their experience but, at the same time, obscure distinctive developments elsewhere. Many legal scholars interested in comparative federalism have followed the lead of these political scientists by examining the same classical cases and seeking to elaborate or complement their arguments (see, for example, Aroney 2006).

The question of what is federalism has raised two derivative questions. First, what is *not* federalism? Historically, scholars were preoccupied with distinguishing federations from confederations on the basis of the mechanism for choosing political office-holders in central institutions. In federations, citizens elect central governments directly, whereas in confederations, delegates of regional governments run central institutions (Watts 1998). More recently, scholars have emphasized the distinction between devolution and decentralization, on the one hand, and federalism, on the other (Cross 2002; Feeley and Rubin 2008). Devolution and decentralization have the same political dynamic and legal form. They both involve the redistribution of authority and capacity from the central government to smaller, subordinate units of government. Consistent with this dynamic, attempts to devolve and decentralize power typically take the form of laws or regulations adopted unilaterally by the central government, in contrast to federal constitutions, which are often understood as compacts among the constituent regions. Although similar in many ways, devolution is thought to entail larger and more powerful

sub-units than decentralization: comparable to provinces and municipalities, respectively (Grindle 2009). In contemporary discussions, devolution is regularly identified with the United Kingdom, while
decentralization is observed in a large number of jurisdictions. However,
the lack of standard definitions for devolution and decentralization make
generalizations of this sort unhelpful. Following Wheare's definition, the
key difference between federalism and these other forms of government
is that the autonomy of the regions that comprise a federation is
guaranteed by a constitution that the central government may not alter
unilaterally, whereas the institutions that exercise delegated powers in a
decentralized or devolved political system may have their powers modified or revoked by the central government, often through the ordinary
legislative process.

Second, which constitutions that appear to be federal truly deserve that
label? Even if the central and regional governments derive their powers
from a constitution, on closer inspection that constitution may fall short
of federal status. Wheare himself originally described India and even
Canada as "quasi-federal" due to their centralizing tendencies. In Canada,
he was concerned with the power of the federal government to prevent
provincial laws from coming into force (disallowance) or to set aside
provincial legislation (reservation); in India, he was bothered by the
power of Parliament to unilaterally create new states and change state
boundaries, as well as the power of the central government to assume the
direct rule of states in an emergency (President's rule) (Wheare 1964).
The difficulties raised by the standard definition prompted Elazar to
pursue a more ambitious project, in which he sought to catalogue the
many institutional manifestations ("species" or "expressions") of the
federal principle, from confederations and federacies to leagues and
condominiums (Elazar 1987: 38–59). Such conceptual and categorical
refinements may help to resolve certain descriptive or theoretical controversies. From the standpoint of public policy, their value is more
ambiguous. On the one hand, they serve to catalogue the variety of
constitutional forms through which states can respect the federal principle. In short, they indicate the broad scope for constitutional choice. On
the other hand, they may draw political actors into debates over categor-
ization (e.g. whether a proposed constitutional design is federal or
confederal) that divert attention from the concrete political problems to
which federalism is a response. Such debates might lead political actors
to conclude that the constitutional forms discussed exhaust the institutional possibilities of federalism, when they are better understood as
variations on a theme that remains open to a great deal of adaptation and
experimentation.

Some scholars working within the traditional paradigm have responded to these concerns by performing empirical surveys of existing federal systems (see, for example, Griffiths 2005; Halberstam and Reimann forthcoming; Kincaid and Tarr 2005; Majeed et al. 2006; Watts 2008). These surveys extend far beyond the four core cases of Australia, Canada, Switzerland and the United States. However, the current literature suffers from shortcomings. Although these studies amass a large amount of material on federalism and its many forms, they are rarely analytical and generally do not seek to explain the commonalities and diversity that exist in the design and operation of federal systems. Moreover, there has been little attempt to evaluate the success of the design choices made by different federations. The flight from prescription is fuelled by the methodology of these studies, which employ a minimal or ecumenical definition of federalism and aim to identify its various manifestations. This line of research should therefore be understood as an important first step that provides the raw material for more analytical and prescriptive work.

B.   Why Federalism?

Classical federalism presupposes a shared account of how federations come into being. Federations form from pre-existing political units that are politically independent from each other. They may be sovereign states or colonies in an imperial order that lack full statehood but enjoy extensive rights of self-government. These political units are the actors that decide to form a new political community, which entails the pooling and surrendering of some of their sovereignty to a central government while retaining an important degree of autonomy. The central government's authority is derived from this political agreement. The federal constitution is a pact, compact or bargain among the regions; this agreement constitutes the central government, creates its institutions and allocates powers to them. Riker built his theory of federalism on this account, which Al Stepan aptly terms "coming-together federalism" (Stepan 2001: 320).

Set against this backdrop, "why federalism?" becomes a two-part question. First, "why should existing political units combine in any form?" Scholars of classical federalism tend to invoke either collective security or economic prosperity (Riker 1964; Wheare 1964). A federation can be understood as a mutual defence alliance against external military threats. Whether the threat comes from a former colonial ruler or another state seeking to expand its territory, the members of a federation can provide a more effective deterrent together than alone. A federation also can be understood as a common market that is larger and more efficient than one in which international borders impede the flow of goods, services and capital.

Since political units that desire such military and economic benefits could choose to pursue them by pooling their sovereignty in a new unitary state, the second part of "why federalism?" is "why federalism and not unitary rule?" As a preliminary matter, federalism may reduce the burden of coming together and thus make union more likely and more durable than if previously independent units sought to form a single unitary state. Federalism allows groups that have a history of self-government or a distinct culture or economy to preserve some measure of autonomy (Watts 1966; Wheare 1964). By definition, it offers the benefits of unity without the costs of imposing uniformity on a diverse population.

Once formed, a classical federal system is believed to offer numerous advantages over a unitary state. For example, it is thought to bolster democracy by guaranteeing the existence of a tier of regional governments. It ensures another set of offices to elect and contest and thus promotes political competition, by ensuring that political parties which lose power at the federal level may wield power at the sub-national level, thereby providing them with the benefits of incumbency to contest for power at the national level. It increases the number of opportunities for political participation, and also improves the quality of political participation by empowering relatively small political communities, in which citizens are more likely to have more in common, individual votes and voices are likely to have more influence, and representatives are likely to be more responsive to their concerns (see, for example, Friedman 1997; Merritt 1988). Classical federalism also is said to enhance efficiency in various ways. The existence of two tiers of government allows a diverse society to allocate responsibilities and assign liabilities in a manner that improves the quantity and quality of public goods by engineering a closer fit between those who benefit from them and those who bear the cost. Those goods, like military defence, that the regions might fail to produce adequately can be assigned to the central government, while those that depend on local knowledge and preferences, like education and perhaps some aspects of environmental regulation, can be left to the regions (Esty 1996; Revesz 1996). In addition, federalism makes it easier for citizens to move from one region to another, which means they can sort themselves into like-minded communities and, through the enduring threat of exit, impel their governments to satisfy their diverse policy preferences as well as or better than another regional government might (Tiebout 1956). Finally, federalism is believed to protect liberty by reinforcing limited government. By dividing power between the two levels of government, it gives politicians at each level the incentives and the means to prevent their counterparts from abusing their constitutional authority (Amar 1991; Hamilton 1788: No. 51; Merritt 1988). By engineering a competition among regional governments for mobile people, resources and money, it also ensures that those governments face economic and political pressure to refrain from infringing upon property rights and markets: a result that just so happens to enhance economic efficiency across the federal system (Weingast 1995).

These arguments prompt an array of critical responses. Some concern the manner in which federalism has been implemented: actual regions are too big, centralized and heterogeneous to deliver the democratic dividends associated with small political units (Briffault 1994; Cross 2002); they are too few and too similar (and the practical constraints on the mobility of individuals and ideas remain too severe) to sustain meaningful inter-jurisdictional competition and thus do not enhance efficiency or promote innovation as promised (Daniels 1991; Feeley and Rubin 2008); they have not, in practice, served as reliable bulwarks against encroachments on individual and group liberties, whether by central governments or other regions (Shapiro 1995); their boundaries are too rigid and arbitrary to capture the myriad externalities their policies produce (e.g. positive and negative, economic and environmental), and agreements to redistribute those burdens and benefits efficiently are too difficult to negotiate and enforce, so they are not likely to supply an optimal bundle of public goods, regulatory or otherwise (Levy 2007). Other criticisms concern inherent characteristics of federalism. Most importantly, federalism has democratic costs that must be weighed against its contested democratic benefits. While it empowers discrete provincial majorities to make certain decisions, it compromises the ability of the national majority to set policies for the entire country. Indeed, by setting constitutional limits on the concentration and exercise of government authority, federalism may frustrate attempts to address our most pressing moral and practical problems (Riker 1964; Stepan 2001).

The arguments for and against federalism are well known. Many of them are drawn from American experience, and together they constitute the intellectual framework for contemporary analytical work on federalism within the classical mould. Although debates about federalism remain vigorous, the classical framework within which they occur is fairly stable. These criteria do not themselves require comparative analysis, and there is a vast body of country-specific work that relies on them without reference to foreign federal examples. Although the bulk of this work is done in economics and political science, legal scholars contribute to and draw upon this literature. In the American legal academy, for example, there has been an extensive debate on environmental policy and federalism. Participants dispute not only the optimal allocation of responsibility for environmental regulation among the federal and state governments but also the proper basis on which to make such decisions (see, for example, Stewart 1977; Revesz 2001).

In addition, there have been a smaller number of comparative studies that draw upon this intellectual framework in specific substantive areas. The work is both analytical and prescriptive. Comparative models offer both negative and positive guidance. Barry Weingast has collaborated with other scholars to elaborate and apply his conception of market-preserving federalism in countries from England and the United States to India and Russia (Figueiredo et al. 2007; Parikh and Weingast 1997). Similar projects have considered topics that range from environmental regulation (Farber 1997; Kimber 1995) and the evolution of corporate law (Deakin 2006; McCahery and Vermeulen 2005; Stith 1991) to the fight against cybercrime (Mendez 2005). The arguments may be familiar but, perhaps for that very reason, "why federalism?" remains a rich and relevant question.

C. What Role for Courts?

Comparative legal analyses of the judicial role in federations present a puzzle. Scholars and statesmen alike have long recognized that courts are an important, if not an integral, component of federal government because of the need for a mechanism to resolve jurisdictional disputes (Madison, Hamilton and Jay: Federalist No. 78; Watts 1966; Wheare 1964). Not surprisingly, constitutional judicial review first developed in three of the classical federations: the United States, Canada and Australia. As federalism spread to Latin America in the nineteenth century, judicial review came along with it. Indeed, the rise and spread of judicial federalism occurred more than a century before the global diffusion of judicial power associated with the "Rights Revolution" and the third wave of democratization. However, whereas this more recent phenomenon has inspired an explosion of comparative literature, judicial federalism has attracted less comparative attention.

In part, this may be a function of the different roles played by courts of final appeal in maintaining different federal systems. In India, debates over state boundaries and the imposition of President's Rule eclipse questions about the role of courts in the federal system. Likewise Ethiopia, where disputes between the ethnic groups that comprise the federation are resolved not by judges but by the upper house of

Parliament (Baylis 2004). By contrast, the United States Supreme Court has been actively engaged in the adjudication of federalism disputes during various periods of American history. This discrepancy, coupled with the passionate American debate over judicial review, may explain why the bulk of the comparative work on judicial federalism is American in origin. But even in the United States, it has been suggested that the primary determinants of the federal balance lie in the political process, and that courts play the role of enforcing constitutional baselines, such as subsidiarity, the right to free movement, the institutional integrity of the federal and state governments, the prohibition on state discrimination against persons, goods and services originating in other states, and the various burdens of justification for government action (Halberstam 2008).

The literature on courts and comparative federalism emphasizes both substance and method. The former involves the constitutional concepts, rules and doctrines appropriate or even necessary for a court operating within a federal system. These include democratic ideals, conflict-of-laws rules, tests for territorial jurisdiction and, more controversially, an anti-commandeering principle (see, for example, Halberstam 2001). Such tools enable courts to maintain and even tinker with the federal structures of their constitutions as circumstances and endeavours evolve. For example, the Supreme Court of Canada has selectively invoked American constitutional text and doctrine to support the introduction of unwritten constitutional principles of order, fairness and efficiency that reconcile elements of Canadian private international law and thus the Canadian federal system to what it perceives as contemporary economic imperatives (Hume 2006).

The latter concerns the risks, benefits and legitimacy of judicial references to foreign law when dealing with federal aspects of the constitution. Some theorists encourage such references because knowledge about foreign arrangements can illuminate new domestic possibilities and clarify existing practices. For example, Halberstam suggests that German constitutional practice could serve as a model for American courts to shift the political morality underlying American federalism jurisprudence from one that emphasizes the entitlements of different orders of government to decide whether to act in a cooperative or competitive manner to a fidelity approach that imposes duties to co-operate and act responsibly in the interest of the entire system (Halberstam 2004). Others are more equivocal about the relevance of foreign federal experiments for domestic judges, since federal constitutions are package deals defined by contextual compromises. More a product of pragmatism than of principle, their lessons often require intimate knowledge of their history and operation, which judges from other countries rarely possess. Nonetheless, Vicki Jackson concedes that judges might profit from studying foreign experience when deciding issues of federal structure and constitutional principle on which the relevant text is silent (Jackson 2004).

These debates are important, but their importance is limited to those countries in which courts play a major part in the federal system. Such issues are unlikely to resonate in federal states where the constitution is viewed predominantly as a contested, contingent political compromise rather than as a settled legal framework for the resolution of political controversies. More generally, arguments that deduce the nature and implications of federalism from a small and increasingly unrepresentative sample of states risk error and irrelevance when applied beyond that narrow realm.

III. POST-CONFLICT FEDERALISM

A. Setting the Stage

Scholars who contribute to the literature of classical federalism disagree on many important issues: the goals served by federalism, their relative priority, the weight of any countervailing considerations and the manner in which the design of a federal system should reflect these calculations. However, this literature also tends to rely on a shared yet generally tacit set of basic assumptions. These assumptions include the following: once pre-existing political units have come together in a federal state, they shall remain members of a single political community bound in a common constitutional order; this new political community is a nation that inhabits the entire territory of the state and possesses the right to self-government; and debates over the design of the federal system are debates about how this nation should organize itself internally and thus do not raise the prior question of whether the nation should continue to exist.

That existential question is precisely what lies at the heart of constitutional politics in what Choudhry has termed a divided society (Choudhry 2008). As a category of political and constitutional analysis, a divided society is not merely a society that is ethnically, linguistically, religiously or culturally diverse. The age of the ethnoculturally homogeneous state, if there ever was one, is long over. What marks a divided society is that these differences are politically salient. That is, they are persistent markers of political identity and bases for political mobilization. In a divided society, ethnocultural diversity translates into political fragmentation: political claims are refracted through the lens of ethnic identity, and political conflict is synonymous with conflict among ethnocultural groups.

Scholars of ethnic politics have long drawn distinctions among different types of ethnic groups. There are many dimensions on which to do so: the relationship they assert between ethnicity and territory, the manner in which they have been incorporated into their respective states, their relative economic and political status, the terms in which they frame their constitutional arguments and the substance of their constitutional claims. One such type is what Will Kymlicka has termed a national minority (Kymlicka 1995). National minorities are regionally concentrated ethnic groups who once enjoyed political autonomy and have become part of states in which they constitute an ethnic minority through conquest, colonization or voluntary incorporation. Other terms for this type of ethnic group include "ethnonationalists" (Gurr 1993: 18–20). They mobilize politically around assertions of national identity and self-determination. The goal of such mobilization is to recover the extensive self-government they claim to have enjoyed historically. The degree of self-government they seek ranges from autonomy to independent statehood, which would entail secession. National minorities accept the premise that states are the means by which nations exercise their right to self-determination over their territory, but they use this premise to challenge particular combinations of state, nation and territory. National minorities argue that the state in which they live contains more than one nation, that each of those nations possesses an inherent and identical right to self-determination, and that they are therefore entitled to their own separate state.

Why do national minorities mobilize, and why do they anchor their specific policy goals around the right to self-determination? The "grievance" or "relative deprivation" school of civil war studies, which focuses on the question of how ethnic conflict becomes violent, offers a leading answer to these questions. On this account, ethnic difference per se is not the spark for the rise of ethnic politics. Rather, ethnic groups mobilize politically in response to their experience of economic and political disadvantage. Political disadvantage entails the systematic limitation of access to political office or basic political rights; economic disadvantage involves the systematic denial of economic goods and opportunities. The different dimensions of disadvantage are often mutually reinforcing: political disadvantage insulates politics from attempts to address economic disadvantage, and economic disadvantage undermines an ethnic group's ability to exercise political influence. Ethnic groups vary in their response to disadvantage. Some groups may demand the reform of those state institutions in which they are consistently outvoted. National minorities entertain secession because they desire the additional protection that comes from forming a political majority in an independent state. Most ethnic groups demand voice; national minorities emphasize exit.

Some states resist political mobilization by national minorities because the very existence of such groups threatens the equation of nation, state and territory on which those states base their claims to political legitimacy. A state that perceives its territory as indivisible and integral to its identity may be more likely to react in that manner (Toft 2003). In such cases, there is a clash between competing nationalisms with parallel logics: a minority nationalism that is confined to one region and seeks to realign nations, states and territories; and a statewide nationalism that asserts the exclusive existence of a single nation throughout the territory of the state and thus denies the need for realignment. Gurr argues that the conflict between competing nationalisms typically escalates in stages: from non-violent protest to violent protest and finally to rebellion. This escalation occurs through a pattern of demands and responses: non-violent protest is met with a lack of political responsiveness, which in turn leads to violent protest, which is met with a violent reaction, and which then leads to rebellion and an armed conflict (i.e. civil war). Indeed, the evidence suggests that self-determination disputes are the most common variety of civil war and are more resistant to settlement than other kinds of disputes, especially when states face more than one potential separatist claim (Walter 2009).

B. Theoretical Debate

This diagnosis suggests that minority nationalism may lead to civil war and secession. The question is whether federalism, either on its own or as part of a larger package of constitutional reforms, is an effective response that diminishes these risks and serves peace and territorial integrity. This question has sparked a vigorous academic debate (Hale 2008). Scholars fall into one of two diametrically opposed camps. One school holds that federalism can dampen secessionist sentiment; the other holds that federalism will in fact fuel it. In other words, federalism is either a solution or a catalyst for ethnic violence. Thus framed, these two positions are mutually exclusive.

Classical federalism cannot answer this question because it focuses on polities in which the existence of the nation is not the crux of constitutional politics. For example, although Wheare and Watts observe how federal systems can accommodate racial, religious and linguistic differences, these concerns are peripheral to their work. By contrast, this is the central question for post-conflict federalism and it is the subject of vigorous and ongoing debate. The core design feature of post-conflict federalism is the drawing of internal borders to ensure that a national minority constitutes a majority in a region. The allocation of jurisdiction between different levels of government ensures that the national minority is not outvoted by the majority and has sufficient powers to protect itself from economic and political disadvantage. These arrangements are constitutionally entrenched and enforced by independent courts. This approach has been variously termed multinational federalism, plurinational federalism, ethnic federalism or ethnofederalism. It even shares some features and sympathies with what Stefan Wolff has labelled "complex power sharing" (Wolff 2009). Here, I refer to "post-conflict federalism" because I want to focus on how federalism in particular can help to contain and perhaps quell ethnic conflict. Although some of the societies that have adopted the arrangements I discuss have not yet suffered secession, ethnic violence or civil war, the term "post-conflict" is still appropriate, since federalism is designed to prevent such conflict from occurring, and those societies are often deployed as positive constitutional models in post-conflict contexts.

The stakes in these debates are very high. Many states in the developing world, such as Ethiopia, Iraq, Nigeria and Sudan, have adopted federal solutions to control ethnic conflict, often as part of a package of post-conflict constitutional design. Moreover, the advocacy of federalism as a tool for managing ethnic conflict continues to gather momentum around the globe. Federalism has also been proposed as a remedy to the frozen conflicts of the former Soviet Union: Armenia, Azerbaijan, Georgia, Abkhazia, South Ossetia, and Nagorno Karabach. In the world of post-conflict constitutional design, it has been "marketed as a palliative to secessionist conflict" (Erk and Anderson 2009: 191). However, while Philip Roeder seems to suggest that post-conflict federalism has emerged as the presumptive policy prescription to manage ethnonationalist conflict, Will Kymlicka has the better view. He carefully charts how, in Eastern and Central Europe, international institutions have taken a much more ambivalent and complex stance on post-conflict federalism, firmly rejecting it as part of the emerging international legal framework regarding the rights of national minorities, while accepting it on a case-by-case basis in order to diffuse violent conflict (Kymlicka 2007; Roeder 2009). But even with that caveat, if federalism exacerbates rather than mitigates conflict, then the most recent wave of constitutional design proceeds from dangerously erroneous premises. It is vitally important to determine how federalism actually performs in such difficult circumstances.

The centre of gravity in this academic debate is firmly anchored in political science. Ethnonationalism and secession have been studied by scholars working from a variety of sub-fields within that discipline: political sociology, comparative politics, international relations and political theory. Although their debates, questions, motivations, frameworks and methodologies may differ, these scholars share a reliance on qualitative research methods that focus on a relatively small number of cases to explain the complex relationship between constitutional design and political behaviour in states with politically mobilized national minorities.

On the one hand, there are those who argue that federalism dampens secessionist sentiment. Kymlicka, a political theorist, is representative of this position (Kymlicka 1998). He proceeds from the starting point that ethnic conflict in states with politically mobilized national minorities is, at root, a conflict between competing nationalisms. This is a zero-sum conflict in which one side will necessarily lose. If secession occurs, a statewide nationalism will lose territory that belongs to the nation as a whole. If secession does not occur, minority nationalists will argue that state and nation must still be brought into alignment. Kymlicka's case for multinational federalism responds by challenging the premise that there must be a one-to-one correspondence between nation and state. Post-conflict federalism acknowledges that the state contains more than one constituent nation and structures its institutions in such a way as to recognize and empower each of them. Post-conflict federalism halts the clamour for secession without dismembering the state because it satisfies the demand for self-determination with powers of self-government that fall short of independent statehood. Although they differ in some respects, many scholars have in essence taken this position: Nancy Bermeo, Rogers Brubaker, Ted Gurr, Yash Ghai, Arend Lijphart, Al Stepan, and John McGarry and Brendan O'Leary (Bermeo 2002; Brubaker 1996; Ghai 2000; Gurr 2000; Lijphart 1977; McGarry and O'Leary 2009; Stepan 1999).

At first blush, post-conflict federalism may superficially resemble Riker's "coming-together" federalism because each bases the legitimacy of federal arrangements on the consent of the constituent units, which create and empower a central entity as part of a constitutional bargain. But upon closer examination, both the process of creating a post-conflict federation and the premises on which it relies are quite different. In most cases, a post-conflict federation is created from a state that already exists, and the constitutional imperative is not to make a new state but to reconstitute the existing one along federal lines in order to prevent it from coming apart. The process of reconstituting an existing state as a post-conflict federation is suitably described as "holding together" an existing political entity for which the alternative to reconstitution is secession or perhaps even dissolution (Stepan 1999). For Riker federalism is just one, often unsatisfactory, way for a nation to exercise its right to self-government. The existence of a single political community, which governs itself through the institutions and procedures created by the constitution, is not in question. For post-conflict federalism, this is the fundamental question. To transform a unitary, devolved or classical federal state into a post-conflict federation entails more than changes to its constitutional structure. It requires a new understanding of the state as the institutional compromise required to preserve a composite or layered political community in which the basic question of constitutional politics is what the terms of political association should be among the constituent nations (Simeon and Conway 2001).

This brief, abstract account of post-conflict federalism contains a number of ambiguities on precise questions of constitutional design that require further research. Consider the causal mechanism whereby federalism dampens the demand for secession. In the world of post-conflict federalism, secession is a defensive response to the policies of the central government. For federalism to be a substitute for secession, it must remedy the disadvantages these policies cause by providing a constitutional self-defence mechanism for the aggrieved minority nation. But scholars differ on the character of the disadvantages against which federalism is a defence. The design of an effective post-conflict federalism will accordingly vary depending on the nature of the harms to which it is a response. Kymlicka (2001) and Brubaker (1996) emphasize culture. They use the concept of nation-building to describe a set of policies that aim to create a shared national identity across a state by promoting a common language and shared historical narrative. For them, regional jurisdiction over education and the language of the public and private sectors will be of paramount importance. Scholars who highlight the failure by central governments to ensure that national minorities receive adequate benefits from the extraction of natural resources in their territories will prioritize regional or local ownership, management and revenue sharing. Gurr dwells on instances of political discrimination, such as the exclusion of national minorities from political power and public sector employment. On this account, any federal arrangements would multiply the opportunities to wield political power.

Set against those who promote post-conflict federalism as a tool to manage and prevent ethnonationalist conflict, there are scholars who argue that it not only will fail to stem secession but will have precisely the opposite effect and intensify the conflict it purports to manage. Philip Roeder has offered the most recent and extended argument of this position. He claims that post-conflict federalism is inherently unstable and is characterized by a constant struggle between the two extremes of centralization and secession: "a recurring crisis of politics" that is oriented around "competing nation-state projects that pit homeland governments against the common-state government" (Roeder 2009: 209). This political pattern is the product of four purportedly unavoidable consequences of post-conflict federalism.

First, post-conflict federalism shapes the development of political identities, in particular, regional political identities. The creation of an ethnically defined region has the effect of institutionally privileging a conception of regional political identity in which the region is imagined as the property and homeland of an ethnic group. Post-conflict federalism also provides regions with the political and economic resources to develop these distinct identities through jurisdiction over education, the adoption of official language policies and cultural policy instruments such as public holidays and monuments. These regional identities will compete with statewide political identities as a source of citizen identification and belonging. They will become political resources for regional political elites to mobilize support during conflicts with central authorities. Second, the multiplication of national identities within post-conflict federations transforms the character of political conflict between the centre and the regions. Moments of high constitutional politics that raise constitutive questions regarding the status and the powers of the national minority and the relationship between the two nation-building projects crowd out ordinary policy disputes; the latter are reframed as raising fundamental questions regarding the right to self-determination. National identity becomes the principal political cleavage. As a consequence, political debate runs the constant risk of escalating from the demand for greater powers toward the existential constitutional question of secession, which would be the logical culmination of the nation-building project of the national minority. Third, post-conflict federalism endows regional governments with coercive policy instruments that national minorities can use as institutional weapons against central authorities, whether by engaging in competitive nation-building or by pushing for enhanced powers and greater autonomy. Such instruments may include the power to interfere with statewide electoral processes and revenue collection. Finally, the constitutional empowerment of the regions entails not just autonomy but also an institutionalized voice in common institutions, up to and including vetoes. These vetoes can weaken the decision-making ability of central authorities and hobble their ability to exercise their authority and thwart minority nationalism. Roeder's views are shared by other scholars (Bunce 1999; Crawford 1998; Leff 1999).

Roeder presents these four features as flowing from the logic of post-conflict federalism and, by implication, as absent from mononational federations. But this is not entirely true. The political resources he identifies – the ability to interfere with the operation of central authorities through coercive means and regional vetoes in central institutions – are contingent features of constitutional design that do not inhere in the very nature of post-conflict federations. To be sure, these were features of the constitution of the Soviet Union, and Roeder generalizes from the failure of the Soviet Union to argue that multinational federalism will fail more generally. But it is legitimate to ask whether the same patterns will hold in post-conflict federations that lack these institutional elements. Roeder himself states that "[t]inkering with the institutional details of different forms of ethnofederalism or autonomy is unlikely to exorcise the demons, for the devil is to be found in ethnofederalism and autonomy arrangements themselves" (2009: 207), which suggests that post-conflict federalism will collapse regardless of their adoption. However, the logic of his account suggests they are necessary for post-conflict federalism to fail. Moreover, if the presence of these features is necessary for federal failure, it is not sufficient, because they are also present in some enduring mononational federations. So Roeder's critique really turns not on the presence of these political resources but on the impact of political agendas on their use. At the root of the political dynamics that he describes are the new political agendas nurtured by post-conflict federalism: in particular, the institutionalization of minority nationalism through the designation of a region as a national minority's homeland. Since this new political orientation is precisely the point of post-conflict federalism, his critique strikes at its very heart.

C. Evidence

Both academic camps – those who advocate the use of post-conflict federalism to manage ethnonational conflict, and those who oppose doing so – support their arguments by reference to examples of federal success and federal failure. This debate was sparked by the collapse of the former communist dictatorships of Eastern and Central Europe (ECE) in the early 1990s (Choudhry 2007). Students of ECE were confronted with a jarring contrast. Three of the former ECE communist dictatorships – Yugoslavia, the Soviet Union and Czechoslovakia – had been post-conflict federations prior to the transition to democracy. All three began to disintegrate within 18 months after embracing democracy. By contrast, unitary states, including several with large national minorities (e.g. Poland, Hungary) and some in which nationalism served as the axis of internal political conflict, did not fall apart. If the ambition of post-conflict federalism is to manage competing nation-building projects within a single state, federalism may in fact have failed to meet its basic objective. Yet the problem went deeper still. Since only the post-conflict federations broke up, and all of them did, the suspicion was that federalism had fuelled secession, whereas unitary state structures prevented it. So in ECE, post-conflict federalism had fuelled precisely those political forces it was designed to suppress. ECE has been central to the case against post-conflict federalism. Indeed, scholars who argue that post-conflict federalism inflames ethnonational conflict have tended to be specialists on ECE who have extended their arguments to indict post-conflict federalism more generally.

The best way to respond to the anti-models of Yugoslavia, Czechoslovakia and the Soviet Union was to identify models where post-conflict federalism had actually worked. In the literature, the leading counter-examples are Canada, India and Spain. The founding of the Canadian federation in 1867 and the creation of Quebec was a direct response to the failure of the United Province of Canada, a British colony that existed from 1840 to 1867 and that had two wings: one with a French-speaking majority and one with an English-speaking majority. Each wing elected equal numbers of representatives to a legislative assembly, although the largely French-speaking citizens of the former outnumbered the largely English-speaking citizens of the latter. The goal behind the merger and the departure from representation by population was linguistic assimilation. The English-speaking wing eventually became more populous and demanded greater representation in the joint legislature, a request that was resisted by the French-speaking wing, which feared it would be outvoted on matters important to its linguistic identity. The result was political paralysis. Federalism was the solution: a compromise that provided representation by population at the federal level, but also created a Quebec with jurisdiction over those matters crucial to the survival of a French-speaking society in that province. Had Quebec not been created, it is likely that the French-speaking parts of Canada would have eventually seceded.

This academic debate has reached an impasse, largely as a consequence of methodology. As Dawn Brancati has argued, the use of qualitative case studies are at best "useful for generating interesting ideas about decentralization" but "do not provide strong evidence of their claims" (Brancati 2006: 653). The reason is that scholars tend to select cases on the basis of the dependent variable, with critics studying the failed communist-era federations of ECE, and advocates analyzing the more successful examples. But recent scholarship in comparative politics that employs large-sample quantitative studies holds the potential to advance our understanding of federalism's capacity to manage ethnic conflict. Such studies can test competing empirical claims across a broad variety of cases and identify the factors that explain when post-conflict federalism succeeds and when it does not.

Three studies warrant discussion.

First, Roeder recently constructed a global database around the notion of the "segmented state", which he defines as a state that "divides its territory and population into separate jurisdictions, and gives the population that purportedly is indigenous to each jurisdiction a distinct political status" (Roeder 2007: 12). In such states, there is a "common state" that possesses jurisdiction over the entire population and territory, as well as separate "segment-states" that have jurisdiction over a portion of that territory and people. A segment-state is not merely a territorial subdivision; it contains "peoples who purportedly have special claim to that jurisdiction as a homeland" (12–13). Roeder observes that, in the twentieth century, 86 per cent of new states had been segment-states prior to independence, from which he concludes that segmented states are far more likely to experience secession than are states that are not segmented. Although Roeder does not use the language of post-conflict federalism, it clearly overlaps with his definition of a segmented state. The interesting question Roeder poses is under what conditions secession from the segmented state (or post-conflict federation) is more likely. Roeder answers this question by reference to a global data set of segmented states created before 1990, with annual observations. The independent variables were (a) the constitutional relationship between the common-state and segment-state, on a spectrum ranging from fully exclusive common-state autocracy to fully inclusive common-state democracy, and (b) whether the segment-state was self-governing or not. His key finding is that, in anocracies and democracies that excluded the population of segment-states from central governance, self-government in a segment-state increased the likelihood of secession. Since self-governing regions are core elements of post-conflict federalism and are designed to prevent secession, Roeder concludes that the evidence does not support this policy prescription and in fact counsels against it.

But Roeder's conclusion does not follow from his results. One of his most striking findings is that the most stable form of post-conflict federalism is a fully inclusive democracy in which the regions enjoy extensive forms of self-government. Two comparisons drawn from his data are important here: (1) inclusive democracies are much more stable than other regimes when their regions are not self-governing; and (2) unlike exclusionary democracies and anocracies, inclusive democracies do not suffer an increased risk of secession when their regions *are* self-governing. What this suggests is that the rise of secessionist politics might instead be a function of the structure of politics at the centre. Roeder's data do not offer an explanation as to why, but it is possible to speculate. The finding that exclusionary democracies are less stable than inclusive democracies is consistent with theories of minority nationalism that explain the rise of minority nationalism as a defensive response to the policies of the central state, whether characterized as nation-building or as economic, political or cultural discrimination. It may be that common states have a freer hand to pursue these policies when they exclude the populations of segment-states from central governance. At a prescriptive level, this suggests that proponents of post-conflict federalism should not neglect the design of central institutions. This points to the need for further research on the link between federalism and central power sharing, as discussed below.

Second, a more recent study by Lars-Erik Cederman and his colleagues supports the conclusion that federalism can reduce the likelihood of secession (Cederman et al. 2010). They work from the grievance school of civil war studies. Ethnic political mobilization can take a variety of forms. One hypothesis they test is that the probability of ethnonationalist conflict increases with the degree of exclusion from central executive power. To test the relationship between political exclusion and violent conflict, Cederman et al. constructed the Ethnic Power Relations data set (EPR), which identified all politically mobilized ethnic groups and measured their access to state power on an annual basis from 1946 to 2005. They draw an important set of distinctions between those groups that are excluded from central power: "regional autonomy" (elites wield local authority within the state, e.g. through federal arrangements), "separatist autonomy" (elites wield local authority coupled with declaration of independence), "powerless" (elites excluded from central and local authority without explicit discrimination) and "discrimination" (elites excluded from central and local authority as a consequence of deliberate discrimination). Violent conflict is linked to any ethnic group in whose name an armed group instigated conflict.

As anticipated, excluded groups are more likely to instigate violent conflict than those that are not excluded. But if one disaggregates excluded groups, those that enjoy regional autonomy are much less likely to instigate violent conflict than those that experience other forms of political exclusion. Even more striking is that groups that are excluded from central power but enjoy regional autonomy are *less* likely than those groups who are *included* in power – either as senior or junior partners – to instigate violent conflict. Although these observations are based on descriptive statistics and they change somewhat with regression analysis, with junior partners less likely to rebel than excluded groups that enjoy regional autonomy, the latter are still less likely to rebel than those that experience more severe forms of political exclusion, such as the power-less and the targets of discrimination. These results support the claims of those who argue that post-conflict federalism may operate as a conflict-management technique.

A third study takes the literature in a different direction. Federal arrangements may stem secession in some contexts but fuel it in others. The outcome may be a function of the central government's commitment to democratic inclusion but, as Brancati points out, federalism may fuel secession even in democratic states (Brancati 2009). The question is what additional factors explain the uneven effects of post-conflict federalism. The answer is to be found in the electoral strength of regional political parties. If they are strong, they can gain power and deploy the institutional resources provided by a federal constitutional structure to foster regional identity and mobilize a national minority around this identity to pursue secession; if they are weak, this is much less likely to happen. Regression analysis demonstrates that federalism reduces ethnic conflict and secession while controlling for the strength of regional parties, but that ethnic conflict increases with regional party electoral strength.

Critics of post-conflict federalism would counter that this constitutional arrangement itself fuels the rise of regional parties. But the evidence is more complex. While post-conflict federalism creates the opportunity for the rise of strong regional parties, they do not emerge in every post-conflict federation. The question is which other features of constitutional design, if any, determine whether that potential is realized. Brancati's principal findings are that regional parties are stronger (a) where there are more regional legislatures, because they provide more opportunities for regional parties to wield power; (b) where regional legislatures select the upper house of the central legislature, which increases the impact of regional parties in central institutions and creates additional incentives to form such parties; and (c) when national and regional elections occur at different times, which offsets the coat-tails effect pursuant to which elections to higher office influence the results in concurrent elections to lower offices.

Taken together, Brancati suggests that, in order to harness the benefits of federalism for managing ethnic conflict while mitigating its dangers, the focus should not be on federal design but on regional political parties.

This leads to two sets of policy proposals. One focuses on the rules governing political parties and electoral competition. For example, it suggests that parties that run in national elections should be required to field candidates in more than one region in order to win seats. Additional research is required to untangle the relationship between the electoral system and the rise of regional parties. But the other set of proposals shifts the focus to the centre, in particular the interaction of central institutions with regional political processes. Here, the prescriptions appear to point in opposite directions. Requiring direct elections for the upper chamber would appear to disentangle the central and regional governments, whereas coordinating the timing of central and regional elections would politically connect the two levels of government. However, if adopted as a package, the two measures should be understood as promoting the autonomy and priority of central political processes at the expense of the electoral strength of regional parties.

IV. POST-CONFLICT FEDERALISM: THREE ASIAN CASES

A. Federalism in Asia

Federalism is an increasingly prominent feature of constitutional design in Asia (Bertrand and Laliberté 2010; Bhattacharyya 2008; He, Galligan and Inoguchi 2009; Kymlicka and He 2005). The histories and trajectories of the Asian federations are diverse. Some federations are long-standing – federal constitutions have existed in India (discussed further below) and Malaysia for several decades, since independence from colonial rule, although they have undergone important reconfigurations since then. In the case of Pakistan, federalism existed in the post-independence period but was a casualty of military rule, and was recently restored after a hiatus of several decades as part of a return to civilian rule. Moreover, there are new federalisms on the horizon, under active discussion, or which are elements of broader political discourses on democratization and post-civil war settlement. Nepal has constitutionally committed itself to restructuring itself along federal lines, as part of its post-civil war transition to a democratic republican form of government. At the time of writing, it is engaged in a constitutional process to realize this commitment, in which the number and borders of sub-units has become a major point of contention. Over several decades, in Sri Lanka (as explored in further detail below), federalism was proffered as a solution to ethnic conflict, by creating a Tamil-majority area in the north-east of the island. As part of broader discussions over political reform in China, the idea of federalism is part of a broad array of constitutional options to institutionalize liberal democracy (Qian and Weingast 1997).

In addition, forms of territorial devolution other than federalism are part of the broader constitutional agenda across Asia. These are often bundled with federalism in constitutional debates as techniques to decentralize power, notwithstanding important conceptual distinctions between federalism and these options. The most relevant are highly asymmetric quasi-federal arrangements in which a high degree of autonomy is given to one or a limited number of territories that account for a small proportion of the national territory and population, on an asymmetric basis, while preserving the unitary character of the rest of the state. The leading examples are in Indonesia, which has adopted this strategy for addressing longstanding demands for territorial autonomy in Aceh and Irian Jaya through the enactment of special autonomy laws. In the Philippines (see below), asymmetric self-governing arrangements have been discussed for decades for the Bagnsamoro, the areas of the Mindanao claimed as the traditional homeland of the Moro. Asymmetric self-governing arrangements – sometimes referred to as federacies – are sometimes viewed as way stations to federalism, since their existence and success may serve as an experiment that may promote its diffusion across the state as a whole by reconstituting the remainder along federal lines. Myanmar is another example. Although the country was originally conceived of as federal, federalism was never adopted. Mayanmar's ethnic minorities now demand federalism as part of a post-authoritarian constitutional settlement. The likely outcome is a quasi-federal arrange-ment.

The justifications for federalism proffered in these jurisdictions trav-erse the divide between classical and post-conflict federalism. The democratic virtue of increased policy responsiveness is often advanced as an argument for federalism in response to distant central administrations that are indifferent or opposed to the policy priorities of regional minorities who are outvoted in central institutions. Another democratic justification for federalism is the promotion of political competition, by creating the possibility for parties in opposition at the statewide level to control a sub-unit where it can harness the advantages of political incumbency to better contest political power at the centre. These justifi-cations are offered side by side with those that anchor federalism as a mechanism to avoid or resolve longstanding conflict rooted in competing nation-building projects. In the three cases discussed below – India, Sri

Lanka and the Philippines – it is the conflict-prevention and resolution functions of federalism that have predominated.

B. India

Federalism has been at the centre of Indian constitutional politics since independence (Choudhry 2009). British India consisted of provinces administered by the British Crown and hundreds of princely states which were nominally self-governing allies of the British Crown. Given India's vast size and population, federalism was an unavoidable necessity. However, the controversial issue was whether provincial boundaries would coincide with linguistic boundaries. The most widely spoken language in India was Hindi, but it is only spoken by about 40 per cent of the population. There are a dozen regional languages in India, each spoken by millions of individuals and accompanied by scripts and literary traditions. Very few speakers of these languages also speak Hindi, and indeed, the principal languages of South India are from entirely different linguistic families. In addition, these languages are spoken in fairly self-confined linguistic regions.

The trauma of the partition of British India into India and Pakistan led India's Constituent Assembly to oppose linguistic provinces out of a fear that they would fuel secessionist mobilization in India's border states and doom the country to disintegration. The decision to organize provinces on a non-linguistic basis was coupled with a constitutional policy to promote Hindi as the official language at the national level after a transitional period of 15 years. The goal of this integrated constitutional strategy was to create a unified nation state whose central institutions would soon operate in a single, indigenous language, and to prevent future threats to India's territorial integrity by deliberately choosing not to create federal sub-units that were linguistically homogeneous and could generate sub-national political identities which could undermine citizens' loyalty and shared sense of political identity. Hindi would knit together a single, unified country capable of mutual intercourse in politics, the economy and public administration. Linguistic homogenization would further the objectives of enabling democratic participation, improving the efficiency of public administration, and enhancing social and economic mobility.

The demand for linguistic states arose as a defensive response to these policies. Advocates of what came to be known as "linguistic reorganization" argued that granting official language status to Hindi would have undemocratic consequences by redistributing economic and political power. Linguistic exclusiveness would consolidate political power in the hands of a Hindi-speaking elite and withdraw it from non-Hindi speakers by restricting access to public office. In addition, official language policies distribute access to public sector employment. Indeed, underlying political competition regarding official language status was economic competition for white-collar public sector employment. Indeed, they argued that far from preserving national integrity, insisting on Hindi alone at the centre would have the perverse effect of undermining it.

The rejection of linguistic provinces began to unravel soon after independence, with the creation of Andhra State (now Andhra Pradesh) in 1953. Once that precedent was established, it sparked a chain reaction of movements for linguistic states across India. The central government struck the States Reorganization Commission with the mandate of recommending the principles for redrawing state boundaries and the specific boundaries of new states. The Commission recommended the redrawing of provincial boundaries on provincial lines. Based on the Commission's recommendations, Parliament created 13 new linguistic states in 1956. In 1960 and 1966, two of these states were further divided into four states. The Indian case is without a doubt the most significant restructuring of political space in modern times in response to competing linguistic nationalisms through a constitutional process. Although India continues to face enormous challenges, it has successfully managed linguistic nationalism through federalism.

There are three broader lessons to be learned from the Indian experience of managing competing nationalisms through a post-conflict federalism. First, language is different from other grounds of group identity that can serve as the basis of political mobilization. If race, ethnicity or religion serves as the grounds of political cleavage, one constitutional strategy for managing these tensions is neutrality. But while the state can be neutral on the basis of race, religion or ethnicity, it cannot be neutral on the question of language. The state must operate in one or more languages for official purposes, in order to communicate internally and externally with its citizens. Thus, it is not possible to take language off the constitutional agenda. Second, the official status of a language does not connote that it operates on a basis of equality with other official languages across the full range of the state's activities. Rather, the question of official language status must be disaggregated into a multiplicity of individual decisions that vary across institutional contexts, and which may be made differently. The scope for linguistic choice across institutional contexts varies. For example, the state can offer services in multiple official languages, but must operate in fewer languages in the judicial system and the legislature. Moreover, multiple official languages can exist within a unitary state structure. Third, linguistic pluralism does create pressure toward federalism in the context of the internal working language of government. There is great pressure toward convergence on one or a very limited number of official languages for intra-governmental communication, for economic and practical reasons. Since the internal working language of government is also the language of government employment, economic competition for these opportunities requires multiple public sectors, each operating in its own language. Federalism is the only mechanism available to meet this political demand.

C. Sri Lanka

Federalism has been on the constitutional agenda for Sri Lanka for several decades, as a tool to manage ethnic conflict on the island (Choudhry 2010). Sri Lanka contains a large, Sinhala-speaking majority as well as a large, Tamil-speaking minority who constitute a majority in the island. Both the Sinhalese majority and Tamil minority are engaged in competing projects of nation-building. The centrepiece of Sinhalese nation-building has consisted of the designation of Sinhala as the official language, especially the internal working language of government. It has also entailed the maintenance of a unitary state inherited from the British, and the refusal thus far to recast Sri Lanka along federal lines. The sources of Sinhalese linguistic nationalism are diverse, ranging from resentment toward the disproportionate professional success enjoyed by Tamils under colonial rule, to the use of official language policies to expand educational and employment opportunities for an increasingly literate and demanding Sinhalese population, to the pressure arising from the growth and consolidation of the state in the post-independence period to interact with the population in indigenous languages.

Tamil nationalism arose as a defensive response to Sinhalese nation-building and has consisted of a series of demands that has escalated from linguistic parity to federalism, and eventually to secession and independence in the northeast of the country. At first, Tamil nationalists advanced their claims through the political process and civil disobedience. The Sri Lankan state was resistant to these claims and responded to Tamil civil disobedience with increasing levels of violence. Frustrated by their lack of success, Tamil nationalists turned to violence. The result was a civil war that lasted from 1983 to 2009, which ended with the defeat of the Liberation Tigers of Tamil Eelam (LTTE), the leading Tamil militant group.

The descent into civil war in Sri Lanka arose from a breakdown in the Sri Lankan constitutional order. One dimension of this breakdown concerned a fundamental disagreement over the constitutional arrangements to frame the relationship between the Sinhalese majority and the

Tamil minority. But there was an equally fundamental disagreement over the precise character of constituent power – the rules governing constitutional amendment. The reason was that those rules were not perceived as being neutral among the competing substantive positions on the constitutional agenda. Tamil nationalists deplored that those rules were based on an understanding of Sri Lanka as a single nation in which the constituent actor was the Sri Lankan people as a whole, in which Tamils had no special standing. In opposition to this vision, Tamil nationalists conceived of Sri Lanka as a multinational or plurinational polity, where the ultimate power of constitutional change vests with its constituent nations, the Tamils and the Sinhalese.

This basic disagreement over the character of constituent power within Sri Lanka played itself out in a debate over whether the Sri Lankan conflict could be resolved from within the Sri Lankan constitutional order. Under Sri Lanka's constitution, amendments must pass by a 2/3 majority in Parliament. In addition, amendments that would alter Sri Lanka's unitary character require approval in a referendum. During over two decades of peace negotiations, a frequent stumbling block was whether a package of constitutional amendments that would meet Tamil demands would pass through these constitutional hurdles, because of opposition from Sinhalese hardliners. These constitutional obstacles produced radical proposals to step outside the constitution entirely. Before the military defeat of the LTTE in 2009, these issues were central to the debate over proposals that the Sri Lankan government legally recognize the LTTE's de facto sovereignty over the northeast of the island. The LTTE sought such recognition to legitimize it as a governmental entity. However, the Sri Lankan government claimed that it would be unconstitutional for it to do so without a constitutional amendment. The most relevant constitutional provision prohibited Parliament from setting up any authority with any legislative power – as the legal recognition of LTTE authority would have required. The LTTE responded by pointing to an international practice of establishing interim governing arrangements with legal force solely based on the agreement of the parties to the conflict.

Ultimately, this issue came before the Sri Lankan Supreme Court, in a case arising out of interim self-governing arrangements agreed to by the Sri Lankan government and the LTTE after the tsunami of 2004. The case was brought by Members of Parliament from the governing coalition (including cabinet ministers). The Court held that the self-governing arrangements circumvented constitutional provisions that gave Parliament the central role in supervising public expenditure, by allowing the self-governing authority to expend public monies from a regional fund entirely outside the structures of the unitary state. After this judgment, many concluded that any ceasefire agreement between the Sri Lankan government and the LTTE would be unconstitutional, because it would amount to a de facto acquiescence of the authority to an armed force acting in breach of law over parts of the country, and would violate the government's constitutional obligation to assert authority over and protect the territorial integrity of Sri Lanka.

There are three broader lessons found in the Sri Lankan case for post-conflict federalism. First, constitutional transitions from unitary states to post-conflict federations must reckon with rules governing constitutional amendment. Those barriers may be insurmountable for political reasons, thereby creating a choice – to maintain fidelity to law and retain the unitary character of the state, or step outside the constitution to achieve the reconstitution of the state. Moreover, since these amending rules may encode a vision of constituent power that pre-supposes a unitary political community as opposed to a multinational or plurinational one, they may not command respect from parties who favour the reconstitution of the state in repudiation of its unitary character. In short, because they may impede constitutional change not perceived as ideologically neutral, constitutional amending rules may be unable to serve one of their basic functions – to enable the politics of constitutional change to occur. In this respect, Sri Lanka repeats a pattern of constitutional politics found in Canada. Second, unitary constitutions may create barriers to the negotiation of interim governing arrangements between warring parties in a civil war over the fundamental character of the state. Such arrangements are important and perhaps even indispens-able stages in the process of moving from violent conflict to political negotiation. They allow the building of trust by setting down mutually agreed norms, procedures and even joint institutions that are necessary for more comprehensive constitutional negotiations. The difficulty is that interim governing arrangements are constitutions in microcosm, and may function as a preliminary form of federal constitutional structure if they grant a rebel party's jurisdiction over a portion of the national territory. This characteristic may render them unconstitutional under existing unitary arrangements. The result may be that the unitary constitution may trap parties who may agree in principle on the idea of post-conflict federalism in a civil war situation. This may be true even if the constitution has no substantive bars on amendments that would convert it from a unitary to federal order. Third, the lead institution for the enforcement of the existing order may be constitutional courts. If they are independent from the government, they may not adhere to even a broad political consensus in favour of post-conflict federalism. Moreover, spoilers who advocate the retention of a unitary state structure – even if a small political minority – can harness the courts to block constitutional change. Judicial review amplifies their political power by providing them with an institutional base within the state to challenge the government.

D. The Philippines

Modern Philippine nationalism has had a different character than in India and Sri Lanka. Whereas in those countries, language has been at the heart of nation-building in the post-colonial area, and has generated defensive linguistic nationalisms in response, in the Philippines, the major axis of nation-building and nationalist conflict has been religion (Bertrand 2010). The Philippines has a Roman Catholic majority, who adopted the faith in the wake of Spanish colonization. Roman Catholicism served to unite the inhabitants of the colony, who came from varied linguistic groups and indeed helped to transcend linguistic differences and prevented them from becoming axes of political cleavage. Islam came to what is now present-day Philippines in the thirteenth century, pre-dating Spanish colonization, and was centred in the southern island of Mindanao. During Spanish rule, Spain never fully established authority over Mindanao's Muslim inhabitants, whom it termed Moros. The Moros never accepted Spanish rule, and indeed, remained free from real Spanish control even after the Spanish defeat of the Moro in the eighteenth century.

The advent of American rule brought a number of fundamental changes that set the stage for contemporary conflict. In the Christian areas of the Philippines, American authorities created the basis for modern Filipino nationalism, through the expansion of education, construction of a national infrastructure, and the creation of a civil service staffed by indigenous officials, and political institutions in which Filipinos were represented by political parties. They also promoted the large-scale settlement of Christians to Mindanao, which profoundly altered its demographic character. While there were major cultural and religious differences between the Christian migrants and the Moro, the major point of conflict was land. American authorities did not legally recognize pre-existing patterns of landholding, and deemed lands long held by the Moro to be public property. They then granted legal titles to these lands to Christian settlers. The net result was a transfer of lands from the Moro to Christians, which also redistributed economic and political power within Mindanao. Alongside conflicts over land was a cultural conflict, whereby Christians saw the Muslim Moros as deviant. The Moro movement arose as a defensive response to Filipino nation-building.

The demand for post-conflict federalism within the Philippines arises from this conflict. The Moro turned to armed struggle in 1969, first under the Moro National Liberation Front (MNLF) and later under the Moro Islamic Liberation Front (MILF). Both the MNLF and the MILF veered between demanding independence and autonomy for traditionally Muslim areas of Mindanao, called the Bangsamoro. While federalism is part of a larger political discourse about democratization and responsiveness, in reality it is centred on Mindanao and is viewed as a means to resolve the conflict with the Moro. As discussed earlier, the proposals under consideration are for a highly asymmetric self-governing framework that leaves the rest of the Philippines structured on a unitary basis.

Since 1976, several agreements have been negotiated between these groups and the Philippines government to grant autonomy to Bangsamoro, with provisions on self-government and natural resource revenue sharing. The most controversial question has been the process for determining the borders of Bangsamoro. The large Christian population of Mindanao has strongly opposed these autonomy agreements, and has demanded plebiscites to determine the territory of Bangsamoro, as is mandated by the Philippines constitution. The high probability that many municipalities would vote against joining Bangsamoro led the MILF, for example, to argue that the parties should step outside the Philippines constitutional order to reach an agreement. Indeed, constitutional issues have been a central issue throughout the negotiations. In 2008, these issues came to a head when the Supreme Court of the Philippines struck down the Memorandum of Agreement on Ancestral Domain (MOA-AD) between the Philippines government and the MILF, which was the result of 11 years of negotiations. The Court found the agreement unconstitutional on substantive and procedural grounds. The MOA-AD referred to the relationship between the central government and Bangsamoro as "associative", but did not define that term. Since this term exists under international law to describe a relationship between two independent states, the Court reasoned that the MOA-AD likewise aimed to confer statehood on the Bangsamoro. Terms of the MOA-AD that empowered Bangsamoro to enter into economic and trade relations with foreign states buttressed this conclusion. The Court held this to be unconstitutional, because the constitution contemplated only one state within the territory of the Philippines. In addition, the Court held that the President had abused her discretion in committing under the MOA-AD to secure the requisite constitutional amendments to implement it. Since the power of constitutional amendment rests with the Philippines Congress, the President had made a promise she could not keep. The judgment led to the collapse of the peace process. In 2012, the MILF and the Philippine government signed a new "framework agreement" that tracked the content of the MOA-AD, to be implemented by a Basic Law, although the constitutional issues remain unresolved.

The Philippines offers three lessons for the study of post-conflict federalism. First, as in Sri Lanka, the rules for constitutional amendment pose a practical barrier to the transition to post-conflict federalism. However, in the Philippines, the challenge they pose is more fundamental. The MOA-AD assumed that amendments would be required to implement Bangsamoro's associative relationship with the rest of the Philippines, but was nonetheless held to be unconstitutional on the basis that it was inconsistent with the existence of a single Philippines state. In effect, this is a basic structure doctrine that limits the substantive scope of possible amendments to the existing Philippine constitution (as opposed to a procedural hurdle that makes such amendments difficult to adopt). Second, the particular character of the separation of powers between the legislative and the executive can profoundly affect the bargaining dynamic of the transitions to post-conflict federalism. The Philippines has a Presidential system with a sharp separation of powers between the President and Congress. The President has led peace negotiations, but the power of constitutional amendment resides with Congress. This creates constitutional difficulties for the President to credibly commit at the bargaining table. These structural barriers might exist even when the same political party controls the Presidency and the Congress, because of the judicial enforcement of the structural constitution. Third, as in Sri Lanka, the courts and judicial review provide institutional resources to spoilers who desire to undermine a negotiated transition to post-conflict federalism. This injects considerable uncertainty into the constitutional process, although it may be countered by the use of standing and political questions doctrines that render peace negotiations non-justiciable (as some dissenting justices of the Supreme Court suggested).

V. CONCLUSION

The familiar conception of classical federalism has fuelled important debates about essential elements of the most stable and successful federal systems. But lessons drawn from states like Australia and the United States often do not apply to more volatile conditions, such as those facing states seeking to recover from ethnic conflict. Post-conflict states must solve a very different set of constitutional problems, and in deciding whether and how to implement federalism, they must respond to a very different set of challenges. By positing that the experiences of post-conflict federal states can support a coherent conception of federalism distinct from that fostered by the experiences of the first wave of federal states, post-conflict federalism offers a new perspective on basic questions like "what is federalism?" and even "what is a constitution?"

Finally, the three analytic narratives offered above (India, Sri Lanka, the Philippines) may inadvertently obscure the extent to which the classical and post-conflict justifications overlap. Indeed, the lesson from the Asian cases may be that the classical and post-conflict justifications for federalism not only overlap in particular cases but often interrelate at a conceptual level. For example, the unresponsiveness of remote centres to peripheries – a democratic concern addressed by classical justifications for federalism – often maps onto a national divide. Statewide nationalism may entail a central elite from one national community that is indifferent or hostile to the interests of a regional minority, whose economic and political exclusion fuel sub-state nationalism (e.g. Sri Lanka). Deploying federalism as a tool to defuse nationalist conflict by giving sub-state minorities access to power at the centre is not distinct from the classical democratic justification for federalism, although the character of the conflict that gives rise to these demands is different than in the classical federations. In parallel, one dimension of nationalist conflict within states may be the permanent exclusion of political parties representing sub-state minorities from power at the centre. Federalism may provide these parties with an institutional base from which to contest power at the centre, not as a majority party but as a member of a governing coalition (as has occurred in India, for example). This overlaps with the justification under classical federalism that federalism promotes political competition. Developing blended accounts of classical and post-conflict justifications for federalism, drawing on Asian materials, may be a fruitful academic agenda for the future.

REFERENCES

Amar, Akhil Reed. 1991. "Some New World Lessons for the Old World." *University of Chicago Law Review* 58: 483–510.

Aroney, Nicholas. 2006. "Formation, Representation and Amendment in Federal Constitutions." *American Journal of Comparative Law* 54: 277–336.

Baylis, Elena A. 2004. "Beyond Rights: Legal Process and Ethnic Conflicts." *Michigan Journal of International Law* 25: 529–604.

Bermeo, Nancy. 2002. "The Import of Institutions." *Journal of Democracy* 13: 96–110.

Bertrand, Jacques. 2010. "The Double-Edged Sword of Autonomy in Indonesia and the Philippines." Pp. 164–195 in *Multination States in Asia: Accommodation or Resistance,* edited by Jacques Bertrand and André Laliberté. New York: Cambridge University Press.

Bertrand, Jacques and André Laliberté, eds. 2010. *Multination States in Asia: Accommodation or Resistance.* New York: Cambridge University Press.

Bhattacharyya, Harihar. 2008. *Federalism in Asia: India, Pakistan and Malaysia.* Oxford: Routledge.

Brancati, Dawn. 2006. "Decentralization: Fueling the Fire or Dampening the Flames of Ethnic Conflict and Secessionism." *International Organization* 60: 651–685.

Brancati, Dawn. 2009. *Peace by Design: Managing Intrastate Conflict through Decentralization.* Oxford: Oxford University Press.

Briffault, Richard. 1994. "'What about the "ism"?' Normative and Formal Concerns in Contemporary Federalism." *Vanderbilt Law Review* 47: 1303–1353.

Brubaker, Rogers. 1996. *Nationalism Reframed: Nationhood and the National Question in the New Europe.* Cambridge: Cambridge University Press.

Bunce, Valerie. 1999. *Subversive Institutions: The Design and the Destruction of Socialism and the State.* Cambridge: Cambridge University Press.

Cederman, Lars-Erik, Andreas Wimmer and Brian Min. 2010. "Why Do Ethnic Groups Rebel? New Data and Analysis." *World Politics* 62: 87–119.

Choudhry, Sujit. 2007. "Does the World Need More Canada? The Politics of the Canadian Model in Constitutional Politics and Political Theory." *International Journal of Constitutional Law* 5: 606–638.

Choudhry, Sujit. 2008. "Bridging Comparative Politics and Comparative Constitutional Law: Constitutional Design in Divided Societies." Pp. 3–40 in *Constitutional Design for Divided Societies: Integration or Accommodation?,* edited by Sujit Choudhry. Oxford: Oxford University Press.

Choudhry, Sujit. 2009. "Managing Linguistic Nationalism through Constitutional Design: Lessons from South Asia." *International Journal of Constitutional Law* 7: 553–576.

Choudhry, Sujit. 2010. "Constitutional Politics and Crisis in Sri Lanka." Pp. 103–135 in *Multination States in Asia: Accommodation or Resistance*, edited by Jacques Bertrand and André Laliberté. New York: Cambridge University Press.

Choudhry, Sujit and Nathan Hume. 2011. "Federalism, Devolution & Secession: From Classical to Post-Conflict Federalism." Pp. 356–384 in *Research Handbook on Comparative Constitutional Law*, edited by Tom Ginsburg and Rosalind Dixon. Northampton, MA: Edward Elgar.

Crawford, Beverly. 1998. "Explaining Cultural Conflict in Ex-Yugoslavia: Institutional Weakness, Economic Crisis, and Identity Politics." Pp. 3–43 in *The Myth of Ethnic Conflict*, edited by Beverly Crawford and Ronnie D. Lipschutz. Berkeley: International and Area Studies.

Cross, Frank B. 2002. "The Folly of Federalism." *Cardozo Law Review* 24: 1–59.

Daniels, Ronald J. 1991. "Should Provinces Compete? The Case for a Competitive Corporate Law Market." *McGill Law Journal* 36: 130–190.

Deakin, Simon. 2006. "Legal Diversity and Regulatory Competition: Which Model for Europe?" *European Law Journal* 12: 440–454.

Elazar, Daniel. 1987. *Exploring Federalism.* Tuscaloosa: The University of Alabama Press.

Erk, Jan and Lawrence Anderson. 2009. "The Paradox of Federalism: Does Self-Rule Accommodate or Exacerbate Ethnic Divisions?" *Regional & Federal Studies* 19: 191–202.

Esty, Daniel C. 1996. "Revitalizing Environmental Federalism." *Michigan Law Review* 95: 570–653.

Farber, Daniel A. 1997. "Environmental Federalism in a Global Economy." *Virginia Law Review* 83: 1283–1319.

Feeley, Malcolm M. and Edward Rubin. 2008. *Federalism.* Ann Arbor: The University of Michigan Press.

Friedman, Barry. 1997. "Valuing Federalism." *Minnesota Law Review* 82: 317–412.

Ghai, Yash. 2000. "Ethnicity and Autonomy: A Framework for Analysis." Pp. 1–26 in *Autonomy and Ethnicity: Negotiating Competing Claims in Multi-Ethnic States,* edited by Yash Ghai. Cambridge: Cambridge University Press.

Griffiths, Ann L., editor. 2005. *Handbook of Federal Countries.* Montreal: McGill-Queen's University Press.

Grindle, Merilee S. 2009. *Going Local: Decentralization, Democratization, and the Promise of Good Governance.* Princeton: Princeton University Press.

Gurr, Ted Robert. 1993. *Minorities at Risk: A Global View of Ethnopolitical Conflicts.* Washington: United States Institute of Peace Press.

Gurr, Ted Robert. 2000. *Peoples versus States: Minorities at Risk in the New Century.* Washington: United States Institute of Peace Press.

Halberstam, Daniel. 2001. "Comparative Federalism and the Issue of Commandeering." Pp. 213–251 in *The Federal Vision: Legitimacy and Levels of Governance in the United States and the European Union,* edited by Kalypso Nicolaidis and Robert Howse. Oxford: Oxford University Press.

Halberstam, Daniel. 2004. "Of Power and Responsibility: The Political Morality of Federal Systems." *Virginia Law Review* 90: 731–834.

Halberstam, Daniel. 2008. "Comparative Federalism and the Role of the Judiciary." Pp. 142–164 in *The Oxford Handbook of Law and Politics,* edited by Keith E. Whittington, R. Daniel Keleman and Gregory A. Caldeira. Oxford: Oxford University Press.

Halberstam, Daniel and Mathias Reimann. Forthcoming. "Federalism and Legal Unification: A Comparative Empirical Examination of 20 Systems."

Hale, Henry. 2008. "The Double-Edged Sword of Ethnofederalism: Ukraine and the USSR in Comparative Perspective." *Comparative Politics* 40: 293–312.

Hamilton, Alexander. 1788. "Federalist No. 78." Pp. 464–72 in *The Federalist Papers,* edited by Clinton Rossiter. New York: Penguin Group, 1961.

He, Baogang, Brian Galligan and Takashi Inoguchi, eds. 2009. *Federalism in Asia.* Northampton, MA: Edward Elgar.

Hume, Nathan. 2006. "Four Flaws: Reflections on the Canadian Approach to Private International Law." *Canadian Yearbook of International Law* 44: 161–248.

Jackson, Vicki C. 2004. "Comparative Constitutional Federalism and Transnational Judicial Discourse." *International Journal of Constitutional Law* 2: 91–138.

Kimber, Clíona J. M. 1995. "A Comparison of Environmental Federalism in the United States and the European Union." *Maryland Law Review* 54: 1658–1690.

Kincaid, John and G. Alan Tarr, eds. 2005. *Constitutional Origins, Structure and Change in Federal Countries.* Montreal: McGill-Queen's University Press.

Kymlicka, Will. 1995. *Multicultural Citizenship: A Liberal Theory of Minority Rights.* Oxford: Clarendon Press.

Kymlicka, Will. 1998. "Is Federalism a Viable Alternative to Secession?" in *Theories of Secession*, edited by Percy Blanchemains Lehning. London: Routledge.

Kymlicka, Will. 2001. *Politics in the Vernacular: Nationalism, Multiculturalism, and Citizenship*. Oxford: Oxford University Press.

Kymlicka, Will. 2007. *Multicultural Odysseys: Navigating the New International Politics of Diversity*. Oxford: Oxford University Press.

Kymlicka, Will and Baogang He, eds. 2005. *Multiculturalism in Asia*. Oxford: Oxford University Press.

Leff, Carol Skalnik. 1999. "Democratization and Disintegration in Multinational States: The Breakup of the Communist Federations." *World Politics* 51: 205–235.

Levy, Jacob T. 2007. "Federalism, Liberalism, and the Separation of Loyalties." *American Political Science Review* 101: 459–477.

Lijphart, Arend. 1977. *Democracy in Plural Societies: A Comparative Exploration*. New Haven: Yale University Press.

Majeed, Akhtar, Ronald L. Watts and Douglas M. Brown, eds. 2006. *Distribution of Powers and Responsibilities in Federal Countries*. Montreal: McGill-Queen's University Press.

McCahery, Joseph A. and Erik P. M. Vermeulen. 2005. "Does the European Company Prevent the 'Delaware Effect'?" *European Law Journal* 11: 785–801.

McGarry, John and Brendan O'Leary. 2009. "Must Pluri-national Federations Fail?" *Ethnopolitics* 8: 5–25.

Mendez, Fernando. 2005. "The European Union and Cybercrime: Insights from Comparative Federalism." *Journal of European Public Policy* 12: 509–527.

Merritt, Deborah Jones. 1988. "The Guarantee Clause and State Autonomy: Federalism for a Third Century." *Columbia Law Review* 88: 1–78.

Nicolaidis, Kalypso and Robert Howse, eds. 2001. *The Federal Vision: Legitimacy and Levels of Governance in the United States and the European Union*. Oxford: Oxford University Press.

Parikh, Sunita and Barry R. Weingast, 1997. "A Comparative Theory of Federalism: India." *Virginia Law Review* 83: 1593–1615.

Qian, Yingyi and Barry R. Weingast. 1997. "Federalism as a Commitment to Preserving Market Incentives." *Journal of Economic Perspectives* 11: 83–92.

Revesz, Richard L. 1996. "Federalism and Interstate Environmental Externalities." *University of Pennsylvania Law Review* 144: 2341–2416.

Revesz, Richard L. 2001. "Federalism and Environmental Regulation: A Public Choice Analysis." *Harvard Law Review* 115: 553–641.

Riker, William. 1964. *Federalism: Origin, Operation, Significance*. Boston: Little, Brown.

Riker, William. 1975. "Federalism." Pp. 93–172 in *Handbook of Political Science: Governmental Institutions and Processes*, edited by Fred I. Greenstein and Nelson W. Polsby. Reading: Addison-Wesley.

Roeder, Philip G. 2007. *Where Nation-States Come From: Institutional Change in the Age of Nationalism*. Princeton: Princeton University Press.

Roeder, Philip G. 2009. "Ethnofederalism and the Mismanagement of Conflicting Nationalisms." *Regional & Federal Studies* 19: 203–219.

Shapiro, David L. 1995. *Federalism: A Dialogue*. Evanston: Northwestern University Press.

Simeon, Richard and Daniel-Patrick Conway. 2001. "Federalism and the Management of Conflict in Multinational Societies." Pp. 338–365 in *Multinational*

Democracies, edited by Alain-G. Gagnon and James Tully. Cambridge: Cambridge University Press.

Stepan, Alfred. 1999. "Federalism and Democracy: Beyond the U.S. Model." *Journal of Democracy* 10: 19–34.

Stepan, Alfred. 2001. *Arguing Comparative Politics*. Oxford: Oxford University Press.

Stewart, Richard. 1977. "Pyramids of Sacrifice? Problems of Federalism in Mandating State Implementation of National Environmental Policy." *Yale Law Journal* 86: 1196–1272.

Stith, Clark D. 1991. "Federalism and Company Law: A 'Race to the Bottom' in the European Community." *Georgetown Law Journal* 79: 1581–1618.

Tiebout, Charles M. 1956. "A Pure Theory of Local Expenditures." *The Journal of Political Economy* 64: 416–424.

Toft, Monica Duffy. 2003. *The Geography of Ethnic Violence: Identity, Interests and the Indivisibility of Territory*. Princeton: Princeton University Press.

Walter, Barbara F. 2009. *Reputation and Civil Wars: Why Separatist Conflicts Are So Violent*. Cambridge: Cambridge University Press.

Watts, Ronald L. 1966. *New Federations: Experiments in the Commonwealth*. Oxford: Clarendon Press.

Watts, Ronald L. 1998. "Federalism, Federal Political Systems and Federations." *Annual Review of Political Science* 1: 117–137.

Watts, Ronald L. 2008. *Comparing Federal Systems*, 3rd ed. Montreal: McGill-Queen's University Press.

Weingast, Barry. 1995. "The Economic Role of Political Institutions: Market-Preserving Federalism and Economic Development." *The Journal of Law, Economics, & Organization* 11: 1–31.

Wheare, K.C. 1964. *Federal Government*, 4th ed. New York: Oxford University Press.

Wolff, Stefan. 2009. "Complex Power-sharing and the Centrality of Territorial Self-governance in Contemporary Conflict Settlements." *Ethnopolitics* 8: 27–45.

8. Constitutions and emergency regimes in Asia

Victor V. Ramraj

I. INTRODUCTION

Since the end of World War II, many governments in Asia have invoked emergency powers in response to a sweeping range of political crises,[1] real or perceived: in 1949, Taiwan proclaimed a *jieyan*[2] as Chiang Kai-shek's nationalist government retreated from the mainland; in 1953 and intermittently thereafter, Sri Lanka invoked emergency powers, with "some measure of emergency regulation … in place for most of its post-independence history" (Nesiah 2009: 123); Hong Kong used emergency powers to regulate social and economic activities from the 1950s to the 1970s (Wong 2011: 449); in 1961, after a coup in South Korea by General Park Chung-hee, a Supreme Council on National Reconstruction was established and enacted an Emergency Measures Law on National Reconstruction, overriding the constitution (a subsequent emergency was declared in 1971) (Chen 2010b: 868–869); in 1962, Brunei's Sultan Omar declared a state of emergency following a dispute between the Sultan and the Legislative Council over a proposed merger with Malaysia (Tey 2008: 7–35); for its part, Malaysia proclaimed a nationwide state of emergency in 1964 in response to Indonesia's "Confrontation" and again in 1969 following widespread post-general election rioting (Das 2007:

---

[1] Emergencies are also invoked to deal with financial crises and natural disasters. The focus of this chapter, however, is on political crises, typically involving violent conflict and often, though not always, a challenge to the legitimacy of the state. I am grateful to Melissa Crouch and Nicolas Cheesman for their helpful comments on a draft.

[2] According to Albert H.Y. Chen, *jieyan* is "often translated in the literature as 'martial law', although 'state of siege' would be a better translation given the continental European and Japanese origins of this Chinese term" (2010a: 69).

101–113);[3] since its independence in 1971, Bangladesh has seen a state of emergency imposed three times, most recently in 2007 in the wake of political unrest following the boycott of a scheduled general election by opposition parties (Haque 2008: 84); in 1975, Indian Prime Minister Indira Gandhi, confronted by an adverse High Court ruling on her continued eligibility to hold office and by public pressure for her resignation, declared a state of emergency and arrested or detained thousands of political opponents (Iyer 2000: 152–7); in 2001, 2003, and 2006, President Arroyo purported to invoke emergency-like powers in the Philippines, inspiring comparisons with Ferdinand Marcos's 1972 proclamation of martial law (Pangalangan 2010: 412–35); in 2005, against the backdrop of a decade-long Maoist rebellion, King Gyanendra of Nepal suspended Parliament and imposed martial law (Human Rights Watch 2005); in 2007, President Pervez Musharraf, who, in the face of an adverse judiciary, drew on a long history of emergency rule (and martial law) in Pakistan (Omar 2002: 113–27) to remove many judges from the court, including the Chief Justice (Kalhan 2010: 96); in 2006 and 2008, post-independence East Timor invoked and later rescinded emergency rule; Thailand invoked states of emergency in the southern provinces in 2005, and since 2008 in response to protests in and around Bangkok, most recently and with lethal consequences in 2010 (International Commission of Jurists 2010: 18); and in 2012, Myanmar declared a state of emergency in Rakhine state in response to communal (Buddhist-Muslim/Rohingya) violence (Fuller 2012).

This survey is hardly exhaustive, but it serves to highlight the pervasive use of emergency rule across a broad swath of Asia, in a vast region marked by social, cultural, economic, political, and legal diversity. Given the practical and theoretical tension between the aspirations of constitutional government and the use of emergency powers, we might in a study of emergency regimes in Asia ask the same analytic questions we might use elsewhere: Should constitutions include emergency powers or should they be prescribed, if at all, only in ordinary legislation? Under what conditions and according to what procedures should emergency powers be invoked? Which institution, the legislature or the judiciary, should provide the primary check on these powers? What legal consequences should follow the invocation of emergency powers and what principles should govern their use? Through what legal mechanisms can emergency powers be contained and ordinary constitutional order restored?

---

[3] Other emergency proclamations limited to particular states have also been issued in relation to Sarawak (1966) and Kelantan (1977).

These are important framing questions, but in many Asian contexts, they seem forced; they draw our attention to constitutional text and principle as if the ability of a constitution to regulate emergency powers depends on these questions, and their interpretation by the courts and other constitutional actors. It is not obvious, however, that this formal approach is always warranted. Emergency powers have been invoked in Asia by drastically different forms of government (from the world's most populous democracy, India, to a military regime in transition in present-day Myanmar) using a variety of distinct mechanisms, many of colonial origin (see Omar 1996: 73–7, on the colonial origins of emergency powers in Malaysia, Sri Lanka, Bangladesh, and India). These powers have been deployed with a diverse array of institutional checks or none at all, and in response to an immense range of social, political, and economic circumstances. This sheer diversity of experiences with emergency powers suggests that to transpose models developed in other settings without reflection, refinement, and a healthy dose of scepticism, would be a mistake.

Although in many instances it is possible and appropriate to analyse emergency powers using liberal-democratic constitutional paradigms, in other contexts, doing so would obscure social and political realities. Understanding emergency powers in Asia, as elsewhere, requires a heightened appreciation of the social context in which formal legal norms and institutions operate. The chapter begins with an overview of the typical framework for analysing emergency powers. It then examines the relevance of this framework in Asia, showing where it makes sense and where it fails to capture the reality of emergency rule. Finally, it considers how, in the context of emergency powers, we might begin to narrow the gap between formal law and social reality.

II. CONSTITUTIONALISM AND EMERGENCY POWERS: A FORMAL ANALYSIS

In his contribution to the companion volume to this collection, Oren Gross offers a helpful overview of the constitutional emergency regimes as they are typically understood in liberal constitutional democracies (2011: 334–55; see also Rossiter 2002). He traces the roots of the modern constitutional model to the Roman dictatorship, which permitted the consuls, when faced with an external threat, to appoint a dictator for a non-renewable period of six months. The dictator, while given "all the powers needed to defend the republic against its enemies", was subject to "well-defined constitutional restrictions ... laid down to prevent abuse of powers" (Gross 2011: 335). The dictator's mandate was limited to addressing a specific threat and he was not permitted to enact new legislation. The other institutions of government continued to function normally. As Gross observes, the emergency provisions of many modern constitutional emergency regimes were inspired by the Roman model, characterized by its "temporary character, recognition of the exceptional nature of emergencies, appointment of the dictator according to specific constitutional provisions that separated, among other things, those who declared an emergency from those who exercised dictatorial powers on such occasions, the appointment of dictators for well-defined and limited purposes" (2011: 335) and, in particular, by its conservative purpose – to preserve and restore the original constitutional order.

Not all modern constitutions contain such powers. The Constitution of the United States notably refers only indirectly to emergencies in providing for the suspension of *habeas corpus* "when in Cases of Rebellion or Invasion the public Safety may require it" (Article I, section 8). But a great many modern constitutions, including many in Asia, and most international human rights instruments, include provisions relating to emergency powers, specifying the circumstances in which they may be used. An analysis of the formal emergency provisions in a particular constitution in Asia might consider the following questions, inspired by Gross's account.

1. Are emergency powers expressly conferred by the constitution? Not all constitutions expressly provide for emergencies, although it is increasingly rare to find constitutions that make no reference at all to emergency powers, even if only to the power or duty of the legislature to provide for them. Indonesia's Constitution provides in Article 12 that it is "the President, with the agreement of the House of Representatives, who has the authority to declare a state of emergency" and the "conditions governing and the consequences of a state of emergency shall be laid down by law".[4] Under President Sukharno, "Indonesia did not have such a law" so "Sukharno's government applied the law on states of emergency inherited by the Dutch" (Hosen 2010: 268). In most other constitutions, emergency powers are set out in considerable detail. East Timor's Constitution provides in Article 25(2) that a state of siege or state of emergency "shall only be declared in case of effective or impending aggression by a foreign force, of serious disturbance or threat of serious disturbance to the democratic constitutional order, or of public

---

[4] Article 22(1) provides further that: "In the event of a compelling emergency, the President has the right to issue government regulations in lieu of law."

disaster". Even when constitutional emergency powers are minimal or unspecified, there remains a question of whether analogous powers are provided by statute or through some other source, such as, in the common law tradition, the controversial martial law power.[5] As Gross observes, there is an extensive controversy in the United States dating back to President Abraham Lincoln's unilateral expansion of the armed forces during the American Civil War, as to whether and to what extent the President has inherent emergency powers in times of war to act without congressional authorization (Gross 2011: 343–4), a controversy that continues to preoccupy US constitutional scholars in the twenty-first century.[6]

2. How are emergencies defined? A second question concerns the definition of an emergency or the triggering conditions that must be met before a state of emergency may be declared. Related to this question is whether the constitution regards an emergency as a singular juridical state that may be declared when the conditions precedent have been met – or whether it recognizes different kinds or degrees of emergency. Whether "emergency" is regarded as one or several categories has important legal consequences.

Where a state of emergency is considered a singular category which, when declared, enables the government to exercise a range of extra-ordinary powers, it would be important, in the interest of moderating those powers, to have some doctrine of proportionality that conditions the government's response. Article 4 of the International Covenant on Civil and Political Rights provides an example of this structure, defining a public emergency as a threat "to the life of the nation" permitting derogation from those rights not specified to be non-derogable, but only "to the extent strictly required by the exigencies of the situation" (a requirement that has been understood to mean that the state's response must be proportionate).

In contrast, some emergency regimes distinguish two or more kinds of emergencies (in some instances, as many as nine, see Gross 2011: 337). For example, the Portuguese distinction between a "state of emergency"

---

[5]   The meaning, scope, and legality of martial law have long been the subject of extensive controversy, both in the common law courts and in the academic literature. See, for example, Dyzenhaus 2009: 1; Holdsworth 1902: 117; Pollock 1902: 152; Townshend 1982: 167.

[6]   See *Hamdi v. Rumsfeld* 542 U.S. 507 2004, the US Supreme Court's first look at the government's response to the attacks of 11 September 2001 and, in particular, the divided opinions of the judges on the inherent powers of the executive branch.

and a "state of siege" is echoed in the East Timorese Constitution (see Article 25(2), discussed above) though constitutions might distinguish between war, riots, and other civil disturbances, natural disasters, financial crises, and so on. The justification for doing so would be to attempt to calibrate the state's response to the nature of the emergency from the outset, as the principle of proportionality seeks to do typically through interpretation and judicial extrapolation after the fact.

3. Who has the power to declare an emergency? Constitutions typically vest the power to declare a state of emergency in the executive, in the legislature, or in the executive subject to ratification by the legislature. For instance, the Constitution of the Republic of India now provides in Article 352(4) that a proclamation of an emergency "shall be laid before each House of Parliament and shall ... cease to operate at the expiration of one month unless before the expiration of that period it has been approved by resolutions of both Houses of Parliament". In Singapore and Malaysia, the power to proclaim an emergency is vested in the President and the Yang di-Pertuan Agong (the King) respectively, on the advice of Cabinet (see Article 150, common to both countries' constitutions).

Where different types or degrees of emergency are specified, different branches or levels of government might be given the power to declare a particular kind of emergency. The Philippine Constitution vests in the President the power to "call out" the armed forces to "prevent or suppress lawless violence, invasion, or rebellion" (Article VII(18)) and in Congress the power to declare the existence of a state of war (Article IV(23)(1)). The power to declare an economic emergency is vested in "the State" which was interpreted judicially to mean Congress (Pangalangan 2010: 422, referring to *David v. Arroyo*, G.R. No. 171396, 3 May 2006, 489 SCRA 160). Among its Asian counterparts, the Philippine Constitution is exceptional in as much as it vests the power to declare some forms of emergency in the legislative branch. A state of emergency might be time-limited and subject, with or without conditions, to renewal. For instance, the Constitution of East Timor specifies that a "suspension shall not last for more than thirty days, without prejudice of possible justified renewal, when strictly necessary, for equal periods of time" (Article 25, paragraph 4). It also declares that the authorities "shall restore constitutional normality as soon as possible" (Article 24, paragraph 6).

4. What are the legal consequences of declaring an emergency? A proclamation of a state of emergency has a range of possible consequences. It might permit the executive to exercise powers that it does not normally have (such as direct legislative powers or, in a federal state, it might confer on the central government powers normally not within its power);[7] it might allow the government to derogate from certain rights or freedoms; and, in some cases, it might permit or enable the executive to make fundamental changes in the structure of government.

As far as derogation is concerned, the substantive legal consequences of a declared emergency might depend on whether the emergency powers regime recognizes different types of emergency, but (as Gross explains) constitutions typically specify either "those rights and freedoms that may be suspended during a declared state of emergency (a positive list approach)" or "those rights and freedoms that may not be restricted or in any way violated even in times of acute exigency (a negative list approach)" (Gross 2011: 241). The Indian Constitution provides an example of the former, specifying that nothing in Article 19 (which guarantees, among others, the right to freedom of speech and expression, peaceful assembly, freedom of association, free movement) "shall restrict the power of the state ... to take any action" it would otherwise be authorized to take.[8] East Timor (Article 25(5)), which sets out an extensive list of non-derogable rights, provides an example of the latter.[9] Singapore's Constitution immunizes emergency measures from invalidity on the ground of inconsistency with other provisions of the constitution, except provisions "relating to religion, citizenship or language" and provisions "authorizing the President to act in his discretion" (that latter when serving as a second check on executive powers relating to government finances, senior government appointments, and security matters).[10] In some constitutions, the regulation of emergency powers is

---

[7]   In India, a Proclamation of Emergency allows the central (Union) government to extend executive power to states and the legislature to confer law-making power on officers and authorities of the central government: Article 353.

[8]   Additionally, Article 359 allows the enforcement of fundamental rights (with the exception now of the right to life and personal liberty in Article 21) to be suspended during an emergency.

[9]   Article 25(5) provides that certain enumerated rights – the rights to life, physical integrity, citizenship, non-retroactivity of the criminal law, defence in a criminal case and freedom of conscience and religion, the right not to be subjected to torture, slavery or servitude, the right not to be subjected to cruel, inhuman or degrading treatment or punishment, and the guarantee of non-discrimination – cannot be suspended.

[10]   Article 150(5)(b). The latter provision enables the President, in his or her discretion, to retain the ability to withhold consent (which must be obtained) in relation to, for example, financial bills, the appointment of key office holders (such as the Prime Minister, the Chief Justice, the Attorney-General, and senior civil service and security positions), the dissolution of Parliament, detention

left to ordinary legislation.[11] As we shall see, while not necessarily anticipated or formally endorsed by the constitutions, one danger in an emergency is the introduction of fundamental institutional changes to the nature of government, including the creation of an unchecked power to legislate or an erosion of judicial independence, or the normalization of the emergency order.

5. *What checks and balances are provided?* Constitutional emergency regimes might include two kinds of checks on the invocation and exercise of emergency powers. First, they might include, as already discussed, legislative checks on the process by which an emergency is formally declared, typically involving legislative ratification of a declaration of a state of emergency. Second, they might attract judicial review of the legality of the declaration or on the powers exercised under it. A substantive notion of rule of law suggests that the courts ought to be able to consider both of these questions, but in practice this does not always happen. For one thing, the constitution might expressly preclude the courts from considering the validity of the proclamation of an emergency, as it does in Malaysia.[12] Alternatively, the courts might on their own initiative adopt a restrictive view of the justiciability of a proclamation

---

under the Internal Security Act, and restriction orders under the Maintenance of Religious Harmony Act.

[11] Article 12 of the Constitution of the Republic of Indonesia provides: "The President may declare a state of emergency. The conditions for such a declaration and the subsequent measures regarding a state of emergency shall be regulated by law." In such circumstances, it may well be open to the courts to infer that no restrictions on fundamental rights and freedoms are constitutionally permissible, although in the face of an emergency, the courts might choose to interpret fundamental rights and freedoms contextually, taking into account the exigencies of the situation, possibly in light of international law instruments governing states of emergency.

[12] Article 150(8) of the Constitution of Malaysia provides: "Notwithstanding anything in this Constitution – (a) the satisfaction of the Yang di-Pertuan Agong mentioned [that 'a grave emergency exists whereby the security, or the economic life, or public order in the Federation or any part thereof is threatened' or 'that certain circumstances exist which render it necessary for him to take immediate action' by promulgating 'such ordinances as circumstances appear to him to require'] shall be final and conclusive and shall not be challenged or called in question in any court on any ground; and (b) no court shall have jurisdiction to entertain or determine any application, question or proceeding, in whatever form, on any ground, regarding the validity of – (i) a Proclamation [of a state of emergency]; (ii) the continued operation of such Proclamation; (iii) any ordinance promulgated under Clause (2B); or (iv) the continuation in force of any such ordinance."

(*ADM Jabalpur v. Shivkant Shukla* 1976 AIR 1976 SC 1207; see also Thiruvengadam 2010: 466–94),[13] often on the basis that the executive is, in their view, in a better position to assess matters of national security.[14]

III. THE RELEVANCE AND LIMITS OF FORMAL ANALYSIS

How useful is the formal approach to emergency powers set out in the previous section for analysing and assessing constitutional emergency powers regimes in Asia? On the one hand, a formal analysis typically adopts an internal perspective on the legal system; it seeks to show how, in principle, the legal system works – in this case, how a state might respond to an emergency within the bounds of the constitution. One key objective is to preserve legality by subordinating emergency powers to law (Dyzenhaus 2006), typically by setting out *ex ante* stringent conditions for their use or supervising their invocation and implementation through *ex post* judicial review (Ramraj 2008). The goal of containing the use of emergency powers is as important in Asia as it is anywhere else. On the other hand, in some parts of Asia, emergency powers do not function as the formal constitutional regime anticipates that they would, and in these circumstances formal analysis takes us only so far. It might nevertheless be a useful first step toward a pathology of emergency powers and constitutional law generally.

A. Formal Analysis of Emergency Powers in Asia

When is formal legal analysis appropriate? The analytic framework set out earlier suggests that constitutional emergency powers provide a way for governments to act in ways that would not normally be open to them

---

[13] I am grateful to Rishad Chowdhury for discussion on the judicial response to the emergency.

[14] See, for instance, the majority opinion of Ray C.J.: "While the courts of law are in normal times peculiarly competent to weigh the competing claims of individuals and government, they are ill equipped to determine whether a given configuration of events threatens the life of the community and thus constitute an emergency. ... Jurists do not have the vital sources of information available to the executive and the legislature" (at 1225). Khanna J., dissenting, held that a Presidential order suspending the enforcement of fundamental rights in an emergency could not prevent the courts from issuing a writ of *habeas corpus* and examining the legality of a person's detention (at 1277).

in response to an extraordinary threat, with a view to restoring the normal legal order. The starting point for a formal analysis, then, assumes a normal state of affairs that the state is seeking to restore. The situation is more complicated in transitional contexts where constitutional government is not or has not long been present (Ramraj 2010: 21–55). Second, formal analysis would be particularly salient in contexts in which there is a high degree of correlation between formal legal rules and the conduct of public officials – that is, situations in which, for public officials, formal law *matters*. In these contexts, there may well be scope to work within the system to articulate and define the scope of and limits on the state's emergency powers.

A restorative model of emergency powers suggests that a key litmus test for a properly functioning emergency powers regime would be whether, in practice, there are examples of judicial intervention or resistance, or of successful legislative opposition or reversal, when an emergency is declared; by the same token, the swift restoration of constitutional normalcy would suggest the existence of a properly functioning emergency regime. One example of the successful use of emergency powers to restore an emerging constitutional "normalcy" can be found in East Timor, against the backdrop of a high degree of international oversight, in February 2008, following an assassination attempt on the President and Prime Minister. A state of emergency was declared on 11 February, initially for 48 hours, restricting assemblies and demonstrations, and imposing a curfew. Police and military were temporarily unified under a joint command. The emergency regime was renewed two days later as a "state of siege" on 13 February and again on 22 February. It was renewed again in March, but only in seven districts, and further in April, but only in one, where rebels were active. In its close adherence to the constitution, the progressive rolling back of restrictions and geographic narrowing of the affected area, and the relatively minor abuses of power, this emergency episode stands out as an almost textbook use of emergency rule under the constitution.[15]

More difficult to demonstrate empirically, however, would be the tendency toward a measured and proportionate response by the state undertaken in the shadow of the law. For instance, although the deferential judicial response to Indira Gandhi's 1975 emergency in India is generally regarded as an example of excessive judicial deference, the

---

[15] This paragraph draws on Ramraj 2010: 29–34, which also discusses reported cases of abuse of powers by the authorities (of the forty cases of abuse reported to the Ombudsman, more were minor, involving "manhandling" by the authorities).

backlash against the Court's decision might be seen as a political and judicial turning point, with the courts subsequently much more willing to engage in judicial review (Thiruvengadam 2010: 489). A deferential decision does not necessarily mean the failure of constitutionalism if, over time, judges remain open to arguments as to why they ought to intervene. At the same time, however, judicial willingness to scrutinize the invocation of emergency powers does not always have the intended result of checking state power where other tools,[16] such as internal security legislation or specialized anti-terrorism statutes can be substituted to achieve similar ends (Thiruvengadam 2010: 476; Harding and Leyland 2011: 113–18).

In some situations, constitutional engagement in relation to emergency powers might be difficult because the emergency powers regime itself creates an obstacle. This might be so where the power to declare an emergency is unchecked legislatively or where judicial review is expressly prohibited, as it is in Malaysia (Thiruvengadam 2010). Elsewhere, legislative checks might be avoided by asserting inherent executive powers not specifically provided for in the constitution. For example, Raul Pangalangan argues that President Arroyo sought in 2001, 2003, and 2006 to declare forms of emergency rule that had little to no basis in the constitutional text (Thiruvengadam 2010: 424–29). Here too, it might yet be possible to amend the constitution or to convince the courts, through litigation, to adopt a different interpretive approach – a strategy that met with mixed success in the Philippine courts (Pangalangan, citing *Sanlakas v. Executive Secretary*, GR No. 159085, 3 February 2004, 421 SCRA 657, the President's declaration of a "state of rebellion" was a nullity; *David v. Arroyo*: the "calling out" power fell within the purview of the President). In other situations, however, a formal analysis might come across as entirely artificial – and an engagement with the courts, even if permissible, would be futile. In these instances, although the "overriding constitutional aim" might be "to create an emergency regime that remains subordinate – both in symbol and actual fact – to the principles of liberal democracy" (Haque 2008: 93), a formal analysis of emergency powers might expose deeper pathologies – or might point toward other kinds of

---

[16] That emergency powers are temporary powers exercised under the authority of the constitution distinguishes them, on the one hand, from "martial law" conceived as the extra-constitutional military assumption of the functions of government and, on the other hand, from standing powers against subversion that purport to authorize the detention without trial of persons deemed to be a threat to national security.

checks beyond those of formal constitutional law, suggesting the presence of informal social or political norms not captured by formal legal analysis.

B. Pathologies of Emergency Powers

A formal account of an emergency powers regime would be particularly deceptive when emergency powers become so entrenched that the gap between formal legality and political reality becomes a chasm. In these situations, the underlying emergency might lead to a concentration of political power in the executive at the expense of the legislative and judicial branches and, in some instances, a fundamental restructuring of government. For example, in the wake of the May 1969 emergency in Malaysia, which was declared in response to post-election ethnic riots, the executive assumed legislative powers for 21 months, until Parliament was reconvened in February 1971. The emergency proclamation of 15 May 1969 was accompanied by an Emergency (Essential Powers) Ordinance (No. 1), which gave the Yang di-Pertuan Agong (the monarch) the power to "make any regulations whatsoever ... which he considers desirable or expedient for securing the public safety, the defence of Malaysia, the maintenance of public order and of supplies and services essential to the life of the community" (Harding 1996: 43). These executive and legislative powers were then delegated (by means of a second emergency ordinance) to a "Director of Operations" assisted by a "National Operations Council" – "special bodies ... not specified in the Federal Constitution" (Das 2007: 109). These bodies, though not specifically recognized in the constitution, "for all practical purposes effectively governed the country" (Das 2007: 109) by promulgating emergency regulations which "extended not just to dealing with the emergency but ... to *all aspects* of government, including foreign policy (Harding 1996: 43). Among the many regulations passed under the emergency regime were fundamental changes to criminal procedure in "security cases" and the imposition of the death penalty for, among other offences, the possession of firearms. Although the second ordinance was repealed in 1971, the emergency proclamation and the first ordinance remained in place; the powers delegated to the Director of Operations were subsequently delegated to the Prime Minister by Ordinance No. 77. As a consequence, while the formal institutions of the emergency were effectively dismantled, the "emergency powers still remained" so the "return to normality was not a return to the pre-1969 Constitution, but to a radically altered version of constitutionality" (Harding 1996: 45). These fundamental changes in the structure and ethos of government would continue to reverberate in the decades that followed, with political power (until recently) increasingly concentrated in the executive.

In Pakistan in 2007, the immediate target of the emergency was judicial, not legislative, power. General Pervez Musharraf, who had come to power in a military coup in 1999, was by 2007 confronted with an increasingly activist court. In March 2007, Musharraf purported to dismiss Chief Justice Iftikhar Muhammad Chaudhry, who was then reinstated in July of that year by the Supreme Court (Lau 2006–2007: 275; Qureshi 2009–2010: 487). Citing the judges' lack of cooperation in the "fight against terrorism and extremism" (Lau 2006–2007: 278), Musharraf declared a state of emergency, suspending the constitution, and removed a number of judges from the bench. He insisted that judges "confirm their loyalty by ... [taking] new oaths of office" and swearing allegiance to the provisional constitutional order (Kalhan 2010: 98). Some judges were not permitted to take the oath, others refused to do so; Chief Justice Chaudhry, who refused to take the oath, was placed under house arrest (Lau 2006–2007: 278). The emergency was lifted in December 2007 to set the stage for elections on 8 January, but the opposition leader, Benazir Bhutto, was assassinated on 27 December. After the elections, a coalition was formed against Musharraf's Muslim League (Q) party. Musharraf, who remained as President, eventually resigned in August 2008, and a "Lawyers' Movement" continued to pressure the government to reinstate the judges who had been removed by Musharraf (Lau 2006–2007: 280). Eventually, on 16 March 2009, Prime Minister Yousaf Raza Gillani reinstated Chief Justice Chaudhry (Ashan 2009: 73), bringing this particular episode to a symbolic close.

These emergency episodes might have been relatively short-lived, at least in their immediate events. In other situations, an emergency decree – particularly one in the hands of a powerful military regime – can have a long-term impact, radically altering the nature and structure of government. Developments in Taiwan in the late 1940s provide a classic example. Against the backdrop of the Japanese defeat in World War II and civil war in China, Taiwan saw the replacement of Japanese rule with a government of the Republic of China, administered by the Chinese Nationalist Party (the Kuomintang, KMT) as it withdrew from the Chinese mainland, where the People's Republic of China was established (Wang 2002: 535). The "western-style" (Chen 2010b: 68) liberal-democratic Constitution of the Republic of China, which was adopted by the National Assembly in Nanjing in 1946 and came into force in December of 1947, was never fully implemented (Chen 2010b: 69). In March–April of 1948, the Nationalist government amended the constitution, introducing "Temporary Provisions for the Period of Nationalist

Mobilization to Suppress the Communist Rebellion", which expanded the President's emergency powers; a *jieyan* decree was issued in relation to the mainland in 1948 and Taiwan in 1949 (Chen 2010b: 69). The decree provided for capital punishment in respect of conduct disruptive of the public order, led to executive measures relating to a range of matters including the restriction of civil liberties and the press, the division of jurisdiction between military and civilian courts, and the implementation of measures relating to entry and exit from Taiwan (Chen 2010b: 70). In the 40 years that followed, the Nationalist government used the "Temporary Provisions" to transform the government into a "dictatorial" presidential system (Wang 2002: 542; Wang and Chou 2010: 1) which was dismantled in stages only from 1987, with the lifting of martial law (Wang 2002: 538–539; see also Ginsburg 2003: 118–120).

Taiwan's experience shows how emergency powers can be used to concentrate state power in the executive branch of government or even in the hands of the president. In other situations, however, it is the instability of public institutions and the inability of those institutions to manage or resolve inter-community conflict through law that prompts the invocation of emergency rule, which in turn weakens those same institutions – a vicious cycle of emergency rule and institutional failure. For instance, the repetitive use of emergency rule in Sri Lanka (Nesiah 2009) might be seen both as a consequence of the failure of formal institutions to resolve a decades-long communal conflict, but equally as a cause of that failure: the indiscriminate use of emergency powers weakens confidence in the ability of formal public institutions to resolve political conflict. The problem, then, is not merely the failure of law or institutions that might be "remedied by better doctrine and institutional reform" but rather "inadequacies with the political culture of constitutionalism" (Nesiah 2009: 131). The result, argues Vasuki Nesiah in the Sri Lankan context, is an "enduring state of exception, of normalized emergencies" (Nesiah 2009: 139).

The pathological use of emergency powers signals a deep, underlying ideological difference in the understanding of the political system itself and its relationship to law, including constitutional law. With the sheer diversity of legal and political systems in Asia, we might expect that constitutionalism would be understood differently in Westminster-inspired democracies (which themselves might be genuine multi-party states or de facto one-party states), communist one-party states, religion-inspired government (even in formally secular or quasi-secular states), constitutional and absolute monarchies, military-controlled or military-dominated governments, and presidential (unicameral or bicameral) systems – to mention but a few variations. Each of these societies might in turn exhibit multiple understandings of the rule of law. Moreover, many of these political systems are in the midst of a transition: as Jane Stromseth and her colleagues observe, in post-conflict and post-intervention societies "there may be only a weak tradition of using law to resolve disputes or no such tradition at all" so "well-intentioned efforts by outsiders to build the rule of law solely by creating formal structures and rewriting constitutions and statutes often have little or no impact" (Stromseth, Wippman and Brooks 2006: 76).

Some legal systems in Asia, as elsewhere, might exhibit greater tendencies toward what Ugo Mattei calls "the rule of professional law" (Mattei 1997: 5–44), in which law is formally separated both from politics and religion and public decisions are adopted "based not on politics but on technical and legal merits as interpreted by a professional legal culture" (Mattei 1997: 23); others might be more inclined toward the rule of "political law" (in which "law in the professional term of the word is not absent, but is extremely marginalized and weak before other sources of social rule making (mainly political power)"(Mattei 1997: 28)) or "traditional law" (in which "the hegemonic pattern of law is either religion or a transcendental philosophy in which the individual's internal dimension and the societal dimension are not separated" (Mattei 1997: 36)). The social significance of formal or "professional" law, then, might differ significantly from one society to another to different degrees, defying simple comparison of formal constitutional provisions, including emergency powers. What this immense variation suggests is that formal constitutional analysis and diagnosis is artificial; the problem is not the legal principles themselves but rather the gap between formal law and social reality. And so for some Taiwanese scholars, even after some two decades of legal and political reform, the basic issue in Taiwan now is not "whether written constitutions guarantee important basic principles, but … whether the people in the culture have accepted and understood these principles" (Wang and Chou 2010: 4).

IV. BRIDGING THE SOCIO-LEGAL GAP: EXPLORING THE OPTIONS

The limits of formal constitutional analysis show how important it is to acknowledge the gap between the formal constitution and its social significance. Understanding the nature of this gap also plays a crucial diagnostic role – the better we understand the nature of the gap, the better able we will be to devise ways of narrowing it. Three options present themselves: first, in some contexts, one response to the chronic abuse of emergency powers is to strengthen adherence to the rule of law, closing the gap between law and society in the direction of formal law. This is no easy task and may not even be appropriate in all situations, particularly where formal legal institutions do not have socio-political legitimacy; in some contexts, it might, in the alternative, be preferable to strengthen existing political institutions by drawing on informal political (or cultural) constitutional norms – closing the law–society gap in the direction of the social norms. Which of these options is preferable is contestable – the answer may well vary depending on the particular context and on one's ideological views as to the importance of formal law. Finally, we might consider the role that civil society organizations can play in mediating between social norms and formal constitutional constraints in an emergency.

A. Engaging Social Norms

It is easy to see why, in a post-authoritarian, post-conflict context, it would be tempting to try to constrain future governments by entrenching liberal constitutional norms of judicial review. Those who endorse this view might even acknowledge the importance of looking beyond formal institutions: "Effective strategies for building domestic justice systems," declares one United Nations report, "will give due attention to laws, processes (both formal and informal) and institutions (official and unofficial)" (Report of the Secretary General 2004: para. 35). However, the "standard-assistance-menu approach" that still prevails, advocating a focus on rewriting laws, training lawyers and judges, and reforming the courts, often fails to acknowledge that promoting the rule of law "is an issue of norm creation and cultural change as much as an issue of creating new institutions and legal codes" (Stromseth, Wippman and Brooks 2006: 75). And this process of social and cultural transformation is evolutionary, not revolutionary. To borrow from Mattei's analysis, it may be futile (particularly in the short term) to reform legal norms and institutions in a socio-political context in which the rule of professional law is not accepted as the dominant "pattern" of law and where political power and traditional norms have a much more significant impact on the outcome of public decisions, including the imposition of emergency powers. Where formal law controls government policy, institutional design, law reform, and litigation will be important. But in many of the societies surveyed in this chapter, it would make more sense to begin not with formal law, but social norms.

The post-colonial and post-conflict experiences of many countries in Asia suggest that formal constitutional design or amendment is insufficient on its own to close the socio-legal gap. Indeed, to secure the legitimacy and efficacy of reforming legal institutions, it may be necessary to close the gap not in the direction of formal law but equally or disproportionately in the direction of social norms. One way of doing so might be to recognize the role played by traditional institutions and customary law within the formal legal system (for a similar observation in the context of domestic violence in East Timor, see Grenfell 2006: 305). It may be, for instance, that a formal declaration of a state of emergency must, within a specified period, be ratified by a traditional political body. The very act of formalizing a traditional institution may well transform it. But acknowledging the role that traditional institutions play in checking formal political power (to the extent that they do[17]), may help to narrow the gap between formal institutions and informal political power in a manner that enhances the legitimacy of both.[18]

More controversially from a liberal-secular perspective is the proposal that constitutional law, rather than distancing itself from religion, should co-opt and incorporate religious directives "not ... for the pure love of religion" but as a "preemptive move aimed at appropriating religion to counter fundamentalist tendencies" (Hirschl 2010: 19). Along similar lines, although avoiding the language of "co-opting", Clark Lombardi shows sympathetically how, in post-colonial Pakistan, a famous Christian judge, A.R. Cornelius, came to defend a particular kind of Islamization as a means of strengthening the rule of law in the face of emergency rule (Lombardi 2010: 436–65). For Lombardi, the gist of Cornelius's extrajudicial speeches was that "whether or not Pakistan's written constitution formally required the government to respect fundamental rights (as understood by the judiciary) or Islamic norms, the military, bureaucracy and judiciary needed to recognize that the majority of Pakistanis would

---

[17]   For example, Tom Ginsburg has argued that a number of informal constitutional conventions govern the conduct of the King and military in Thailand, constraining what they do when faced with civil unrest (see Ginsburg 2009: 83). These informal conventions include the prescription that "the monarch ... is highly respected and will limit his interventions in the political sphere", that when he does exercise his power, "he will be respected", and that "violence against the people is rarely, if ever, legitimate, and no political force is entitled to excessively restrict the freedoms of the people".

[18]   There are, of course, parallels elsewhere: the incorporation of the House of Lords and the monarchy into the English, and later British, constitution can be understood as co-opting political power into a constitutional framework.

consider Pakistani law illegitimate if they deemed it inconsistent with their core expectations" – among which was the expectation that "their government would respect Islamic norms" (p 454). As with the formal recognition of customary law, the goal is not to promote traditional values to the exclusion of, say, human rights, but rather to promote dialogue and co-evolution.

In those societies, then, where formal legality does not carry great social weight (but at least some segments of society would prefer that it did), the aspirations of formal legality might be advanced by engaging with traditional social or legal norms. This kind of engagement comes with a cost, however, and will likely find resistance from two directions. On the one hand, those who see traditional values as normatively lacking might resist formally recognizing them in the constitution, preferring to focus on transforming social attitudes toward the rule of law, even if this makes formal law less effective initially and possibly in the longer term as well;[19] on the other hand, those who value traditional norms might resist replacing them with formal legal norms and structures which might be perceived as alien (Grenfell 2009: 228). Reconciling these competing world-views is perhaps *the* challenge of constitutional reform in transitional contexts and in societies where a formal rule-of-law culture is weaker, but it often arises against a backdrop of civil society engagement, suggesting a possible way forward.

B. Civil Society and Legal Transformation

Although civil society organizations are often targeted by oppressive governments, which might use the instruments of emergency rule against them,[20] these organizations, which are often linked (as are modern governments (Slaughter 2004)) to like-minded groups beyond national borders, increasingly play a significant role in constitutional governance. For example, while the government of East Timor deserves much of the credit for its textbook use of emergency powers in 2008, the presence of

---

[19] Commenting on difficulties with access to the formal justice system in cases of domestic violence in East Timor, Laura Grenfell observes that "the persistence of these problems in the state legal system are pushing people toward reliance on customary law, marginalizing the role of the courts and weakening public confidence in the concept of the 'rule of law'" (2009: 226).

[20] For example, Haque reports that in Bangladesh, emergency powers were used to intimidate political opponents, including human rights activists, with the emergency legislation used, in some instances, retrospectively, relating to events that took place seven years before the emergency was proclaimed (2008: 91).

a vast array of international agencies and advisors and a plethora of NGOs[21] may well have provided an additional incentive for the government to be judicious in the exercise of these powers. What is more, the explosion of information communication technology makes it that much more difficult for governments to remain isolated and for their excesses to avoid international scrutiny. Of course, a determined government might be able to keep some of its excesses secret for some time – but to do so as standard operating procedure would be imprudent. For instance, to the extent that China's emergency powers legislation has teeth, it is in large measure because of an assumption shared by government and civil society that the invocation of emergency powers must be publicly justified (deLisle 2010: 382–8).

Crucially, however, it is not only domestic civil society that is watching, but a better-informed global civil society, including not only well-known human rights watchdogs and journalists, but also bar associations and judicial networks. For instance, in support of the Lawyers' Movement in Pakistan, the New York Bar used its influence to put additional pressure on Musharraf during the 2007 emergency.[22] In the same vein, in 2009, after three years of hearings in approximately 40 countries around the world, the International Commission of Jurists released a comprehensive report on the impact of the 11 September 2001 attacks in the United States on human rights and the rule of law more generally (International Commission of Jurists 2009). Although more research is needed on civil society organizations and governance, there is a growing recognition of the significant impact of civil society organizations on international governance (Woodward 2010), constitutionalism (Teubner 2012: 17–21), and even emergency powers (see Thiruvengadam 2010: 475, noting that in India after Indira Gandhi's emergency, "the pressure to avoid using [emergency powers] appears to have come not from the judiciary but from civil society"). Civil society organizations (including, but not limited to those within the legal elite (Dezalay and

---

[21]   According to Grenfell, while some the rule-of-law promotion effort in East Timor is direct "much of it is performed through indirect means such as the funding of non-governmental organisations and Timor's formal rule-of-law institutions such as the courts and the Provedor" (2009: 231).

[22]   After Chief Justice Mohammad Chaudhry was dismissed and while he was detained under house arrest, the New York City Bar bestowed honorary membership on him *in absentia* (New York City Bar 2008). More recently, in the context of military rather than formal emergency rule, domestic and foreign lawyers worked together to lobby for the reinstatement of lawyers disbarred during the 1988 uprising in Burma/Myanmar (Law Society of Upper Canada 2012).

Garth 2010)) can play an indirect role in limiting the power of the state (Alagappa 2004: 11). By exposing abuses of power, mobilizing political opposition, and challenging the state's claims to political legitimacy, civil society organizations can play the role of "shadow" constitutional courts – as they have sought to do by resisting emergency rule in Pakistan (Ahmed and Stephan 2010: 492; Ashan 2009) and Nepal (see, in the context of the 2005 emergency in Nepal and its aftermath, Karki and Joshi 2010: 223), and facilitating democratic transition in Indonesia (Aspinall 2004: 84).

C.   Formal Emergency Regimes Revisited

Understanding the social significance of formal law and the role of civil society in mediating between law and society helps to put formal legal analysis and reform in perspective. Certainly, it is not everywhere the case that formal constitutional law is ineffective, and in many "new democracies" the place of the constitutions and constitutional courts is rapidly changing in the direction of greater significance and influence (Ginsburg 2003). We should be wary of underestimating the power of law or the ability of the courts, through judicial review (or the prospect of judicial review) – particularly under favourable social conditions – to be able to influence the conduct of government. But the diversity of legal experiences and cultures in Asia recommends a mindfulness of the relative significance of formal law and a healthy scepticism as to how far it might take us in our efforts to moderate political power, particularly in the context of emergency rule.

How, then, should constitutional lawyers approach emergency regimes with a view to limiting their potential abuse? First, we must be wary of assuming that one size fits all when it comes to designing an emergency powers regime capable of constraining government. Transitional and post-conflict states, even those committed to liberal constitutional principles, face unique challenges (e.g., communal dispute resolution, institution building, policing reform) as compared to, say, socially stable but politically turbulent states or executive-dominated but formal rule-of-law states, and the ideal emergency regime in each of these situations may vary considerably. Second, although threshold criteria and formal checks might be introduced at different stages of the process and different types of emergencies might be enumerated with different keys for unlocking them, it is important to recognize that the viability of these constraints is less a function of their formal relationship with one another as their "fit" within the legal and political culture; socio-legal research is therefore an indispensable component of comparative constitutional analysis. Finally, while formal constitutional constraints might be most effective when governments commit themselves to govern within the bounds of the constitution, it is contestable whether formal constitutional law can *only* work in a full-blown liberal democracy complete with an activist, reform-minded judiciary. It is therefore important for comparative constitutional law scholars to look beyond the usual assumptions about how constitutional law operates in liberal democracies. And while it might be challenging to show empirically that constitutional law can be effective even without the backing of the courts,[23] an examination of the socio-political context of emergency powers suggests that even in states not committed to a "Western" understanding of liberal-democratic constitutionalism, such as modern-day China, the government might yet have pragmatic reasons to take their constitutional commitments seriously and to justify their conduct publicly in legal terms (deLisle 2010). This kind of formally articulated but socially enforced constitutionalism might find an important place in the regulation of emergency powers when judicial review is absent – all the more when it is clear that civil society organizations, at home and abroad, are watching.

V. CONCLUSION: EMERGENCIES, COMPARATIVE METHODOLOGY, AND CONSTITUTIONALISM IN ASIA

It is unwise to generalize about constitutional emergency powers in the many diverse jurisdictions in Asia, let alone to offer any prescriptions. What we might nevertheless bear in mind is that more than any other area of constitutional law, emergency powers implicate a government's very commitment to constitutional government – a constitutional emergency powers regime, while occasionally necessary for self-protection, also opens the door to a legal regime's constitutional self-destruction. There are far too many instances of emergency powers invoked by governments as a way of consolidating political power, with emergency rule providing a thin "veneer of legality" (Dyzenhaus 2008: 33) to the abuse of political power. A pathology of emergency powers regimes, then, exposes the weaknesses of constitutional government itself, but it also suggests a variety of ways of narrowing the gap between the

---

[23]   The work of Tom Ginsburg and Tamir Moustafa on authoritarian states provides one example of how this sort of empirical inquiry might be approached: see their edited collection (2008).

aspiration of a legally accountable government and the reality of constitutionalism as it works (or not) in practice.

Comparative constitutional analysis in an Asian context has to walk a fine line between a formal, internal, and normative approach to constitutionalism, detached from the multiple realities of legal practice and socio-political context, and a contextual, empirical approach that abandons prescription altogether. A survey of emergency powers suggests the importance of acknowledging the diversity of constitutions and their socio-legal contexts in Asia, while recognizing that, amid this diversity, we might yet be able to reflect on the higher aims of constitutionalism and find multiple ways of realizing those aims. It also demonstrates the importance of being able to shift our perspective from internal to external and to deploy the relevant tools of analysis and statecraft, depending on the requirements of the context. Formal constitutional analysis provides a useful way of approaching the problems of governance, but it rarely provides a complete solution.

REFERENCES

Ahmed, Zahid Shahab and Maria J. Stephan. 2010. "Fighting for The Rule of Law: Civil Resistance and the Lawyers' Movement in Pakistan." *Democratization* 17(3): 492–513.

Alagappa, Muthiah, ed. 2004. *Civil Society and Political Change in Asia: Expanding and Contracting Democratic Space.* Stanford: Stanford University Press.

Ashan, Aitzaz. 2009. "The Preservation of the Rule of Law in Times of Strife." *The International Lawyer* 43(1): 73–76.

Aspinall, Edward. 2004. "Indonesia: Transformation of Civil Society and Democratic Breakthrough." Pp. 61–96 in *Civil Society and Political Change in Asia: Expanding and Contracting Democratic Space*, edited by Muthiah Alagappa. Stanford: Stanford University Press.

Chen, Albert H.Y. 2010a. "Emergency Powers: The East Asian Experience." Pp. 56–88 in *Emergency Powers in Asia*, edited by Victor V. Ramraj and Arun K. Thiruvengadam. Cambridge: Cambridge University Press.

Chen, Albert H.Y. 2010b. "Pathways of Western Liberal Constitutional Development in Asia: A Comparative Study of Five Major Nations." *International Journal of Constitutional Law* 8(4): 849–884.

Das, Cyrus. 2007. "The May 13th Riots and Emergency Rule." Pp. 101–113 in *Constitutional Landmarks in Malaysia: The First 50 Years 1957–2007*, edited by Andrew Harding and H.P. Lee. Petaling Jaya: Malayan Law Journal.

deLisle, Jacques. 2010. "States of Exception in an Exceptional State." Pp. 342–390 in *Emergency Powers in Asia*, edited by Victor V. Ramraj and Arun K. Thiruvengadam. Cambridge: Cambridge University Press.

Dezalay, Yves and Bryant G. Garth. 2010. *Asian Legal Revivals: Lawyers in the Shadow of Empire.* Chicago: University of Chicago Press.

Dyzenhaus, David. 2006. *The Constitution of Law: Legality in a Time of Emergency.* Cambridge: Cambridge University Press.

Dyzenhaus, David. 2008. "The Compulsion of Legality." Pp. 33–59 in *Emergencies and the Limits of Legality*, edited by Victor V. Ramraj. Cambridge: Cambridge University Press.

Dyzenhaus, David. 2009. "The Puzzle of Martial Law." *University of Toronto Law Journal* 59(1): 1–64.

Fuller, Thomas. 2012. "Crisis in Myanmar Over Buddhist-Muslim Clash." *New York Times*, June 10. (www.nytimes.com/2012/06/11/world/asia/state-of-emergency-declared-in-western-myanmar.html).

Ginsburg, Tom. 2003. *Judicial Review in New Democracies: Constitutional Courts in Asian Cases.* New York: Cambridge University Press.

Ginsburg, Tom. 2009. "Constitutional Afterlife: The Continuing Impact of Thailand's Postpolitical Constitution." *International Journal of Constitutional Law* 7(1): 83–105.

Ginsburg, Tom and Tamir Moustafa. 2008. *Rule by Law: The Politics of Courts in Authoritarian Regimes.* Cambridge: Cambridge University Press.

Grenfell, Laura. 2006. "Legal Pluralism and the Rule of Law in Timor Leste." *Leiden Journal of International Law* 19(2): 305–337.

Grenfell, Laura. 2009. "Promoting the Rule of Law in Timor-Leste." *Conflict, Security & Development* 9(2): 213–238.

Gross, Oren. 2011. "Constitutions and Emergency Regimes." Pp. 334–355 in *Comparative Constitutional Law*, edited by Tom Ginsburg and Rosalind Dixon. Cheltenham: Edward Elgar.

Haque, A.K.M. Masudul. 2008. "Emergency Powers and Caretaker Government in Bangladesh." *Journal of the Australasian Law Teachers Association* 1(1–2): 81–94.

Harding, Andrew. 1996. *Law, Government, and the Constitution in Malaysia.* Kuala Lumpur: Malayan Law Journal Sdn Bhd.

Harding, Andrew and Peter Leyland. 2011. *The Constitutional System of Thailand: A Contextual Analysis.* Oxford: Hart Publishing.

Hirschl, Ran. 2010. *Constitutional Theocracy.* Cambridge, Massachusetts: Harvard University Press.

Holdsworth, W.S. 1902. "Martial Law Historically Considered." *Law Review Quarterly* 18: 117–132.

Hosen, Nadirsyah. 2010. "Emergency Powers and the Rule of Law in Indonesia." Pp. 267–293 in *Emergency Powers in Asia*, edited by Victor V. Ramraj and Arun K. Thiruvengadam. Cambridge: Cambridge University Press.

Human Rights Watch. 2005. "Nepal: State of Emergency Deepens Human Rights Crisis." February 2. Retrieved September 6, 2012 (www.hrw.org/news/2005/01/31/nepal-state-emergency-deepens-human-rights-crisis).

International Commission of Jurists. 2009. *Assessing Damage, Urging Action: Report of the Eminent Jurists Panel on Terrorism, Counter-terrorism, and Human Rights.* Geneva: International Commission of Jurists.

International Commission of Jurists. 2010. "Press Release: Emergency Decree in Bangkok Thai Provinces Must be Revoked Immediately." July 9. (www.icj.org/wp-content/uploads/2012/06/Thailand-emergency-decree-revoked-press-release-2010.pdf)

Iyer, Venkat. 2000. *States of Emergency: The Indian Experience.* New Delhi: Butterworths.

Kalhan, Anil. 2010. "Constitution and 'Extra-Constitution': Colonial Emergency Regimes in Postcolonial India and Pakistan." Pp. 89–120 in *Emergency Powers in Asia*, edited by Victor V. Ramraj and Arun K. Thiruvengadam. Cambridge: Cambridge University Press.

Karki, Arjun and Neeraj N. Joshi. 2010. "Civil Society and Struggle for Human Rights in Nepal." Pp. 213–226 in *Democratic Process, Foreign Policy and Human Rights in South Asia*, edited by Joseph Benjamin. New Delhi: Gyan Publishing.

Lau, Martin. 2006–2007. "Pakistan." *Yearbook of Middle Eastern and Islamic Law* 13: 275.

Law Society of Upper Canada. 2012. "Law Society Efforts Bolster Rule of Law in Myanmar." *LSUC Gazette*, August 8. Retrieved September 9, 2012 (www.law societygazette.ca/news/law-societys-efforts-bolster-rule-of-law-in-myanmar/).

Lombardi, Clark B. 2010. "Islamism as a Response to Emergency Rule in Pakistan: The Surprising Proposal of Justice A.R. Cornelius." Pp. 436–465 in *Emergency Powers in Asia*, edited by Victor V. Ramraj and Arun K. Thiruvengadam. Cambridge: Cambridge University Press.

Mattei, Ugo. 1997. "Three Patterns of Law: Taxonomy and Change in the World's Legal Systems." *The American Journal of Comparative Law* 45(1): 5–44.

Nesiah, Vasuki. 2009. "The Princely Impostor: Stories of Law and Pathology in the Exercise of Emergency Powers." Pp. 121–145 in *Emergency Powers in Asia*, edited by Victor V. Ramraj and Arun K. Thiruvengadam. Cambridge: Cambridge University Press.

New York City Bar. 2008. "Honorary Membership Bestowed upon Pakistan Chief Justice Iftikhar Muhammad Chaudhry." January 14. (www.nycbar.org/media-aamp-publications/press-releases/2008/689-press20080114).

Omar, Imtiaz. 1996. *Rights, Emergencies, and Judicial Review*. Boston: Kluwer Law International.

Omar, Imtiaz. 2002. *Emergency Powers and the Courts in India and Pakistan*. The Hague: Kluwer Law International.

Pangalangan, Raul. 2010. "Political Emergencies in the Philippines: Changing Labels and the Unchanging Need for Legitimacy." Pp. 412–435 in *Emergency Powers in Asia*, edited by Victor V. Ramraj and Arun K. Thiruvengadam. Cambridge: Cambridge University Press.

Pollock, Frederick. 1902. "What is Martial Law?" *Law Quarterly Review* 18: 152–158.

Qureshi, Taiyyaba Ahmed. 2009–2010. "State of Emergency: General Pervez Musharraf's Executive Assault on Judicial Independence in Pakistan." *North Carolina Journal of International Law and Commercial Regulation* 35: 485.

Ramraj, Victor V. ed. 2008. *Emergencies and the Limits of Legality*. Cambridge: Cambridge University Press,

Ramraj, Victor V. 2010. "The Emergency Powers Paradox." Pp. 21–55 in *Emergency Powers in Asia*, edited by Victor V. Ramraj and Arun K. Thiruvengadam. Cambridge: Cambridge University Press.

Ramraj, Victor V. and Arun K. Thiruvengadam, eds. 2010. *Emergency Powers in Asia*. Cambridge: Cambridge University Press.

Report of the Secretary General. 2004. *The Rule of Law and Transitional Justice in Conflict and Post-Conflict Societies*. August 23, UN Security Council, S/2004/616.

Rossiter, Clinton L. 1948, reprinted in 2002. *Constitutional Dictatorship: Crisis Government in Modern Democracies*. New Brunswick, NJ: Transaction Publishers.

Slaughter, Anne-Marie. 2004. *A New World Order*. Princeton: Princeton University Press.

Stromseth, Jane, David Wippman and Rosa Brooks. 2006. *Can Might Make Rights? Building the Rule of Law After Military Interventions*. New York: Cambridge University Press.

Teubner, Gunter. 2012. *Constitutional Fragments: Societal Constitutionalism and Globalization*. Oxford: Oxford University Press.

Tey, Tsun Hang. 2008. "Brunei: Entrenching an Absolute Monarchy." Pp. 7–35 in *Constitutionalism in Southeast Asia*, vol. 2, edited by Clauspeter Hill and Jörg Menzel. Singapore: Konrad Adenauer Stiftung.

Thiruvengadam, Arun. 2010. "Asian Judiciaries and Emergency Powers: Reasons for Optimism?" Pp. 466–494 in *Emergency Powers in Asia*, edited by Victor V. Ramraj and Arun K. Thiruvengadam. Cambridge: Cambridge University Press.

Townshend, Charles. 1982. "Martial Law: Legal and Administrative Problems of Civil Emergency in Britain and the Empire." *Historical Journal* 25(1): 167–195.

Wang, Tay-sheng. 2002. "The Legal Development of Taiwan in the 20th Century: Toward a Liberal and Democratic Country." *Pacific Rim Law & Policy Journal* 11(3): 531–560.

Wang, Tay-sheng and I-Hsun Sandy Chou. 2010. "The Emergence of Modern Constitutional Culture in Taiwan." *National Taiwan University Law Review* 5(1): 1–38.

Wong, Max W.L. 2011. "Social Control and Political Order – Decolonisation and the use of Emergency Regulations in Hong Kong." *Hong Kong Law Journal* 41(1): 449–480.

Woodward, Barbara K. 2010. *Global Civil Society in International Lawmaking and Global Governance: Theory and Practice*. Leiden: Martinus Nijhoff.

PART III

CONSTITUTIONAL RIGHTS

9. The comparative constitutional law of freedom of expression in Asia

Adrienne Stone, Rishad Chowdhury and Martin Clark

Constitutional protection of freedom of expression is virtually universal (Barendt 2005; Currie and de Waal 2005; Krotoszynski 2006; Rishworth et al. 2003; Stone 2005). While freedom of expression has particularly strong roots in the Western liberal political tradition, the arrival of constitutionalism in Asia has brought constitutional protection of freedom of expression with it. Most Asian constitutions, reflecting the international consensus evident in the Universal Declaration of Human Rights and the International Covenant on Civil and Political Rights (which were either in existence or in the pipeline at the time most Asian constitutions were adopted) afford explicit protection, in one form or the other, to the right to speech and expression.

However, just as Western forms of constitutional law have been adapted to the particular contexts of Asian countries, understandings of freedom of expression too have been shaped by the distinctive political contexts and traditions of Asia. As in the West, the scope and reach of the right varies greatly across Asian nations, on paper as well as in its actual enforcement on the ground (Thio 2003; Zhang 2010; Chen 2010, for an exploration of the effect of historical contingencies on the actualization of constitutional rights in Asia).

Despite these variations, there are significant common factors across many Asian countries. A majority of Asian nations gained independence from foreign rule only in the twentieth century. Governance is generally weaker, the strength of enforcement of formally entrenched constitutional rights often varies widely (Chen 2010) and these features can significantly affect the protection afforded to the freedom of expression. Common accounts of Asian approaches to legal relations often emphasize that Asian legal cultures have fewer formal legal rules (Kahler 2000). Speaking generally, Asian cultures tend to prefer cultural expectations or principles and customary codes of conduct over strict obligations. Where disputes arise between parties, informal negotiation and mutual agreement is preferred over recourse to adversarial adjudication of disputes by a third party.

Although this account is necessarily general, these broad preferences are reflected in both the political culture of expression and in the legal rules protecting freedom of expression in Asian countries. Alongside the sometimes uncertain enforcement of constitutional rights, there are particular sensitivities that are relevant to the right to freedom of expression. Social and cultural values often vary significantly from Western ones, and this affects both the conceptualization and the enforcement of the freedom of expression in certain contexts (Thio 2003; Zhang 2010).

The chapter will review how the distinctive political and constitutional cultures of four Asian countries – Japan, Singapore, Malaysia and India – affect the articulation of freedom of expression principles by courts in those countries. Rather than attempting an exhaustive analysis of particular categories of freedom of expression protection and limitations in each of these four jurisdictions, our analysis will draw out particular aspects of protections and limitations that help to illustrate the broader constitutional cultures in each of these jurisdictions. Before doing so, we will review the fundamental elements of any constitutional principle of freedom of expression (including its formal manifestation, structural elements and doctrinal forms), noting some particularities evident in Asian countries.

I. FUNDAMENTAL ELEMENTS OF FREEDOM OF EXPRESSION RIGHTS

A. Constitutional Text

As elsewhere in the world, there is some variation among Asian constitutions in the nomination of "speech," "expression" and "communication" as the subjects of constitutional protection. The Constitution of India protects "freedom of speech and expression" (Article 19(1)(a)) as do the Constitutions of Malaysia and Singapore; the Bill of Rights Ordinance of Hong Kong refers to "freedom of opinion and expression;" and the Constitution of Japan (in the translation provided by the Ministry of Justice) refers to "speech, press and all other forms of expression."

Most commonly, these provisions are expressed as a declaration that all persons hold a certain right, following the model of the International Covenant on Civil and Political Rights, which provides that "everyone shall have the right to freedom of expression." The form of the First Amendment to the Constitution of the United States, which is expressed as a limitation on government ("Congress shall make no law ... abridging the freedom of speech") is not common in Asia. One clear counter-example, which reflects the American influence on Filipino constitution-making, is provided by Article III s 4 of the Constitution of the Republic of the Philippines which provides: "No law shall be passed abridging the freedom of speech, of expression, or of the press ..." This low level of influence is consistent with the generally waning influence of the wording of the US Constitution (Law and Versteeg 2012).

In Asia, as in other parts of the world, freedom of expression guarantees are often accompanied by related guarantees, typically of rights of assembly and association and protection for the press, though these too vary somewhat. To provide two examples: the Constitution of the Republic of Korea protects "freedom of assembly and association" along with "freedom of speech and the press" (Article 21) and the Constitution of the Republic of the Philippines (Article III s 4) similarly guarantees freedom "of the press, [and] the right of the people peaceably to assemble ..." These textual details are no doubt important in some contexts but there are more significant points of convergence and divergence among rights of freedom of expression and the law derived from them.

B. The Structure of a Freedom of Expression Principle

The shape of any constitutional right of freedom of expression will depend on at least three structural issues: (1) the coverage of the principle (the acts or things to which the principle applies); (2) the nature and degree of limitations permitted; and (3) whether the right has a positive aspect and/or a horizontal aspect.

1. What is expression?
Any guarantee of freedom of expression contains, at least implicitly, some conception of "expression" or "speech." In Asia, as elsewhere, it is usually accepted that a right of freedom of expression extends to speaking and writing, as well as many non-linguistic means of communi-cation, and to expressive conduct. For instance, the recognition that flag burning is a form of expression covered (though not necessarily pro-tected) by freedom of expression rights is widespread (Stone 2011) and extends to some Asian jurisdictions. Flag desecration, for instance, is recognized as expression in Hong Kong (*H.K.S.A.R. v Ng Kung Siu* [2001] 1 HKC 117 (Hong Kong Court of Final Appeal)). On a somewhat

different note, the Supreme Court of India has invalidated extremely restrictive guidelines that prohibited the common citizen from displaying the national flag, reasoning that displaying the national flag is a facet of a citizen's right to expression under the Constitution (*Union of India v Naveen Jindal* (2004) 2 SCC 510).

2.　Limiting freedom of expression

Because all rights of freedom of expression are subject to limits, determining the "coverage" of a right of freedom of expression is only the first step in resolving a question about its application. As a general proposition, Asian legal systems are, in varied contexts, willing to restrict speech to an extent that would be impermissible in many Western nations. Laws criminalizing blasphemy or proselytization in certain Islamic nations, including Malaysia, Indonesia and Pakistan, form one example, while another illustration is the controversial *lèse-majesté* law in Article 112 of Thailand's Criminal Code, which criminalizes defaming, insulting or threatening the monarchy (and by extension the Thai government: Harding and Leyland 2011: 237–247).

The reasons for this willingness to limit freedom of expression will be explored more fully in Section II of this chapter. For the moment, we simply note a few pertinent issues of constitutional structure prevalent in Asia. In most Asian constitutions, limitations on freedom of expression are explicitly or implicitly delineated by the constitutional text itself. Sometimes limitations are expressed in general terms, for example through a provision for "reasonable restrictions," such as Article 19(2) of the Indian Constitution, or a general limitation applicable to most or all rights listed in the constitution, as seen in Articles 12 and 13 of the Japanese Constitution. Indeed, constitutional rights of freedom of expression are universally limited and thus all constitutional systems must address the question of how, and in what circumstances, freedom of expression can be restricted.

3.　The application of freedom of expression guarantees: positive and negative application

A final set of structural considerations relates to the application, or scope, of a right of freedom of expression. Conceptually, like other rights, rights of freedom of expression might be "positive," entitling the rights holder to demand that enjoyment of the right be ensured, or "negative," protecting the rights holder only from interference. Although the drawing of this distinction is much criticized (Sunstein 2006: 207), it remains significant in the constitutional law of freedom of expression.

In the common law world, constitutional rights are usually thought to have an exclusively negative cast. However, in many other countries, there is no general reticence about positive constitutional rights and in some countries the recognition of a positive duty of protection has influenced even free speech jurisprudence.

Several Asian constitutions guarantee "duties of protection" (see for instance the reading of Article 21 of the Indian Constitution in *Francis Coralie Mullin v Administrator, Union Territory of Delhi* (1981) 1 SCC 608). However, the effect of the recognition of such positive obligations on the part of the State on the conceptualization of free speech is not always clear.

In India, the concept of a duty of protection has helped justify outright proscriptions on freedom of expression in certain situations. For example, in upholding the ban on a work of fiction alleged to offend the religious sentiments of a particular community, the Supreme Court reasoned that the State had an obligation to protect and safeguard the interests of minorities (*Baragur Ramachandrappa v State of Karnataka* (2007) 5 SCC 11). Such limitations on expression are fairly common in other Asian countries too (for example, see Thio 2003 for an analysis of the community-oriented approach of the Singapore judiciary in interpreting the constitutional guarantee of freedom of speech).

II. COMPARATIVE CONCEPTIONS OF FREEDOM OF EXPRESSION IN ASIA

The structural issues analyzed above are undoubtedly important when considering the law governing freedom of expression in Asian jurisdictions. But the most interesting points at which Asian constitutions have departed from the more widely studied Western systems of constitutional protection of freedom of expression are found in the clear differences in the conceptions of substantive values – about freedom of expression specifically, and rights more generally – that underlie Asian constitutions.

There are certain underlying characteristics common to a large number of countries that are important to bear in mind while engaging in such a comparative exercise. For one thing, democratic norms are undoubtedly weak in many Asian nations. While some countries are per se undemocratic on any fair understanding (North Korea and China) (Chen 2010: 882–884; Zhang 2010: 915), others are democracies but susceptible to coups or the imposition of martial law (for example, Pakistan) (Qureshi

2010), and still others are formally democratic but not always accompanied by strong democratic institutions or norms (Sri Lanka) (Coomaraswamy and Reyes 2004). Others are functioning democracies, but ones that see their governments change rarely (Japan) or never, or at least not yet (Malaysia and Singapore). The weakness of democratic norms is the first and foremost challenge to the enforcement of rights that might be formally entrenched in a written constitution.

The challenge for judicial bodies in Asia will often be that the indifferent commitment to democratic values is often accompanied by a lack of respect for judicial independence. Therefore, even where courts have a strong normative commitment to certain civil liberties, it would be necessary for them to act strategically to advance those values without jeopardizing their long-term institutional viability. Interestingly, however, there is scholarship that suggests that courts have been performing reasonably well on that score in certain East Asian countries (Chang 2010; Ginsburg 2003).

We now turn to the particular Asian countries that we propose to explore in greater detail. As we said above, the aim is not to flesh out every detail of constitutional jurisprudence pertaining to this right in any of these nations. It is, rather, to try to obtain a better and deeper understanding of the core themes that play out in this sphere of constitutional law, in different though related forms, in much of Asia.

A. Japan

Even before the decline of democracy in the 1930s, civil liberties in Japan were regarded as quite weak: those political rights that were enumerated in the Meiji Constitution had long been subject to stringent "public order" regulations used to suppress civil unrest. Pre-war rights guarantees were not constitutionally entrenched, and there was no mechanism for judicial review of legislation (Chen 2010: 853; Krotoszynski 2006: 139). In contrast, the post-war Constitution has been held up as a "success story" of transplanting Western liberal constitutional democracy into an Asian context (Chen 2010: 855, cf Law 2011). Since 1946, Japan has had a robust democratic constitutional system, with relatively strong constitutional rights and courts with strong, if infrequently exercised, powers of judicial review under Article 81 of the Japanese Constitution (Matsui 2011a; Oda 2009: 88).

In relation to freedom of expression, Article 21 of the Japanese *Constitution* provides that:

Freedom of assembly and association as well as speech, press and all other forms of expression are guaranteed. No censorship shall be maintained, nor shall the secrecy of any means of communication be violated.

Article 19 provides that: "Freedom of thought and conscience shall not be violated." However, Articles 12 and 13 limit all constitutional rights and freedoms, including freedom of expression and conscience, on the basis of a broad "public welfare" limitation. Article 12, the principal limiting clause in freedom of expression cases, reads:

The freedoms and rights guaranteed to the people by this Constitution shall be maintained by the constant endeavour of the people, who shall refrain from any abuse of these freedoms and rights and shall always be responsible for utilising them for the public welfare.

That clause is implemented through a "balancing of interests" test that weighs the value of the right against the value achieved by restricting that right, and requires that any restriction be "reasonable and necessary" (Oda 2009: 92–93). The doctrinal development of this test resembles some aspects of United States law: where prior-restraint of speech is involved (as in censorship), the court applies the most exacting standard of scrutiny; where a content-based restriction is challenged, the government must show that it is narrowly tailored to achieve a compelling interest, or that there is a clear and present danger of significant harm that the law avoids; and content-neutral restrictions require the government to show that it is the least restrictive means to achieving an important objective (Matsui 2011a: 196–197; Matsui, 2011c: 1398; Oda 2009: 91).

However, this superficial similarity looks quite different in context. In Asian courts as elsewhere, formal doctrine does not always fully reveal the values that actually animate judicial decision-making. Most significantly in the Japanese case, the Supreme Court has never applied these tests to rule a law invalid. This aspect of Japanese constitutional law reflects a more general feature: the rarity of judicial overruling. Indeed, the Court has only exercised its power to strike down unconstitutional legislation on eight occasions since 1946 (Matsui 2011a: 146). Thus, although the Court apparently takes a United States-style approach to investigating questions of the constitutional permissibility of limitations on expression, it is somewhat difficult to make any clear statement of what would constitute an impermissible restriction on speech. Whether or not this means the Court is hostile or unsympathetic towards individual rights, or should be labeled "conservative," is a matter of contention among Japanese legal scholars and judges (Fujita 2011, contra Watanabe,

Etoh and Odanaka 1995). The more general question of how the justices of the Supreme Court consider their own role in constitutional adjudication is likewise contentious (see Krotoszynski 2006: 142–145; Matsui 2011b: 1375). These constitutional practices can perhaps be fully understood only in the context of the broader political and constitutional culture. The traditional view of Japanese social and political culture is that social harmony and consensus are prioritized and promoted over individual freedoms and strong dissent (Matsui 2011a: 210–211) though it is also contended, to the contrary, that strong opinions are held and voiced, but through non-individual channels that are unfamiliar to Western observers (Beer 1990; Law 2011).

The picture is further complicated when the nature of judicial review in Japan is taken into account. When assessing the Japanese Supreme Court's approach to freedom of expression it is important to bear in mind that the failure to formally invalidate any legislation on the ground of violation of Article 21 does not imply that judicial decisions in this realm have had no effect on free expression in Japan. Significantly, in several decisions, the Supreme Court has employed the guarantee of free expression in Article 21 to inform its interpretation of the statute in question. In the *Tokyo Metropolitan Security Regulation Case* (20 July 1960, *Keishu* 14-9-1243), for instance, a majority of the Court interpreted a statute governing public assemblies to require that an application be rejected only "under very rare circumstances," such as where "the mass movement is recognized as clearly and directly dangerous to the maintenance of the public peace." Similarly, in the *Narita Airport Case*, the Supreme Court considered a law that granted the Minister of Transport a power to prohibit free expression near a controversial airport development. In upholding the power, the Court again read the law narrowly as applying only where "violent and destructive activities" were "highly likely" (Krotoszynski 2006: 153–154).

A strong emphasis on consensus, order and communal values is detectable in the Japanese case law in the realm of free expression, consistent with the social norms highlighted earlier. Two cases, both decided in 2011, and both relating to limitations on expression connected with the national anthem, are illuminating. The first case, Case No 2008 (A) No 1132 ("*Obstruction Case*"), involved a person indicted under Article 234 of the Penal Code, which makes it a criminal offense to forcibly obstruct the business of another. The accused, who had served as a teacher at a Tokyo high school, arrived before a graduation at the school, distributed leaflets to parents, ignored the principal's request to stop, voiced his opposition to the requirement to stand and sing the national anthem and shouted loudly when confronted.

The Supreme Court held that Article 21 of the Constitution did not preclude the accused from being held criminally responsible under Article 234 of the Penal Code. Characterizing the accused's actions as "rough speech and behavior" that caused "uproar," the Court concluded "[t]he acts of the accused in question were performed in an inappropriate manner that was unsuitable to the occasion, and caused interference with the smooth implementation of the graduation ceremony, which is supposed to be held in a peaceful and quiet atmosphere, to the extent that such interference could not be overlooked." (Notably however, the Supreme Court upheld the lower court's imposition of a fine even though a prison sentence was sought by the prosecutor.)

Case No 2010 (O) No 951 (*"Anthem Case"*) involved similar circumstances. By way of protest, a group of teachers and an official employed at various Tokyo Metropolitan high schools refused to comply with official orders issued by the principals at those schools to stand, face the national flag and sing the national anthem during official ceremonies. The Supreme Court held that the orders did not violate Article 19 (freedom of thought and conscience) because they did not force the appellants "to have a particular thought or prohibit them from having an objection thereto, nor ... compel the [appellants] to confess whether they have or do not have a particular thought." The "indirect" constraint involved in forcing the appellants to perform actions at odds with "their views of history" was held to be "necessary and reasonable" as the orders were directed to securing the "well-ordered" and "smooth" procession of official school events and to the performance of the appellants' legal duties as public servants.

This emphasis on public order over individual rights can be seen as far back as the *Tokyo Metropolitan Security Regulation Case* (1960) in which a majority of the Court upheld the constitutional validity of a Tokyo city ordinance prohibiting the use of a park for a May Day assembly on the basis of the "public welfare" served by maintaining the public peace within the park. While this attention to public order distinguishes the Japanese Supreme Court's approach from that of the Supreme Court of the United States, however, it is not obviously far outside the international mainstream. Courts have given considerable weight to concerns of this kind in Western countries too. They are especially notable in decisions of the courts in the United Kingdom upholding s 5 of the Public Order Act (*Hammond v DPP* [2004] EWHC 69; *Norwood v DPP* [2003] EWHC 1564) and have received widespread, though not yet dominant, judicial attention in Australia (*Attorney-General (SA) v Corporation of the City of Adelaide* [2013] HCA 3 (27 February 2013); *Coleman v Power* (2004) 220 CLR 1). However the recent cases drive home the strength of that commitment and the distinctiveness of the contexts in which it can be invoked in Japan. In those cases, laws aimed at public order at official events were upheld as "necessary and reasonable" even though they were directed to disruptions that preceded the events, and even where they involve conduct primarily involving abstaining from participation in the ceremony.

B. Singapore

Article 14 of the *Constitution of Singapore* provides "every citizen of Singapore ... the right to freedom of speech and expression" subject to any restriction contained in a law of the Parliament that it

> considers necessary or expedient in the interest of the security of Singapore ... friendly relations with other countries, public order or morality, and restrictions designed to protect the privileges of Parliament or to provide against contempt of court, defamation or incitement to any offence.

Article 14(1)(b) grants "all citizens of Singapore ... the right to assemble peaceably and without arms" subject to any restriction contained in a law of the Parliament. "Special powers" relating to subversion and emergencies may also operate to further limit free expression (Articles 149, 150).

Article 14 is to be read in the context of an unusually well-defined, explicit state ideology. Since the first Singaporean elections in 1959, the People's Action Party (PAP) has held unassailable control of the government, and opposition parties have never held more than three seats at any one time (Tey 2011: 235). The PAP's ideology – and hence the legal and political culture of Singapore – is often broadly described as neo-Confucianist or "communitarian," meaning that there is a greater emphasis on community values and social harmony through respect for hierarchical relations, which trumps individual rights and plural conceptions of the good (as evident in the 1991 Parliamentary Report "White Paper on Shared Values"). The Singaporean government embraces and frequently re-affirms its commitment to "Asian values" though some commentators discern a gradual shift away from its tight restrictions on expression, and towards permitting "disagreement without being disagreeable or treating critics as rebels" (Tan and Thio 2010: 984–985).

When considering limitations on freedom of expression, the central test for Singaporean courts grants Parliament "an extremely wide discretionary power and remit that permits a multifarious and multifaceted approach towards achieving any of the purposes specified in Article 14(2) of the *Constitution*" (*Chee Siok Chin v Minister for Home Affairs* [2005]

1 Sing L. R. 582). When called upon to interpret the powers of Parliament to limit Article 14, Singapore's courts "have tended to defer to the government's assessment of the needs of public order, without requiring that the restrictions be informed by substantive standards of reasonableness, proportionality, or necessity within a democratic society" (Thio 2003: 516).

An array of laws restrict both the content and mode of expression, many of them justified on "public morality" grounds. Various statutes provide for the censorship of obscene or indecent films, books, music, advertisements and posters. Others create offenses relating to "unlawful" public assembly, nuisance offenses, and offenses against public order (Tan and Thio 2010: 991). Consequently, the power of censorship boards to effect prior-restraints on expression by banning particular material is not meaningfully constrained by Article 14. To take one example, the Board of Film Censors is empowered under the Films Act to ban "party political films," defined as films that it considers to be "sensationalistic," not "factual and objective" or presenting a "dramatised" or "distorted picture" of political issues.

In addition, the news media are subject to significant restrictions in Singapore that are not typical of other democracies. Foreign press ownership and licenses to operate or distribute foreign newspapers are especially strictly controlled at the Attorney-General's discretion. In *Dow Jones Publishing Company (Asia) Inc v Attorney-General* (1989), the Court of Appeal upheld a decision to reduce the circulation of the *Asian Wall Street Journal* from 5000 to 400 after the paper had questioned the government's intentions in establishing a second stock exchange and refused to print a government reply.

This sensitivity to criticism of government is evident also in the law of defamation and in the robust interpretation of the common law offense of "scandalizing the court". Like much of the rest of the world, the Singaporean courts have considered, but not adopted, the United States Supreme Court's decision in *New York Times v Sullivan* (Stone and Williams 2000) but in Singapore the position is more than usually permissive of defamation actions. Singaporean courts have considered and rejected the approaches to political defamation in the US, UK and Australia that limit defamation law in the interests of freedom of expression (Tan 2011). In *Review Publishing Co Ltd v Lee Hsien Loong*, the Court of Appeal declined to adopt either the House of Lords' approach to responsible journalism (established in *Reynolds v Times Newspapers* [2001] 2 AC 127), or the Australian rules (established in *Lange v Australian Broadcasting Corporation* (1997) 182 CLR 520) (Thio 2003: 523). Also, damages awards are quite high, and have been described as "crippling" and no PAP politician has ever lost a defamation suit (Tey 2011: 458). There is some suggestion (Tan 2011), however, that the Court of Appeal might apply the House of Lords' test in the future in defamation cases involving Singaporean citizens (as opposed to foreigners who are not entitled to Article 14 protections: *Review Publishing Co Ltd v Lee Hseien Loong* [2010] 1 Sing L. R. 52). As to criticisms of judges or the courts generally, any speech that "scandalizes" the judiciary is criminalized, and can be prosecuted by the Attorney-General. The offense does not require that any "real risk" of prejudicing the administration of justice be proven, rather it requires only proof that the speech has the "inherent tendency to interfere with the administration of justice" (*Attorney-General v Wain* [1991] SLR 383) without any need for proof of an intention to do so (*Chee Soon Juan's Case*, Lia Siu Chiu J).

One recent development, indicative of prevailing attitudes to freedom of expression, is the establishment of a "Speakers' Corner" in 2000. The Public Entertainments (Speakers' Corner) (Exemption) Order of 2000 creates a "free expression" area within Singapore's central business district. However, use of the area is still strictly controlled: potential speakers must be Singaporean citizens, must apply for a government-issued permit 30 days prior to speaking, must not use amplification, must only address the audience in an official language, and must only speak for a limited time on administration-approved subjects (Thio 2003: 517–520). Speakers who violate the conditions may be suspended for 30 days from using the corner, and may be charged with violating the Public Entertainments and Meetings Act, which carries a maximum penalty of a $10,000 fine. Several speakers have been prosecuted for violating the regulations. In one such instance, *Chee Soon Juan v Public Prosecutor*, a speaker was fined $3,000 for breaching regulations aimed at preventing social unrest, after he spoke critically of Singapore's ban on wearing a particular form of Muslim headscarf, the *tudung*, in schools, which had led to the suspension of four primary school girls. Judge Kow Keng Siong held that "some members of the public" believed the speech to be "racially and religiously divisive" and stated that "any disturbance to the delicate equilibrium in our multi-racial and multi-religious country can have potentially catastrophic consequences" (Thio 2003: 521–522).

In conclusion, then, freedom of expression in Singapore is tightly controlled both through political culture and legal restrictions. Any valid statute is capable of curtailing expression, and courts take a permissive and deferential approach to limitations on free expression.

C. Malaysia

Malaysia and Singapore share a close and intertwined political and cultural history and hence many constitutional similarities. Since the state's inception in 1957, Malaysia's constitutional system has provided for a strong central federal executive, and is said to be typical of the "East Asian developmental states" that aimed at strong economic progress and later the development of democracy over time (Harding 2012: chapter 2). It has also been dominated by a single political party: the National Alliance coalition, which has obtained a clear majority in each of the 12 elections held so far, and its Chairman – who has in each instance also been the president of the largest political party in the coalition, the United Malays National Organisation (UMNO)) – has each time been appointed prime minister.

While in this context, broad restrictions on freedom of expression are not surprising, the breadth of permissible limitations on expression contained in the Constitution itself is especially notable. While Article 10 of the Constitution outlines the freedom of expression, and guarantees "every citizen ... the right to freedom of speech and expression," in Article 10(2) that right is significantly qualified by a provision that Parliament may impose by law, any restriction "it deems necessary or expedient in the interest of the security of the Federation ... friendly relations with other countries, public order or morality and restrictions designed to protect the privileges of Parliament ... or to provide against contempt of court, defamation, or incitement to any offence."

Moreover the Constitution explicitly requires courts to take a deferential approach to the interpretation of limitations on expression by limiting the power of the courts to inquire into the necessity for laws directed at restrictions mentioned in Article 10(2). (Article 4(2)(b); Vohrah, Koh and Ling 2004: 108). In addition, Article 10(4) allows content-based restrictions on "sensitive issues": it provides that as to restrictions to free expression on the grounds of national security or public order,

> Parliament may pass law prohibiting the questioning of any matter, right, status, position, privilege, sovereignty or prerogative protected by the provisions of Part III [citizenship], article 152 [national languages], 153 [duties, responsibilities and powers of the Monarch] or 181 [savings for the powers of the Ruling Chiefs of various states] ...

Article 10 is also further limited by executive emergency powers (Article 150), legislation aimed at combating "subversion" or "action prejudicial to public order" (Article 149) even absent a state of emergency being declared (Harding 2012: 164). Finally, as the text of Article 10 suggests, free expression rights are enjoyed only by Malaysian citizens (Tan and Thio 2010: 989).

In the regulation of freedom of expression in Malaysia, matters of race and religion have proved to be particularly sensitive flashpoints. Sedition and security laws extend to matters that in other jurisdictions would come under the banner of hate speech regulation. Section 22(1) of the Internal Security Act 1960 empowers the Minister to prohibit any publication that the Minister considers likely to cause violence, disobedience, a breach of the peace, or hostility between races or classes of the population. Section 4 of the Sedition Act 1948 criminalizes making, preparing or conspiring to do a "seditious act," which includes uttering seditious words or producing or importing any seditious publication. The definition of sedition in s 3 is wide, and extends to inciting hatred or contempt against the government or judiciary, fomenting revolt, discontent, disaffection, ill-will or hostility among the citizenry and there is no requirement that the speaker intended to incite violence, tumult or public disorder (*Public Prosecutor v Ooi Kee Saik* [1971] 2 MLJ 108 (High Court of Malaysia) [16]). Strict limits on criticizing the judiciary, derived from Article 125 of the Constitution, also exist (*Majlis Peguam Malaysia v Raja Segaran a/l Krishnan* [2005] 1 MLJ 15; Harding 2012: 219).

Limitations on religious expression – in particular strict curtailment of blasphemy and certain forms of proselytization – have take on especially high prominence in Malaysian law. Articles 295–298A of Malaysia's Penal Code make it an offense to utter words that are intended to offend another's religion. The states have enacted a wide range of specific prohibitions relating to religious offense, some applicable only to Muslims, and others applicable to both Muslims and non-Muslims alike. For Muslims, certain statutes prohibit apostasy, worshipping in an incorrect manner, defying religious authorities, and falsely claiming to be a religious authority. Blasphemy offenses, which protect only Islam, apply to all persons, and include insulting, bringing into contempt or ridiculing the religion of Islam, Islamic ceremonies or practices, Islamic religious authority figures or the verses of sacred Islamic texts. These offenses can carry penalties of heavy fines and severe prison sentences (Masum 2009).

Propagation of religious belief is likewise heavily regulated. Nine of Malaysia's 14 states have enacted laws that limit the ability of non-Muslims to propagate their religious beliefs. These include outlawing the conversion of Muslims, and, in certain states, an offense of subjecting a Muslim to speech or literature concerning a non-Islamic religion, including distributing that literature in public (see, eg, Enactment for Malacca No 1 of 1988, Kedah No 11 of 1988, cited in Tan and Thio 2010: 1339).

In the context of religions whose practice includes a duty to proselytize, the regulation of proselytizing may in fact amount to a regulation on practice, to which Art 11(4) does not extend (Tan and Thio 2010: 1339).

The extensive regulation of expression in Malaysia has been somewhat limited by the courts. Typically, however, limitations on religious expression have been struck down on federalism grounds, rather than to preserve constitutional rights. In *Mamat bin Daud v Government of Malaysia* [1988] 1 MLJ 119, the Federal Court struck down s 298A of the Penal Code, which prohibited a wide range of offensive acts aimed at causing "religious disunity" (including making the imputation that another person was an apostate). The Court held that the substance of s 298A did not relate to "public order" but rather religious matters or affairs; that legislative power is reserved to the states alone.

In an important 2011 decision, however, there appears to be some strengthening of judicial approaches to Article 10. In previous cases, it had been held that while a law that limits Article 10(1) "must be sufficiently connected" to the subjects enumerated under Article 10(2)(a), the courts would not inquire into the reasonableness of the restriction (*Public Prosecutor v Pung Chen Choon* [1994] 1 MLJ 566). However, in a significant recent case, the Federal Court (Malaysia's highest court) read a "reasonableness" requirement into Article 10. In *Sivarasa Rasiah v Badan Peguam Malaysia* [2010] 2 MLF 333, the Federal Court held that an act aimed at preventing conflicts of interest in the legal profession did not infringe Article 10's guarantee of freedom of association. In doing so, the Court held that Article 10 required a standard of "reasonableness" because, as a general matter, limits to constitutional rights were to be read restrictively. In addition, the Court appeared to adopt a "basic structure" doctrine finding that "certain features that constitute [the Constitution's] basic fabric", and that '[u]nless sanctioned by the Constitution itself, any statute (including one amending the Constitution) that offends the basic structure may be struck down as unconstitutional". Part II rights guarantees constituted one part of that basic fabric (*Sivarasa Rasiah v Badan Peguam Malaysia* [2010] 2 MLF 333, 342). These principles were applied to Article 10's freedom of expression guarantee in *Muhammad Hilman bin Idham* [2011] 6 MLJ 507, in which a majority of the Court of Appeal struck down a provision that curtailed university students from expressing or doing anything that could be reasonably construed as supporting, sympathizing with, or opposing any political party, on the basis that, following *Sivarasa Rasiah* and reading the word "reasonable" into the provisions of Article 10, the statute unreasonably restricted freedom of expression and did not serve the government's alleged "public order" interest. (*Muhammad Hilman* is also of consider-able methodological interest. In contrast to the general reluctance among Malaysian judges to consider foreign materials in constitutional cases, Mohd Hishamudin JCA in *Muhammad Hilman* quoted two United States cases, including Justice Brandeis' famous opinion in *Whitney v California*, 274 US 357 [1927]).

In keeping with this overall trend, a recent lower court decision overruled the Home Minister's rejection of an application for a print publishing license as a violation of the freedom of the press, which the Court read into Article 14. The case is yet to go to appeal, but it marks a possible landmark expansion in freedom of expression in Malaysia ("Malaysiakini" 2011).

D. India

India is an especially interesting case for freedom of expression in Asia (as well as generally). An independent republic since the end of British rule in 1950, India has a well-developed constitutional jurisprudence; a long-standing commitment to democracy (albeit with a significant ques-tion mark with respect to the two-year period when a proclamation of emergency was made by Prime Minister Indira Gandhi in the 1970s); and a commitment to liberal constitutional values that sits alongside deep-rooted societal and cultural norms and values that affect freedom of expression.

Protection for freedom of expression is found in Part III of the Constitution of India, which sets out the fundamental rights of the people of the country. Many though not all of these rights are enjoyed against the State, but there are other rights that are enforceable against private persons too (at least in certain contexts).

The right to freedom of speech and expression is to be found in Article 19 of the Constitution. Article 19(1)(a) states that all citizens shall have the right "to freedom of speech and expression," part of a set of rights contained in Article 19, which also include the right of peaceable assembly, the right to form associations and unions, and the right to move freely throughout and to reside in any part of India.

Like many constitutions, express limitations are found in the same article. Clauses (2) to (6) delineate "reasonable restrictions" that can lawfully be imposed on the exercise of each of these rights. As it stands today, Article 19(2) states that the State shall not, by virtue of Article 19(1)(a), be prevented from making any law imposing "reasonable restrictions on the exercise of the right ... in the interests of the sovereignty and integrity of India, the security of the State, friendly relations with foreign States, public order, decency or morality, or in relation to contempt of court, defamation or incitement to an offence."

When the Constitution first came into being, the exception carved out in Article 19(2) was worded differently, and pertained to "any law relating to libel, slander, defamation, contempt of Court or any matter which offends against decency or morality or which undermines the security of, or tends to overthrow the State." In response to an early Supreme Court judgment (*Romesh Thapar v Union of India* AIR 1950 SC 124) that invalidated certain statutes authorizing broad measures to ensure public safety and the maintenance of public order, the Constitution (First Amendment) Act 1951 was passed, enlarging the heads of permissible restrictions to include "friendly relations with foreign States," "public order" and "incitement to an offence." However, and very significantly, the word "reasonable" was inserted before the word "restrictions."

As in the case of the other Asian jurisdictions analyzed in this chapter (although perhaps not to the same extent), the Indian Supreme Court has been willing to defer to the executive with respect to restrictions on the right to free expression in different contexts, and most of all in the realm of speech on sensitive topics such as religion. The Indian Penal Code 1860 contains a number of provisions imposing limitations on the exercise of free speech in various contexts, including the type of limitations that would fall within the category of content-based (and viewpoint-based) restrictions. Section 153A of the Indian Penal Code 1860 criminalizes the promotion, "on grounds of religion, race, place of birth, residence, language, caste or community or any other ground whatsoever, disharmony or feelings of enmity, hatred or ill-will between different religious, racial, language or regional groups or castes or communities." The provision further criminalizes the commission of "any act which is prejudicial to the maintenance of harmony between different religious, racial, language or regional groups or castes or communities, and which disturbs or is likely to disturb the public tranquility." Section 95 of the Criminal Procedure Code 1973 permits the forfeiture of any book or written material that appears to the State government to contain material that is punishable inter alia under s 153A or s 153B.

The Court has upheld the constitutional validity of these penal provisions, reasoning that they fall within the ambit of "reasonable restrictions" on the constitutional right. While upholding the power of forfeiture in s 95, the Court has held that, in order for the provision to be compatible with the constitutional right to free speech, it must be interpreted restrictively. The Court has noted that the power to order forfeiture of a book is a drastic power that has a direct impact upon a cherished right, and as such ought to be construed narrowly, and the exercise of the power must be strictly in accordance with the procedure envisaged in the statutory provision (*State of Maharashtra v Sagharaj Damodar Rupawate* (2010) 7 SCC 398).

Bijoe Emmanuel v State of Kerala (1986) 3 SCC 615 is another significant case, and one of the most pro-speech decisions given by the Indian Supreme Court. In this case, a school had expelled three children belonging to the Jehovah's Witnesses faith, on account of their failure to join in the singing of the national anthem. The Supreme Court set aside the expulsion of the children, holding that their refusal to participate in the singing of the national anthem was on account of genuine religious objections. Hence, the action taken was violative of their constitutional right to practice their religion as also their right to freedom of speech and expression under Article 19(1)(a).

In the relatively recent case of *S Khushboo v Kanniammal* (2010) 5 SCC 600, the appellant was a well-known actress who had commented on the increasing incidence of pre-marital sex in the state of Tamil Nadu, and expressed an opinion that there was no harm caused. A number of criminal complaints were filed against her, alleging that the statements were offensive and defamatory in nature. Quashing the criminal complaints, the Supreme Court held that notions of societal morality were inherently subjective, and the criminal process could not be used to interfere unduly with the domain of personal autonomy. The remarks have to be judged keeping in mind the average, prudent reader, and the law ought not to be employed in a manner that would have a chilling effect on free expression. Hence, the Court concluded that even a prima facie case was not made out against the appellant, and accordingly quashed the criminal complaints.

In the context of the law of defamation, the Supreme Court has recognized the possible adverse impact effect on freedom of expression of permitting public officials to sue too readily for libel. In the landmark case of *R Rajagopal v State of Tamil Nadu* (1994) 6 SCC 632, the Supreme Court approved the *New York Times v Sullivan* rule, and held that a case for defamation would not be made out "even where the publication is based upon facts and statements which are not true, unless the official establishes that the publication was made ... with reckless disregard for truth." Nonetheless, from a practical perspective, defamation in India appears to be less relevant to the constitutional jurisprudence governing free speech than in other jurisdictions such as the United States (or Singapore, as discussed earlier). This is possibly on account of particular features of the Indian legal system. While defamation is a civil wrong, defamation suits (like most civil cases) take inordinately long in the Indian court system. Further, heavy damages are rarely imposed and so the prospect of civil defamation does not perhaps have the same "chilling effect" on free speech as is the case in other jurisdictions (such as Malaysia). Defamation is also a criminal offense under the Indian Penal Code 1860 and this is probably a greater deterrent to controversial speech. Even in the context of criminal law, though, the penal provisions relating to causing offense to different classes of persons appear to be more frequently invoked in the context of controversial political or artistic speech, and it is these that are most significant for the exercise of the right to free expression in India.

Contempt of court law in India is also extremely relevant to a discussion of a possible "chilling" of the right to free speech and expression. Arguably, the Supreme Court has been less than consistent in this sphere. In cases such as *In Re: Mulgaonkar* (1978) 3 SCC 339, the Supreme Court has advocated cautious resort to the contempt jurisdiction, observing that judges should not be hyper-sensitive and that the press should be given free play within reasonable limits. However, in *In Re: Arundhati Roy* (2002) 3 SCC 343, the Court sentenced Ms Roy to a day's imprisonment, holding that she had committed contempt of court by stating on affidavit (in pending contempt proceedings) that the Court displayed a "disquieting inclination ... to silence criticism and muzzle dissent, to harass and intimidate those who disagree with it." In this case, the Court acknowledged that outspoken criticism of the courts is permissible, but concluded that the contemnor had exceeded her constitutional right to speech by imputing motives to the Court, and therefore convicted her for contempt of court.

While freedom of the press is not independently guaranteed in Article 19(1)(a) or elsewhere, the Supreme Court has held it to be an integral part of the broader constitutional right to free speech and expression (Sorabjee 2000: 335). A number of interesting cases in the 1970s dealt with situations where ostensibly neutral regulatory measures were alleged to be intended to coerce the press. In *Bennett Coleman & Co v Union of India* AIR 1973 SC 106, the Supreme Court held that a policy significantly restricting the import of newsprint would be violative of Article 19(1)(a), since it would directly affect the circulation (and viability) of the newspaper in question.

It is hard to assess the extent to which any of the cases discussed above are indicative of a real and meaningful trend in the context of free expression jurisprudence in India. Generalizing too broadly from a few landmark decisions is always hazardous. This is particularly the case with a constitutional court consisting of a large number of justices, like the Indian Supreme Court. (In response to mounting arrears, Parliament has increased the strength of the Supreme Court several times since 1950, and the Court today is comprised of a Chief Justice and a maximum of 30 other justices. The Court ordinarily conducts judicial business in panels of two or three justices, with five or more justices sitting together only rarely, normally for constitutional questions of first impression.)

Inconsistency in Indian constitutional jurisprudence is a very real phenomenon (Seervai 1996: 2964–5), and there is no reason to believe that this sub-set of constitutional law is left unaffected. The contrasting approach of the Court in two cases highlighted above, *Bijoe Emmanuel* and *Baragur Ramachandrappa*, is revealing. While efforts to reconcile the decisions doctrinally could perhaps be made, the more plausible explanation may well be the one advanced by the legal realist, that the judicial ideology and personal predilections of the justices in question played a significant role.

In conclusion, India presents an interesting study of the often uneasy meshing of liberal constitutional values with significantly more conservative religious and social values. A further complicating factor is India's judicial structure (particularly the phenomenon of a high number of panels in the Supreme Court) and the uncertainty and fluidity of Indian constitutional jurisprudence. The cumulative effect of this is a constitutional structure and jurisprudence that values and protects the constitutional right to free expression, but far from perfectly.

III. CONCLUSION: COMPARATIVISM AND FREEDOM OF EXPRESSION IN ASIA

Comparative constitutional law analysis in the Asian context poses its own, distinctive challenges. The "elephant in the room," of course, is the overarching debate regarding the universality or otherwise of human rights principles and norms (including the right to free speech), and the question of whether principles generally developed in liberal Western democracies are well suited to transplantation in Asian jurisdictions (Harding and Lee 2007, analyzing but ultimately rejecting such concerns).

But the challenges are both greater and more varied than that. The temptation to view Asia as a monolithic entity must be scrupulously avoided. Indeed, Asia within itself arguably contains all the complexities and variations that are to be seen on a survey of the globe as a whole. One analysis of five Asian nations classifies their constitutional practices, over time, as falling within one of three types: Classical Constitutionalism, Party-State and Hybrid Constitutional Practices (Chen 2010). Chen concludes that there is reason for cautious optimism about the "prospects of constitutionalism in Asia and its adaptability to Asian soil" (Chen 2010: 884).

Related to the caveat about Asian nations themselves varying widely with respect to constitutional institutions and practices, there is a need to consider comparative constitutional law within Asia. As a matter of practice, do Asian nations borrow more willingly from other Asian nations than from the outside world? Normatively, should they?

Future scholarship on comparative constitutional law in Asia generally, and free speech jurisprudence in particular, might also consider whether Asian countries can or should look differently upon constitutional principles that might have originated outside Asia, but have since been "tested" in other Asian jurisdictions. For an Asian country that is similar in institutional structure or cultural norms to another Asian nation, it might be easier to incorporate constitutional principle or doctrine that has already been adopted by the latter.

In any event, this debate regarding the potential use of comparative insights in Asian constitutional law goes only to one use of comparative analysis in constitutional law: the use of foreign law as an interpretive resource. There remain of course many other circumstances in which comparative inquiry may be useful. Constitutional design is one obvious instance, and the process of framing of new constitutions in Asian countries such as Afghanistan and Iraq drew heavily on comparative insights. Comparative inquiry will also be required in cases that do not involve the straightforward application of freedom of expression principles. For instance, courts may consider foreign law on freedom of expression under choice of law rules where expression originating in one jurisdiction causes or is alleged to have caused harm in other jurisdictions or when questions arise as to the enforceability of foreign judgments.

Comparativism in one context or another is, therefore, an almost inevitable element of constitutional analysis in all legal systems, and one that Asian nations cannot avoid. This fact poses a challenge for constitutionalists to which comparativists are well placed to respond. Successful comparativism within the field of freedom of expression, as elsewhere, requires a deep and critical engagement with foreign law that encompasses critical legal and philosophical literature on freedom of expression as well as case law. In the case of Asia, it also requires close attention to the ways in which the countries in question differ from those to which comparative constitutional law scholarship has thus far primarily addressed itself, and the manner in which such differences can be accounted for without sacrificing the core values of free speech.

REFERENCES

Austin, Granville. 1966. *The Indian Constitution: Cornerstone of a Nation*. Oxford: Clarendon Press.

Barendt, Eric. 2005. *Freedom of Speech*, 2nd ed. Oxford: Oxford University Press.

Beer, Lawrence W. 1990. "Freedom of Expression: The Continuing Revolution." *Law and Contemporary Problems* 53(2): 39–69.

Chang, Wen-Chen. 2010. "Strategic Judicial Responses in Politically Charged Cases: East Asian Experiences." *International Journal of Constitutional Law* 8(4): 885–910.

Chen, Albert H.Y. 2010. "Pathways of Western Liberal Constitutional Development in Asia: A Comparative Study of Five Major Nations." *International Journal of Constitutional Law* 8(4): 849–884.

Coomaraswamy, Radhika and Charmaine de los Reyes. 2004. "Rule by Emergency: Sri Lanka's Postcolonial Constitutional Experience." *International Journal of Constitutional Law* 2(2): 272–295.

Currie, Iain, and Johan de Waal. 2005. *The Bill of Rights Handbook*, 5th ed. Lansdowne: Juta and Co Ltd.

Fujita, Tokiyasu. 2011. "The Supreme Court of Japan: Commentary on the Recent Work of Scholars in the United States." *Washington University Law Review* 88(6): 1507–1526.

Ginsburg, Tom. 2003. *Judicial Review in New Democracies: Constitutional Courts in East Asia*. Cambridge: Cambridge University Press.

Harding, Andrew. 2012. *The Constitution of Malaysia: A Contextual Analysis*. Oxford: Oxford University Press.

Harding, A.J. and H.P. Lee. 2007. "Constitutional Landmarks and Constitutional Signposts: Some Reflections on the First Fifty Years." Pp. 291–295 in *Constitutional Landmarks in Malaysia: The First 50 Years 1957–2007*, edited by Andrew Harding and H.P. Lee. Petaling Jaya, Malaysia: LexisNexis.

Harding, Andrew and Peter Leyland. 2011. *The Constitutional System of Thailand: A Contextual Analysis*. Oxford: Hart Publishing.

Kahler, Miles E. 2000. "Legalization as Strategy: The Asia-Pacific Case." *International Organization* 54(3): 549–571.

Krotoszynski, Jr., Ronald J. 2006. *The First Amendment in Cross-Cultural Perspective: A Comparative Legal Analysis of the Freedom of Speech*. New York and London: New York University Press.

Law, David S. 2011. "Why Has Judicial Review Failed in Japan?" *Washington University Law Review* 88(6): 1425–1466.

Law, David S. and Mila Versteeg. 2012. "The Declining Influence of the U.S. Constitution." *New York University Law Review* 87(6): 761–858.

"Malaysiakini: We maintain editorial independence." *New Straits Times*, September 24, 2011.

Masum, Ahmad. 2009. "Freedom of Religion under the Malaysian Constitution." *Current Law Journal* 2(1).

Matsui, Shinegori. 2011a. *The Constitution of Japan: A Contextual Analysis*. Oxford: Hart Publishing.

Matsui, Shinegori. 2011b. "Constitutional Precedents in Japan: A Comment on the Role of Precedent." *Washington University Law Review* 88(6): 1669–1680.

Matsui, Shinegori. 2011c. "Why is the Japanese Supreme Court So Conservative?" *Washington University Law Review* 88(6): 1375–1423.

Oda, Hiroshi. 2009. *Japanese Law*, 3rd ed. Oxford: Oxford University Press.

Parliament of Singapore. 1991. "White Paper on Shared Values." Singapore: Singapore National Printers.

Qureshi, Taiyyaba A. 2010. "State of Emergency: General Pervez Musharraf's Executive Assault on Judicial Independence in Pakistan." *North Carolina Journal of International Law & Commercial Regulation* 35(2): 485–538.

Rishworth S., G. Huscroft, S. Optican and R. Mahoney. 2003. *The New Zealand Bill of Rights.* Melbourne: Oxford University Press.

Seervai, H.M. 1996, Reprint 2012. *Constitutional Law of India: A Critical Commentary*, 4th ed. New Delhi: Universal Law Publishing Co. Pvt. Ltd.

Sorabjee, Soli J. 2000. "Constitution, Courts, and Freedom of the Press and the Media." Pp. 334–335 in *Supreme but not Infallible: Essays in Honour of the Supreme Court of India*, edited by B.N. Kirpal et al. New Delhi: Oxford University Press.

Stone, Adrienne. 2005. "Australia's Constitutional Rights and the Problem of Interpretive Disagreement." *Sydney Law Review* 27(1): 29–48.

Stone, Adrienne. 2011. "The Comparative Constitutional Law of Freedom of Expression." In *Comparative Constitutional Law*, edited by Tom Ginsburg and Rosalind Dixon. Edward Elgar, 2011, 406–422.

Stone, Adrienne and George Williams. 2000. "Freedom of Speech and Defamation in the Common Law World." *Monash University Law Review* 26: 362–378.

Sunstein, Cass. 2006. "A New Progressivism." *Stanford Law and Policy Review* 17(1): 197–231.

Tan, Kevin Y.L. 2011. *An Introduction to Singapore's Constitution*, rev. ed. Singapore: Talisman Publishing.

Tan, Kevin Y.L. and Thio Li-Ann. 2010. *Constitutional Law in Malaysia and Singapore*, 3rd ed. Singapore: LexisNexis.

Tey, Tsun Hang. 2011. "Contempt of Court Singapore-Style: Contemptuous of Critique." *Common Law World Review* 40(3): 235–262.

Thio, Li-ann. 2003. "Singapore: Regulating Political Speech and the Commitment 'To Build a Democratic Society'." *International Journal of Constitutional Law* 1(3): 516–524.

Vohrah, Dato K.C., Philip T.N. Koh and Peter S.W. Ling (eds.). 2004. *Sheridan & Groves – The Constitution of Malaysia*, 5th ed. Kuala Lumpur: Malayan Law Journal Sdn Bhd.

Watanabe, Yozou, Hiroshi Etoh and Toshiki Odanaka. 1995. *Nihon no Saiban [The Japanese Trial System]*. Tokyo: Iwanami Shoten.

Zhang, Qianfan. 2010. "A Constitution without Constitutionalism? The Paths of Constitutional Development in China." *International Journal of Constitutional Law* 8(4): 950–976.

10. The right to property in Asia

Tom Allen

Eminent domain – the power to take private property for public use – is an inherent aspect of sovereignty. However, the institution of private property would have little meaning if governments expropriated property without restraint. Hence, most constitutions impose restrictions on eminent domain. These constitutional restraints can take a variety of forms, but the most common is the right to property.

This chapter provides a comparative overview of the right to property in Asia. The doctrine, history and broader context of the right to property in Asia share a number of common features. For example, the right to property is often prominent in transitions, whether from colonial systems, or from military or communist governments to democracy, or from capitalism to socialism and back again. Many Asian countries also face continuing social or economic issues that can affect, or be affected by, the development of constitutional law. The dislocation caused by "land grabs" is one example; gross inequities in the distribution of land and wealth is another.

Accordingly, the chapter gives an overview of the key issues relating to the right to property, with the focus on those aspects of particular importance to Asian countries. Section I provides a framework for examining the issues, as it contrasts the liberal and social democrat perspectives on the right to property. Liberalism, with its emphasis on the individual, equality and autonomy, has had an obvious appeal for those seeking to challenge colonialism or traditional feudal or caste systems. Social democracy has appealed to those arguing for an enhanced role for the State in planning economic development that does not submerge the private sector or private capital. The chapter assesses their influence on constitutional law in Asia, and explains how liberalism has come to dominate the judicial application of rights to property.

The remaining sections are organized around the main doctrinal issues concerning the right to property. Constitutional property clauses tend to follow a common structure (Daintith 2004; Mann 1959; Van der Walt 1999). Most provide that the government may only acquire property by a process laid down by law, for a public use or purpose, and on terms that provide the owner with compensation. Accordingly, Section II examines the meaning of "property" as used in constitutional property clauses, and Section III concentrates on the meaning of "taking" (or similar terms). There is some overlap between these two sections, as together they determine the scope of the property clause. Questions of scope raise interesting issues on the relationship between public and private law in any jurisdiction, but in some Asian countries they are particularly challenging because the systems of private law are either undeveloped or do not recognize informal interests. In China, for example, a fairly strong property guarantee was added to the Constitution in 2004, but the law on real property was not enacted until 2007. Until then, the constitutional guarantees were something of an empty vessel, awaiting content from the development of private law.

Section IV examines the public purpose requirement, and Section V the compensation guarantee. These two sections also consider two issues with particular relevance for Asia: the impact of takings for private purposes on "land grabs", and the impact of compensation standards on redistributive land reform programmes. The Philippines and India provide two case studies on land reform and compensation: in both cases, constitutional law has, arguably, limited the success of reform pro-grammes and preserved enormous disparities in wealth and power.

I. CONSTITUTIONAL PROPERTY CLAUSES IN LIBERAL AND SOCIAL DEMOCRAT THEORY

The liberal view of human rights concentrates on the protection of individual autonomy from the State (Epstein 1985; Grey 1986). Property describes a zone of autonomy that should be kept free of interference from the State. This does not mean that autonomy is absolute: every legal system includes rules that prevent owners from using their property to harm others. Individuals may bring private claims for nuisance; similarly, the State may prevent uses of property that cause undue harm to others. The State also has the power of eminent domain (the focus of this chapter), which it may exercise in the public interest, if it pays compensation that indemnifies the owner. Liberals argue that the protection of individual liberty means that, as far as possible, decisions regarding the use and disposition of property should be left to the owners. Expropriation should only be allowed where it is necessary for the State to own the property and ordinary market processes for acquiring property are unavailable or inappropriate. Moreover, expropriation can only be justified if it leaves the owner no worse off than he or she would have been under an ordinary consensual transaction with other private persons. In other words, expropriation should be conditional on payment of market value compensation.

Liberal values, with their emphasis on individual equality and personal autonomy, had an appeal to many nationalists in colonial regimes. In India, for example, ideas of individual equality cut across the exclusions of both the colonial and traditional caste systems. However, in post-World War II Western Europe, social democrats challenged the economic aspects of liberalism, from a perspective that accepted democracy and a continued role for private capital (Berman 2006; Callaghan 2000). The social democrats agreed that the law of human rights should protect autonomy and dignity. However, they believed that human rights were not solely concerned with individual autonomy and limitations on State power. Human rights included claims to the basic goods needed to live a meaningful life. The State had a crucial role to play in ensuring that these basic goods were provided. Hence, constitutions and human rights instruments should ensure that these basic goods – housing, education, health care, and the like – were available to all.

The social democrat philosophy had important implications for the right to property. For social democrats in Europe, the pre-War experience demonstrated that the boom-and-bust pattern of business cycles could make it impossible for many people to gain access to basic goods. This was attributed to a failure to regulate the economy. In effect, the absence of an effective government could itself jeopardize human rights, even if the government itself did not seek to encroach on liberty. However, social democrats were not socialists, as they saw a continued role for private capital. Nevertheless, private capital would operate within a system with a strong State, where regulation, planning and central control of key industries would ensure that a market economy would produce wealth and ensure that human rights received respect.

In Western Europe, after World War II, the conflict between liberal and social democrat thinking drove a long debate on the merits of including a right to property in the European Convention on Human Rights (Allen 2010). Social democracy was also influential in Asia. For example, in the debates in the Indian Constituent Assembly on proposals for a constitutional right to property, Jawaharlal Nehru argued that the State had an important role in protecting the vulnerable, including vulnerable property owners. However, the threat to property did not come exclusively from the State: a strong State was needed to support small capitalists and landowners. They needed protection from monopolies, which "can crush out the little shop-keeper by their methods of business and by the fact that they have large sums of money at their command". Their survival could only be ensured if the State pursued "large schemes of social reform, social engineering etc" (Constituent Assembly of India 1949; Austin 1966: 87–99).

This faith in ownership, and in the need for the State to intervene to protect the more vulnerable capital holders, also underpinned the extensive land reform programmes in Japan, South Korea, Taiwan and India. These countries sought to improve agricultural productivity by increasing the peasant control over the land that they farmed. They achieved it through compulsory redistribution, rather than market-led reforms (as liberals would advocate, and as found in the Philippines; Borras et al 2009) or the collectivization of farms (as the communists advocated in China, see below, Section V).

However, except for these specific programmes, social democracy has lacked influence in Asia (Haggard and Kaufman 2008). Democracy itself has struggled, although there have been notable transitions from authoritarian rule in a number of countries, such as South Korea, Thailand, the Philippines and Taiwan. A number of countries have also seen some growth in social commitment, with increased spending on education, health and social welfare. However, as the rest of the chapter demonstrates, they have tended not to follow the social democrat model of economic planning and regulation and market-oriented reforms are largely prevalent.

Some of the most interesting recent developments have been in China. The present Constitution was enacted in 1982 and amended in 1988, 1993, 1999 and 2004. It is avowedly socialist: Article 1 declares that "The People's Republic of China is a socialist state under the people's democratic dictatorship led by the working class and based on the alliance of workers and peasants" and that "the socialist system is the basic system of the People's Republic of China". Article 6 declares that the system is based on the "socialist public ownership of the means of production". The Constitution originally gave little scope for private ownership, as individuals could not own land or capital (this is still the case with respect to land). Given the degree of State control, there was little practical need for a law of eminent domain or compensation, especially in relation to land: all land belonged to the State or collectives; individuals did not pay to acquire land use rights, and could not sell them anyway; and those dispossessed of their home were, in theory, still entitled to housing from the State, which would normally be arranged through their work.

As is well known, the Chinese economy has undergone a radical transformation since the era of "reform and opening up" began in 1978. These changes have been reflected in the Constitution. In 1988, an amendment allowed for the transfer of land use rights and for a private sector to develop, within the law and under State "guidance, supervision and control" (Articles 10 and 11; see the discussion in Abramson 2011; Hu 2012). The 1993 amendments declared that "the state has put into practice a socialist market economy" (Article 15). In 1999, amendments acknowledged the growing importance of the private sector, by declaring that, in this "primary stage of socialism", the basic system of public ownership would be "dominant", but with "diverse sectors of the economy developing side by side". Moreover, it declared that "individual, private and other non-public economies that exist within the limits prescribed by law are major components of the socialist market economy" and that "the State protects the lawful rights and interests of individual and private economies, and guides, supervises and administers individual and private economies".

The development of a market in land use rights has led to social dislocation and increasing unrest (Erie 2007; Hess 2010). It is not merely a case of governments failing to take action to protect citizens, as local governments have often acted in concert with developers. A frequent pattern sees local officials requisition land use rights, evict the tenants, and then transfer the land into government investment vehicles for use as collateral for debt or for transfer to commercial enterprises (Hu 2012). Tenants lose their homes, but compensation is often non-existent, delayed or inadequate, and (unlike earlier periods) no alternative housing is provided. In 2004, a further set of constitutional amendments guaranteed property rights and compensation: the property of citizens is now declared to be "inviolable" and the State undertakes to protect "the rights of citizens to private property and to its inheritance" (Abramson 2011; Hu 2012). Article 10 provides that the State "may, in the public interest, appropriate or requisition land for its use in accordance with the law, while making compensation"; Article 13 includes a similar provision, applicable to all private property. However, the protests have not abated, and the rise of the "Nail House" phenomenon after 2004 suggests that the amendment did not have the impact that was desired or expected (Erie 2007; Hess 2010). Instead, the declaration of inviolability may have been more important in legitimating the wealth accumulation of senior Party officials.

The lack of a strong system of judicial review, and the political monopoly of the Communist Party, means that the constitutional right to property must be read against the Communist Party Constitution of 2007

(Xing 2009). It declares that China is still in "the primary stage of socialism and will remain so for a long time to come ... at least a hundred years". The basic economic system will remain in place, "with public ownership playing a dominant role and different economic sectors developing side by side". It says that the system will "gradually eliminate poverty and achieve common prosperity" but, quite strikingly, this is preceded by the statement that it will "encourage some areas and some people to become rich first". The Party Constitution puts forward the idea of "Scientific Outlook on Development" as a central element of policy; as it also makes numerous references to "socialist democracy", the "rule of law" and "human rights", it appears that there is a shift to something resembling social democracy as it is understood elsewhere. A minimum standard of living is the objective, rather than equality or an egalitarian distribution of wealth and power or the socialist structures of State and collective ownership. According to Xing, the Scientific Outlook entails "the transformation of the Chinese economy into a capitalist one, and within this arena, they address mounting inequality through social welfare plans" (2009: 216–17). As in European social democracy, the market economy and capitalist growth are the important drivers of growth, but the State is expected to act as a kind of supervisory authority in economic and distributive matters, where it guarantees the delivery of the basic goods needed for a meaningful life.

Whether social democracy will gain strength in Asian politics is uncertain. Neo-liberal economic theory, with its emphasis on market-led programmes and strong property rights, has dominated policy in recent years. As part of this, there has been considerable international pressure to adopt property guarantees of various kinds. The emphasis on property, and especially on markets, suggests that social democrat thinking is not in the ascendancy. As a further challenge, social democracy requires a strong and capable public sector to operate successfully. This has been notably lacking in much of Asia. In countries where there are issues concerning corruption or institutional capacity, social democracy can easily fail to deliver on promises. For example, it is doubtful that China has the institutions of governance that will allow it to deliver on the Scientific Outlook. The privatization of State-owned enterprises has removed the institutions that previously supplied the basic goods of housing and employment. It is now only through the market that one can obtain housing in urban areas, and it is doubtful that the governing authorities, local or national, have the resources to supervise market activity or to provide social welfare on the scale that is needed. Hence, it is uncertain how the right to property fits within the Chinese system (Erie 2007; Cao 2009).

II. THE INTEREST THAT IS PROTECTED: WHAT IS "PROPERTY"?

Constitutions vary in their descriptions of the interest protected by property clauses, but all raise similar issues concerning the relationship of constitutional law and the private law of property. To what extent is the scope of the constitutional clause determined by private law? Does property have the same meaning in constitutional law as it does in private law? And to what extent does a constitution create or modify private property interests?

There are important differences in liberal and social democrat views on the meaning of "property", but in some Asian countries, a preliminary question concerns the scope of the constitutional property clause where the law of private property is relatively undeveloped or unevenly implemented. In China, for example, the property guarantees were added to the Constitution in 2004, but there was no comprehensive law of property until the enactment of the Real Property Rights Law in 2007 (Lee 2010). The Civil Code was in force, but its focus lies on State ownership of land and it provides little guidance on general principles of private ownership. There were also a number of statutory regimes governing specific types of property, but they were more concerned with international trade and relations (Lee 2010: 32). The constitutional guarantee was, in many respects, waiting for content: it protected property in a system where, to a significant extent, the institution of private property had yet to be constituted. For that reason, the Real Property Rights Law of 2007 was more than a "private" law, as the State was more than a neutral arbiter in cases of dispute. It was a transformative law, making a political statement regarding the relationship of citizens to land, with the potential to be as significant in China as the Civil Code was in France (Erie 2007). The Civil Code ended feudalism and championed the autonomy of the individual; in China, the 2007 Law marks a highly significant step away from socialist ownership. It brings to an end the individual's dependence on local government and especially on the place of work as the source of the basic goods of housing and social support. In doing so, it gave content to the constitutional guarantee and the constitutional relationship between the State and the individual.

The Chinese experience is particularly interesting because it tests the liberal view that the scope of the constitutional property clause should be determined by private law. By the liberal view, private property exists prior to constitutional or even ordinary public law. Hence, private law defines the interests that are recognized as property; moreover, through doctrines such as the law of nuisance, it defines the limits on the owner's rights of use (see e.g. *Lucas v. South Carolina Coastal Council* 1992: 1029, *per* Justice Scalia). Conversely, it imposes limits on the scope of the constitutional right to property; that is, the right to property applies only to existing property interests, and does not provide a mechanism for modifying or creating new forms of private property (see e.g. *Hacienda Luisita, Inc. v. Presidential Agrarian Reform Council* 2011; 2012; cf. *Sagong bin Tasi v. Kerajaan Negeri Selangor* 2005; Van der Walt 1997: 58).

For social democrats, the State's continuing duty to control markets and property requires it to regularly define and re-define the zone of autonomy that is protected by private property. Constitutions often express this in terms of the social function of property or the social obligations of ownership. While the property guarantee seeks to protect an area of personal autonomy, it must be balanced against the State's obligation to ensure that the use of property serves the public good. The State's obligation is not subordinate or external to the owner's autonomy: both liberty and the public good are inherent values of the law of property. Plainly, they are often in tension, but the Constitution requires the legislature (and courts) to ensure that an appropriate balance is struck between them, without giving one priority over the other (see e.g. *'Green Belt Case'* 1998).

The Philippines provides one of the most interesting examples on the development of the social function of property in constitutional language. The property clauses are taken directly from the Fifth Amendment to the United States Constitution, with no reference to the social obligations or social function of ownership. The Philippine Supreme Court has often borrowed from the doctrines laid down by the United States Supreme Court. In the early part of the twentieth century, the Philippine Court followed *Lochner v. New York* (1905; Choudhry 2004) and related the cases of the United States Supreme Court, in which socially progressive laws were declared unconstitutional (e.g. *People v. Pomar* 1924). Partly to reverse this trend, the 1935 Constitution included a "Declaration of Principles". In Section 5, it stated that "The promotion of social justice to insure the well-being and economic security of all the people should be the concern of the State." In *Calalang v. Williams* (1940), the Supreme Court, through Laurel J., rejected the idea that "social justice" could be equated with the idea of autonomy in the use of property:

> Social justice ... must be founded on the recognition of the necessity of interdependence among divers and diverse units of a society and of the protection that should be equally and evenly extended to all groups as a

combined force in our social and economic life, consistent with the fundamental and paramount objective of the state of promoting the health, comfort,
and quiet of all persons, and of bringing about "the greatest good to the
greatest number".

Calalang v. Williams is significant for its rejection of the *Lochner*
approach, even though it is not particularly radical. Laurel J. talks of the
"protection that should be equally and evenly extended to all groups", but
not about a more equal distribution of wealth, or even land or economic
reform. As such, the Constitution's declaration regarding social justice
did not take the Philippine Supreme Court further than the United States
Supreme Court had already gone without a similar clause: by 1940, when
Calalang v. Williams was decided, the Supreme Court of the United
States had reversed its *Lochner*-era jurisprudence (see e.g. *West Coast
Hotel Co. v. Parrish* 1937). In other contemporaneous cases on the
relationship between constitutional law and economic policy, the Philippine Supreme Court did not even raise Section 5, but preferred to rely on
the American jurisprudence reversing *Lochner* (see e.g. *Leyte Land
Transportation Company, Inc. v. Leyte Farmer's and Laborer's Union*
1948).

The Constitutions of 1973 and 1987 contain even stronger statements.
For example, social justice requires the State to "equitably diffuse
property ownership and profits" (Declaration, 1973 Constitution). The
use of property "bears a social function", and the State has a duty to
"promote distributive justice" (Section 6, Article XII, 1987 Constitution).
However, the idea of the "social function" is used more as a defence to
expropriation and redistribution. For example, it has been argued that
there is no need to redistribute land that is used productively and
provides employment (Putzel 1992: 177; *Hacienda Luisita v. Presidential
Agrarian Reform Council* 2011; 2012). Similarly, it appears that the idea
of "social justice" has not taken on the social democrat meaning, as the
following statement by Mr Justice Isagani Cruz, made as a member of
the 1986 Constitution Commission, indicates:

> social justice – or any justice for that matter – is for the deserving, whether he
> be a millionaire in his mansion or a pauper in his hovel. It is true that, in case
> of reasonable doubt, we are called upon to tilt the balance in favor of the
> poor, to whom the Constitution fittingly extends its sympathy and compas-
> sion. But never is it justified to prefer the poor simply because they are poor,
> or to reject the rich simply because they are rich, for justice must always be
> served, for poor and rich alike, according to the mandate of the law (quoted in
> *Land Bank of the Philippines v. Honeycomb Farms Corporation* 2012).

It appears that social justice allows, or even requires, the expenditure of State resources on social programmes; however, judges would be very wary of any reform programme that puts an economic burden on property owners as a class. The social obligations of ownership allow for some regulation, but have a very limited role in bringing about the reforms of a social democrat agenda.

III. TAKINGS OF PROPERTY AND "REGULATORY TAKINGS"

The scope of the constitutional property clause is also determined by the interpretation of a "taking", "compulsory acquisition", or the corresponding term. In all systems, it is necessary to distinguish the types of interference with property that would normally require compensation from those that would not. The most difficult cases concern the regulation of property: when, if ever, are restrictions on the enjoyment of property rights so severe that they should be treated as takings? This brings up the key difference in the liberal and social democrat theories of the right to property. For liberals, the regulation of property interferes with liberty. As such, it represents a threat to the human rights of the individual, and the courts should be vigilant in safeguarding the individual's autonomy. For social democrats, regulation and takings can threaten human rights, but it is the failure to regulate that is the greater threat. Regulation may limit the owner's autonomy, but those limitations may be necessary to ensure the welfare (and autonomy) of many other citizens. As I have said elsewhere, "for social democrats, regulation is not an interference with a natural or normal state of affairs; regulation *is* the normal state of affairs in a nation that respects human rights" (Allen 2010: 1058).

In doctrinal terms, interpretation usually focuses on the distinction between takings and regulatory controls on property. In relation to impact, most jurisdictions hold that regulations that permanently appropriate all of the economic benefits of ownership for the benefit of the State should be treated as a taking, even if there is no formal acquisition of legal title (*Lucas v. South Carolina Coastal Council*, 1992; *Sporrong and Lönnroth v. Sweden* 1983; *La Compagnie Sucriere de Bel Ombre Ltee v. The Government of Mauritius* 1995). This raises both the purpose and the impact of the regulation: public safety may require restrictions on the use of property or even its destruction, without compensation; similarly, in most jurisdictions, regulations do not constitute a taking if the owner's interests retain some economic value.

While this is the general rule, there have been some notable exceptions. For example, in its early years, the Indian Supreme Court treated some regulatory controls as compulsory acquisitions, for which compensation would be required. It did so on the basis of the original Article 31(1) of the Constitution, which provided that "No person shall be deprived of his property save by authority of law." Article 31(2) dealt with acquisitions, and included a compensation guarantee. On its face, it appeared that a deprivation of property was broader than an acquisition. It seemed to include regulatory restrictions on rights of use, and hence they would not be covered by the compensation guarantee of Article 31(2). However, in *Dwarkadas Shrinivas v. Sholapur Spinning and Weaving Co. Ltd.* (1954), the Court conflated Article 31(1) and (2) and held that the legislature could not deprive an individual of rights of property without adequate compensation. Mahajan J., with the liberal's concern for the individual, stated that only a "close and literal construction" of Article 31 could justify limiting the duty to compensate to an acquisition of property, since "[i]t is immaterial to the person who is deprived of property as to what use the State makes of his property or what title it acquires in it. The protection is against loss of property to the owner …" (128). Parliament reversed the Supreme Court's ruling by constitutional amendment, and other Commonwealth jurisdictions have been less protective of property than the Indian Supreme Court. For example, nearly 25 years after *Dwardakas Shrinivas v. Sholapur Spinning and Weaving Co.*, the Privy Council reached the opposite conclusion on similar provisions of the Malaysian Constitution (*Selangor Pilot Association v. Government of Malaysia* 1978).

The general rule leaves open the possibility that legislation might have a very serious impact without offering the property owner any recourse. If a technical rule is adopted – for example, that there is no taking unless the owner is left with no value whatsoever – there would be the risk of serious unfairness. Some Asian courts have borrowed from the continental European approach, by importing a general principle of proportionality into rights to property. For example, under the European Convention on Human Rights, regulatory controls are not treated as "deprivations of possessions" (for which compensation would normally be required), but the Court of Human Rights has held that the core principle is fairness: any interference with the enjoyment of possessions, whether or not formally regarded as a deprivation, must strike a fair balance between public and private interests. In some cases, compensation may be necessary to strike a fair balance, even in the case of a regulatory control on property (see e.g. *Chassagnou v. France* 1999). Similarly, in some continental systems, the State may be required to pay damages for lawful acts, including the regulation of property, if it imposes a disproportionate burden on an individual for the general benefit of the public. In South Korea, the Constitutional Court applied this doctrine under Article 23 of the Constitution in the '*Green Belt Case*' (1998). The Court stated that Article 23 requires a balance between the individual autonomy associated with property and the State's obligation to ensure that its use serves the public good. However, unlike many common law jurisdictions, the balance applies to both regulation and expropriation. Hence, the Court held that, although the restrictions on land use did not amount to an expropriation, Article 23(1) and (2) could apply so as to require compensation for the special or unique sacrifice made by the landowner. In South Korea, and the other jurisdictions with this kind of flexibility, there may be less pressure on courts to devise doctrinal tests that distinguish between takings or acquisitions and other forms of interference with property.

IV. PUBLIC INTEREST/USE IN TAKINGS

Constitutional property clauses normally provide that property may only be taken for a public use or in the public interest. In most jurisdictions, courts defer to the legislature and executive on this issue (Allen 2000: 201–220). Even the taking of property for the use of a private person is permitted, so long as some benefit accrues to the public. In recent years, the nature of that benefit has come under close scrutiny in many jurisdictions.

The key issue concerns "private takings", where eminent domain is used to take property from one private person for transfer to another private person (e.g. *Kelo v. City of New London* 2005). For liberals, these "private takings" undermine several key principles. To begin with, the property owner should be free to choose whether to sell at the market price, except in cases of public necessity. The usual justification for a private taking – that the transfer to another private person will increase overall productivity and economic growth – does not justify making one person serve the interests of another, even in this indirect manner. Moreover, the economic argument applies only where there has been a market failure. In practice, there is too much risk that the true reasons for the taking will be found in improper favouritism or corruption. There are also issues concerning the fairness of the impact. Many of the cases concern takings of land for redevelopment, but this tends to affect people who are not well off, if only because governments and developers are anxious to reduce costs and therefore look for relatively inexpensive land.

Indeed, in the last decade, the impact of "land grabs" on poorer occupants and indigenous peoples has been the subject of concern in much of Asia and the developing world (Azuela and Herrera 2007; Erie 2007; De Schutter 2011). The impact varies: in southeast Asia, the pressure on indigenous peoples in forested land is very heavy. However, in China, land grabs often occur in urban areas and can affect relatively recent migrants. Many cases involve the exercise of the power of eminent domain. Local or state governments acquire smallholdings or residential property for transfer to private developers, who evict the occupants in the course of converting the land to large-scale agricultural, industrial or residential use. These concerns are not unique to Asia: similar experiences are reported from South and Central America, as well as in Africa (Azuela and Herrera 2007; De Schutter 2011). Indeed, in terms of the pressure on owners of low-value land, the situation is not unlike that of *Kelo*: all other things being equal, the greatest profit is likely to be found by acquiring relatively inexpensive land. In the developing world, this puts the focus on land that is occupied by poor or transient populations. This not only justifies the taking, but also the argument that any harm is minimal and hence that compensation may be modest. Indeed, Baka's work on India demonstrates that the public officials tended to classify land as waste, even when it was regularly used by those without formal title. In many cases, corporate and government stakeholders believed that land was not used productively, but civil society and village stakeholders believed that all land was used in ways that were important to the community (Baka 2011; see also Roy 2011).

One common theme of these "land grabs" is the failure of the legal system. For example, in China, local officials are widely reported to have pursued dispossessions, with no interest in protecting occupiers (Erie 2007; Liu 2008). Indeed, in some cases, they have subjected the occupiers to illegal threats to circumvent their own processes for expropriation. Writing in 2008, Liu stated that

> there is no single case in which a homeowner has even attempted to challenge the public purpose of a particular government project. No such case exists because "public interest" is an extremely elusive term in Chinese law, which in practice grants the government the absolute power to make decisions based on local leaders' preferences (p 318).

The practical difficulties are present because neither lawyers nor the courts were willing to take such cases, despite the constitutional guarantees. The result is that "there is no legal remedy when the government abuses the 'public purpose' requirement in the takings law" (Liu 2008: 318).

From a comparative perspective, *Kelo* and the land grab cases provide a reminder that the constitutionalization of property does not necessarily ensure the protection of the vulnerable. Indeed, on this issue, it is likely that both liberals and social democrats would agree. For liberals, all property requires protection, and State power is always vulnerable to abuse. Hence, the courts ought to use the right to property to prevent the private capture of sovereign power. Social democrats are more likely to concentrate on the vulnerable, and there is no doubt that the most vulnerable people in many Asian countries are at risk in these situations. Faith in planning, and the sense of social obligation of ownership, means that social democrats are more accepting of projects that require individual sacrifice for the greater good. However, the impact of these private takings and land grabs raises the point made by Jawaharlal Nehru on the role of the State in a social democrat state: it must intervene to protect the small property owner from the monopolies that would crush them. In Asia, it appears that the concentration of power is often aided by public officials: in such circumstances, where legislative power has failed, there should be a role for the courts.

V.   COMPENSATION IN TAKINGS CASES

Most constitutions explicitly guarantee compensation for takings, although they vary in the degree of detail on valuation and manner of payment. Some simply promise "compensation" (India, Article 31(2) as originally enacted), or "just compensation" (United States, Fifth Amendment) or "just terms" (Australia, Section 51(xxxi)); others go into considerable detail about matters such as the convertibility of the currency of payment and the speed of payment (Hong Kong Basic Law; Art. 110).

It is on the question of compensation that the strongest differences between liberal and social democrat views emerge. The liberal view holds that the purpose of compensation is essentially indemnification: compensation should restore the owner to their pre-taking position. As Blackstone asserted, the legislature may force a sale only by giving the owner "a full indemnification and equivalent for the injury thereby sustained" (1765–1769: 135). Of course, practical considerations may make it impossible to achieve a perfect balance. For example, it may not be possible to measure all intangible or subjective gains and losses. If so, it may be necessary to rely on objective measures, and usually this is done by paying the market value of the property. Hence, true indemnification is rarely achieved. However, the key point is that it would not be legitimate to pay something less than the market value merely because the State is seeking to save capital for other purposes. Similarly, the individual's claim is based on the fact of ownership; it would not be legitimate for the State to pay less than the market value because the individual was not morally deserving of full compensation.

The social democrat view holds that compensation should ensure that a fair or equitable balance is struck between public and private interests (Berman 2006: 177–199; Callaghan 2000: 1–25; Allen 2010). Payment of the market value of the property would usually represent the fair or equitable balance, but the legislature should have the discretion to pay something below the market value in some circumstances. These circumstances relate to the purpose of taking: for example, there may be more justification to pay something below the market value for nationalization of an entire industry, as opposed to the taking of a plot of land for a specific project.

In Asia, questions of compensation have been particularly important, because of their impact on land reform. In Asia, as in much of the developing world, social democrats have supported redistributive land reform programmes (see generally Lipton 2009). The liberals also see value in land reform, but tend to oppose redistribution. In their view, the root cause of rural poverty is low agricultural productivity, which should be addressed by increased investment and greater efficiency. The emphasis should fall on the development of a market in land and enhancing the availability of credit. Hence, liberals often promote programmes for land titling, improved registration schemes, and the modernization of tenure. They see little value in the compulsory expropriation of land for redistribution, because they believe that the interference with the market would lead to an inefficient allocation of resources and ultimately to even greater rural poverty. In addition, compulsory redistribution infringes liberal values relating to the autonomy of the property owner, and could discourage investment in the country as a whole. In those rare cases where expropriation would be appropriate, full market value compensation should be paid, without delay. A different standard should not be applied simply because land reform is a priority: the owner is under no greater obligation to make a sacrifice to support reform than any other citizen.

The social democrat supporters of redistribution agree that increased productivity is a key aim of land reform. They also believe that private property is essential for enhancing productivity. However, they see large estates, functioning as near-feudal monopolies, as a threat to productivity. The aim of reform is to increase the number of land owners, especially from the peasant class. From this, increases in productivity would follow.

As they support private property, they also agree that the confiscation of property can amount to a violation of basic human rights. Hence, it would be appropriate to provide compensation on expropriation. However, they fear that the cost of compensation could make redistribution so expensive that it would become necessary to abandon reforms.

These fears regarding compensation are borne out by the experience in Japan, South Korea and Taiwan, especially when contrasted with that of the Philippines and India. After World War II, Japan, South Korea and Taiwan embarked on extensive redistribution programmes that were largely successful. Different reasons have been given for these successes or failures (see generally Putzel 1992: 101–105; Tai 1974; You 2008; on Japan, see Nathanson 1958; Õchi 1966; on Taiwan, see Koo 1968; on South Korea, see Jeon and Kim 2008: 254–258; on India, see Merillat 1970; on the Philippines, see Hanstad 1988; Putzel 1992). For example, the American influence in these countries was clearly important. American policy would harden against redistribution in the 1950s, but in the immediate post-War period, redistribution was seen as a means of checking the advance of communism. In addition, political circumstances had left agricultural landlords with little political influence. Even in South Korea, where landlords had more influence than in Japan or Taiwan, they recognized that the threat of a peasant revolution meant that they were better off accepting reforms than challenging them.

From the point of view of the constitutional law on property, it is the compensation standard that has had the most significant impact. In the countries where land reform succeeded, compensation was paid for the acquisition of land for redistribution, but at rates that fell considerably below the market value. Instead, it was calculated on the basis of formulae of general application, based on previous yields. At the time, there was no effective system for judicial review in either Taiwan or South Korea. In Japan, landowners did challenge the relevant legislation, on the basis that the compensation formula did not take into account the timing of valuation and the effects of subsequent inflation. Compensation was based partly on prices (and hence earnings) for rice over a five-year period prior to the enactment of the legislation, when price controls had been in effect. Compensation therefore depended on wartime conditions that no longer applied. Nevertheless, the majority in the Supreme Court stated that compensation could be based on yields and profits; price controls were legitimate; and the issue of timing did not invalidate the legislation (*Tanaka v. The State* 1958; Nathanson 1958: 211–215).

In the Philippines and India, where there has been less success with land reform, at least one key factor has been compensation standards imposed under constitutional law. Both jurisdictions are worthy of closer study, as the constitutions themselves give the courts the discretion to relax compensation standards so as to achieve social goals. Indeed, in India, one could argue that the Constitution was written so as to avoid any presumption of market value compensation.

A.   Compensation and Land Reform in the Philippines

Land reform, and the failure to reform, has been a central aspect of constitutional history in the Philippines (Putzel 1992). In 1986, Corazon Aquino's campaign for the presidency put agrarian reform high on the list of priorities, but she avoided making clear statements on the nature of the reform. Her support lay with the landed elite; indeed, her own family owned one of the largest estates in the Philippines. Accordingly, the Constitutional Commission that was set up in 1986 was designed to ensure that the conservative position was entrenched in the Constitution. This applied not only to the process – only one of the eight members of the Commission was drawn from the peasant class – but also to the outcome. While the Constitution included provisions on social justice and the social function of ownership (described above), the Commission was less progressive on the question of compensation (Hanstad 1988).

Like the Commission, the Supreme Court has taken the classic liberal position on compensation. It first rejected the compensation standards issued under decrees issued by Ferdinand Marcos, which had directed assessors to determine compensation on the basis of average harvest yields, or, in some cases, on the owner's declaration of value for tax purposes. As stated above, similar rules were applied in the successful redistribution programmes in Japan, South Korea and Taiwan. In *Export Processing Zone Authority v. Honorable Ceferino E. Dulay* (1987), the Court held that such fixed formulae were unconstitutional because the final determination of "just compensation" should always lie with the courts. Recently, in *Land Bank of the Philippines v. Honeycomb Farms* (2012), the Court reiterated the view it took in the "definitive" case *Association of Small Landowners in the Philippines v. Hon. Secretary of Agrarian Reform* (1989):

> Just compensation is defined as the full and fair equivalent of the property taken from its owner by the expropriator. It has been repeatedly stressed by this Court that the measure is not the taker's gain but the owner's loss. The word "just" is used to intensify the meaning of the word "compensation" to convey the idea that the equivalent to be rendered for the property to be taken shall be real, substantial, full, ample. (p. 812)

The Supreme Court has also rejected the social democrat argument that the nature and importance of agrarian reform, and its separate treatment in the Constitution, justify a different approach. In *Apo Fruits Corporation and Hijo Plantation, Inc. v. Land Bank of the Philippines* (2008), it stated that

> nothing is inherently contradictory in the public purpose of land reform and the right of landowners to receive just compensation for the expropriation by the State of their properties. That the petitioners are corporations that used to own large tracts of land should not be taken against them.

As explained below, the Indian Supreme Court fell into conflict with Parliament over a similarly liberal view of compensation. In the Philippines, however, there has been no real conflict with Congress, which has been reluctant to force redistribution on landowners, even at full compensation (Borras et al. 2009). As a result, land reform has failed to achieve the objectives set out in the Constitution. Indeed, the Philippine idea of social justice seems to exclude the argument that landowners are under any kind of obligation to accept something less than full market value in order to allow the State to achieve a more equitable distribution of wealth.

B. Compensation and Land Reform in India

In India, a range of views on the right to property and compensation were expressed in the Constituent Assembly. Jawaharlal Nehru gave the social democrat case against a justiciable compensation standard. While full compensation should be provided for "petty acquisitions" such as the expropriation of a house for the construction of a school, it should not be assumed that market values were appropriate for larger projects, such as land reform or the nationalization of an entire industry (Constituent Assembly of India 1949; Austin 1966: 87–99). In such cases, different interests and values had to balance against each other. Crucially, he argued that the scale, complexity and importance of reform meant that "ultimately the balancing authority can only be the sovereign legislature of the country which can keep before it all the various factors – all the public, political and other factors – that come into the picture". There should be no place for judicial review of compensation on substantive grounds. Accordingly, the second paragraph of Article 31 provided that:

> (2) No property, movable or immovable, including any interest in, or in any company owning, any commercial or industrial undertaking, shall be taken possession of or acquired for public purposes under any law

> authorising the taking of such possession or such acquisition, unless the law provides for compensation for the property taken possession of or acquired and either fixes the amount of the compensation, or specifies the principle on which, and the manner in which, the compensation is to be determined and given.

Nehru informed the Assembly that "[e]minent lawyers have told us that on a proper construction of this clause, normally speaking, the Judiciary should not and does not come in." The courts would become involved only where "there has been a gross abuse of the law, where, in fact, there has been a fraud on the Constitution" (Constituent Assembly of India 1949).

As written, Article 31(2) appears to give the legislature a great deal of discretion. However, further provisions were included to deal with land reform (Austin 1966: 87–99; Gae 1973; Merillat 1970). The first stage of reform would involve the abolition of the near-feudal *zamindari* form of tenure. The *zamindari* estates carried the right to collect revenues from tenant farmers. The *zamindaris* were seen as allies of the colonial administration; indeed the right to property of the Government of India Act 1935 was drafted with a view to securing their position.

Article 31(2) seems to give legislatures the power to set their own principles for compensation, but in any case, Article 31(4)–(6) exempted land reform legislation from review under Article 31(2). (The exemptions were not based on the subject matter of the legislation, as they applied to any legislation that had already been passed by a state legislature and had received or were awaiting presidential assent, or would do so within 18 months and were certified by the President to be exempt; this was intended to apply to *zamindari* legislation that was going through State legislatures.)

As one might expect, a number of *zamindaris* challenged the reform programme in the courts. It soon became clear that the judiciary would only interpret the right to property in the liberal framework. In *Kameshwar Singh v. State of Bihar* (1951), the Patna High Court held that a progressive scheme of compensation for *zamindari* estates violated the right to equality of Article 14, although it satisfied Article 31(2). It appeared that the types of graduated or progressive compensation schemes of other countries would not be permitted in India. In response, Parliament enacted amendments to extend the exemptions to challenges under all fundamental rights, with retroactive effect. Article 31A insulated legislation dealing with estates from review under any of the fundamental rights. For good measure, Article 31B added a Ninth Schedule to the Constitution, containing a list of statutes that were declared to be immune from any constitutional challenge. The *zamindari* abolition was therefore able to proceed without full compensation.

In 1974, Tai commented that the *zamindari* reform was a remarkable success: "The termination within a decade of a 150-year old agrarian institution that encompassed nearly half of India's land is an extraordinary act that required the political elite to demonstrate unusual resolution" (p. 218). Whether this could have been achieved if full compensation had been payable is doubtful. In any case, the second phase of reform, with the ceilings on landholdings, was much less successful. For some, the Supreme Court's interpretation of the constitutional standard was the major issue. Where legislation fell outside the specific exceptions, or had not been added to the Ninth Schedule, the Supreme Court held that compensation had to represent an equivalent value for the property. In *West Bengal v. Bela Banerjee* (1954), the Court held that Article 31(2) set a "basic requirement of full indemnification of the expropriated owner" (563). The Court suggested that this still left the legislature with "free play" to set the principles for determining the amount payable, but it was clear that statutory principles for determining compensation "must ensure that what is determined as payable must be compensation, that is, a just equivalent of what the owner has been deprived of". Moreover, the courts would engage in fairly close scrutiny: the statutory principles must take into account the "true value of the property" and exclude irrelevant matters.

The ruling in *West Bengal v. Bela Banerjee* was plainly contrary to the meaning that many Congress Party members, including Nehru, ascribed to Article 31(2). As the Party controlled Parliament, it secured the passage of the Fourth Amendment in 1955, which added the italicized words to the provision:

> (2) No property, movable or immovable, including any interest in, or in any company owning, any commercial or industrial undertaking, shall be taken possession of or acquired for public purposes under any law authorising the taking of such possession or such acquisition, unless the law provides for compensation for the property taken possession of or acquired and either fixes the amount of the compensation, or specifies the principle on which, and the manner in which, the compensation is to be determined and given, *and no such law shall be called into question in any court on the ground that the compensation provided by that law is not adequate.*

The Amendment also added another seven statutes to the Ninth Schedule.

In principle, the amended Article 31(2) should have permitted flexibility in setting compensation. However, within ten years, the Supreme

Court again declared that an equivalent value was still required. As long as Article 31(2) required the acquiring law to set out principles on "compensation", the Court held that it could only mean indemnification: nothing could be said to "compensate" if it did not fully counterbalance the loss (see e.g. *Vajravelu v. Special Deputy Collector, West Madras* 1965; cf. *State of Gujarat v. Shantilal Mangaldas* 1969). Plainly, the amendments did not resolve the issue of substantive review of compensation. Parliament moved to water down Article 31 by the Seventeenth Amendment (1964), which added another 45 land reform enactments to the Ninth Schedule. It appeared that the Parliament was determined to restrict the Supreme Court's scrutiny of the land reform programme.

These issues came to a head in *Golak Nath v. State of Punjab* (1967), which concerned a challenge to ceilings on land holdings. The impugned law had been included in the Ninth Schedule. The Court held that Parliament did not have the power to amend the "basic structure" of the Constitution. The right to property, along with other fundamental rights, was part of the basic structure. The Court allowed previous amendments to stand, but declared that Parliament could not pass further amendments in future or, for that matter, add to the list in the Ninth Schedule. It appeared that the Supreme Court had decided that the market liberal view of fundamental rights was not only part of the Constitution but that it was beyond the power of Parliament or the state legislatures to modify it.

The Congress Party reacted by campaigning in the next election on a platform of economic reform, with a strong anti-judicial rhetoric. They won substantial majorities in both Houses and enacted the Twenty-Fourth and Twenty-Fifth Amendments, which were intended to reverse *Golak Nath*. They also pursued further reform, including the nationalization of key sectors of the economy. This led to *R.C. Cooper v. Union of India* (1970), in which the Supreme Court decided that the compensation provisions of the bank nationalization legislation were unconstitutional. Perhaps inevitably, the issue returned to the Court, in *Kesavananda Bharati v. State of Kerala* (1973). This case raised issues of immense constitutional importance: who, ultimately, had the power to determine the meaning and content of the Constitution? Were fundamental rights in conflict with the programme of transformation? If so, which one should prevail?

By a 7–6 majority, the Court held that Parliament did not have the power to undermine the "basic structure" of the Constitution. It could amend fundamental rights, but not if the amendment destroyed the essence or core of the right. However, in a key part of the decision, a majority also held that the right to property was not part of the basic structure of the Constitution. In 1978, after the election of the Janata

Government, Parliament repealed Article 19(1)(f) and Article 31 in the Forty-Fourth Amendment. As explained above, it enacted Article 300A, but placed it in Part XIII of the Constitution ("Finance, Property, Contracts and Suits").

One might have thought that the Forty-Fourth Amendment severely curtailed the Supreme Court's power to review legislation on substantive grounds. Nevertheless, the Supreme Court has continued to review statutory compensation provisions on substantive grounds and, to some extent, restored the position that applied under *Bela Banerjee*. Just how far the Court will go is uncertain, as it has been careful to allow more discretion to the legislature. In *K.T. Plantation Pvt. Ltd. v. State of Karnataka* (2011; para. 121), it stated that "Measures designed to achieve greater social justice may call for lesser compensation and such a limitation by itself will not make legislation invalid or unconstitutional or confiscatory." In *Rajiv Sarin v. State of Uttarakhand* (2011; para. 68), it declared that the Constitution "does not require payment of market value or indemnification to the owner of the property expropriated. Payment of market value in lieu of acquired property is not a condition precedent or sine qua non for acquisition."

The Indian record on land redistribution is patchy. Politicians have frequently blamed the lack of progress on the courts, although Merillat, writing in 1970, at the height of the conflict between the Supreme Court and Parliament, argued that it was unfair to blame the courts for the lack of progress:

> In the total context the courts appear not to have impeded the reforms seriously. They occasionally accepted the legal and constitutional arguments of those hurt by reform measures, but the main reasons for delay and lack of depth in land reforms lay in the apathy or inaction of legislatures and administrators serving the interests of the substantial peasantry. (p 124)

Tai (1974) argues that land reform fell in importance as national political debates shifted to religion and caste, rather than class. As the Congress Party was itself primarily a middle class party, it had little to gain from investing in the administrative machinery that was necessary to make land reform effective. The initiative has shifted to the local level, where there has been some movement, but only in some of the states (Lipton 2009: 95, table 2.1).

VI. CONCLUSION

One theme of this chapter is the tension between liberal and social democrat theories of the State and property. In Asia, the right to property is often understood as a liberal right: it limits the State's powers in order to protect the individual's liberty. Property, as a form of liberty, is not constituted by the State. Of course, positive law helps to define property interests, as our modern societies need some measure of precision in order to form relationships over property. However, the State is still seen as a threat to the liberty that is conferred by property, and hence a strong judiciary is needed to keep the threat under control. In India, for example, Sikri C.J. stated that the Supreme Court's protection of property ensured that "a social and economic revolution can gradually take place while preserving the freedom and dignity of the individual" (*Kesavananda Bharati v. State of Kerala* 1973: para. 296). For Sikri C.J., social and economic revolution itself represents a threat to the "freedom and dignity of the individual", whereas social democrats would argue that the failure to engage in radical reform was the greater threat to freedom and dignity.

This position has come about despite the social democrat or even socialist outlook of many constitution framers. In many of the jurisdictions discussed in this chapter, comparative law has been important in this regard, as it has driven the sense of what a property clause does or should do (on India, see e.g. Dhavan 1977; *Kesavananda Bharati v. State of Kerala* 1973; *K.T. Plantation Pvt. Ltd. v. State of Karnataka* 2011; on the Philippines, see e.g. *Leyte Land Transportation Company, Inc. v. Leyte Farmer's and Laborer's Union*, 1948; *People v. Pomar* 1924; on South Korea, see e.g. *'Green Belt Case'* 1998). This extensive citation of foreign law may be intended as little more than a rhetorical device. That is, the courts may be seeking to emphasize their own independence and neutrality from the executive and legislature. However, the impact goes further, as it has meant that the liberalism of relatively stable Western jurisdictions is imported into Asian countries undergoing transitions, with great disparities in wealth and, in some cases, greater uncertainty over the function and extent of judicial review. In addition, constitutional issues that relate to property are only seen as coming within the scope of a constitutional property clause if they have already been treated as "right to property" issues in other jurisdictions (especially Western jurisdictions). For example, social democrat concerns with issues such as access to land are not seen as "right to property" issues; indeed, measures to promote access are more often seen as intrusions on the right to property (e.g. *Hacienda Luisita, Inc. v. Presidential Agrarian Reform Council* 2011; 2012). It will be interesting to follow the future course of the right to property in Asia, to see whether a uniquely Asian focus develops.

REFERENCES

Abramson, Daniel. 2011. "Transitional Property Rights and Local Developmental History in China." *Urban Studies* 48: 533–568.

Allen, Tom. 2000. *The Right to Property in Commonwealth Constitutions*. Cambridge: Cambridge University Press.

Allen, Tom. 2010. "Liberalism, Social Democracy and the Value of Property under the European Convention on Human Rights." *International and Comparative Law Quarterly* 59 (4): 1055–78.

Austin, Granville (1966). *The Indian Constitution: Cornerstone of a Nation*. Oxford: Clarendon Press.

Azuela, Antonio and Carlos Herrera. 2007. *Taking Land Around the World: International Trends in the Expropriation for Urban and Infrastructure Projects*. Cambridge, MA: Lincoln Institute of Land Policy.

Baka, Jennifer. 2011. "Biofuels and Wasteland Grabbing: How India's Biofuel Policy is Facilitating Land Grabs in Tamil Nadu, India." Paper presented at the International Conference on Global Land Grabbing, 6–8 April 2011. Sussex: University of Sussex Institute of Development Studies.

Berman, Sheri. 2006. *The Primacy of Politics: Social Democracy and the Making of Europe's Twentieth Century*. New York: Cambridge University Press.

Blackstone, William. 1765–1769. *Commentaries on the Laws of England*. Oxford.

Borras, Saturnino M. Jr. et al. 2009. *Anti-Land Reform Land Policy?: The World Bank's Development Assistance to Agrarian Reform in the Philippines*. Retrieved July 13, 2012 (http://www.acaoterra.org/IMG/pdf/wb-final.pdf).

Callaghan, John T. 2000. *The Retreat of Social Democracy*. Manchester: Manchester University Press.

Cao, J. Albert. 2009. "Developmental State, Property-led Growth and Property Investment Risks in China." *Journal of Property Investment & Finance* 27(2): 162–179.

Choudhry, Sujit. 2004. "The *Lochner* Era and Comparative Constitutionalism." *International Journal of Constitutional Law* 2(1): 1–55.

Constituent Assembly of India, Debates, Volume IX, 10th September 1949. Retrieved July 5, 2012 (http://www.indiankanoon.org/doc/797053/).

Daintith, Terence. 2004. "The Constitutional Protection of Economic Rights." *International Journal of Constitutional Law* 2(1): 56–90.

Dhavan, Rajeev. 1977. *The Supreme Court of India: A Socio-Legal Analysis of its Juristic Techniques*. Bombay: N.M. Tripathi Pvt. Ltd.

Epstein, Richard A. 1985. *Takings: Private Property and the Power of Eminent Domain*. Cambridge MA: Harvard University Press.

Erie, Matthew S. 2007. "China's (Post-)Socialist Property Rights Regime: Assessing the Impact of the Property Law on Illegal Land Takings." *Hong Kong Law Journal* 37(3): 919–949.

Gae, R.S. 1973. "Land Law in India: With Special Reference to the Constitution." *International and Comparative Law Quarterly* 22(2): 312–328.

Grey, Thomas C. 1986. "The Malthusian Constitution." *University of Miami Law Review* 41: 21–47.

Haggard, Stephen and Robert R. Kaufman. 2008. *Development, Democracy and Welfare States: Latin America, East Asia and Eastern Europe*. Princeton: Princeton University Press.

Hanstad, Timothy Milton. 1988. "Philippine Land Reform: The Just Compensation Issue." *Washington Law Review* 63(2): 417–433.

Hess, Steve. 2010. "Nail-Houses, Land Rights, and Frames of Injustice on China's Protest." *Asian Survey* 50(5): 908–926.

Hu, Richard. 2012. "Understanding Chinese Real Estate: The Property Boom in Perspective." Pp. 87–100 in *Law and Policy for China's Market Socialism*, edited by John Garrick. Oxford: Routledge.

Jeon, Y.D. and Y.Y. Kim. 2000. "Land Reform, Income Redistribution, and Agricultural Production in Korea." *Economic Development and Cultural Change* 48(2): 253–268.

Koo, Anthony Y.C. 1968. *The Role of Land Reform in Economic Development: A Case Study of Taiwan*. New York: Praeger.

Lee, Wei-chin. 2010. "Yours, Mine, or Everyone's Property? China's Property Law in 2007." *Journal of Chinese Political Science* 15(1): 25–47.

Lipton, Michael. 2009. *Land Reform in Developing Countries: Property Rights and Property Wrongs*. London and New York: Routledge.

Liu, Chenglin. 2008. "The Chinese Takings Law from a Comparative Perspective." *Washington University Journal of Law and Policy* 26: 301–351.

Mann, F.A. 1959. "Outlines of a History of Expropriation." *Law Quarterly Review* 75: 188–219.

Merillat, Herbert Christian Laing. 1970. *Land and the Constitution in India*. New York: Columbia University Press.

Nathanson, Nathaniel L. 1958. "Constitutional Adjudication in Japan." *American Journal of Comparative Law* 7(2): 195–218.

Ōchi, Tsutomu. 1966. "The Japanese Land Reform: Its Efficacy and Limitations." *The Developing Economies* 4(2): 129–150.

Putzel, James. 1992. *A Captive Land: The Politics of Agrarian Reform in the Philippines*. Quezon City: Ateneo de Manila University Press.

Roy, Devparna. 2011. "Gujarat's Gain and Bengal's Loss? 'Development,' Land Acquisition in India and the Tata Nano Project: A Comparison of Singur with Sanand." Paper presented at the International Conference on Global Land Grabbing, April 6–8, 2011. Sussex: University of Sussex Institute of Development Studies.

De Schutter, Olivier. 2011. "The Green Rush: The Global Race for Farmland and the Rights of Land Users." *Harvard International Law Journal* 52(2): 503–559.

Tai, Hung-Chao. 1974. *Land Reform and Politics: A Comparative Analysis*. Berkeley: University of California Press.

Van der Walt, A.J. 1997. *The Constitutional Property Clause*. Kenwyn: Juta & Co.

Van der Walt, A.J. 1999. *Constitutional Property Clauses: A Comparative Analysis*. Cape Town: Juta & Co.

Xing, Guoxin. 2009. "Hu Jintao's Political Thinking and Legitimacy Building: A Post-Marxist Perspective." *Asian Affairs: An American Review* 36(4): 213–226.

You, Jong-Sung. 2008. "Inequality and Corruption: The Role of Land Reform in Korea, Taiwan, and the Philippines." Paper presented at the annual conference of the Association for Asian Studies, April 3–6, 2008. Atlanta.

CASES

Apo Fruits Corporation and Hijo Plantation, Inc. v. Land Bank of the Philippines (2011), G.R. No. 164195.

Association of Small Landowners in the Philippines. v. Hon. Secretary of Agrarian Reform (1989), G.R. No. 78742.

Bihar, State of v. Kameshwar Singh (1952), 1 S.C.R. 889.

Calalang v. Williams (1940), G.R. No. 47800.

Chassagnou v. France, 1999-III Eur. Ct. H.R. 21.

Dwarkadas Shrinivas v. Sholapur Spinning and Weaving Co. Ltd., A.I.R. 1954 S.C. 119.

Export Processing Zone Authority v. Honorable Ceferino E. Dulay (1987), G.R. No. 59603.

Golak Nath v. State of Punjab, [1967] 2 S.C.R. 762.

'Green Belt Case', Constitutional Complaint against Article 21 of the Urban Planning Act (1998) 10-2 KCCR 927, 89 Hun-Ma 214 (http://www.ccourt.go.kr/home/english/decisions/mgr_decision_view.jsp?seq=250&code=4&pg=8&sch_code=&sch_sel=&sch_txt=&nScale=15; last accessed 8 July 2012).

Gujarat, State of v. Shantilal Mangaldas, A.I.R. 1969 S.C. 634.

Hacienda Luisita, Inc. et al. v. Presidential Agrarian Reform Council et al. (decision) (2011), G.R. No. 171101.

Hacienda Luisita, Inc. et al. v. Presidential Agrarian Reform Council et al. (resolution) (2012), G.R. No. 171101.

Kameshwar Singh v. State of Bihar, A.I.R. 1951 Patna 91.

Kelo v. City of New London (2005), 545 U.S. 469.

Kesavananda Bharati v. State of Kerala (1973), 4 S.C.C. 225.

K.T. Plantation Pvt. Ltd. v. State of Karnataka (2011), Civil Appeal No. 6520 of 2003, No. 6521-6537 of 2003, No. 6538 of 2003 (<http://indiankanoon.org/doc/1524072/; last accessed 6 July 2012).

La Compagnie Sucriere de Bel Ombre Ltee v. The Government of Mauritius, [1995] 3 L.R.C. 494 (P.C.).

Land Bank of the Philippines v. Honeycomb Farms Corporation (2012), G.R. No. 169903.

Leyte Land Transportation Company, Inc. v. Leyte Farmer's and Laborer's Union (1948), G.R. No. L-1377.

Lochner v. New York (1905), 198 U.S. 45.

Lucas v. South Carolina Coastal Council (1992), 505 U.S. 1003.

People v. Pomar (1924), G.R. No. L-22008, 46 Phil. 440.

R.C. Cooper v. Union of India, [1970] 3 S.C.R. 530.

Rajiv Sarin v. State of Uttarakhand (2011), 8 S.C.C. 708.

Sagong bin Tasi v. Kerajaan Negeri Selangor, [2005] 6 M.L.J. 289.

Selangor Pilot Association (1946) v. Government of Malaysia, [1978] A.C. 337 (P.C.-Malaysia).

Sporrong and Lönnroth v. Sweden (1983), 52 Eur. Ct. H.R. (ser. A).

Tanaka v. The State (1953), 7 Supreme Court Reports 1523 (as discussed in Nathanson 1958: 211–215).
Vajravelu v. Special Deputy Collector, West Madras, A.I.R. 1965 S.C. 1017.
West Bengal, State of, v. Bela Banerjee, 1954 S.C.R. 558.
West Coast Hotel Co. v. Parrish (1937), 300 U.S. 379.

11. Equality in Asia

Kate O'Regan and Madhav Khosla[1]

> "Equality is not only the Leviathan of Rights; it is also a Tantalus.
> It promises more than it can ever deliver."
> Chief Justice of Canada, Beverley McLachlin (2001: 20)

If the right to equality promises more than it can ever deliver, it is also a right whose text and application reflects the history of the society in which it applies. The right to equality is thus particularly challenging for comparative law. Although it is found in nearly every modern democratic constitution, the formulation, interpretation and application of the right varies markedly and it accordingly presents acutely difficult questions for a study such as this. The difficulties not only arise from the differences in historical, socio-economic and political context, but also from differing conceptions of equality itself. In this brief chapter we shall identify some of the difficult questions that arise in developing an equality jurisprudence and then consider how different legal systems in Asia (India, Malaysia and Japan) have approached these questions.

At the outset, we should acknowledge that because each of the three jurisdiction's response to equality is in significant ways dependent on the constitutional text in question (and the legislative framework) as well as each jurisdiction's social and political history, understanding the equality jurisprudence of any one of the jurisdictions will generally require some understanding of the social and economic circumstances of that society. Comparative analysis is not futile in this field, but it must be approached with circumspection (see the useful discussions in Kahn-Freund 1974; Watson 1976; 1978).

[1] We would like to thank Aqeel Noorali for his great assistance with research in the preparation of this chapter. We would also like to thank Professors Akiko Ejima, HP Lee and Tokujin Matsudaira for their advice and guidance.

I. THE CONCEPTION OF EQUALITY

The idea of equality as an enforceable right is modern (Fredman 2002: 4), but as a philosophical principle it is ancient, stretching back to Aristotle's principle that "persons who are equal should have assigned to them equal things" (Barker 1946: ch XII §1). Although equality has been entrenched in constitutions since the eighteenth century, direct reliance on equality as the basis of a justiciable legal claim only developed widespread currency in the twentieth century.

There are two prominent models of equality jurisprudence. Sometimes, as in the United States of America, both are present. Sometimes only one is present. Moreover, the precise character of each model also varies across legal systems. The origins of both models can be found in the ancient Aristotelian concept of equality, which suggests that the meaning of equality is that like should be treated alike. This definition focuses on treatment as the core of equality and recognizes that if groups are different, they should be treated differently: whereas if they are alike, they should be treated alike.

The first model of equality jurisprudence, which we can call the rational classification or rational review model, requires governments to have a reason for all classifications. Thus, if a government awards a benefit to a certain class of people and not others, it must have a reason for this differentiation. The extent to which the courts will scrutinize the reason varies from legal system to legal system, and also in relation to the basis of the classification. So, where the classification is based on prohibited or suspect grounds, such as race or gender, courts may require the reason to be an important or persuasive one. It will be seen that all three jurisdictions under consideration in this chapter, India, Malaysia and Japan, have adopted some form of the rational classification model of equality jurisprudence. It will also be seen that the level of scrutiny by courts of the reasons given by government for classifications is greater, in most cases, in India than elsewhere. In Malaysia, in particular, the courts have been particularly deferential to reasons proffered by government for classifications.

The second model of equality jurisprudence can be called the anti-discrimination model of equality jurisprudence. It does not require scrutiny of all grounds of differentiation but seeks to prevent discrimination on specified grounds, particularly those based on personal characteristics. In countries that adopt an anti-discrimination model of equality jurisprudence, differentiation based on personal characteristics, such as race, sex, gender, age, and, increasingly, sexual identity, is impermissible unless a very powerful reason exists for it. The anti-discrimination model generally recognizes that past patterns of discrimination have made certain groups particularly vulnerable to discriminatory classification and seeks to prevent such classification, and even, in some cases, reverse the consequences that the past pattern of discrimination caused.

As mentioned, the rational classification model ordinarily focuses on equal treatment, but the anti-discrimination model does not always do so. Although the principle of equal treatment in relation to the discriminatory treatment of groups is full of promise in societies which routinely exclude certain people from a range of benefits, it does not immediately undo the effects of past discriminatory practices. Thus, while the discriminatory practices persist in obvious and direct ways, the doctrine of equal treatment will be valuable. So, for Black South Africans under apartheid, Roma people throughout Europe, Jewish people in Nazi Germany or women in patriarchal societies all over the world, the principle of equal treatment – that people may not be treated differentially because of their race, ethnicity or sex – is a deeply affirming principle (see the similar remarks by Wintemute 2004: 1180).

Once, however, direct discrimination on the basis of race, gender, sexual orientation or religion ends, the doctrine of equal treatment often does little to undo the existing patterns of disadvantage which may remain. The reason for this is that at times treating people equally can serve to entrench their inequality. Anatole France's ironic remark about the "majestic equality of the law, which forbids the rich as well as the poor to sleep under bridges, to beg in the streets and to steal bread" (Fredman 2002: 1) illustrates the fact that a facially neutral law may impact more harshly on some than others. At times too, patterns of deep social inequality may require special treatment for those who are disadvantaged in order to give them real access to opportunities.

Accordingly, the shortcomings of the equal treatment approach in the anti-discrimination model of equality jurisprudence have resulted, in some jurisdictions, in the development of other approaches. One of these is to single out particular groups for special treatment to assist them to overcome the discriminatory treatment of the past. We see such a response in both India and Malaysia.

A second response is to develop an equality jurisprudence focusing on impact rather that treatment. The earliest example of this approach is to be found in *Griggs* v. *Duke Power Company* (1971), a case brought under Title VII of the Civil Rights Act, in which the United States Supreme Court held that a law that does not appear to be facially discriminatory may in its impact have a discriminatory effect. The shift from focusing on treatment to impact is important. It places the disadvantaged group at the centre of the enquiry, and has become the starting point for what has been referred to as a jurisprudence of substantive equality, rather than formal equality.

The more divided a society, the deeper the consequences of a discriminatory impact jurisprudence, as Justice White observed in *Washington* v. *Davis* (1976: 248):

> A rule that a statute designed to serve neutral ends is nevertheless invalid, absent compelling justification, if in practice it benefits or burdens one race more than another would be far reaching and would raise serious questions about and perhaps invalidate, a whole range of tax, welfare, public service, regulatory and licensing statutes that may be more burdensome to the poor and to the average black than to the average white.

There can be no doubt that often there is a tension between an equal treatment approach to equality and a disparate impact approach (see the extended discussion of this in Collins 2003). This tension is ordinarily best illustrated by the manner in which the two approaches view the lawfulness of remedial action or affirmative action programmes.

An approach to equality that focuses on effect or impact rather than treatment or discriminatory intent will ordinarily accept that establishing programmes to benefit those who have been disadvantaged by patterns of discrimination in the past is not inconsistent with equality, if such programmes will contribute to the eradication of disadvantage in the future.

None of the three jurisdictions we consider here has developed a jurisprudence based on disparate impact. This may be because, in India and Malaysia, in any event, there are explicit constitutional provisions that provide for affirmative action in favour of specifically identified previously disadvantaged groups. The existence of such provisions may attenuate the jurisprudential urge to subject classifications on the grounds of this disadvantage to stringent review.

We can see from the above that different conceptions of and approaches to equality will have a material impact on the jurisprudence of a particular jurisdiction. In considering the three jurisdictions below, some of the questions that have arisen from this very brief introduction should be borne in mind. They are the following:

(a)   Does the equality guarantee establish a rational classification model of equality? If so, how intense is the scrutiny by the courts of the government's reason for a classification?

(b) Does the equality guarantee establish an anti-discrimination model of equality jurisprudence? If so, is the focus still equal treatment? Or have the courts developed a disparate impact model?

(c) Does the Constitution permit remedial action (or affirmative action) programmes for specific groups? To what extent are these programmes subject to judicial oversight and on what principles? Are the remedial action programmes permanent or temporary?

We now turn to a consideration of the first of three jurisdictions, India.

II. INDIA

The Indian Constitution is one of the world's first major post-colonial constitutions. It is also the Constitution of the most populous democracy in the world. The Indian population is now estimated at more than one billion. Drafted over three long years, the Constitution's adoption in 1950 marked the end of dominion status and the birth of the Indian republic (see Austin 1966; Guha 2007: 103–23). The moment was striking in many respects. For instance, unlike in the West, in India universal adult suffrage was granted at once, and came before industrialization and the growth of wealth. It came before the creation and nurturing of public institutions. A further striking feature of the Constitution was its affirmation of the state: its belief and faith in the necessity and potential of state power (Mehta 2010).

In a country with deep social cleavages and conflict, it is not surprising that one of the most contentious issues before India's Constituent Assembly was the idea of equality and the concept of citizenship, in particular the question of how minorities and especially vulnerable groups would be safeguarded and kept secure in the new nation. Group rights had been steadily expanded by the British from the late nineteenth century to the mid-twentieth century. Often this involved separate electorates and reserved seats. Groups were often characterized on the basis of religion or caste identity. There is a considerable literature describing how group identities, such as caste, were created, consolidated and perpetuated by the British (Dirks 2001). In this respect, the crafting of the Constitution marked a period of radical historical rupture. For instance, political safeguards for minorities, through mechanisms such as representation in legislatures or in public employment, were abolished. Separate electorates had, at the time of constitutional drafting, already been abandoned as a result of Gandhian agitation that focused on the creation of a unified political community. The constitutional text also rejected the concept of reserved seats for religious groups; and religious minorities were instead ensured protection in a new nation through an elaborate scheme of rights.

The debates of the Constituent Assembly engaged deeply with political concepts such as equality and justice. Many members were at pains to emphasize the importance of individuals rather than groups, and the idea of national citizenship. Women rejected special treatment: they sought instead to be treated as equal participants in a new country, in need of no schemes that granted special privileges based on their gender.

In the end, the emphasis on national citizenship and unity – influenced in part by the traumatic events that led to partition – resulted in the recognition and protection of only a narrow class of group – low castes and tribal groups. The deliberations of the Constituent Assembly mark, as Rochana Bajpai has recently suggested, "a dynamic of attenuation with regard to most group rights, although this trend was more pronounced in the case of political safeguards than cultural rights, and in the case of some groups, notably religious minorities, than others such as the 'backward classes'" (2011: 63).

The final document contained an elaborate set of equality guarantees. According to Article 14 of the Constitution, the "state shall not deny to any person equality before the law or the equal protection of the laws within the territory of India". Article 15 contains an intricate set of provisions relating to the "prohibition of discrimination on grounds of religion, race, caste, sex or place of birth". Article 16 is similar to Article 15 in certain respects, and concerns itself with the equality of opportunity in public employment. India's equality jurisprudence has centred on these three provisions, their interrelationship and changing character over time, and they shall be the focus of our analysis.[2]

Before we begin, however, it is worth taking note of certain additional textual guarantees. Article 17 abolishes untouchability and its practice "in any form" and articulates the constitutional aspiration of transcending caste. This provision applies horizontally and while there is statutory support backing this provision and tackling caste-based discrimination, it is worth noting that India lacks a general legislative prohibition of discrimination in the private sphere. Article 18 abolishes titles. The Supreme Court has held that while this provision does not bar the state from recognizing achievements and granting awards, no honour conferred by the state can be used as a title, either in the form of prefixes or

---

[2]　For the text of Articles 14–16 see Appendix 1.

suffixes, by recipients.[3] Two provisions, Articles 29 and 30, are also worth mentioning as they relate to how the Indian Constitution understands minority groups. These two provisions have been the subject of vexed constitutional litigation over the past two decades, and the difficult question has been the relationship between Article 29(2) – declaring that "no citizen shall be denied admission into any educational institution maintained by the state or receiving aid out of state funds on grounds only of religion, race, caste, language or any of them" – and Article 30(1) which ensures that "minorities, whether based on religion or language, shall have the right to establish and administer educational institutions of their choice". Through cases such as *St. Stephen's College*[4] and *T. M. A. Pai Foundation*,[5] the latter provision has been held to be independent of the former, granting minority educational institutions a wide sphere of autonomy.

It is useful to start our discussion with a consideration of the jurisprudence that has developed in relation to Article 14, and, in particular, the series of cases that has explicated the principles that inform the guarantees of "equality before the law" and "equal protection of the laws". A key case in this regard is *State of West Bengal* v. *Anwar Ali Sarkar*.[6] Examining the constitutionality of a law that empowered the government to classify offences and determine which cases could be decided by a special court, *Anwar Ali Sarkar* gave the Supreme Court an opportunity to establish the general test for determining whether a legal rule that differentiates between two different groups of people constitutes a breach of Article 14. It is, in effect, a rationality review test. It is called the "nexus test" and permits the state to differentiate between individuals or objects if two conditions are satisfied. First, the classification that the measure involves – i.e. what is included in and excluded from the group – must be based on an intelligible differentia. Second, that differentia must be rationally related to the object to be performed by the measure. That is to say, a causal connection must be present.

The classification requirement is central to the nexus test. For instance, in *D. S. Nakara* v. *Union of India*,[7] the Supreme Court struck down the revision of a retirement pension scheme that was applicable only to government servants who retired after a specific date. The Court held that pensioners form a class by themselves, and may not be sub-classified on

---

[3]   *Balaji Raghavan* v. *Union of India*, (1996) 1 SCC 361.
[4]   *St. Stephen's College* v. *University of Delhi*, (1992) 1 SCC 558.
[5]   *T. M. A. Pai Foundation* v. *State of Karnataka*, (2002) 8 SCC 481.
[6]   AIR 1952 SC 75.
[7]   (1983) 1 SCC 305.

the basis of an eligibility criterion based on an arbitrary date. The Court "found no rational principle ... for granting these benefits only to those who retired subsequent to that date, simultaneously denying the same to those who retired prior to that date" (para. 43).

In an early case dealing with taxation statutes, the Supreme Court held that a legislature may classify persons into different categories and subject them to different rates of taxation with respect to income or property, and may also subject different kinds of property to different rates of taxation, so long as the classification rests on a rational basis. It cannot, however, tax property of the same character differently, as such a measure would rest on no classification: it would treat holders of the same kind of property unequally.[8]

In general, Indian courts have read Article 14 as granting latitude to the state in the matter of taxation laws, and economic legislation more generally.[9] So, for example, in *R. K. Garg* v. *Union of India*,[10] the Supreme Court upheld a law that created special bonds to encourage those in possession of money unlawfully or improperly acquired to invest their concealed wealth and thus effectively "launder" their wealth. Among other things, the impugned law guaranteed anonymity and security to tax evaders. Rejecting the contention that the measure conferred special benefits on persons who had violated the law, the Court found that the classification was "clearly based on intelligible differentia having rational relation with the object of the Act". It emphasized that the "validity of a classification has to be judged with reference to the object of the legislation and if that is done, there can be no doubt that the classification made by the Act is rational and intelligible ...".[11]

The principles that mould the application of the nexus test were summarized by the Supreme Court in *Ram Krishna Dalmia* v. *Justice S. R. Tendolkar*,[12] a case that is often cited, not only in India, but also in other jurisdictions, including Malaysia, as we shall mention below. The question is whether a reasonable basis for classification exists and its relationship to the object sought to be achieved by the law.[13] Many of the principles highlighted in *Justice S. R. Tendolkar* were again revisited in

---

[8]   *K. T. Moopil Nair* v. *State of Kerala*, AIR 1961 SC 552.

[9]   See *Mafatlal Industries* v. *Union of India*, (1997) 5 SCC 536. See also *Federation of Hotel & Restaurant Association of India*, (1989) 3 SCC 634; *Elel Hotels and Investments Ltd.* v. *Union of India*, (1989) 3 SCC 698.

[10]   (1981) 4 SCC 675.

[11]   Ibid at 703.

[12]   *Ram Krishna Dalmia* v. *Justice S. R. Tendolkar*, AIR 1958 SC 538.

[13]   Ibid at paragraphs 11–12.

an important case in 1978, *In re Special Courts Bill, 1978*.[14] The Court emphasized that the classification under Article 14 must be rational in the sense that it cannot be based on qualities which are found in those persons grouped together and not in those excluded, but rather on those that are related to the object of the law. Thus, while Article 14 does not permit the conferring of benefits or liabilities on persons arbitrarily selected from a group of persons who are similarly situated, it does not bar classification for the purpose of the legislation.[15]

One of the major criticisms to be raised against the version of rationality review encapsulated in the nexus test is that it sets a rather low threshold for constitutionality. In an important essay four decades ago, P.K. Tripathi observed that the test "notices only the object and criterion of classification and their mutual relationship. It altogether ignores ... the special treatment the statute devises for the selected class of persons, and the relationship of this element with the other two" (1972: 58–9). Such a standard stands in striking variance with global trends. Consider, for example, the proportionality test often adopted in a disparate impact model of equality jurisprudence, which is used in a wide range of countries as the means through which rights-based violations are assessed (see Sweet and Mathews 2008). The test demands significantly more than the nexus test, and examines, *inter alia*, whether there are any other means available that are equally effective in pursuing the objective, and that impair the right less than the measure chosen.[16]

Over time, the courts have begun to employ a more rigorous reasonableness standard to assess claims under Article 14.[17] In *Tata Cellular*, for instance, the Supreme Court reviewed the awarding of government contracts, and held that in considering state action dealing with tenders, the decision-making process and not the merits of the decision itself would be reviewable.[18] This review of the decision-making process under Article 14 is based on the principles of arbitrariness and unreasonableness. The reasonableness standard may impose a more rigorous standard of scrutiny than the rationality requirement in the nexus test. So far, however, most cases that have invoked it have been squarely concerned with administrative law review. It is thus not entirely clear whether legislative action will be subjected to the reasonableness standard of

---

[14]   (1979) 1 SCC 380.

[15]   Ibid at 423–36.

[16]   See *Rocket* v. *Royal College of Dental Surgeons* [1990] 2 S.C.R. 232; *S* v. *Manamela*, 2000 (3) SA 1 (CC).

[17]   See *E. P. Royappa* v. *State of Tamil Nadu*, (1974) 4 SCC 3.

[18]   *Tata Cellular* v. *Union of India*, (1994) 6 SCC 651.

review, and if it is, how that standard of review would compare to a reasonableness standard applied to administrative conduct.

A recent decision has recognized the ambiguity of Indian constitutional law doctrine on this point.[19] Some recent decisions have also explored the possibility of incorporating the American strict scrutiny standard into Indian law, but no clear and definitive doctrinal development has yet taken shape. Until that occurs, or courts explore the possibility of a disparate impact approach, the equality guarantee in the world's largest democracy will continue to remain relatively weak.

Another important issue is gender equality. Debates surrounding women's rights have, for the most part, focused their attention on India's personal law system, which provides differential rules for different religious communities within the sphere of family law. Many of these rules discriminate on the grounds of sex and gender (see Agnes 2011: 1–113). Article 44 calls on the state to work towards a uniform civil code but this provision is unenforceable as per Article 37 of the Constitution, as it forms part of the chapter on Directive Principles of State Policy. So far courts have dealt with the constitutionality of personal laws on the basis of interpreting provisions in different personal laws in liberal and gender-neutral terms.

Outside the sphere of personal laws, the judiciary has now and again played an active role in emphasizing women's rights (Agnes 2011: 133–95). In *C. B. Muthamma* v. *Union of India*, for instance, the Supreme Court struck down a regulation of the Indian Foreign Services that prohibited the appointment of married women to the service.[20] In another prominent case, *Air India* v. *Nergesh Meerza*, the Supreme Court examined employment regulations governing Air India, a national airline carrier.[21] The Court held unconstitutional a bar on pregnancy and conditions relating to retirement, but upheld a lower retirement age for women on the ground that it was not based on sex alone. It is interesting to contrast this decision with the Malaysian decision in *Beatrice a/p AT Fernandez* v. *Sistem Penerbangan Malaysia and Another* [2005] 3 MLJ 681 (see the discussion below).

In later cases, courts struck down regulations that violated the principle of equal pay for equal work for men and women;[22] and in a recent case, the Supreme Court highlighted the importance of equal opportunity in

---

[19]   *Subramanian Swamy (Dr.)* v. *Director, CBI*, (2005) 2 SCC 317.

[20]   AIR 1979 SC 1868.

[21]   AIR 1981 SC 1829.

[22]   *Mackinnon Mackenzie* v. *Audrey D'Costa*, (1987) 2 SCC 469; *Uttarakhand Mahila Kalyan Parishad v. State of U. P.*, AIR 1992 SC 1695.

employment for both sexes.[23] In a prominent and widely discussed case in 1997, the Supreme Court incorporated provisions of the United Nations Convention on the Elimination of All Forms of Discrimination Against Women (CEDAW) and laid down guidelines relating to the sexual harassment of women at the workplace.[24] Another provision, Article 15(3), has also been relied upon to uphold certain provisions for affirmative action in public employment. The 73rd and 74th Amendments to the Constitution (1992) introduced reservations for women in local bodies, and currently pending before the Indian Parliament is the Constitution (One Hundred and Eighth Amendment) Bill, 2008 which aims to reserve one-third of all seats for women in the House of the People (*Lok Sabha*) and the state legislative assemblies.

As we observed, the Constituent Assembly did not seek to entrench and protect the rights of a wide range of groups. Special treatment was limited to "backward" castes and tribal groups. The interim recognition of such groups was considered essential, and it was "assumed that [their identities] were transient, and would yield finally to the more permanent claims of citizenship; but in the interim, both transient and permanent forms had to be acknowledged" (Khilnani 2002: 76). The achievement of this constitutional aspiration was sought through Articles 15 and 16. As it originally stood, Article 15 contained only three clauses. Clause (1) bars discrimination "on grounds of religion, race, caste, sex or place of birth" and clauses (2) and (3) prohibit restrictions, on such grounds, on access to public spaces, and enable the state to make "any special provision for women and children", respectively. Article 16 relates to equal opportunity in public employment, and clause (4) of the provision enables the state to make "the reservation of appointments or posts in favour of any backward class of citizens" underrepresented in state services. There was no equivalent provision to clause (4) in Article 15, suggesting that the founding constitutional vision appreciated a difference between reservations in public employment and in education, which is the sector with which Article 15 has become primarily associated.

Controversy surrounding these provisions arose soon after the Constitution was founded, with the case of *State of Madras* v. *Champakam Dorairajan*.[25] Here, an executive order proportioning seats according to caste and religion in engineering and medical colleges in Madras was

---

[23]   *Anuj Garg* v. *Hotel Association of India*, AIR 2008 SC 663.
[24]   *Vishaka* v. *State of Rajasthan*, (1997) 6 SCC 241.
[25]   AIR 1951 SC 226.

struck down as being unconstitutional. The Court was careful to distinguish between reservations in public employment and education. It held that while reservations in state services were constitutionally permissible, very different considerations were involved as regards admission to an educational institution, and no person had a right to admission as a member of a particular religion or caste. The Court held that it was for this reason that Article 29 did not adopt a clause similar to Article 16(4).

Champakam Dorairajan led to an amendment to the Constitution and the inclusion of a fourth clause in Article 15. The newly inserted Article 15(4) declared that the other provisions of Article 15 as well as Article 29(2) did not "prevent the state from making any special provision for the advancement of any socially and educationally backward classes of citizens or for the Scheduled Castes and the Scheduled Tribes". Naturally, the introduction of this provision invited debate over what constitutes backwardness. In *M. R. Balaji* v. *State of Mysore*,[26] the Supreme Court held that caste could not be the dominant, let alone sole, criterion for determining backwardness. The Court emphasized the importance of social *and* economic backwardness for groups that could receive special treatment by way of Article 15(4). As regards the quantum of reservations, *Balaji* placed a cap on 50 per cent. Such measures were, the Court reasoned, special in nature; and as exceptions to a general rule they would have to be employed within reasonable limits.

A series of decisions during the three decades following *Balaji* oscillated on questions of beneficiary identification and the logic of reservations. A significant nine-judge decision of the Supreme Court in the early 1990s, *Indra Sawhney* v. *Union of India*, attempted to clarify matters.[27] This case arose in the context of two executive orders proposing a certain scheme of reservations in public employment under Article 16, though it also addressed the nature of Article 15. The most significant finding of the Court was its generous endorsement of the usage of caste in reservation policies: caste could be the dominant criterion as well as the starting point for determining backwardness. The Court also held that the reservations, and Articles 15 and 16, were not exceptions to Article 14. Rather they were only articulations of what was already implicit in the provision: a commitment to substantive equality. That is to say, the Constitution affirmed the principle that like cases must be treated alike and different cases must be treated differently. This reasoning thus supports a conception of equality focused on impact rather

---

[26]   AIR 1963 SC 649.
[27]   AIR 1993 SC 477.

than treatment and thus a step, at least in relation to reservations, in the direction of a disparate impact approach. As regards the quantum of reservations, *Indra Sawhney* highlighted the importance of the 50 per cent cap, permitting 49.5 per cent reservations in public employment.

The Court's cap on 50 per cent was not necessarily grounded in the rule-exception logic that had motivated the decision in *Balaji*. Instead, one way to read the judgment, and to view the nature of the equality guarantee under India's Constitution more generally, is to argue that the Constitution, after the aforementioned amendment, embraces an asymmetric anti-discrimination principle (Khosla 2012a: 94–106). That is to say, it is asymmetric towards the use of caste: caste may be used as a criterion for benign discrimination but not for invidious discrimination (see Dworkin 1985: 293–303). Viewed in this way, *Indra Sawhney*'s rationale can be understood as not considering Articles 15(4) and 16(4) as exceptions to the norm but rather as clarifying the overarching equality guarantee. If this is correct, *Indra Sawhney* may mark the start of a jurisprudence based on disparate impact, at least as far as caste and reservations are concerned. It is too early to tell. While *Indra Sawhney* gave the state much leeway to determine "backwardness", that leeway was not unlimited. The Court placed a 50 per cent cap on reservations.

The reluctance of the Supreme Court in *Indra Sawhney* to scrutinize backwardness closely came into sharp focus again recently. In 2005, the 93rd Amendment to the Indian Constitution was enacted and placed a fifth clause in Article 15. Aiming to undo the consequences of an earlier judicial decision,[28] Clause (5) enabled the state to reserve seats for "other backward classes" (OBCs) in higher education in both public as well as private educational institutions, although the statute following the amendment was limited to public educational institutions. This amendment was challenged in *A. K. Thakur* v. *Union of India*.[29] The Supreme Court declined to decide whether the applicability of reservations to private educational institutions was constitutional (as no petitioner raised this issue), but upheld reservations for OBCs in public educational institutions. By permitting reservations for a vaguely defined category such as the OBCs, the Court effectively treated Scheduled Castes and Scheduled Tribes as equivalent to OBCs. This is a controversial approach, given the different historical experience of OBCs to Scheduled Castes and Tribes.

This is a very difficult area of the law, but arguably the weakness of the Supreme Court's jurisprudence lies in its failure to distinguish clearly

---

[28] *P. A. Inamdar* v. *State of Maharashtra*, (2005) 6 SCC 537.
[29] (2007) 4 SCC 361.

between different groups of beneficiaries, particularly OBCs as opposed to Scheduled Castes and Tribes, and to provide a clear map as to how the Constitution understands different groups.

One of the ways the Supreme Court has tried to distinguish between groups and prevent abuse has been through the development of the "creamy layer" doctrine. In *Indra Sawhney*, this measure aimed to exclude economically non-backward sections within a group from benefiting from reservations. The Court held, however, that this doctrine was inapplicable to Scheduled Castes and Scheduled Tribes, and later cases have struggled with determining which groups fall within the ambit of this doctrine. The doctrine illustrates the difficulty of identifying the criterion for preferential treatment within India's political and legal discourse. In part the problem has arisen because of the use of forms of immutable identity as the criterion. Identities like caste or religion are immutable unlike groups defined by reference to economic or social disadvantage. The use of an immutable criterion leads naturally to its institutionalization (Mehta 2012: 23–7). Whatever degree of social or economic mobility the beneficiary obtains, she cannot abandon her immutable identity. She will always remain of a certain caste or religion, as the case may be.

A lack of clarity over the idea of backwardness has only been compounded by different understandings as to the meaning of equality. This is most vividly revealed in the amendments to Article 16 (Khosla 2012b). This provision enables reservations in public employment, and in *Indra Sawhney* the Supreme Court held that such reservations could only exist at the entry level. Reservations were certainly part of the idea of substantive equality, but they too had an internal logic. Thus, the Court held, reservations in promotions in public employment could not be permitted, since the justification for reservations was unequal starting positions and the aspiration was the creation of a level playing field. In 1995, Parliament responded to this by adding Article 16(4A) to the Constitution to permit promotional reservations. This was followed by a further controversy – the "carry forward" problem. Could vacancies in reserved seats be carried forward into future years? *Indra Sawhney* adopted a halfway house approach to this, holding that carry forwards were permissible but could not exceed 50 per cent of the total vacancies available for posts in the following year. Again, Parliament amended the Constitution, to nullify this requirement. In the past, if reserved seats were unfilled, the demands of state capacity required that other general candidates fill those seats. Now, as a result of the amendment, either unfilled posts will remain vacant indefinitely or more posts would have to be created to accommodate the carry forwards.

The next controversy arose because promotional reservations had given rise to a peculiar phenomenon. Scheduled Castes and Scheduled Tribes' civil servants began to dominate higher civil service jobs, to an extent that far exceeded their prescribed quotas. Why was this so? As Rajeev Dhavan's important work captured, these candidates rose higher in the hierarchy because the result of their being promoted earlier rendered them senior to their colleagues who had not been appointed to reserved posts (Dhavan 2008). Scheduled Castes and Scheduled Tribes' candidates sought entry into a non-reserved promotional post on the ground that they were eligible for both such posts and quota posts, and "accelerated promotion" to a lower post had given them an "accelerated seniority". For years, the Supreme Court held that accelerated promotion could not result in accelerated seniority. This was, at least in some eyes, a double promotion, and the Supreme Court evolved a catch-up rule prescribing circumstances under which seniority could be regained by a non-quota candidate. Again, Parliament amended the Constitution. The 85th Amendment altered Article 16(4A) to enable "reservation in matters of promotion, with consequential seniority". Along the way, Parliament also amended Article 335 – which requires reservation claims to be considered along with concerns of efficiency in administration – to permit the lowering of standards of evaluation for Scheduled Castes and Scheduled Tribes' employees.

Recently, the Congress-led government has attempted to institute reservations on the basis of religion although the measure was struck down by the Andhra Pradesh (AP) High Court.[30] The proposed quota carved out 4.5 per cent reservations for religious minorities as a sub-quota within the overall 27 per cent reservations allotted towards OBCs in public employment and educational institutions. The AP High Court struck down the minority sub-quota, in part because it claimed that it was based entirely on religion. Sub-classification has been a tricky, and not entirely clear, question within Indian constitutional law; but in general *Indra Sawhney* permitted sub-classification among backward classes on the extent of backwardness. The question here is whether the minority groups in the sub-quota are more backward than the OBCs from whom the quota has been carved out and do not form part of the sub-quota. If not, as the AP High Court argued, then the carving out had been done solely on the basis of religion, thus violating Article 15(1) (see Reddy 2012).

---

[30] *R. Krishnaiah* v. *Union of India* (Andhra Pradesh High Court, 28 May 2012).

The Indian experience with affirmative action in the form of compulsory quota-based reservations warrants careful reflection (see Shourie 2012). Studies of Indian parliamentary behaviour reveal that the amendments to Articles 15 and 16 over the past two decades have been passed without any deliberation or scrutiny whatsoever, resulting in commentators asserting that the amendments reflect the rise of certain political groups and may have been used as forms of vote-buying (Dhavan 2008; 2012).

In 1984 Marc Galanter in his book *Competing Equalities* – which remains the most comprehensive study of reservations in India – concluded that India's experience demonstrated how formal equality could coexist with schemes for specific groups, although, in order to prevent the former from collapsing into the latter, we must have clear boundaries "with self-liquidating devices built into preference programs" (1984: 567). Two decades later, Galanter began to recognize the absence of any serious re-evaluation of such policies, and acknowledged "the threat that the essentially transitional and exceptional arrangements contemplated by the Constitution will ossify into permanent arrangements" (2002: 315).

Contrary to the intention of the framers, electoral politics and the recognition of caste in the form of reservations have solidified rather than undermined identities like caste. Equality is now, as Sudipta Kaviraj once observed, being claimed on the basis of caste (2000: 109). The most devastating consequence of this has been the idea that people from a certain community can only trust individuals who belong to the same community; and that different people are represented by different groups. If it continues to be extended, this argument "would completely undermine the impersonal rules of the operation of political power. It will make trust wholly segmentary, and make it impossible to run a modern democratic polity" (Kaviraj 2000: 112–113). Apart from carrying us away from the vision of a casteless society, this politics – and the structuring of equality around groups rather than individuals – has revealed insidious consequences for civic life. As Pratap Bhanu Mehta has argued, the advancement of democracy in India has proceeded through hostile pacts between groups and social conflict, resulting in the focus of political mobilization being access to the state and its power rather than state accountability (2003; 2012: 21). As India looks to the future and other countries hope to learn from its vast experience with quotas, it is important to notice how the creation of social categories can affirm them, allowing reservations to take on a life of their own. The ultimate risk is that the Indian Constitution will no longer recognize citizens as individuals but only on the basis of their community, caste and gender (Béteille 1999; 2012). At present, the Indian equality debate remains at an impasse; as India stands at the cusp of major economic and political change, it remains to be seen whether it can invent new idioms of equality.[31]

Another Asian country that has developed a vigorous affirmative action policy is Malaysia, to which we now turn.

III. MALAYSIA

Having only 28 million inhabitants, Malaysia's population is much smaller than India's, yet like India its population is both ethnically and religiously diverse. Ethnic Malays and the natives of Sabah and Sarawak comprise approximately two-thirds of the population. Jointly these groups are referred to as Bumiputera (loosely this translates as "sons of the earth"). People of Chinese descent constitute a quarter of the population while those of Indian descent constitute less than 10 per cent. Approximately 61 per cent of the population are adherents of Islam, while just under 20 per cent are Buddhist, just under 10 per cent are Christian and approximately 6 per cent are Hindu (Department of Statistics 2010).

Like India too, Malaysia was a British colony. It gained its independence in 1957 and is now a constitutional monarchy. The King, the Yang di-Pertuan Agong, is the head of government and is elected every five years from among the hereditary rulers of the nine states of peninsular Malaysia. Since the 1990s, Malaysia has experienced rapid economic growth and it now has the 35th largest economy in the world according to the World Bank (2010).

Again, like India, the question of ethnic relations is a defining characteristic of Malaysia's political economy. The Malaysian Constitution entrenches the policy of affording affirmative action to the Bumiputera, although again the Malaysian model is different to the model adopted in India. The policy of providing affirmative action measures to protect ethnic Malays is an old one which originated during the colonial era (Castellino and Dominguez Redondo 2006).

---

[31] For a major reflection on the equality debate in India, its historical character, analytical frameworks, and many challenges, see Pratap Bhanu Mehta, "Breaking the Silence: Why we don't talk about equality – and how to start again", *The Caravan* (November 2012); available at: http://www.caravan magazine.in/essay/breaking-silence.

The Federal Constitution of Malaysia is the supreme law of the country.[32] Article 8 of the Constitution is the equality clause. Its first two sub-clauses provide that:

(1) All persons are equal before the law and entitled to equal protection of the law.
(2) Except as expressly authorized by this Constitution, there shall be no discrimination against citizens on the ground only of religion, race, descent, place of birth or gender in any law or in the appointment to any office or employment under a public authority or in the administration of any law relating to the acquisition, holding or disposition of property or the establishing or carrying on of any trade, business, profession, vocation or employment.

Article 8(5) then provides a series of exceptions to the application of the clause:

This article does not invalidate or prohibit –

(a) any provision regulating personal law;
(b) any provision or practice restricting office or employment connected with the affairs of any religion or of an institution managed by a group professing any religion, to persons professing that religion;
(c) any provision for the protection, wellbeing or advancement of the aboriginal peoples of the Malay peninsula (including the reservation of land) or the reservation to aborigines of a reasonable proportion of suitable positions in the public services;
(d) any provision prescribing residence in a State or part of a State as a qualification for election or appointment to any authority having jurisdiction only in that State or part, or for voting in such an election;
(e) any provision of a Constitution of a State, being or corresponding to a provision in force immediately before Merdeka (Independence) Day;
(f) any provision restricting enlistment in the Malay Regiment to Malays.

In addition to the exceptions created in subparagraph (5), Article 8 is narrow in several other respects. First, it applies only to Malaysian citizens, rather than providing for all inhabitants of Malaysia. Second, it contains a closed list of prohibited grounds of discrimination. Unlike Section 9 of the South African Constitution and Article 15 of the Canadian Constitution (O'Regan and Friedman 2011), it does not permit other grounds of prohibited discrimination to be identified by courts. The

---

[32] Article 4(1) of the Constitution provides that: "This Constitution is the supreme law of the Federation and any law passed after Merdeka Day which is inconsistent with this Constitution shall, to the extent of the inconsistency, be void."

list in Article 8 was amended in 2001 to include a prohibition on discrimination on the grounds of gender. This amendment followed Malaysia's ratification of CEDAW, albeit with several reservations,[33] on 5 July 1995.

Third, Article 8 is also narrow in specifying the areas in which the prohibition of discrimination will apply, rather than providing a general prohibition of discrimination on the listed grounds. Article 12 of the Federal Constitution does expand the field somewhat. It provides that:

> Without prejudice to the generality of Article 8, there shall be no discrimination against any citizen on the grounds only of religion, race, descent or place of birth:
>
> (a) in the administration of any educational institution maintained by a public authority, and in particular, the admission of pupils or students or the payment of fees; or
> (b) in providing out of funds of a public authority financial aid for the maintenance or education of pupils or students in any educational institution (whether or not maintained by a public authority and whether within or outside the Federation).

Perhaps the most obvious aspect of Article 8, however, is the introductory phrase to Article 8(2) – "Except as expressly authorized by this Constitution ...". This express qualification on the operation of Article 8(2) means that Article 153 which provides for express quotas for Bumiputeras operates without reference to Article 8. Article 153 is in broad terms. It provides:

> (1) It shall be the responsibility of the Yang di-Pertuan Agong to safeguard the special position of Malays and natives of any of the States of Sabah and Sarawak and the legitimate interests of other communities with the provisions of this Article.
> (2) Notwithstanding anything in this Constitution, but subject to the provisions of Article 40 and of this Article, the Yang di-Pertuan Agong shall exercise his functions under this Constitution and federal law in such manner as may be necessary to safeguard the special position of the Malays and natives of any of the States of Sabah and Sarawak and to ensure the reservation for Malays and natives of any of the States of Sabah and Sarawak of such proportion as he may deem reasonable of positions in the public service (other than the public service of a State) and of scholarships, exhibitions and other similar educational or training

---

[33] The initial list of reservations recorded in 1995 was reduced in 2010 so that now the remaining reservations affect articles 9(2), 16(1)(a), 16(1)(f) and 16(1)(g) of the Convention.

> privileges or special facilities given or accorded by the Federal Govern-
> ment and, when any permit or licence for the operation of any trade or
> business is required by federal law, then, subject to the provisions of that
> law and this Article, of such permits and licences.

The ambit and application of Article 153 appears never to have been the
subject matter of litigation before a Malaysian court (Bari 2002). One of
the key reasons for this may well be the fact that in the Sedition Act,
1948, as amended, a "seditious tendency" is defined to include the
questioning of "any matter, right, status, position, privilege, sovereignty
or prerogative established by or protected by the provisions of Part III of
the Federal Constitution or Article 152, 153 or 181 of the Federal
Constitution".[34] A person who commits a seditious tendency commits an
offence[35] and is liable for a first offence to imprisonment for a period not
exceeding three years.

A recent report by the Equal Rights Trust has concluded that Article
153 "falls short of the international standards for legitimate positive
action" and has called for the repeal of this provision on the grounds that
it constitutes discrimination on the grounds of race (2012: 314 and 325).

A. Jurisprudential Approach to Article 8

The leading case on the interpretation of Article 8 is *Datuk Haji Harun
bin Haji Idris* v. *Public Prosecutor* [1977] 2 Malaysian LJ 154. The case
concerned an appellant who had been convicted of three counts of
corruption. He challenged section 418A of the Criminal Procedure Code
which permitted the Public Prosecutor to issue a certificate requiring a
lower court to remove a particular case to a High Court. The appellant
argued that the provision was in conflict with the constitutional principle
of equality before the law entrenched in Article 8 as it afforded the Public
Prosecutor a discretion to require a particular case to be heard by the
High Court without regard to the question whether other similarly placed
cases should also be removed to the High Court.

After a consideration of the Indian jurisprudence under Article 14 of
the Indian Constitution, Suffian LP, on behalf of a unanimous Court,
distilled ten principles to determine whether a litigant has established a
breach of Article 8. Those principles are:

---

[34] Section 3(1)(f) of the Sedition Act.
[35] Section 4 of the Act.

1. The equality provision is not absolute. It does not mean that all laws must apply uniformly to all persons in all circumstances everywhere.
2. The equality provision is qualified. Specifically, discrimination is permitted within clause (5) of Article 8 and within Article 153.
3. The prohibition of unequal treatment applies not only to the legislature but also to the executive – this is seen from the use of the words "public authority" in clause (4) and "practice" in clause (5)(b) of Article 8.
4. The prohibition applies to both substantive and procedural law.
5. Article 8 itself envisages that there may be a lawful discrimination based on classification – thus Muslims as opposed to non-Muslims (para. (b) of clause (5) of Article 8); aborigines as opposed to others (para. (c)); residents in a particular State as opposed to residents elsewhere (para. (d)); and Malays and natives of Borneo as opposed to others who are not (Article 153).
6. In India, the first question they ask is, is there classification? If there is and subject to other conditions, they uphold the law. If there is no classification, they strike it down. With respect we would agree with the Solicitor-General's submission that the first question we should ask is, is the law discriminatory, and that the answer should then be – if the law is not discriminatory, if for instance, it obviously applies to everybody, it is good law, but if it is discriminatory, then because the prohibition of unequal treatment is not absolute but is either expressly allowed by the constitution or is allowed by judicial interpretation we have to ask the further question, is it allowed? If it is, the law is good, and if it is not, the law is void.
7. In India discriminatory law is good law if it is based on "reasonable" or "permissible" classifications, using the words used in the passage reproduced above from the judgment in *Shri Ram Krishna Dalmia*,[36] provided that:
    (i)   the classification is founded on an intelligible differentia which distinguishes persons that are grouped together from others left out of the group; and
    (ii) the differentia has a rational relation to the object sought to be achieved by the law in question. The classification may be founded on different bases such as geographical, or according to objects or occupations and the like. What is necessary is that there must be a nexus between the basis of classification and the object of the law in question. ...

    As regards the narrower question whether or not the courts should leave it to the legislature alone to go into the reasonableness of the classification, we think that the courts should not that in other words, the court should consider the reasonableness of the classification.
8. Where there are two procedures existing side by side, the one that is more drastic and prejudicial is unconstitutional if there is in the law no

---

[36] *Shri Ram Krishna Dalmia and Others* v. *Shri Justice SR Tendolkar and Others*, AIR 1958 SC 191.

guideline as to the class of cases in which either procedure is to be resorted to. But it is constitutional if the law contains provisions for appeal, so that a decision under it may be reviewed by a higher authority. The guideline may be found in the law itself; or it may be inferred from the objects and reasons of the bill, the preamble and surrounding circumstances, as well as from the provisions of the law itself. The fact that the executive may choose either procedure does not in itself affect the validity of the law. ...

9. In considering Article 8 there is a presumption that an impugned law is constitutional, a presumption stemming from the wide power of classification which the legislature must have in making laws operating differently as regards different groups of persons to give effect to its policy. ...

10. Mere minor differences between two procedures are not enough to invoke the inhibition of the equality clause. ... "[37]

Applying these principles, the Court concluded that section 418A did not give rise to discrimination because of, among other things, the presumption of constitutionality. Suffian LP reasoned that "though differing procedures might involve disparity in the treatment of persons under them, such disparity is not by itself sufficient to outwit the presumption and establish discrimination unless the degree of disparity amounts to a denial of a fair and impartial trial" (at 167 E).

The Court continued by stating that even if the law was discriminatory, contrary to the conclusion of the Court, the classification was nevertheless reasonable. "The [Criminal Procedure] Code classifies cases into those triable in a magistrate's court, in a Sessions Court and in the High Court, putting the least serious cases in the first class, the most serious in the third and those in between in the second", the Court reasoned. It continued

In our view, this classification is made in the interest of the efficient administration of justice. This classification in our view also affords the necessary guideline to the Attorney-General when acting under section 418A who will be expected to transfer to the High Court only cases of unusual difficulty or of unusual importance, and there is no doubt that the case against the accused is one of great difficulty, considering that the trial took nine days and the appeal alone 13 days, the longest time taken to argue an appeal in Malaysia (167 H–I).

The approach developed in this case has been followed in many cases since. Most of the jurisprudence under Article 8 relates to "equality before the law". In a well-known case in 1987, the Supreme Court of

---

[37]   At 165–6.

Malaysia was divided on the question whether a statutory provision, section 46A of the Legal Profession Act, which restricted membership of the Bar Council and other organizations to lawyers of not less than seven years' standing was in breach of Article 8. The majority held that although the purpose of the provision was not expressly stated in the legislation, the Court could "infer the real object of the Act from the whole scheme" of the Act.[38] The majority held that the purpose of the differentiation was to ensure that the legal profession would be effectively and independently run by persons of considerable experience in the legal profession, and concluded that the provision was not in conflict with Article 8. The Lord President of the Court, Judge Salleh Abas, reached a different conclusion. He found that the provision prevented 45 per cent of the number of lawyers then in practice from having "a say through representatives of their class in the running of the affairs of their profession".[39] This result he found to be discriminatory.

Most of the cases under Article 8 approach the issue on the basis of the rational connection model which, given that many of them are dealing with the principle of equality before the law, is perhaps not surprising. There are very few cases dealing with alleged discrimination. The first case dealing with gender discrimination was *Beatrice a/p AT Fernandez v. Sistem Penerbangan Malaysia and Another* [2005] 3 MLJ 681 (Federal Court). The applicant was an air stewardess for a national carrier. The collective agreement between the airline and the union provided that pregnant air stewardesses were required to resign. If they did not resign, the airline was entitled to dismiss them. The applicant had become pregnant and, after refusing to resign, had been fired. She challenged her dismissal in the courts, arguing, among other things, that the provision in the collective agreement was an infringement of Article 8. She lost in the two lower courts, and the Federal Court dismissed her application for leave to appeal.

The Court reasoned that Article 8(2) of the Constitution did not apply to a collective agreement as it only regulated the relationship between citizens and the government. The Court also observed that the situation of female flight attendants is different from that of other employees because of the nature of the work. The Court reasoned "… that the nature of the job requires flight stewardesses to work long hours and often flying across different time zones. They have to do much walking on board

---

[38] *Malaysian Bar and Another* v. *Government of Malaysia* [1987] 2 MLR 165 at 170 H (per Mohamed Azmi SCJ).

[39] Ibid at 168 H–I.

flying aircraft. It is certainly not a conducive place for pregnant women to be." Accordingly, the Court concluded that its hands were tied and that "[r]egardless of how we try to interpret Article 8 of the Federal Constitution, we could only come to the conclusion that there was obviously no contravention."

This judgment has been heavily criticized (Abdul Aziz 2008; NEO 2007). The question whether private individuals and corporations are bearers of obligations under Article 8 of the Constitution is difficult. This difficulty is one of the reasons that many countries have enacted legislation to promote equality and prohibit discrimination. Indeed, Article 2(b) of CEDAW, which Malaysia has ratified, provides that states parties undertake "to adopt appropriate legislative and other measures, including sanctions where appropriate, prohibiting all discrimination against women". Yet, like India, Malaysia has not enacted such legislation. In fact, Malaysia has not enacted legislation outlawing discrimination on any ground (Equal Rights Trust 2012). It has enacted legislation relating to people with disabilities,[40] but that legislation does not include an operative provision prohibiting discrimination on the grounds of disability.

Nevertheless the reasoning in the *Beatrice Fernandez* judgment is disappointing, especially on the question whether Ms Fernandez was the subject of discrimination. Many courts have battled with the question whether discrimination on the grounds of pregnancy constitutes discrimination on the ground of sex or gender.[41] The reason for this, of course, is that because men do not fall pregnant, courts fail to find a comparator group for pregnant women. Yet, in *Beatrice Fernandez*, the collective agreement singled out pregnant air stewardesses as the only group who would be dismissed on grounds of pregnancy. The Court set a very low bar for the rationality of this distinction. The low bar was particularly disappointing given Malaysia's ratification of CEDAW, Article 11(a) of which provides that:

> In order to prevent discrimination against women on the grounds of marriage or maternity and to ensure their effective right to work, States Parties shall take appropriate measures:

---

[40] The Persons with Disability Act, 2008.

[41] See, for example, *Bliss* v. *Canada (Attorney-General)* [1979] 1 SCR 183 where the Supreme Court held that "any inequality between the sexes in this area is not created by legislation but by nature". *Bliss* was overturned in *Brooks* v. *Canada Safeway Ltd* [1989] 1 SCR 1219.

(a) To prohibit, subject to the imposition of sanctions, dismissal on the grounds of pregnancy or of maternity leave and discrimination in dismissals on the basis of marital status.

The Court thus failed to adopt an anti-discrimination approach to discrimination in this case which would have required a greater level of justification for the classification drawn.

As mentioned earlier, unlike in India, there is no jurisprudence on the relationship between Article 8 and Article 153. This is not surprising given that any questioning or discussion of the extent of the "special position" of Bumiputera may fall within the definition of sedition under the Sedition Act (Sani 2011). Similarly, it is very difficult to find information on the effects that Article 153 has in practice. The consequence is that it is very difficult to assess the special affirmative action measures enabled by Article 153 within Malaysia.

IV. JAPAN

India and Malaysia have many similar features: a shared history of colonization by Britain, and culturally and linguistically diverse population groups. Japan does not share these features. It is situated in eastern Asia and its landmass comprises a group of islands, approximately 378,000 square kilometres in extent. Relatively speaking, its population of approximately 128 million people is culturally and linguistically homogeneous. And Japan was never colonized by a European nation.

Historians generally divide Japanese history into two parts: the period prior to 1868, which is often referred to as pre-Meiji Japan and the period thereafter. In the mid-nineteenth century a dispute arose between the Tokugawa Shogunate, the governing elite, and others partly concerning a commerce treaty that had been entered into with the United States of America. The dispute led to a civil war and resulted in the 1868 restoration of imperial authority, an event known as the Meiji Restoration (Matsui 2011b: 7–8).

Prior to the Meiji Restoration – and for some time after – Japan was a feudal society with a rigid system of social stratification: at the top were the daimyo or feudal lords and samurai warriors, below were peasants, artisans and merchants. Outside of the system were the Burakumin, who were outcasts. The feudal system was abolished by law, after the Meiji Restoration, in 1871. Vestiges of the feudal social stratification persist, however, particularly in relation to the Burakumin.

The 1889 Meiji Constitution was based on the Prussian Constitution and premised on the sovereignty of the Emperor. Under the 1889 Constitution, judges were under the direction and control of the Ministry of Justice and accordingly, it is suggested, behaved cautiously and conservatively (Law 2011: 1435). A distinguished former Chief Justice of Japan, Chief Justice Yaguchi, suggested that the history of the judiciary as "a second-class bureaucracy" might have continued to influence judicial decisions throughout the twentieth century (cited in Law 2011: 1437).

Following Japan's defeat at the end of World War II, the 1889 Constitution was amended extensively. Three principles guided the amendment of the Constitution: popular sovereignty, the renunciation of war and the dismantling of the feudal system (Matsui 2011b: 13–16). Accordingly, the Emperor's role became titular, and a liberal democracy was established premised on the protection of fundamental human rights. Article 81 of the Constitution expressly gives the Supreme Court the power of judicial review over legislation and executive conduct. Despite the clear textual authority for judicial review, it is only on rare occasions that the Supreme Court has declared legislation to be inconsistent with the Constitution. According to Matsui, this had happened only eight times by 2011 (2011a: 1388; see also Law 2011: 1426). Compare this to the German Constitutional Court, established at about the same time, which has declared in excess of 600 legislative provisions to be in conflict with the Basic Law in roughly the same period (Law 2011: 1426).

Many different reasons for the deferential jurisprudence of the Japanese Supreme Court have been suggested in the academic literature (Holland 2009; Law 2011: 1426; 2009: 1547; Martin 2010; Matsui 2011a). What is plain, as will emerge from the discussion that follows, is that the Supreme Court's jurisprudence in relation to the equality guarantee of the Constitution is also clearly deferential. In this regard, it is more similar to the Malaysian Court than it is to the Indian.

The key provisions of the Japanese Constitution, for the purposes of the right to equality, are Articles 13, 14 and 24. Article 13 provides that:

> All of the people shall be respected as individuals. Their right to life, liberty and the pursuit of happiness shall, to the extent that it does not interfere with the public welfare, be the supreme consideration in legislation and in other government affairs.

Article 13 has been interpreted as a limitations clause which permits the abridgement of rights where government can point to a "public welfare" need that is served. But it has also served to focus on the importance of individuals and their need to be treated with respect (Martin 2010: 175). In a case concerning the aboriginal rights of the Ainu people in Hokkaido, the Sappor District Court reasoned that Article 13 imposes an obligation on government to have the "highest regard" for an individual in his relationship with the state. (Martin 2010: 175)

Article 14 is the equality clause and reads as follows:

(1) All of the people are equal under the law and there shall be no discrimination in political, economic or social relations because of their race, creed, sex, social status or family origin.
(2) Peers and peerage shall not be recognized.
(3) No privilege shall accompany any award of honor, decoration or any distinction, nor shall such award be valid beyond the lifetime of the individual who now holds or hereafter may receive it.

From the text of Article 14, it is clear that the Constitution reinforces the abolition of the feudal system in several ways. It provides that discrimination may not take place on the grounds of social status or family origin. It prohibits recognition of hereditary titles and asserts that honours may not be valid beyond the lifetime of an individual.

Article 24 relates to marriage and the family and provides as follows:

(1) Marriage shall be based only on the mutual consent of both sexes and it shall be maintained through mutual co-operation with the equal rights of husband and wife as a basis.
(2) With regard to choice of spouse, property rights, inheritance, choice of domicile, divorce and other matters pertaining to marriage and the family, laws shall be enacted from the standpoint of individual dignity and the essential equality of the sexes.

The Supreme Court has affirmed that the words "All of the people" in Article 14 include foreigners (see commentary in Martin 2010: 174).[42] It has also affirmed that the list of grounds in Article 14 is not exhaustive, but merely illustrative.[43] The Supreme Court has held, for example, that age is a prohibited ground of discrimination. Yet, as in India and Malaysia, the equality clause applies only to the relationship between government and individuals (with the only exception being Article 17 of the Indian Constitution, discussed above, which prohibits discriminatory

---

[42] Supreme Court judgment 18 November 1964, 18 Keishu 9: 579.
[43] Supreme Court judgment of 4 April 1973, the *Patricide* case.

treatment of "untouchables").[44] Again as in India and Malaysia, there is no comprehensive anti-discrimination legislation which prohibits discrimination by private individuals and corporations.

An attempt to introduce a prohibition on unreasonable private discrimination failed in the Diet, the Japanese Parliament, in 2002. The Human Rights Vindication Bill failed, apparently because of provisions in the draft which related to the prohibition of discriminatory speech. There are some legislative provisions which prohibit discrimination in specific circumstances. An example is Article 3 of the Labour Standards Law, which provides that an employer may not discriminate against employees with regard to wages, working hours or other conditions of employment on the grounds of nationality, creed or social status. The provision does not prohibit discrimination on the grounds of sex or gender.

Nevertheless, the Supreme Court has held that an employer may not discriminate against female employees. In the *Nissan Motors* case, decided in 1981, the Supreme Court held that a lower compulsory retirement age for women than for men constituted discrimination against women on the basis of their gender. It held that such discrimination was contrary to Article 90 of the Civil Code which prohibits juristic acts whose purpose is contrary to public policy or good morals. In interpreting Article 90 of the Code, the Court had regard to the constitutional norm of equal treatment. This decision may be contrasted with the decision in the *Mitsubishi Plastics* case. In that case, a university graduate had not disclosed his political activities as a student to Mitsubishi Plastics during the recruitment process. During his probationary period, his employer found out about his activities and refused to confirm his employment. The Supreme Court held that the dismissal was not unlawful.[45]

The Court has only upheld a challenge to legislation on the basis of Article 14 twice in its history. The first case, the *Patricide* case, concerned a challenge to Article 200 of the Criminal Code which imposed as a minimum sentence a mandatory life term of imprisonment for the murder of a lineal ascendant. Article 199 of the Criminal Code, on the other hand, imposes a minimum of three years' imprisonment for other forms of murder. The facts of the case that came before the Court were dreadful. A young woman had killed her father after having been

---

[44] Supreme Court judgment of 12 December 1973, the *Mitsubishi Plastic* case.
[45] Supreme Court judgment of 12 December 1973.

being effectively imprisoned by him since she was a teenager, raped on numerous occasions, and being forced to bear five of his children. She successfully challenged the constitutionality of the minimum sentence imposed by Article 200. The Court held (14–1) that the discrimination in Articles 199 and 200, as far as the sentences imposed in respect of the two forms of murder, was "unreasonable" and "disproportionate". A significant minority (six judges), who concurred in the majority outcome, held that, in light of the value of the individual, as reflected in Article 13 of the Constitution, the differential treatment between one form of murder and another was in itself discriminatory.

The test adopted by the majority is a form of the "rational classification" model, which is also followed in both India and Malaysia, and requires a discriminatory provision to be rational or reasonable ("gorisei"). The test as applied in the *Patricide* case has been criticized for being "rudimentary", "tautological" and "result-oriented" (Martin 2010: 170). As mentioned above, commentators criticize the Japanese Supreme Court for being conservative, and for failing to develop a robust jurisprudence for the protection of fundamental rights. The weak reasonableness test to determine whether there has been a breach of Article 14 is considered to be an exemplar of this practice.

A well-known example of the Supreme Court's willingness to defer to executive or legislative choices in the field of equality is the *Tokyo Metropolitan Government* case.[46] The case concerned a female health care professional in the Tokyo metropolitan government. She was a Japanese-born permanent resident of Japan who was a Korean national and who had applied for, but been refused, permission to take the test set for promotion to managerial level. The reason for the refusal was that only Japanese nationals could perform managerial functions. Although the Tokyo High Court upheld the claim, the Supreme Court dismissed it reasoning that the policy asserted by the City was necessary to maintain the functioning of the City's integrated management appointment system. This judgment has been criticized for failing to test the reason for the policy and for failing to consider meaningfully the effect of the policy on permanent residents such as the claimant (Martin 2011: 1550).

In 2008, however, the Supreme Court handed down judgment in the *Nationality Act* case,[47] which may be a harbinger of a more rigorous approach to the test of reasonableness. The case concerned the acquisition of Japanese nationality by children born to only one Japanese parent,

---

[46] Supreme Court decision of 26 January 2005.
[47] Supreme Court decision, 4 June 2008.

as well as the question of legitimate and illegitimate children. The effect of Articles 2(1) and 3(1) of the Nationality Act was that children of Japanese fathers, but non-Japanese mothers, whose parents were not married at the time of their birth, did not obtain Japanese citizenship if their fathers did not acknowledge paternity prior to their birth. The provisions thus constituted discrimination in several ways: as between children born within and without wedlock, as between children whose Japanese parent was male as opposed to children whose Japanese parent was female, and as between children whose male Japanese parent acknowledged paternity before their birth and those who did not.

The Court held that a legislative distinction must have a reasonable basis and that if there is not "reasonable relevance between the distinction in question and the ... legislative purpose" the legislative provision will be in violation of Article 14. The Court held that the purpose of the legislative distinction was to ensure that there was a "sufficiently close connection" between a child and Japan before conferring Japanese nationality on a child. The Court held that although originally the legislation may have met this requirement, changing social mores meant that the fact that a child's parents were not married was not a predictor of the connection between the child and Japan. The Court also assessed the harm done to children to whom nationality was effectively denied as a result of these provisions, and concluded that the relevant provision was in conflict with Article 14.

At least one commentator has suggested that the decision in the *Nationality Act* case is a departure from earlier jurisprudence (Martin 2010) in that it imposed a more rigorous standard of scrutiny to determine whether legislation was in conflict with Article 14. It is too early to declare this to be so, and, indeed, at least one of the cases that has followed the *Nationality Act* case[48] suggests that the decision in the *Nationality Act* case may be the assertive exception to an otherwise deferential rule (Martin 2010: 241–242).

Given the deferential flavour of the rational classification jurisprudence described above, it may not be surprising that there has been no sign of the emergence of an anti-discrimination model of jurisprudence under Article 14. It was mentioned above that Japan, compared to India and Malaysia, is a relatively homogeneous society. Yet, although that is true as a relative proposition, Japan is not entirely homogeneous. There are

---

[48]   Supreme Court judgment 30 September 2009, the *Illegitimate Child Inheritance* case.

groups of citizens in Japan who might well benefit from an anti-discrimination jurisprudence.

One such group would be the Ainu who have faced a long history of discrimination in Japan (Goodman 2010: 105–110; Matsui 2011b: 177). The Ainu are the indigenous people of Japan, although there is a debate as to whether they are indigenous to Hokkaidu only or to a wider part of Japan. In the late 19th century, the Meiji government adopted a policy of assimilation towards the Ainu that has been compared to the Native American assimilation programme in the United States of America (Goodman 2008: 105). The programme imposed mandatory Japanese medium schooling, forbade the practice of Ainu religious rituals and deprived the Ainu of their ancestral lands.

The question of the expropriation of Ainu lands arose in the *Nibutani Dam* case before the Sapporo District Court in 1997.[49] The regional Hokkaido government intended to develop the Sara River area in south central Hokkaido, which was historically the home of the Ainu people. In pursuance of this goal, the regional government expropriated land from the Ainu community. The land in question was traditional Ainu land which was considered sacred. The community relied on Article 27 of the International Covenant on Civil and Political Rights (ICCPR) and Article 13 of the Constitution. The Court held that Article 13 "fulfills the basic tenets of democracy by meaningfully respecting the individual while striving for the majority's compensation of and respect for the circumstances faced by the socially weak". Although the dam was subsequently built, the Court's recognition that the Ainu were a community entitled to rely on Article 27 of the ICCPR was an important acknowledgement of their status (Stewart 2003: 393–394). Shortly after the judgment was handed down, the Diet enacted the Act for the Promotion of Ainu Culture and Dissemination of Knowledge Regarding Ainu Traditions. Unfortunately, the Act does not contain a provision prohibiting discrimination against the Ainu.

There is a second group, the Ryukyuan, who might be thought to be similar to the Ainu. The Ryukyuan lived independently in the region around Okinawa until the 17th century. There is a dispute in Japan as to whether the Ryukyuan have a distinct cultural heritage. The United Nations Human Rights Committee advised the government to designate both the Ainu and Ryukyuan as indigenous peoples and to afford them assistance to protect and promote their culture and traditions, but as yet,

---

[49] *Kayano et al.* v. *Hokkaido Expropriation Committee*, 38 ILM 394, 27 March 1997.

the Japanese government does not consider the Ryukyuan to be an indigenous people although it does acknowledge their unique culture and history.

A third group that could benefit from anti-discrimination jurisprudence are the Burakumin (also known as the Dowa). They are not a distinct ethnic group but are a group who have been historically discriminated against in Japan, stemming back at least to the feudal era under the Tokugawa. The Burakumin performed tasks that were considered undesirable though indispensable, such as butchery. They were subjected to official discrimination until the late 19th century. There remains strong social prejudice against the Burakumin (Goodman 2008: 91–92; Matsui 2011b: 181– 182). It is widely accepted that, if proved, discrimination against the Burakumin would fall foul of Article 14 as discrimination on the ground of social status, but there has been as yet little or no jurisprudence on the question. Moreover, despite demands that the government enact civil rights legislation prohibiting private discrimination against the Burakumin, no such legislation has been enacted (Matsui 2011b: 181–182). Private agencies have been known to compile and sell "Burakumin lists" which foster discriminatory practices. The government has sought to reach a consensus that the publication of such lists violates the rights of citizens, but has not yet taken steps to outlaw them (Goodman 2008: 104–105).

As mentioned above, the Constitution contains a provision expressly asserting the equality of spouses within a marriage (Article 24). Despite the clear constitutional affirmation of the equality of the sexes in both Article 14 and Article 24, there have been several judgments of the Supreme Court, in which the Court has demonstrated a disappointing willingness to accept the rationality of discrimination on the grounds of sex and/or gender. For example, in the *Waiting Period for Remarriage for Divorced Women* case,[50] the Supreme Court upheld a provision preventing women from remarrying for six months after divorce, although there was no equivalent provision for men. The Supreme Court upheld the provision stating that the Diet has a broad discretion to determine the conditions of marriage and that the provision is not "utterly unreasonable" as it makes certain who is the presumed father of any child born during the period (Matsui 2011b: 180).

This brief overview of the Japanese jurisprudence on equality illustrates that the Japanese Supreme Court is deferential in scrutinizing the reasons proffered by government to justify legislative differentiation. The

---

[50]   Supreme Court judgment of 5 December 1995.

dominant mode of jurisprudential analysis is a rational classification test, where the executive and legislature's reasons for discriminatory conduct are rarely rigorously interrogated.

V. CONCLUSION

The value of comparative analysis across legal systems is evident in the above account. We have seen that there are significant differences in constitutional text between India, Malaysia and Japan as well as significant differences in historical, cultural and social context.

It is interesting to observe that in these three Asian countries, unlike in Canada, the United Kingdom and South Africa – the three countries studied in the earlier volume (O'Regan and Friedman 2011) – the dominant mode of equality jurisprudence is the rational classification test. There is little sign of the emergence of a vigorous anti-discrimination jurisprudence. One of the reasons for this may be courts' reluctance to challenge legislative and executive choices that implicate equality rights. In Malaysia and Japan in particular, the courts have been willing to adopt a deferential rational classification model of equality jurisprudence that has left the legislative and executive arms of government considerable leeway. In these jurisdictions, courts have often seemed reluctant to acknowledge the harmful effect of discriminatory laws and practices. Perhaps this is not surprising. Adjudicating equality claims brings courts close to questions at the heart of the democratic process. Developing a principled and predictive theory of judicial deference that acknowledges the proper role of the democratic arms of government yet at the same time recognizes the importance of affirming the principle of equality is a challenge for courts all over the world, not only in the three jurisdictions we have considered in this chapter.

The comparative analysis we have undertaken has enabled us to consider the recurrent conceptual, methodological and institutional issues that arise in equality jurisprudence from different angles. Doing so enables us to identify and interrogate unarticulated assumptions in the way we approach these issues. Here lies the real value of comparative legal study.

REFERENCES

Abdul Aziz, Zarizana. 2008. "Mechanisms to Promote Gender Equality in Malaysia: the Need for Legislation." *Mechanisms and Structures to Promote and Protect*

Women's Human Rights and Gender Equality Women Living Under Muslim Laws Dossier 29: 79–94.

Agnes, Flavia. 2011. *Family Law.* Vol. 1, *Family Laws and Constitutional Claims.* New Delhi: Oxford University Press.

Austin, Granville. 1966. *The Indian Constitution: Cornerstone of a Nation.* New Delhi: Oxford University Press.

Bajpai, Rochana. 2011. *Debating Difference: Group Rights and Liberal Democracy in India.* New Delhi: Oxford University Press.

Bari, Abdul Aziz. 2002. "Constitutional Bases for Affirmative Action – Comparing the Malaysian Position with that of India and the United States." *Lawasia Journal*: 127–136.

Barker, Ernest ed. 1946. *The Politics of Aristotle.* Book III, *The Theory of Citizenship and Constitutions.* Oxford: Clarendon Press.

Béteille, Andre. 1999. "Empowerment." *Economic & Political Weekly* 34(10): 589–97.

Béteille, Andre. 2012. *Democracy and Its Institutions.* New Delhi: Oxford University Press.

Castellino, Joshua and Dominguez Redondo, Elvira. 2006. *Minority Rights in Asia: A Comparative Legal Analysis.* Oxford: Oxford University Press.

Collins, Hugh. 2003. "Discrimination, Equality and Social Inclusion." *Modern Law Review*, 66(1): 16–43.

Department of Statistics, Malaysia. *Population and Housing Census, Malaysia 2010.* (http://www.statistics.gov.my/portal/index.php?option=com_content&view=article &id=1215&Itemid=89&lang=en/).

Dhavan, Rajeev. 2008. *Reserved! How Parliament Debated Reservations 1995–2007.* New Delhi: Rupa & Co.

Dhavan, Rajeev. 2012. "How Parliament Discusses Reservations: Examining the Debates on the Central Educational Bill." Pp. 168–201 in *Equalizing Access: Affirmative Action in Higher Education in India, US, and South Africa*, edited by Zoya Hasan and Martha C. Nussbaum. New Delhi: Oxford University Press.

Dirks, Nicholas B. 2001. *Castes of Mind: Colonialism and the Making of Modern India.* Princeton: Princeton University Press.

Dworkin, Ronald. 1985. *A Matter of Principle.* Cambridge MA: Harvard University Press.

Equal Rights Trust in partnership with Tenaganita. 2012. *Washing The Tigers*: *Addressing Discrimination and Inequality in Malaysia.* http://www.equalrights trust.org/ertdocumentbank/Malaysia%20CR.pdf.

Fredman, Sandra. 2002. *Discrimination Law.* Oxford: Oxford University Press.

Galanter, Marc. 1984. *Competing Equalities: Law and the Backward Classes in India.* New Delhi: Oxford University Press.

Galanter, Marc. 2002. "The Long-Half Life of Reservations." Pp. 306–138 in *India's Living Constitution: Ideas, Practices, Controversies*, edited by Zoya Hasan et al. New Delhi: Permanent Black.

Goodman, Carl F. 2008. *The Rule of Law in Japan: A Comparative Analysis*, 2nd Revised Edition. Alphen aan den Rijn: Wolters Kluwer.

Goodman, Carl F. 2010. *The Rule of Law in Japan: A Comparative Analysis*, 3rd Revised Edition. Alphen aan den Rijn: Wolters Kluwer.

Guha, Ramachandra. 2007. *India After Gandhi: The History of the World's Largest Democracy.* London: Macmillan.

Holland, Kenneth M. 2009. "Rights Protection in Japan: the Political Dimension." *Australian Journal of Political Science* 44(1): 79–96.

Kahn-Freund, Otto. 1974. "On Uses and Misuses of Comparative Law." *Modern Law Review* 37(1): 1–27.

Kaviraj, Sudipta. 2000. "Democracy and Social Inequality." In *Transforming India: Social and Political Dynamics of Democracy*, edited by Francine R. Frankel et al. New Delhi: Oxford University Press.

Khilnani, Sunil. 2002. "The Indian Constitution and Democracy." Pp. 64–82 in *India's Living Constitution: Ideas, Practices, Controversies,* edited by Zoya Hasan, Eswaran Sridharan, R. Sudarshan. New Delhi: Permanent Black.

Khosla, Madhav. 2012a. *The Indian Constitution.* New Delhi: Oxford University Press.

Khosla, Madhav. 2012b. "Down Reservation Road", *Indian Express*, 15 August.

Law, David S. 2009. "The Anatomy of a Conservative Court: Judicial Review in Japan" *Texas Law Review* 87: 1545 at 1547.

Law, David S. 2011. 'Why has Judicial Review failed Japan?' *Washington University Law Review* 88(6): 1425–1463.

Martin, Craig. 2010. "Glimmers of Hope: The Evolution of Equality Rights Doctrine in Japanese Courts from a Comparative Perspective." *Duke Journal of International and Comparative Law* 20: 167–243.

Martin, Craig. 2011. "Decision-making on the Japanese Supreme Court: The Politics of Supreme Court Adjudication: the Japanese Constitution as Law and the Legitimacy of the Supreme Court's Constitutional Decisions: A Response to Matsui." *Washington University Law Review* 88(6).

Matsui, Shigenori. 2011a. "Why is the Japanese Supreme Court so Conservative?" *Washington University Law Review* 88(6): 1375–1423.

Matsui, Shigenori. 2011b. *The Constitution of Japan: A Contextual Analysis.* Oxford: Hart Publishing.

McLachlin, Beverley. 2001. "Equality: The Most Difficult Right." *Supreme Court Law Review* 14 (2nd) 17, 20.

Mehta, Pratap Bhanu. 2003. *The Burden of Democracy.* New Delhi: Penguin.

Mehta, Pratap Bhanu. 2012. "The Politics of Social Justice." *Business Standard*, 2011, pp 1–30.

Mehta, Pratap Bhanu. 2012. "Breaking the Silence: Why we don't talk about equality – and how to start again." *The Caravan*, October 2012. (http://www.caravan magazine.in/essay/breaking-silence).

Mehta, Uday. 2010. "Constitutionalism." Pp. 15–27 in *The Oxford Companion to Politics in India*, edited by Niraja Gopal Jayal and Pratap Bhanu Mehta. New Delhi: Oxford University Press.

Neo, Jaclyn Ling-Chien. 2007. "Malaysia's First Report to the CEDAW Committee: A Landmark Event for Women's Rights in Malaysia." *Asian Yearbook of International Law* 13: 303–313.

O'Regan, Kate and Nick Friedman. 2011. "Equality." Pp. 473–503 in *Comparative Constitutional Law*, edited by Rosalind Dixon and Tom Ginsburg. Cheltenham: Edward Elgar.

Reddy, K. Vivek. 2012. "Lessons on How Not to Pitch a Quota." *The Hindu*, 21 June.

Sani, Mohd Azizuddin Mohd. 2011. "Free Speech in Malaysia: From Feudal and Colonial Periods to the Present." *The Round Table*, 100(416): 531–546.

Shourie, Arun. 2012. *Falling Over Backwards: An Essay on Reservations and on Judicial Populism*, 2nd edition. New Delhi: HarperCollins.

Stewart, Andrew Daisuke. 2003. "*Kayano v Hokkaido Expropriation Committee* Revisited: Recognition of Ryukyuans as a Cultural Minority under the ICCPR, an Alternative Paradigm for Okinawan Demilitarization." *Asian Pacific Law and Policy Journal* 4: 382–430.

Sweet, Alec Stone and Jud Mathews. 2008. "Proportionality Balancing and Global Constitutionalism." *Columbia Journal of Transnational Law* 47: 72–164.

Tripathi, P.K. 1972. *Some Insights into Fundamental Rights*. Bombay: University of Bombay.

Watson, A. 1976. "Legal Transplants and Law Reform." *Law Quarterly Review* 92: 79–84.

Watson, A. 1978. "Comparative Law and Legal Change." *Cambridge Law Journal* 37(2): 313–336.

Wintemute, Robert. 2004. "Sexual Orientation and the Charter." *McGill Law Journal* 49(4): 1143–1180.

The World Bank. 2010. "Gross Domestic Product 2010." (http://siteresources.world bank.org/DATASTATISTICS/Resources/GDP.pdf).

CASES

Canada

Bliss v. *Canada (Attorney-General)* [1979] 1 SCR 183.
Brooks v. *Canada Safeway Ltd* [1989] 1 SCR 1219.
Rocket v. *Royal College of Dental Surgeons* [1990] 2 S.C.R. 232.

India

Air India v. *Nergesh Meerza* AIR 1981 SC 1829.
A. K. Thakur v. *Union of India* (2007) 4 SCC 362.
Anuj Garg v. *Hotel Association of India* AIR 2008 SC 663.
Balaji Raghavan v. *Union of India* (1996) 1 SCC 361.
C. B. Muthamma v. *Union of India* AIR 1979 SC 1868.
D. S. Nakara v. *Union of India* (1983) 1 SCC 305.
Elel Hotels and Investments Ltd. v. *Union of India* (1989) 3 SCC 698.
E. P. Royappa v. *State of Tamil Nadu* (1974) 4 SCC 3.
Federation of Hotel & Restaurant Association of India (1989) 3 SCC 634.
Indra Sawhney v. *Union of India* AIR 1993 SC 477.
In re Special Courts Bill, 1978 (1979) 1 SCC 380.
K. T. Moopil Nair v. *State of Kerala* AIR 1961 SC 552.
M. R. Balaji v. *State of Mysore* AIR 1963 SC 649.
Mackinnon Mackenzie v. *Audrey D'Costa* (1987) 2 SCC 469.
Mafatlal Industries v. *Union of India* (1997) 5 SCC 536.
P. A. Inamdar v. *State of Maharashtra* (2005) 6 SCC 537.
R. K. Garg v. *Union of India* (1981) 4 SCC 675.
R. Krishnaiah v. *Union of India* (Andhra Pradesh High Court, May 28, 2012).
Ram Krishna Dalmia v. *Justice S. R. Tendolkar* AIR 1958 SC 538.
St. Stephen's College v. *University of Delhi* (1992) 1 SCC 558.

State of Madras v. *Champakam Dorairajan* AIR 1951 SC 226.
State of Uttar Pradesh AIR 1992 SC 1695.
State of West Bengal v. *Anwar Ali Sarkar* AIR 1952 SC 75.
Subramanian Swamy (Dr.) v. *Director, CBI* (2005) 2 SCC 317.
Tata Cellular v. *Union of India* (1994) 6 SCC 651.
T. M. A. Pai Foundation v. *State of Karnataka* (2002) 8 SCC 481.
Uttarakhand Mahila Kalyan Parishad v. *State of U. P.* AIR 1992 SC 1695.
Vishaka v. *State of Rajasthan* (1997) 6 SCC 241.

Japan

Supreme Court judgment 27 May 1964, *Tateyama Mayor* case.
Supreme Court judgment 18 November 1964, 18 Keishu 9.
Supreme Court judgment of 4 April 1973, *Patricide* case.
Supreme Court judgment of 12 December 1973, *Mitsubishi Plastic* case.
Supreme Court judgment 1981, *Nissan Motors* case.
Supreme Court judgment of 5 December 1995, *Waiting Period for Remarriage for Divorced Women* case.
Supreme Court judgment of 26 January 2005, *Tokyo Metropolitan Government* case.
Supreme Court judgment of 4 June 2008, *Nationality Act* case.
Supreme Court judgment of 30 September 2009, *Illegitimate Child Inheritance* case.
Kayano et al. v Hokkaido Expropriation Committee 38 ILM 394 (27 March 1997) (Sapporo District Court).

Malaysia

Beatrice a/p AT Fernandez v. *Sistem Penerbangan Malaysia and Another* [2005] 3 MLJ 681.
Datuk Haji Harun bin Haji Idris v. *Public Prosecutor* [1977] 2 Malaysian LJ 154.
Malaysian Bar and Another v. *Government of Malaysia* [1987] 2 MLR 165 at 170 H.
Shri Ram Krishna Dalmia and Others v. *Shri Justice SR Tendolkar and Others* AIR 1958 SC 191.

South Africa

S v. *Manamela* 2000 (3) SA 1 (CC).

United States of America

Griggs v. *Duke Power Company* 401 US 424 (1971).
McCleskey v. *Kemp* 481 US 270 (1987).
Washington v. *Davis* 426 US 229 (1976).

APPENDIX: ARTICLES 14–16 OF THE CONSTITUTION OF INDIA

Article 14: Equality before law – The State shall not deny to any person equality before the law or the equal protection of the laws within the territory of India.

Article 15: Prohibition of discrimination on grounds of religion, race, caste, sex or place of birth – (1) The State shall not discriminate against any citizen on grounds only of religion, race, caste, sex, place of birth or any of them.

(2) No citizen shall, on grounds only of religion, race, caste, sex, place of birth or any of them, be subject to any disability, liability, restriction or condition with regard to –

(a) access to shops, public restaurants, hotels and places of public entertainment; or

(b) the use of wells, tanks, bathing ghats, roads and places of public resort maintained wholly or partly out of State funds or dedicated to the use of the general public.

(3) Nothing in this article shall prevent the State from making any special provision for women and children.

(4) Nothing in this article or in clause (2) of Article 29 shall prevent the State from making any special provision for the advancement of any socially and educationally backward classes of citizens or for the Scheduled Castes and Scheduled Tribes.

(5) Nothing in this article or in sub-clause (g) of clause (1) of Article 19 shall prevent the State from making any special provision, by law, for the advancement of any socially and educationally backward classes of citizens or for the Scheduled Castes or the Scheduled Tribes insofar as such special provisions relate to their admission to educational institutions including private educational institutions, whether aided or unaided by the State, other than the minority educational institutions referred to in clause (1) of Article 30.

Article 16: Equality of opportunity in matters of public employment – (1) There shall be equality of opportunity for all citizens in matters relating to employment or appointment to any office under the State.

(2) No citizen shall, on grounds only of religion, race, caste, sex, descent, place of birth, residence or any of them, be eligible for, or discriminated against in respect of, any employment or office under the State.

(3) Nothing in this article shall prevent Parliament from making any law prescribing, in regard to a class or classes of employment or appointment to an office under the Government of, or any local or other authority within, a State or Union territory, any requirement as to residence within that State or Union territory prior to such employment or appointment.

(4) Nothing in this article shall prevent the State from making any provision for reservation in matters of promotion, with consequential seniority, to any class or classes of posts in the services under the State in favour of the Scheduled Castes and Scheduled Tribes which, in the opinion of the State, are not adequately represented in the services under the State.

(4-B) Nothing in this article shall prevent the State from considering any unfilled vacancies of a year which are reserved for being filled up in that year in accordance with any provision for reservation made under clause (4) or clause (4-A) as a separate class of vacancies to be filled up in any succeeding year or years and such class of vacancies shall not be considered together with the vacancies of the year in which they are being filled up for determining the ceiling of fifty per cent reservation on total number of vacancies of that year.

(5) Nothing in this article shall affect the operation of any law which provides that the incumbent of an office in connection with the affairs of any religious or denominational institution or any member of the governing body thereof shall be a person professing a particular religion or belonging to a particular denomination.

12. Comparative constitutional law and religion in Asia

Ran Hirschl[1]

I. INTRODUCTION

Asia – the birthplace of many faith traditions – is not only the most populous continent, home to over four billion people; it is also the most religiously diverse continent. Hundreds of millions follow Islam, Christianity, Hinduism, and Buddhism in its Shinto, Thervada, Mahayana, and Confucian-Taoism versions. Crude estimates suggest that followers of Islam account for approximately 28 percent of Asia's population (Islam is the majority religion in 26 of the 48 Asian countries); 24 percent follow Hinduism (the vast majority of them in India and Nepal); 18 percent of the continent's population (constituting the majority religion in eight countries) follow varieties of Buddhism; and followers of all other religions make up the remaining 30 percent (Mahmood 2010; Esposito et al. 2011). The varied post-colonial legacy – British in India and Pakistan, French in Vietnam, Spanish in the Philippines, Portuguese in Macao and East Timor, and Dutch in Indonesia – alongside post-war (e.g. Japan) and post-Soviet (six Asian nations were once part of the USSR) reconstruction, add another layer of complexity. It is hardly surprising that when it comes to the comparative constitutional law of religion, Asia has it all. It sports the entire array of "religion-and-state" models (see Hirschl 2011), ranging from India's "secularism" to Iran's "constitutional theocracy," and from North Korea's atheism to the transplantation of American constitutional vocabulary of "free exercise" and "(dis)establishment" in the predominantly Catholic Philippines.

The extraordinary scope and variance of constitutional law and religion in Asia renders a comprehensive survey of the topic well beyond the

[1] I thank Madhav Khosla, Diane Desierto, Kate Brookson-Morris, and the volume editors for their helpful comments and suggestions.

scope of this chapter. Instead, I chart below the contours of three common constitutional configurations of religion-and-state relations in Asia, covering over three-quarters of the continent's national constitutions: (i) constitutional "secularism" alongside religious pluralism (e.g. India); (ii) preferential constitutional treatment of a particular religion or group of religions, but without exclusive establishment of a single faith as a "state religion" or a mandatory source of legislation (e.g. Thailand, Cambodia, Sri Lanka and other predominantly Buddhist countries); and (iii) varieties of "Islamic constitutionalism" in Asia (i.e. full endorsement of Islam as the single state religion and its establishment as "a" or "the" source of legislation). Taken as a whole, these three prototypical modes of religion-and-state relations represent a continuum, ranging from pro-active advancement of secularism to strong establishment of religion.

I conclude by suggesting that it is hard to identify a uniform or coherent "Asian" approach to religion-and-state relations or detect a distinctly "Asian" aspect of constitutional law of religion in that continent. At the same time, Asia does feature several prototypical models of religion-and-state relations that defy the Western ideal of separating religion and state along private/public lines. In fact, there appears to be far less adherence to the classic separation of church and state model in Asia than in any other continent. A closer look at the constitutional law of religion in Asia may thus complement and enrich, perhaps even put in a modest light, the countless, purportedly comparative accounts of constitutional law and religion in North America and Europe. The study of constitutional law and religion in Asia may also question the feasibility and wisdom of advocating a single paradigm for arranging the relations between politics and religion worldwide.

II. INDIA: CONSTITUTIONAL "SECULARISM" AND RELIGIOUS PLURALISM

Of all the Asian countries, India features what is arguably the clearest example of constitutionally backed secularism. India has long been a member of the world's nuclear club, has recently become one of the world's major information technology centers, and has also seen its urban middle-class population grow rapidly. At the same time, India is not only the second most populous country in the world but also one of the most religious ones. Comparative sociological studies consistently rank India as one of the most religious polities in the world. Most Indians (much like Americans or Turks) view religion as a crucial marker of identity, as well as a significant source of reference and guidance in their day-to-day lives. The Hindu ethnic-nationalist impulse has grown considerably over the last three decades, a fact that is reflected in the rise of Hindu right-wing parties, such as the Bharatiya Janata Party (BJP). The populist social-democratic establishment Congress Party continues to portray itself as secular, although in the 2009 general election, much as in the two general elections before it, religion cast a wide shadow over the entire political spectrum. Even the explicitly secularist left has been playing the religious card; in the states of West Bengal, Kerala, and Uttar Pradesh, left-leaning regional parties have been collaborating with religious leaders to advance their cause and attract Muslim voters. Meanwhile, India has a huge Muslim minority that numbers approximately 160 million and constitutes about 14 percent of India's population. India is home to the third-largest Muslim population in the world (after Indonesia and Bangladesh), although some unofficial reports suggest that the Muslim population is actually distinctly larger than these official numbers. Muslim Indians do occasionally come to the fore in public, from sports stars Zaheer Khan (cricket) and Sania Mirza (tennis) to A.P.J. Abdul Kalam, India's eleventh president (2002–2007). However, the Muslim community continues to claim that it suffers from systemic discrimination against its members and Hindu-orchestrated attempts to erode its autonomy and clout. At times these claims and counterclaims fuel severe sectarian violence. To add further complexity, Christians (who account for slightly over 2 percent of India's population) constitute the dominant majority in the three north-eastern states of Meghalaya, Mizoram and Nagaland.

The tension between religiosity and secularism has dominated Indian politics from the outset. In fact, as several observers (e.g. Goodman 2009) have pointed out, the very concept of secularism has multiple meanings in the Indian context: the universalist, neutralist, separation-of-religion-and-state notion of secularism often associated with Western-like modernization and social progress; the populist vision of secularism often associated with Hindu right-wing parties, such as the BJP, which advocate secularism with the understanding that it will reflect the perspectives of the dominant Hindu majority; and a "multicultural" or pluralist conception of secularism, which reflects the status quo in India and whereby members of different religious communities are afforded some legal recognition and jurisdictional autonomy in the realm of personal-status law.

The Supreme Court of India's pertinent jurisprudence has generally endorsed the first vision of secularism described in the preceding paragraph, advocating a neutral, uniform civil code. However, as Josh Goodman suggests, some of the Court's rhetoric and some well-known recent decisions seem to align the Court with the second, Hindu populist version of secularism (Goodman 2009). This is hardly surprising, given the increasing pro-Hindu sentiment in India's political sphere. In several rulings involving personal-status law, the Court has appeared overtly hostile to the third, pluralist model, casting it as contrary to the principles of secularism and in violation of the spirit of the Indian Constitution.

The Constitution (as amended in 1976) depicts India as a secular state. In the landmark *Kesavananda Bharati* case (1973) the Supreme Court introduced the "basic-structure" doctrine, according to which the basic features and structure of the Constitution of India are beyond the powers of amendment of the Parliament of India. The Court held that amendments and other laws that violated or attempted to change the basic structure or basic features of the Indian Constitution would be held invalid. The response of the legislature to this ruling was the 42nd Amendment, passed in 1976, which attempted to reverse the "basic-structure" doctrine. However, the Court voided the provisions of the 42nd Amendment that contradicted the "basic-structure" doctrine, and the doctrine has since remained established in Indian jurisprudence. Nonetheless, the 42nd Amendment did insert into the preamble to the Constitution the words "socialist" and "secular" so that it reads: "We, the people of India, having solemnly resolved to constitute India into a sovereign, socialist, secular democratic republic." Thus "secularism" has formally been incorporated into the Constitution. The Court has since held that secularism is indeed part of the basic structure of the Constitution.[2]

At the same time, the Court has not advocated a notion of militant secularism in the Turkish sense. Article 25 of India's Constitution (1950) protects "Freedom of conscience and free profession, practice and propagation of religion." On many occasions, the Court has protected the rights of religious minorities and their members to hold genuine, conscientious beliefs followed as part of the authentic practice of their religion. In the landmark case of *Bijoe Emmanuel v. State of Kerala* (1986), the Supreme Court of India ruled that Jehovah's Witness students may be exempt from singing the national anthem at school as compelling them to join in such singing would violate their "genuine, conscientious religious objection" to such practice. The decision went on to add that standing up during the anthem singing showed sufficient respect towards the anthem, and stated that "Our tradition teaches tolerance, our philosophy teaches tolerance, our Constitution practices tolerance, let us not

---

[2] *S. R. Bommai v. Union of India* AIR 1994 SC 1918.

dilute it."[3] With that said, the Supreme Court of India has developed a sophisticated interpretive matrix to delimit the scope of religious practice protected under Article 25. In a nutshell, it provides that constitutional protection of religious practice extends only to such religious practices considered "essential" or "integral" to a particular religion. In the Court's words:

> protection under Article 25 extends a guarantee for rituals and observances, ceremonies and modes of worship which are *integral* parts of religion and as to what really constitutes an essential part of religion or religious practice has to be decided by the courts with reference to the doctrine of a particular religion or practices regarded as parts of religion.[4]

One of the perennial bones of contention in the Indian context is the struggle between advocates of universal secularism (and by extension, the adoption of a uniform civil code) and proponents of the status quo, in which religious minorities, most notably Muslims, enjoy certain jurisdictional autonomy in matters of personal status, primarily marriage and divorce. Section 44 of the Indian Constitution states that: "The State shall endeavour to secure for the citizens a uniform civil code throughout the territory of India." However, for a host of political reasons, not least the pressure to preserve the religious jurisdictional enclaves, little has been done in practice to enact such a uniform law. At the more abstract level, the tension between these competing visions of secularism has taken the form of a clash between group rights and the individual rights of potentially vulnerable group members, e.g. women (see Shachar 2001).[5]

The *Shah Bano* saga is a good illustration. It involved an elderly Muslim woman who was divorced by her husband of 43 years through the Muslim practice of *talaq*, which allows a husband to effect a unilateral, immediate divorce. However, lacking the resources to support herself and her five children, Shah Bano sought maintenance payments in the courts. Under Muslim personal law, Shah Bano's ex-husband was only obligated to pay her a small sum of maintenance money during the three months after the divorce, known as the period of *iddat*. Section 125 of the Code of Criminal Procedure stipulates that a husband may be

---

[3]　*Bijoe Emmanuel v. State of Kerala* AIR 1987 SC 748.

[4]　*N. Adithyan v. Travancore Devaswom Board* AIR 2002 SC 106.

[5]　Similar tensions between group rights and women's rights, and more generally between a quest for uniformity, equality and modernization on the one hand, and accommodation of group-based religious difference and jurisdictional autonomy on the other is evident in virtually all countries where the religious jurisdictional enclaves model is in place.

ordered to pay maintenance to his wife or ex-wife if she is unable to maintain herself. However, according to Section 127 of the same law, these maintenance payments are to be reassessed by the court where the woman has received the sum due to her under the personal law.

In its famous ruling in *Mohammed Ahmed Khan v. Shah Bano Begum*, the Supreme Court of India held that the state-defined statutory right of a neglected wife to maintenance stood regardless of the personal law applicable to the parties.[6] In other words, individual rights and gender equality norms are more fundamental than India's long-standing practice of Muslim self-jurisdiction in personal-status matters. The Court held that the right to maintenance under Section 125 was a secular legal right that could be "exercised irrespective of the personal law of the parties," and that "section 125 overrides the personal law, if there is any conflict between the two." It also rejected the husband's argument that Section 127 was automatically satisfied by his payment of a dowry (*mahr*).

Traditionalist representatives of the Muslim community considered this to be proof of Hindu homogenizing trends that threatened to weaken Muslim identity. India's Parliament, led by Rajiv Gandhi's Congress Party, bowed to massive political pressure by conservative Muslims and overruled the Indian Supreme Court's decision in *Shah Bano* by passing the Muslim Women's (Protection of Rights of Divorce) Act. Despite its reassuring title, this new bill undid the Court's ruling by removing the rights of Muslim women to appeal to state courts for post-divorce maintenance payments. It also exempted Muslim ex-husbands from other post-divorce obligations. So harsh was the Muslim reaction to *Shah Bano* that notable commentators see it as one of the reasons for the subsequent ascent of right-wing Hindu politicians. The Muslim Women's Act served to agitate many Hindus and galvanize support for the Hindu right wing, which accused the Congress Party of compromising the principles of secularism in order to appease Islamic fundamentalists and get Muslim votes (Sathe 2003: 192). Some commentators also tie the ruling to the volatile public atmosphere that led to the notorious destruction of the historic Babri mosque by Hindu militants at a disputed religious site in the city of Ayodhya in 1992, and the spate of sectarian violence that followed (Jacobsohn 2003: 106). Thus, whereas the Court has been effective at stoking significant public controversy concerning personal laws, its secularist jurisprudence on the matter has been quite counter-productive in achieving its declared goals of a uniform civil code and national integration.

---

[6] *Mohammed Ahmed Khan v. Shah Bano Begum* AIR 1985 SC 985.

In 2001, the Court returned to the issue of personal-status laws in *Danial Latifi v. Union of India*.[7] Here, the abovementioned Muslim Women's Act was challenged on various constitutional grounds, including the violation of Article 14 (equality) and Article 15 (non-discrimination) of the Constitution, as well as for violating the basic constitutional feature of secularism. The Court upheld the constitutionality of the Act, but did so through a broad, liberal construction of its requirement that the husband make a "reasonable and fair provision and maintenance within the period of iddat." The Court commented that if the statute only authorized maintenance for three months, this would appear to violate the constitutional rights provisions on equality and discrimination. However, applying the constitutional avoidance canon (an interpretive device of reading legislation such that it complies with the Constitution), the Court construed the statute to authorize maintenance orders for "reasonable and fair" sums that may provide support for the divorced wife for much longer than just the three-month period of *iddat*, so long as the payment itself is made during the period of *iddat*.

This ruling, although contrary to the common understanding of the Act's purpose, followed the actions of lower courts at the state level, which had already been interpreting the statute in this fashion and awarding relatively generous lump sum maintenance payments to divorced Muslim women. Thus, the *Latifi* ruling used creative statutory interpretation to dodge constitutional controversy, while still preserving judicial discretion in determining the size of maintenance awards based on the facts of each case. This strategy suggests that the Court understood the not-so-subtle message sent by the public outcry and legislative response in the wake of *Shah Bano*. Its ruling in *Danial Latifi* was less ambitious and notably more moderate and diplomatic than its original ruling in *Shah Bano*.

On other occasions, the Supreme Court of India has consistently sided with secularist uniformity even at the cost of occasional clashes with the political sphere. In *Sarla Mugdal v. Union of India* (1995), a case that involved married Hindu men who were converting to Islam in order to practice polygamy, which is legal under Muslim personal law, Justice Kuldip Singh wrote:

> Those who preferred to remain in India after the partition, fully knew that the Indian leaders did not believe in two-nation or three-nation theory and that in the Indian Republic there was to be one Nation – Indian nation – and no community could claim to remain a separate entity on the basis of religion ...

---

[7]   *Danial Latifi v. Union of India* AIR 2001 SC 3958.

The Successive Governments till-date have been wholly remiss in their duty of implementing the constitutional mandate under Article 44 of the Constitution of India.[8]

In the *Vallamattom* case (2003) – a successful challenge to the constitutionality of Section 118 of the Indian Succession Act that prohibited bequests to religious or charitable organizations made less than a year prior to the grantor's death – the then Chief Justice V.N. Khare stated that:

> Article 44 provides that the State shall endeavor to secure for the citizens a uniform civil code throughout the territory of India. The aforesaid provision is based on the premise that there is no necessary connection between religious and personal law in a civilized society ... It is a matter of regret that Article 44 of the Constitution has not been given effect to. Parliament is still to take steps for framing a common civil code in the country. A common civil code will help the cause of national integration by removing the contradictions based on ideologies.[9]

In sum, the Supreme Court of India has been standing at the vanguard of reformist attempts by the Indian state to contain religion and to modernize and "rationalize" it under an overarching secularist platform. To retain its legitimacy, the Court must constantly take into account the complex, religion-laden socio-political setting within which it operates. This may occasionally result in retreats from its overall secularizing jurisprudential line. Although it may be argued that the Supreme Court's reading of Hinduism has legitimized the concept of Hindutva, the Court has consistently been in pursuit of what Gary Jacobsohn (2003) calls "ameliorative secularism" viewed as a project of betterment – a supposed counter-narrative to India's long tradition of religiosity, charged Hindu–Muslim relations, and strong undertones of religion-based political symbolism.

III. STATE-ENDORSED RELIGION(S)

This broad category of religion-and-state relation models includes systems that do not advance secularism or adhere to a strict separation of church and state, yet at the same time do not subscribe to a "strong establishment" model and fall short of formally affirming one particular

---

[8]   *Sarla Mugdal v. Union of India* AIR 1995 SC 1531.
[9]   *John Vallamattom v. Union of India* AIR 2003 SC 384.

religion as the official or state religion. Placed in the elusive space between these two ends, these systems either (i) acknowledge that a particular religion has a special status in the country's constitutional hierarchy, often reflecting the historical role of that religion as a marker of political sovereignty, ethnic or national identity; or (ii) list a small number of "state-approved" religions that may be practiced under varying degrees of government monitoring, while non-state-controlled denominations or alternative voices within "certified" religions are banned.

Outside of Asia, relatives of this mode of religion-and-state relations come in two main forms: formal separation alongside de facto pre-eminence of a single religion, and weak (or symbolic) religious establishment. The first variant is featured in countries where formal separation of church and state, and religious freedoms more generally, are constitutionally guaranteed, but where long-standing patterns of politically systematized church hegemony and church-centric morality continue to loom large over the constitutional arena. Many countries where the vast majority of the population is Roman Catholic and where the history of Catholic Church dominance dates back to the pre-independence era fall in this category. The closest example in Asia for such a setting is the Philippines (see Pangalangan 2008).[10]

In the second variant (weak establishment) there is a formal, mainly ceremonial, designation of a certain religion as "state religion," but this designation has few or no implications for public life. Several European countries illustrate this model. A case in point is the designation of the Evangelical Lutheran Church as the "state church" in Norway, Denmark, Finland and Iceland – arguably some of Europe's most liberal and progressive polities. Norway's head of state, for example, is also the leader of the church. Article 2 of the Norwegian Constitution guarantees freedom of religion, but also states that Evangelical Lutheranism is the official state religion. Article 12 requires more than half of the members of the Norwegian Council of State to be members of the state church. Similarly, Greece and Cyprus formally designate the Greek Orthodox Church as their state church. In England, the monarch is "Supreme Governor" of the Church of England and "Defender of the Faith." The Crown has a role in senior ecclesiastical matters and, by the same token, the church is involved in the coronation of a new monarch, and senior bishops are represented in the House of Lords.

---

[10]   A second predominantly Catholic country in Asia is East Timor. Alongside constitutional guarantees for freedom of religion and worship, the Constitution (2002) provides that: "The State acknowledges and values the participation of the Catholic Church in the process of national liberation of East Timor."

In Asia, variants of this model have taken a considerably more substantive direction. To begin with, several Asian polities have a long history of state-endorsed religion. In imperial Japan during the Meiji era and through the end of World War II, to pick one example, Shinto was the state-endorsed religion. The post-World War II reconstruction Constitution rejected the Meiji era's concept of state-endorsed Shinto, and followed the pattern adopted in many liberal constitutions by setting a rigid separation of church and state, and by moving religion to the private sphere (Kobayashi 2010). Prior to the 2006 sacking of King Gyandera and the transition to democracy, Nepal, to pick another example, was the last country in the world to endorse Hinduism as its constitutive faith.

This model continues to be quite prevalent today. Over 90 percent of the Thai population (approximately 67 million), are adherents of Theravada Buddhism. There is no state religion; having debated the matter for months, drafters of the 2007 Constitution (which replaced the 1997 Constitution, which was scrapped during a military coup in 2006) elected not to include a clause designating Buddhism as the national religion, or a diluted "Buddhism defines Thailand" clause. Instead, five religious denominations are officially recognized: Buddhism, Islam, Brahmin-Hinduism, Sikhism, and Christianity. However, Buddhism and Siamese peoplehood have been closely entangled for over two millennia. Buddhism remains a key element of national ideology and constitutional identity in contemporary Thailand (see Harding and Leyland 2011); the support of Buddhist monkhood is essential to maintaining the regime's political legitimacy.

Theravada Buddhism receives significant government support, and the Constitution retains the requirement that the monarch be Buddhist.[11] Tellingly, the 2007 Constitution is officially marked as signed in year 2550 of the Buddhist Era. Section 79 of the Constitution specifies that the state shall "protect Buddhism as the religion observed by most Thais for a long period of time and other religions, and shall also promote a good understanding and harmony among the followers of all religions as well as encourage the application of religious principles to create virtue and develop the quality of life." While freedom of speech is constitutionally protected, laws prohibit the defamation or insult of Buddhism and the Buddhist clergy. A roughly similar structure exists in Sri Lanka, where Article 9 of the Constitution (1978) states that: "The Republic of Sri Lanka shall give to Buddhism the foremost place and accordingly it shall be the duty of the State to protect and foster the Buddha Sasana,

---

[11] Section 9 reads: "The King is a Buddhist and guardian of all religions."

while assuring to all religions the rights granted by Articles 10 and 14(1)(e)." The Constitution of Bhutan (2008) states that Buddhism is the spiritual heritage of the country, and that the Buddhist Drupka Lineage is practically the state religion of Bhutan. Buddhism enjoys a de facto preferential status in other countries in the region, most notably Burma and Cambodia, where Theravada Buddhism has long been a pillar of collective identity and the faith of an overwhelming majority of the population.

The "state-endorsed religion(s)" model is often accompanied by close government monitoring of the religious market. For example, in Tajikistan and Uzbekistan, Muslim followers of non-state-approved religious organizations may be arrested for holding "unsanctioned gatherings" or are labeled "extremists" by state courts and by leaders of registered religious organizations. In 2007, for example, the Supreme Court of Tajikistan declared a dozen such unregistered organizations, including the Islamic Movement of Turkestan, to be "extremist." The practice is by no means confined to predominantly Muslim countries. Most Vietnamese, for instance, follow Mahayana Buddhism. Driven by anti-American suspicions, Vietnamese law closely monitors political associations, and thus requires that religious groups register with the government (see generally, Sidel 2009). Those groups that do not join one of the officially authorized religious organizations, the governing boards of which are under government control, are considered illegal. This has led to effective infringement of religious freedom of various Christian and non-state-controlled Buddhist sects.

Indonesia provides another interesting example. It has one of the largest Muslim populations in the world; approximately 90 percent of its roughly 250 million citizens identify themselves as Muslim. One of the five core precepts of the *Pancasila* (the foundational national philosophy) established by the Indonesian Constitution (1945, reaffirmed 1959) is that "the state shall be based on the belief in the one and only God." Buddhism, Catholicism, Hinduism, Islam, Protestantism, and, as of 1998, Confucianism, enjoy equal status as state-recognized religions. At the same time, government monopoly over the definition of official religion is maintained. Two recent landmark rulings of the Indonesian Constitutional Court illustrate this approach.

The Indonesian Religious Courts Law lists a number of areas (e.g. marriage, divorce, inheritance, trusts, gifts, and Islamic finance) over which Shari'a tribunals have jurisdiction. In the *Religious Court Law Case* (2008), the Constitutional Court unanimously rejected a claim made by a religious student who argued that the state-imposed limitation of the jurisdiction of religious courts to particular civil matters is unconstitutional because it prevents his full observance of Islam.[12] The Court held that expanding the list of subject-matters falling within the jurisdiction of religious courts is within the exclusive prerogative of the federal government, and is not something the Court can do (Butt 2010: 297).

In 2010, the Indonesian Constitutional Court upheld (8:1) the legality of the country's controversial 1965 Blasphemy Law.[13] The law officially acknowledges six religions: Buddhism, Catholicism, Confucianism, Hinduism, Islam, and Protestantism, and prohibits "religious based activities" that "resemble the religious activities of the religion in question, where such interpretation and activities are in deviation of the basic teachings of the religion." This amounts to a prohibition on alternative teachings and has been used to clamp down on "unofficial" Islamic voices ranging from the Ahmadiyya sect to militant Wahhabism. Proponents of Western-style rights argued that the law in its current form infringes basic religious freedoms as well as group rights, and violates the International Covenant on Civil and Political Rights. Drawing on a "war on terror" impulse (Bali and other parts of Indonesia have been targets of bombings tied to Islamic militants), the government countered that the law must be upheld to avoid interpretation-at-will of Islamic and Shari'a law. Upholding the law, the government argued, would "maintain social harmony and prevent an explosion of new religions." The Court agreed. Repealing the Blasphemy Law, it ruled, could bring "misuses and contempt of religion and trigger conflicts in society." By upholding the law, the Court has thus aided authorities in preventing "runaway" radical Islamization by keeping the process of religious interpretation under official check.

Malaysia and Israel feature a strong variant of the "state-endorsed religion" model. Here, there is no constitutional entrenchment of a single religion as "a" or "the" source of legislation; however, religious ascription (Islam in Malaysia, Judaism in Israel) is the key marker of national identity, and the basis for preferential treatment granted to followers of that religion, at the expense of members of the polity who are not Muslims (Malaysia) or Jews (Israel). The problems stemming from Israel's self-definition as a "Jewish and democratic state" (approximately 20 percent of Israel's citizenry are not Jewish) have been widely debated.

---

[12]   Constitutional Court Decision No 19/PUU-VI/2008.
[13]   Constitutional Court Decision No 140/PUU-VII/2009. For a detailed analysis of the decision *see* Crouch (2012). This ruling was upheld by the Court in 2013. See Constitutional Court Decision No 84/PUU-X/2012.

Considerably lesser attention has been given to Malaysia, where non-Muslims comprise approximately 40 percent of the citizenry. The Constitution of Malaysia (1963) states that "Islam is the religion of the Federation; but other religions may be practiced in peace and harmony in any part of the Federation" (Article 3), and where "every person has the right to profess and practice his religion and to propagate it" (Article 11.1). Further, "every religious group has the right to manage its own religious affairs" (Article 11.3), while state law (and, in the Federal Territories of Kuala Lumpur and Labuan, federal law) "may control or restrict the propagation of any religious doctrine or belief among persons professing the religion of Islam" (Article 11.4). To add further complication, Malaysian law draws on religious ascriptions to establish what has been termed "ethnic democracy," where, despite the existence of some ethnic power-sharing mechanisms and an accompanying façade of inter-racial harmony, Malay political dominance is ensured. Core elements of the political system are organized so as to benefit members of the Malay ethnic group to the detriment of others, and members of minority ethnic groups are not granted proportional access to power. Ethnic Malays (Bumiputra or "sons of the soil"), generally Muslim, are granted constitutionally entrenched preferential treatment in various aspects of public life over members of other ethnic groups (Article 153 of the Constitution). Malay citizens who convert out of Islam are no longer considered Malay under the law and hence forfeit the Bumiputra privileges afforded to Malays under Article 153.

The religious-secular duality embedded in the Malaysian legal system is further reflected in the changing jurisdictional interrelation between the civil and Syariah courts. Muslims (and non-Muslims who marry Muslims) are obliged to follow the decisions of Syariah courts in matters concerning their religion, most notably marriage, inheritance, apostasy, conversion, and custody. Historically, the civil and Syariah courts existed side by side in a dual court structure established at the time of Malaysia's independence, with the prevalent understanding that Syariah courts were subordinate to the civil courts and that the common law was superior to other laws. In the landmark case *Che Omar bin Che Soh* (1984) the Federal Court, then known as the Supreme Court of Malaysia, ruled that the common law had not been ousted or otherwise affected by the introduction of the Federal Constitution, and that it would allow secular courts to resolve legal issues, even where the parties to the case were Muslims.[14] However, in 1988 an amendment to the constitution, Article

---

[14]   *Che Omar bin Che Soh v. Public Prosecutor* (1984) 1 MLJ 113.

121(1A), was introduced; it provided that civil courts "shall have no jurisdiction in respect of any matter within the jurisdiction of the Syariah Courts."

Even after the 1988 amendment the civil court system continued to view Syariah courts as subordinates and, at any rate, subject to general principles of administrative and constitutional law. The civil courts consistently interpreted the jurisdictional boundaries between the two court systems so as to prevent the expansion of the Syariah court system. Likewise, the Malaysian Bar Council has continued to argue that Article 121(1A) does not exclude the supervisory review power of the Federal Court. However, because Islam has become a major political force in Malaysia, taking an all-out anti-Islamist stand on the question of jurisdictional boundaries is no longer a feasible option for the Court. It opted instead for a dual approach of respecting Syriah courts' jurisdiction in matters assigned to them, and at the same time maintaining the Federal Court's overarching jurisdiction in all matters constitutional, religious or otherwise.[15]

In short, the state-endorsed religion model as it has been practiced in Asia reflects complex, perhaps even blurry, state–religion relations that draw on religious tradition and heritage for collective identity and nation building purposes, while hovering in a space between Western-style rights discourse and what is perceived as overly permissible religious freedoms on the one hand, and overly restrictive strong establishment of religion as the source of public morality on the other.

IV. VARIETIES OF ISLAMIC CONSTITUTIONALISM

The term "Asia" (as in, say, "Asian food" or "Asian values") is often invoked to refer to what is actually a sub-region that includes East and Southeast Asia. But the continent is larger than that. Over half (26) of the world's predominantly Muslim countries (48) are in Asia, stretching from the Middle East to the edge of the Pacific Rim. These include countries that are considered part of the so-called "Arab world," small countries such as the Maldives and Brunei alongside giants such as Iran, Pakistan, Indonesia and Bangladesh. In many of these countries, public support for the principles of theocratic governance has grown considerably over the last few decades. At the same time, principles of constitutionalism,

---

[15] For illustrations of this duality, see *Lina Joy v. Majlis Agama Islam Wilayah Persekutuan* (2007) 4 MLJ 585; *Latifa Mat Zin v. Rosmawati Binti Sharibun et al.* (2007) 5 MLJ 101.

human rights, economic development and other modernizing pressures dictate a moderate approach to what may be termed the "Islamic state." The result has been the rise of "Islamic constitutionalism" – a constitutional system based on an inherently dual commitment to religious fundamentals and constitutional principles, or a bi-polar system of constitutional *and* sacred texts and authority. This model comes close to what I have termed elsewhere "constitutional theocracy" (Hirschl 2010). The "ideal" version of this model can be summarized by outlining four main cumulative elements: (1) the presence of a single religion or religious denomination that is formally endorsed by the state, akin to a "state religion;" (2) the constitutional enshrining of the religion, its texts, directives and interpretations as *a* or *the* main source of legislation and judicial interpretation of laws – essentially, laws may not infringe upon injunctions of the state-endorsed religion; (3) a nexus of religious bodies and tribunals that often not only carry tremendous symbolic weight, but are also granted official jurisdictional status on either regional or substantive bases, and which operate in lieu of, or in uneasy tandem with, a civil court system; and (4) adherence to some or all core elements of modern constitutionalism, including the formal distinction between political authority and religious authority, qualified protection of religious freedoms for minorities, and the existence of some form of active judicial review. Most importantly, their jurisdictional autonomy notwithstanding, some key aspects of religious tribunals' jurisprudence are subject to constitutional review by apex courts, often state created and staffed.

The 1979 Islamic revolution in Iran established a paradigmatic example of a constitutional theocracy. The preamble of the 1979 Islamic Republic of Iran's Constitution enshrines the Shari'a as the supreme law – superior even to the Constitution itself. Articles 2 and 3 declare that the authority for sovereignty and legislation has a divine provenance (from the Shari'a) and that the leadership of the clergy is a principle of faith. According to Article 6, the administration of the state is to be conducted by the wider population: the general public participates in the election of the President, the Majlis representatives (members of parliament) and municipality councils. Article 8 further entrenches principles of popular participation in deciding political, economic and social issues. Most notably, Iran has seen the emergence of the Guardian Council – a de facto constitutional court armed with mandatory constitutional "preview" powers and composed of six mullahs appointed by the Supreme Leader – and six jurists proposed by the head of the judicial system of Iran and voted in by the Majlis. The Supreme Leader has the power to dismiss the religious members of the Guardian Council, but not its jurist members (Article 91). At the same time, Iran's constitutional regime combines religious supremacy, pragmatist institutional innovations (e.g. Ayatollah Khomeini's 1989 introduction of the Regime's Discernment Expediency Council to serve as the final arbiter between the generally more progressive Consultative Assembly and the distinctly more conservative Guardian Council), alongside carried-over legacies of the 1906 Imperial Constitution, primarily with respect to the notion of popular sovereignty, elected parliament and some separation of powers principles.

While Iran features what is arguably one of the strictest manifestations of strong establishment, several considerably softer versions of this model have emerged in Asia's predominantly Islamic countries. It is well known that Afghanistan has long been torn between conflicting values of tradition and modernism. From 1994 to 2001 the country was ruled by the radical Islamist Taliban, but the U.S.-led military campaign removed the Taliban from power and installed a more moderate regime representing an array of groups hitherto in opposition: moderate religious leaders and the country's elites and intellectuals in exile. The new Constitution of Afghanistan came into effect in January 2004. It states that Afghanistan is an Islamic republic (Article 1); that the "sacred religion of Islam is the religion of the Islamic Republic of Afghanistan" (Article 2); and that "[n]o law shall contravene the tenets and provisions of the holy religion of Islam in Afghanistan" (Article 3). Courts are allowed to use Hanafi jurisprudence in situations of constitutional lacunae (Article 130). At the same time, the Constitution also enshrines the right to private property (Article 40) and resurrects a woman's right to vote, as well as to run for and serve in office (Article 22). The 2004 Constitution also establishes a Supreme Court (Stera Mahkama) composed of nine judges appointed by the president for a term of ten years (Articles 116–117). All members of the Court "[s]hall have higher education in legal studies or Islamic jurisprudence" (Article 118).

The newly adopted Iraqi Constitution of 2005 offers another variant of this amalgam. Article 2.1 states that "Islam is the official religion of the state and a basic source of legislation." No law can be passed that contradicts settled Islamic (legal) rules. At the same time, Article 2.1(b) states that "[n]o law can be passed that contradicts the principles of democracy," and Article 5 declares: "The law is sovereign and the people are the sources of power and its legitimacy." The Federal Supreme Court, states Article 92, "shall be made up of a number of judges, experts in Islamic jurisprudence, and legal scholars, whose number, the method of their selection, and the work of the Court shall be determined by a law enacted by a two-thirds majority of the members of the Council of Representatives." Influenced by the circumstances of its adoption, the Iraqi Constitution also emulates Western constitutional catalogues of rights by protecting a host of rights and liberties, such as religious freedoms (Articles 2.2, 41, and 42), formal equality, including anti-discrimination on the basis of religion (Articles 14 and 16), privacy (Article 17), and personal freedom and dignity (Article 37). More important still, it incorporates into Iraqi law (via Article 44) provisions of international human rights treaties to which Iraq is a signatory, so long as they do not conflict with the Constitution. The commitment to rights and liberties is also affirmed by a declarative umbrella section (Article 2.1(c)), which reads: "No law can be passed that contradicts the rights and basic freedoms outlined in this constitution." To pass comprehensive constitutional scrutiny, then, a law has to conform to the common tenets of Islam, democracy, individual rights and liberties, and international human rights – a difficult task, to put it mildly, even for distinctly more stable polities.

Another variation on the strong establishment model is essentially a mirror image of the religious jurisdictional enclaves discussed earlier. Here, most of the law is religious; however, certain areas of the law, such as economic law or certain aspects of gender equality, are "carved out" and insulated from influence by religious law. An interesting case in point is Saudi Arabia, arguably one of the countries whose legal system comes the closest to being fully based on *fiqh* (Islamic jurisprudence). Article 1 of the Saudi Basic Law (1993) reads: "The Kingdom of Saudi Arabia is a sovereign Arab Islamic state with Islam as its religion; God's Book and the Sunnah of His Prophet, God's prayers and peace be upon him, are its constitution." Article 23 establishes the state's duty to advance Islam: "The state protects Islam; it implements its Shari'a; it orders people to do right and shun evil; it fulfills the duty regarding God's call." At the same time, Chapter 4 of the Basic Law (titled: Economic Principles) protects private property, provides a guarantee against the confiscation of assets, and suggests that "economic and social development is to be achieved according to a just and scientific plan." Moreover, whereas Saudi courts apply Shari'a in all matters of civil, criminal or personal status, Article 232 of a 1965 Royal Decree provides for the establishment of a commission for the settlement of all commercial disputes. Although judges of the ordinary courts are usually appointed by the Ministry of Justice from among graduates of recognized Shari'a law colleges, members of the commission for the settlement of disputes are appointed by the Ministry of Trade. In other words, Saudi Arabia has effectively exempted the entire finance, banking and corporate capital sectors from application of Shari'a rules. Softer examples of this model are common in the Islamic world, from Qatar or the United Arab Emirates to exotic destinations such as the Maldives in the Indian Ocean.

A fascinating aspect of such strong establishment constitutional settings is the role constitutional courts play in mediating the often conflicting commitments of constitutional rights and radical religion. The Supreme Court of Pakistan's jurisprudence provides a prime example. The process of "Islamization" of Pakistani law goes back to 1973 and has known many twists and turns. Its pinnacles have been the 1978–1980 establishment of a Shari'at court system at the provincial and federal levels, as well as the Shari'at Appellate Bench (SAB) at the Supreme Court; and the introduction in 1985 of a set of amendments to the Constitution, effectively stipulating that "[a]ll existing laws shall be brought in conformity with the Injunctions of Islam as laid down in the Holy Qur'an and Sunna, in this Part referred to as the Injunctions of Islam, and no law shall be enacted which is repugnant to such Injunctions." In theory, this means that legislation must be in full compliance with principles of Shari'a. The Supreme Court of Pakistan (SCP), however, has begged to differ.

In response to the possible conclusiveness of the Islamization reforms, the Court developed its "harmonization doctrine," according to which no specific provision of the Constitution stands above any other provision. In a landmark ruling in 1992, the SCP held that the "Islamization amendment" shall not prevail over the other articles of the Constitution, as the amendment possessed the same weight and status as the other articles of the Constitution and therefore "could not be placed on a higher pedestal or treated as a *grund norm.*"[16] The Court's subsequent judgments of this key issue have firmly precluded and strongly warned against an interpretation of the Islamization amendments which would "raise it to the point of being a litmus test for gauging, evaluating, and potentially justifying the judiciary to strike down any other constitutional provisions" (Siddique and Hayat 2008: 368). Any reading of the amendments as elevated "special clauses" would undermine the entire Constitution. The Constitution as a whole must be interpreted in a harmonious fashion so that specific provisions are read as an integral part of the entire Constitution, not as standing above it. In the words of the Court: "It may be observed that the principles for interpreting constitutional documents as laid down by this Court are that all provisions should be read together and harmonious construction should be placed on such provisions so that no provision is rendered nugatory."[17]

---

[16]   *Hakim Khan v. Government of Pakistan* P.L.D. 1992 S.C. 595.
[17]   *Qazi Hussain Ahmed et al. v. General Pervez Musharraf* P.L.D. 2002 S.C. 853.

To be sure, although it has shown some secularizing tendencies, the SCP, like its counterparts elsewhere, does not operate in a political or ideological vacuum. To some extent, it may be considered an extension of the executive branch rather than a fully autonomous organ. It is hardly surprising that in several rulings it sided with the Islamist face of the Constitution. A notable example is the Court's approval in 1993 of part of the 1984 blasphemy laws that made members of the Ahmadiyya community liable to prosecution for engaging in activities associated with Islam. Likewise, in the politically charged area of personal-status and family-law matters, the equality provisions of the Constitution are seldom invoked by the Court. Indeed, the constitutional status of women in Pakistan is a far cry from any Western liberal standards. Women's groups pushing for greater gender equality face intense opposition. As Sadia Saeed notes, the initial containment of religious zeal via constitutionalization may have the effect of subsequent entrenchment of more moderate, but nonetheless illiberal, rights discourses. That said, the SCP has managed to block calls for major Islamic-based family-law overhaul.

In addition to its refusal to accept the Islamization amendments as a supra-constitutional norm, the Court has retained its overarching jurisdictional authority, including its de facto appellate capacity over the SAB at the Supreme Court. This has proved time and again to be a safety valve for secular interests. In 2002, for example, the Supreme Court ordered the SAB to reconsider its 1999 ruling that interest or usury *(riba)* in any form contravened Shari'a principles and was therefore impermissible.[18] The Supreme Court accepted the government's argument that the transition to a *riba*-free economy, as it had been defined by the SAB, was effectively infeasible. It noted concerns about the economic stability of Pakistan should the reforms occur and stated that they were simply impractical. The Court also accepted the government's claim that the reasoning employed by the SAB misinterpreted both the Qur'an and Sunna, had invoked only one conception of *riba,* and thus lacked the objectivity needed to render an adequate verdict in the case. The Court thus ordered the SAB "to conduct thorough and elaborate research, and comparative study of the financial systems which are prevalent in the contemporary Muslim countries of the world."[19]

In 2003, to give another example, the Pakistani Supreme Court ruled that the Hudood Ordinances (adopted in 1979 to introduce harsh penalties for offenses described in the Qur'an) had been drafted hastily, had

---

[18] *United Bank Ltd. v. M/S Farooq Brothers* P.L.D. 2002 S.C. 800.
[19] Ibid, 815–16.

many gaps, were defective, and were the source of many challenges to the establishment of human rights in the country. The enforcement of the ordinances, stated the Court, was not in line with the justice-seeking purpose of enforcing Islamic law. In 2004, the SCP went on to curtail the Federal Shari'at Court's competence to overturn any legislation judged to be inconsistent with the tenets of Islam. The Court held that any Shari'a-related jurisprudence that involves significant constitutional law aspects must take a cohesive view of Pakistan's constitutional law, as well as the supremacy of federal legislation over provincial legislation.[20]

In short, religion has made a major comeback over the last few decades, and is now a de facto and often de jure pillar of collective identity, national meta-narratives and constitutional law in numerous predominantly Muslim countries in Asia (as well as parts of Africa). The strong establishment model is back in vogue in these places, albeit subject to various constitutional and jurisprudential ingenuity aimed at mitigating the tensions between religious directives and modern-life necessities, worldviews and interests.

V. CONCLUSION

Much has been written over the past decade about the migration of constitutional ideas across legal systems, and the formation of an Esperanto-like, "generic" form of constitutional law, at least with respect to rights and liberties. These trends are said to hold true even in Asia, arguably the most politically and culturally diverse continent (see Chen 2010). But as we have seen, when it comes to the comparative constitutional law of religion in Asia, clear patterns of divergence persist. Asia is a vast, densely populated continent that features tremendous cross-country variance in regime types, colonial legacies, economic development levels, faith traditions, as well as histories of religion-and-state relations. In fact, it is hard to think of a pertinent factor that is common to Oman (Islamic sultanate), Laos (mix of communist atheism and Buddhist prevalence) and East Timor (predominantly Catholic new democracy) other than the classification of all three as Asian countries. Such multiplicity and lack of substantive common denominator defy attempts to identify a common "Asian" approach to constitutional law and religion, and question the intellectual merit of invoking concepts such as "Asian values" in dealing with law and religion in that continent.

---

[20] *Muhammad Siddique et al. v. Government of Pakistan* (decision released on Nov. 5, 2004).

What may be said with confidence is that three broad approaches for arranging the relationship between state and religion are common in Asia: (i) constitutional secularism, which may be accompanied by enclaves of religion-based jurisdictional autonomy; (ii) state endorsement of religion as a source of national heritage and a marker of collective identity; and (iii) strong establishment of religion (so-called "Islamic constitutionalism"). Obviously, there is considerable variance within these prototypical or "ideal" models; each comes in different shapes, forms and sizes, with local nuances and idiosyncrasies abounding. This variance is often rooted in distinctive political legacies, differences in constitutional structures and aspirations, dissimilarities in historical inheritances and formative experiences, as well as non-trivial differences in value systems and foundational national meta-narratives. These differences often feed and shape the specific ways in which the tension between religion and constitutional governance manifests itself. But taken as a whole, and despite all the differences and nuances, constitutional law in Asia is arguably the most religion steeped of all continents, with over three-quarters of national constitutions assigning special status to religion as a pillar of collective identity, and with no more than a handful of countries that adhere to a Western-style separation of religion and state. In short, few regions pose a greater challenge to the simplistic "modernization equals secularization" argument.

REFERENCES

Butt, Simon. 2010. "Islam, the State and the Constitutional Court in Indonesia." *Pacific Rim Law & Policy Journal* 19(2): 279–301.

Chen, Albert H.Y. 2010. "Pathways of Western Liberal Constitutional Development in Asia: A Comparative Study of Five Major Nations." *International Journal of Constitutional Law* 8(4): 849–884.

Crouch, Melissa. 2012. "Law and Religion in Indonesia: The Constitutional Court and the Blasphemy Law." *Asian Journal of Comparative Law* 7(1): 1–46.

Esposito, John et al. 2011. *Religions of Asia Today*. Oxford: Oxford University Press.

Goodman, Josh. 2009. "Divine Judgment: Judicial Review of Religious Legal Systems in India and Israel." *Hastings International and Comparative Law Journal* 32: 477–528.

Harding, Andrew and Peter Leyland. 2011. *The Constitutional System of Thailand: A Contextual Analysis*. Oxford: Hart Publishing.

Hirschl, Ran. 2010. *Constitutional Theocracy*. Cambridge MA: Harvard University Press.

Hirschl, Ran. 2011. "Comparative Constitutional Law and Religion." Pp. 422–440 in *Comparative Constitutional Law*, edited by Tom Ginsburg and Rosalind Dixon. Cheltenham: Edward Elgar.

Jacobsohn, Gary J. 2003. *The Wheel of Law: India's Secularism in Comparative Constitutional Context.* Princeton: Princeton University Press.

Kobayashi, Hiroaki. 2010. "State and Religion in Japan: Yasukuni Shrine as a Case Study." In *Law and Religion in the 21st Century*, edited by Silvio Ferrari and Rinaldo Cristofori. Farnham: Ashgate.

Mahmood, Tahir. 2010. "Religious Communities and the State in Modern India." In *Law and Religion in the 21st Century*, edited by Silvio Ferrari and Rinaldo Cristofori. Farnham: Ashgate.

Pangalangan, Raul C. 2008. "Transplanted Constitutionalism: The Philippine Debate on the Secular State and the Rule of Law." *Philippine Law Journal* 82(3): 1–23.

Sathe, S.P. 2003. *Judicial Activism in India: Transgressing Borders and Enforcing Limits.* Oxford: Oxford University Press.

Shachar, Ayelet. 2001. *Multicultural Jurisdictions: Cultural Differences and Women's Rights.* Cambridge: Cambridge University Press.

Siddique, Osama and Zahra Hayat. 2008. "Unholy Speech and Holy Laws: Blasphemy Laws in Pakistan – Controversial Origins, Design Defects, and Free Speech Implications." *Minnesota Journal of International Law* 17(2): 303–85.

Sidel, Mark. 2009. *The Constitutional System of Vietnam: A Contextual Analysis.* Oxford: Hart Publishing.

Index

Ackerman, B. 73–4
Adegbenny v. Akintola (1963) 88
Afghanistan 247, 331
Ainu, Japanese minority group 307–8
Air India v. Nergesh Meerza (1981) 286
Albania 41
Anthem Case (2010) 235
anti-discrimination equality model
    278–78
Apo Fruits Corp. and Hijo Plantation v.
    Land Bank of Philippines (2008)
    267
Aristotle 278
Association of Small Landowners in the
    Philippines v. Hon. Secretary of
    Agrarian Reform (1989) 266–7
Att.Gen. v. Corporation and City of
    Adelaide (2013) 235
Att.Gen. v. Wain (1991) 238
Aucoin, L. 34
Australia 40
authoritarian pluralism 47

Bajpai, R. 282
Balaji v. State of Mysore (1963) 288
Bangladesh 95–7, 201
Bannon, A. 31
Barangar Ramachandrappa v. State of
    Karnataka (2007) 231
Beatrice a/p A.T. Fernandez v. Sistem
    Penerbangan Malaysia (2005)
    286, 299–301
Belarus 41
Bennett Coleman v. Union of India
    (1973) 245
Bharati v. State of Kerala (1973)
    269–70
Bhutan 326

Bijoe Emmanuel v. State of Kerala
    (1986) 244, 246, 319–20
blasphemy, criminalizing 6, 230, 240,
    327
Brancanti, D. 181, 184–5
Brandt, M. 34
Brubaker, R. 178
Brunei 145, 200
Buddhism 11, 325–6, 328
Burakumin, Japanese minority group
    308
Burma 145

Calalong v. Williams (1940) 257–8
Cambodia 35, 145
Canada 112–13, 167, 181
Cederman, L.-E. 183
Chad 31
Chang, W.-C. 2, 82–3
Che Omar bin Che Soh (1984) 328
Chee Siok Chin v. Minister for Home
    Affairs (2005) 236–7
Chee Soon Juan v. Public Prosecutor
    (2011) 238
Cheibub, J. 134
Cheng, T.-J. 153
Chernykh, S. 134
Cherokee Nation 39
China
    Confucian tradition 10
    constitutional development 10–11,
        105–6
    emergency powers 218
    post-conflict federalism 186
    right to property 251, 253–6, 259
    Scientific Outlook on Development
        255
Choudhry, S. 90–91, 173